CORNISH STUDIES

Second Series

FIFTEEN

INSTITUTE OF CORNISH STUDIES

EDITOR'S NOTE

Cornish Studies (second series) exists to reflect current research conducted internationally in the inter-disciplinary field of Cornish Studies. It is edited by Professor Philip Payton, Director of the Institute of Cornish Studies at the University of Exeter, Cornwall Campus, and is published by University of Exeter Press. The opinions expressed in *Cornish Studies* are those of individual authors and are not necessarily those of the editor or publisher. The support of Cornwall County Council is gratefully acknowledged.

CORNISH STUDIES

Second Series

FIFTEEN

edited by
Philip Payton

UNIVERSITY
of
EXETER
PRESS

First published in 2007 by
University of Exeter Press
Reed Hall, Streatham Drive
Exeter EX4 4QR
UK

www.exeterpress.co.uk

British Library Cataloguing in Publication Data
A catalogue record for this book is available from the British Library.

ISBN 978 0 85989 808 9

Typeset in Adobe Caslon
by Carnegie Book Production, Lancaster
Printed in Great Britain by Printed in Great Britain by
Athenaeum Press Ltd, Gateshead, Tyne & Wear

Contents

Notes on contributors

Bernard Deacon is Senior Lecturer in Cornish Studies at the Institute of Cornish Studies, University of Exeter, Cornwall Campus, and has written extensively on Cornish topics. His most recent book is *Cornwall: A Brief History* (2007). He is also director of the Master of Arts in Cornish Studies degree programme.

John Dirring has recently completed the Master of Arts in Cornish Studies degree programme at the Institute of Cornish Studies, University of Exeter, Cornwall Campus. He has a particular interest in economic theory and its relevance for policy-making in regions such as Cornwall.

Charles Fahey is Senior Lecturer in the History Program at the Bendigo Campus of La Trobe University in Victoria, Australia. His main research interests are labour history, rural history and the history of the Victorian goldfields, with particular reference to the Cornish. He is also leading a collaborative research project 'Beyond the Black Stump', a history of the wheat and mining industries of inland Australia to be written by a consortium of historians brought together from across Australia.

D. H. Frost is the Acting Principal of St David's Catholic College, Cardiff. He is author of 'Sacrament an Alter: A Tudor Cornish Patristic Catena' in *Cornish Studies: Eleven* (2003), and has also contributed several patristic references and commentary to the online *Valorium Edition* of *John Foxe's Book of Martyrs*. He is currently a member of the advisory committee assisting in the attempt to rescue and restore at the National History Museum (St Fagan's) what is left of the medieval parish church of Llandeilo Talybont.

Ronald M. James is State Historic Preservation Officer for the State of Nevada, United States of America. He has written widely on the history and folklore of the western mining frontier of North America, with particular reference to the Cornish. He is the author of *The Roar and the Silence: A History of Virginia City and the Comstock Lode* (1998).

Alan M. Kent is Lecturer in Literature at the Open University and Visiting Lecturer in Celtic Literature at the University of Coruna in Galicia, Spain. He has written widely on the literary and cultural history of Cornwall. His most recent academic works include several entries in John T. Koch, *Celtic Culture: A Historical Encylopedia* (2005), essays in *Cornish Studies: Thirteen* (2005) and *Celtic Englishes IV* (2006), and a contribution on the literature of Robert Morton Nance to a volume celebrating his life and work. Other recent publications include his latest collection of verse *Stannary Parliament* and his plays *Nativitas Christi: A Cornish Nativity* and *Oggly es Sin*.

Philip Payton is Professor of Cornish and Australian Studies at the University of Exeter, Cornwall Campus, where he is also Director of the Institute of Cornish Studies. Recent books include *A. L. Rowse and Cornwall: A Paradoxical Patriot* (University of Exeter Press, 2005; paperback 2007) and *Making Moonta: The Invention of Australia's Little Cornwall* (University of Exeter Press, 2007). During 2007 he was also Visiting Fellow in the Humanities Research Centre at the Australian National University in Canberra.

Garry Tregidga is Senior Lecturer in Cornish Studies and Assistant Director of the Institute of Cornish Studies, University of Exeter, Cornwall Campus. He also directs the Cornish Audio Visual Archive, based at the Institute. He has published widely in the general area of Cornish Studies, especially oral history and twentieth-century Cornish politics. His most recent book is *Camborne, Killerton and Westminster: The Political Correspondence of Francis Acland* (2006).

Nicholas J. A. Williams is Associate Professor of Celtic Studies at University College Dublin. He has published and lectured extensively on the Cornish, Manx and Irish languages, and is editor with Graham Thomas of *Bewnans Ke/The Life of St Kea: A Critical Edition with Translation* (University of Exeter Press, 2007).

Introduction

The publication in 2002 of *Cornish Studies: Ten* was an opportunity to look back on a decade's progress. The volume contained contributions by leading practitioners in the general field of Cornish Studies, who each took stock of their particular specialisms, presenting a comprehensive survey of our subject area that ranged from consideration of recent archaeological advances to contemporary work in the social sciences and cultural studies. There was a wealth of new research to report, and the mood was overwhelmingly positive – even celebratory. But the review was also reflexive and self-critical, and as well as identifying (and to a degree challenging) the normative assumptions that underpinned much of 'New' Cornish Studies, it was also quick to point out gaps and flaws in recent work, and to suggest new avenues for the future. The collection concluded, therefore, with a firm eye on the years ahead, each specialism sketching an agenda for the future, and with a strong expectation that the next decade's efforts would be at least as rewarding as that reviewed in *Cornish Studies: Ten*.

We are already halfway through that decade, and although this book – *Cornish Studies: Fifteen* – is not the occasion to consider the sum of new work since 2002, it is an opportunity to reflect that much of the promise detected five years ago has already born fruit. Nowhere is this more evident than in the study of the Cornish language and literature of the late medieval/early modern period. When *Cornish Studies: Ten* went to press in 2002, the Cornish Studies community was only just waking up to the implications and significance of the then very recent find of a new Cornish-language 'miracle play' amongst papers bequeathed to the National Library of Wales. Now we are in no doubt as to the importance of this discovery. 'Beunans (or Bewnans) Ke' – the 'Life of St Kea' – proved to be a sixteenth-century copy of a previously unknown play in Middle Cornish, probably composed in the second half of the fifteenth century. It has some of the features of what we might guardedly term its 'sister' composition, 'Beunans Meriasek' – the 'Life of St Meriasek'. It is a late-medieval *vita* with numerous Cornish topographical allusions, and features the tyrant Teudar. But among the play's distinctive elements is a wealth of material on King Arthur, a fascinating insight into the strength of the Arthurian tradition in Cornwall in that period. Additionally, the play's text has added new words and phrases to the extant Cornish language, and is in itself a major contribution to the corpus of Cornish-language literature. Not surprisingly, the discovery of 'Bewnans Ke' has provoked considerable excitement in Cornish-language circles, culminating in the appearance in early 2007 of *Bewnans Ke/The Life of St Kea: A Critical Edition with Translation*, edited (with a substantial introduction) by Nicholas J.A. Williams and Graham Thomas, and published by University of Exeter Press in association with the National Library of Wales.

The preparation of Williams's and Thomas's scholarly edition of *Bewnans Ke* has also prompted other discoveries within the text itself. In his article in this collection, for example, Nicholas J.A. Williams alights upon the word *englyn* ('stanza' or 'verse'), a word hitherto known only in Welsh and unattested in Cornish, though discussed in a comparative context by Edward Lhuyd towards the end of his Cornish grammar of 1707. The term appears in 'Bewnans Meriasek', however, as Williams notes, in the second part of the drama when King Arthur and his court are at Caerleon upon Usk, where the king has just received legates from the Roman emperor. King Arthur says: *'Dun ow amors ha'm cuvyon,/ gans solas hag* **eglynnyon**/ *ha mirth ha melody whek'* – 'Come, my friends and my dear ones,/ with entertainment and *englynion*/ and mirth and sweet melody'. As Williams observes, the word *eglynnon* is clearly the plural of a Cornish word *eglyn* (*englyn*), meaning 'verse'. Williams goes on to make further comparisons between Welsh and Cornish in such 'metrical matters', and finds that in Middle Cornish there was an *englyn* metre similar in form to the Welsh *englyn milwr*, and that three such *englynion* have survived in Cornish literature of the period.

Alongside Williams's work on *Bewnans Ke* has been much other research on late medieval and (most especially) early modern Cornwall. Recent editions of *Cornish Studies* have included important contributions by Matthew Spriggs, and in this volume D.H. Frost returns to his specialist interest in the life and times of John Tregear, the supposed translator into Cornish of Bishop Bonner's Catholic homilies composed during Mary's reign. Building upon his Tregear article in *Cornish Studies: Eleven* (2003), Frost looks in considerably more detail into the backgrounds of John Tregear, Thomas Stephyn, Ralph Trelobys, Richard Ton (the elusive Rad Ton of 'Beunans Meriasek' fame, perhaps?) and other sixteenth-century Cornish characters. In a remarkable scholarly *tour de force*, Frost sheds startling new light on the period, suggesting that much of the ecclesiastical writing in the Cornish language conducted under the aegis of Glasney was actually undertaken in the nearby parishes of mid- and West Cornwall, rather than at the college itself. It was 'the humble clergy that ran the parishes in West Cornwall from which Glasney drew its tithes' who performed much of 'the work to preserve traditional religion through the medium of Cornish', argues Frost, and we can pinpoint the localities where these men grew up and learned to speak their native tongue. In contrast to the later picture of Cornish lingering in the coastal communities of Mount's Bay, here we have a sketch of an earlier epicentre on the borders of North Kerrier and East Penwith, around Crowan, Sithney, Wendron, Helston, Camborne and Redruth, with an outlying area extending to Mylor, St Allen and Newlyn East.

John Tregear himself appears to have translated Bonner's homilies when he was vicar of St Allen in the 1550s. This was in the aftermath of the Prayer Book Rebellion (or Western Rising) of 1549, in which Tregear may have been implicated, and, unlike other Cornish clergy who were evicted (and even executed), Tregear managed to remain in his parish until his death in 1583. As Frost observes, at some point Tregear's manuscript must have passed to Thomas Stephyn, vicar of Newlyn East during Mary's reign, and in time it found its way to Chirk Castle in Flint in North Wales – either via some tortuous journey through Brittany or Iberia, or more simply by way of South Wales and the Welsh Marches. In 1871 it was erroneously classified as 'Welsh' by the Historical Manuscripts Commission, and in the twentieth century was first noticed as Cornish in 1949.

Alongside these recent advances in the history of the Cornish language and its literature, new work on Cornwall's nineteenth-century 'Great Emigration' stands out as one of the key areas in Cornish Studies where significant progress has been made over the last few years. Here an important trajectory may be observed. Moving from the earlier 'classic' histories of the Cornish overseas – which dealt with specific national destinations (the United States of America, Mexico, Australia, South Africa) – Cornish emigration studies had by the turn of the new millennium branched in several new directions. There were attempts at overview, at achieving a new synthesis which would construe Cornish emigration as a global process, and allied to this initiative was the suggestion that recent scholarly 'transnational' perspectives developed elsewhere might usefully be applied to understanding the cultural and economic dimensions of Cornwall's international identity. But there was also a new emphasis on the 'micro' dimension, on movement to and from specific 'micro' localities, together with an important reminder that emigration from Cornwall was matched by an internal migration within the British Isles which was also significant in its scale and impact. Indeed, it was argued, we could not fully understand population movement in nineteenth-century Cornwall without considering both processes in tandem – external (overseas) emigration and internal (British Isles) migration – for the two were inextricably linked and were twin faces of the same phenomenon. At the same time, it was added, Cornish emigration studies had for too long relied overwhelmingly on qualitative material. Now, with new census and other quantitative data readily available in digitized form on the world wide web and elsewhere, and with new software techniques to manipulate such data with relative ease, it was high time that historians attempted to quantify Cornish emigration and offer statistical analyses.

In this volume, there are three articles which reflect this new 'micro' and 'quantitative' mood. The first is Bernard Deacon's major reconstruction of nineteenth-century Cornish migration patterns, an extended statistical analysis which at a stroke establishes 'surer empirical grounds for the discussion of migration processes' and opens new doors for our understanding in detail the movement from Cornwall. Deacon asks important questions that earlier historians have shied away from or felt ill-equipped to pose (let alone answer). How many people left Cornwall, he asks, what were their ages, and from areas did they leave? Where did they go? And what were the processes in operation behind these movements? Why did so many people leave some places in Cornwall, and so few leave others? As Deacon admits, there are sometimes problems in dealing with the data – not least the difficulties modern transcribers have with Cornish-language placenames – but the end-result is impressive.

By the middle of the nineteenth century, as Deacon shows, migration from Cornwall was of three broad times. There were the short-distance moves, common to all regions in Britain. There was also the drift from smaller settlements to larger villages and towns. But in addition there was significant long-distance emigration, some of it to overseas destinations. In the 1860s and 1870s the sudden contraction of mining in Cornwall disrupted these trends. There was a surge in long-distance migration but, interestingly, much of this was first to other industrial regions in Britain, stepping-stones (as Deacon describes them) from which individuals might move on to mining frontiers overseas once they had amassed sufficient funds. By the 1890s, however, overseas migration was waning, partly because of the reduced demographic base in Cornish mining communities, and partly as a result of the greater attraction of internal migration. There were also important changes in the nature of migration overseas, with family migration declining and an increased number of short-stay migrations by young, single males who returned to Cornwall. It was a fluid and complex process, Deacon concludes, 'where economic changes encouraged new and expanded old migration streams but where pre-existing migration chains and established networks led to recognizable continuity in the pattern of movement across generations'.

The quantitative turn is also pursued by Charles Fahey in his discussion of Cornish emigration to nineteenth-century Victoria in Australia. Complaining, like others before him, that the historian's gaze has been all too easily attracted to the overtly 'Cornish' mining communities of South Australia, Fahey focuses instead on the goldmining districts of neighbouring Victoria, where the Cornish may have been less visible but were certainly at least as numerous. He notes that, while census data may have conflated the Cornish with the English, making statistical separation impossible, the Registrations of Birth, Deaths and Marriages are a different matter. Here place of birth (or marriage or death) complements a wealth of other useful social data, making identification of the Cornish and their activity far easier. Concentrating on what he describes as 'regional Victoria' – from the main goldfields settlements of Ballarat and Bendigo in 1861 to a wider focus towards the end of the century when the area of European settlement had expanded – Fahey uses such registrations to track and quantify the Cornish. As he explains, by 1871 there were probably at least 15,000 Cousin Jacks and Jennys on the central goldfields of Victoria; although by this time Ballarat had already eclipsed Bendigo as the centre of Cornish activity, a trend which reflected the relative mobility of the Cornish in Victoria.

Fahey's discussion is leavened with illustrative qualitative material, notably the diary of Richard Pope. Born in Breage in 1834, Pope had mined in the United States and in Ireland before emigrating to Victoria. He worked there for eighteen years before moving on to Broken Hill in New South Wales in 1886, and later tried to find employment in the Transvaal. He died in Broken Hill in 1900. In this typically 'Cousin Jack' career, Pope had risen to the rank of 'captain' or mine manager. But, like many of his compatriots, he had been continually on the move, following a precarious existence as he was forced by economic circumstances to shift from one mine to the next or on to the latest mineral strike. Although, like other Cornish miners in Victoria, Pope was certainly better-off than in his native Cornwall it was hardly an easy life or a secure existence. As Pope himself once observed, 'taking everything into consideration it appears to me that the poor man does not improve his position by emigrating'. His assessment was overly pessimistic, perhaps, but, as Fahey observes, Pope was 'absolutely typical' of the majority of Cornish miners in Victoria. They did not expect to make their fortunes but they had to work hard and to be prepared to move often if they were to support their families through waged work.

In Nevada, on the western mining frontier of the United States, there was a slightly different story to tell – as Ronald M. James makes plain in his article on the subject. As in Victoria, the Cornish in nineteenth-century Nevada were a mobile population, moving from one mining district to the next as the relative fortunes of the different mines waxed and waned. But the Cornish were shrewd and, confident of their reputation and employability as 'Cousin Jacks', they could afford to bide their time. It was for others to scramble breathlessly to the latest rush in the hope (probably vain) of striking it rich, struggling to be the first on the new field so as to have a head start over competitors. The Cornish, meanwhile, as James shows, preferred to wait until a new mining area had proved its worth, only then deciding to move in (often in groups) to take the best hard-rock mining jobs. Districts of only fleeting or marginal value, the Cornish avoided altogether. Moreover, the Cornish were on the whole well-paid. In the 1870s underground miners on the Comstock in Nevada earned a minimum of four dollars for an eight-hour shift, making them the best paid industrial workers in North America – if not the world – and more experienced miners (such as the Cornish) could attract up to six dollars a day.

As James explains, detailed 'micro' research into settlement patterns in Nevada in the second half of the nineteenth century has been facilitated by the recent availability of online Federal census data. Although, as in Victoria, the Cornish are conflated with the English in these official statistics, making absolute identification impossible, James argues that it is possible to use distinctive Cornish surnames as a guide. Acknowledging the shortcomings of this method, not least the strong likelihood that resultant figures will be on the conservative side, he nonetheless concludes that surnames analysis provides a good indicator of Cornish movement and settlement trends, as well as a reliable estimate of their overall numbers. He maps Cornish preferences over time – the destinations they ventured to, the ones they avoided – and shows how particular venues, such as Gold Hill, near Virginia City, and Austin in Lander County, became especially associated with Cornish settlement. Unlike the Irish and the English, who 'arrived early and scattered everywhere', the Cornish in Nevada were patient and discerning. As always, they deployed their 'Cousin Jack' network to good effect, gaining reliable intelligence which allowed them to make informed, reliable choices about where and when to settle and work.

For those Cornish who did not migrate to Victoria, Nevada or the multiplicity of other destinations overseas or in the British Isles, Cornwall at the end of the nineteenth century and into the early twentieth was a much changed place. Reliant to a considerable degree on remittances sent home from abroad or up-country, Cornish mining communities exhibited all the deleterious socio-economic signs of early de-industrialization. Attempts at economic diversification – the growth of market gardening, for example, or the continued expansion of china clay – combined with the entrepreneurial zeal of returned migrants to provide at least some optimism for the future in the years before the Great War. But by the early 1920s Cornwall had already slipped back into its 'paralysis', events on the international stage thereafter doing little to foster economic regeneration, despite the growth of tourism.

As Garry Tregidga shows in his article on Francis Acland and Cornish politics in the years 1910–22, much the same could have been written about the political scene in Cornwall during the same period. Focussing on the career of Francis Acland, elected Liberal MP of Camborne in 1910 – a position he was to hold until his resignation in 1922 – Tregidga discusses what was 'a critical period in Cornwall's political history'. In the early years of the twentieth century, before and after Acland's election, there was evidence of uncertainty in the Cornish political scene. Continuing conflict between Liberals and Liberal Unionists reflected unease over Irish Home Rule, where many in Cornwall feared for the future of their fellow Nonconformists in Ulster should a self-governing Ireland become a reality. Yet there were others, as Tregidga shows, who, as early as 1912, and taking their cue from the rhetoric of the Cornish-Celtic Revival, argued for Home-Rule-All-Round and advocated instead self-government for both Ireland and Cornwall. As Alfred Browning Lyne, editor of the Bodmin *Cornish Guardian*, wrote that year: 'There is another Home Rule movement on the horizon. Self-government for Cornwall will be the next move'.

At the same time, there were the first signs of potential Labour penetration in Cornwall. Although a Social Democratic Federation candidate had polled a mere 1.5 per cent of the vote in the 1906 election in Camborne, the china-clay strike in mid-Cornwall in 1913 had, argues Tregidga, 'a radicalizing effect on the Labour movement throughout the region'. After the Great War, this 'radicalization' of the Cornish working class was felt in Camborne, with Labour coming remarkably close to a breakthrough and winning 48 per cent of the vote in a straight fight with Acland. As Acland admitted privately at the time, if the Tories had put forward a candidate, then he would surely have lost his seat. Yet this radical upsurge was not sustained, and Cornwall signally failed to participate in what Christopher Cook has called the 'age of alignment', when British politics generally was transformed into a Labour–Conservative contest, with the Liberals reduced to minor third-party status. The election of Isaac Foot as Liberal MP for Bodmin did much to rally traditional Liberal-Nonconformity as the Cornish radical alternative to Conservatism, helping to nip Labour in the bud in Cornwall. Additionally, as Tregidga admits, the socio-economic condition of Cornwall in the 1920s was hardly conducive to major political change: 'The lack of a trade union tradition, following the decline of mining in the previous century, along with the strength of small family businesses in sectors like agriculture, certainly presented obstacles to Labour'. As Tregidga concludes, by the early 1920s there was a return to the 'old order' in Cornwall, with Cornish politics confirmed in its Tory versus Liberal mould at a time of rapid change elsewhere. Acland, meanwhile, had become increasingly frustrated with Cornwall and the Cornish, preferring the 'high politics' of Westminster, and resigned from Camborne in 1922.

Here we see Acland as 'outsider' – the Aclands were an old Devon family – and in his growing impatience with Cornwall and the Cornish we can detect his cultural distance from the place and its people. There were issues of class at play but this essentially was a question of identity. For all his knowledge of the Cornish and their homeland, for Acland they remained the sometimes unfathomable 'other'. The boundaries and complexities of Cornish identity also underpin the discussion in this volume of the relationship between John Betjeman and Cornwall. As Betjeman devotees will know, John Betjeman's 'foreign' surname and his German (Dutch?) family origins were for him a source of angst and uncertainty, leading him sometimes to doubt his 'English' credentials. As A.L. Rowse reminded him, he was not 'Cornish' either, and Betjeman was the first to admit that he was a 'foreigner' in Cornwall. Worse still, Betjeman thought, was the fact that he was a 'visitor', an interloper who was actively contributing to the ruin of Cornwall by the tourist industry. Moreover, as a writer and broadcaster who regularly extolled the beauty and fascination of Cornwall, he felt guiltily complicit in the promotion of Cornwall as a tourist destination. Yet Betjeman went out of his way to claim common cause with the Cornish, discovery of his own 'Welsh' descent opening up for him the possibilities of pan-Celticism and fostering an anti-'Whitehall' anti-metropolitanism. Moreover, he was attracted by the imagery of the Cornish-Celtic Revival, not least its Anglo-Catholic element, which spoke directly to Betjeman's search for religious faith.

North Cornwall in particular became the stage on which John Betjeman acted out his personal 'quest for the Holy Grail', a search for personal identity and faith which followed in the footsteps of, and drew inspiration from, Robert Stephen Hawker and Sabine Baring-Gould. It was also guided by Prebendary Wilfred Johnson, Rector of St Ervan, who when Betjeman was still an adolescent lent him a copy of Arthur Machen's novel, *The Secret Glory*. For Betjeman, this was to be a life-changing book, such was his identification with its fictional school-boy hero, Ambrose Meyrick. Meyrick struggled (just as Betjeman had done) to cope with his public school existence, all the while nurturing a devotion to Celtic Christianity and a childhood memory of the Holy Grail hidden in the depths of his native Gwent. For 'Gwent' Betjeman read 'Cornwall', and although he felt that he could never really be 'Cornish', his 'Welshness' gave him the confidence to claim affinity and insight, an identification with Cornwall that was on the whole welcomed and approved of by Cornish opinion – even in nationalist circles.

Of course, John Betjeman was not the only twentieth-century figure seduced by the idea of 'Celtic Cornwall'. As Betjeman knew, such Celticity was a powerful draw for those outsiders in search of the exotic and the 'other'. But if the notion of 'Celticity' continued to exercise its fascination for visitors to Cornwall, then it was also a significant influence in the lives of many of those who lived here. This was true in Betjeman's day, and remains the case in early twenty-first-century Cornwall. For example, as Alan M. Kent shows in his survey of popular music in Cornwall in the period 1967–2007, the Cornish-Celtic Revival has long exerted – and continues to exert – a strong influence over the interpretation, composition and performance of Cornish music. This influence has extended to choice of genre, instruments, costume, record or CD cover design, and associated dance or other performance, together with a desire by Cornish musicians to be perceived as 'Celtic' – not least by the bench-markers of 'Celtic music' in Brittany and (especially) Ireland. To some extent this pursuit of the 'Celtic' merely reflects the imperatives of the Cornish-Celtic Revival. But, as Kent detects, it is has been, until very recently at least, evidence of a lack of self-confidence in Cornwall – first of all, a fear that traditional Cornish music is not really Celtic enough, and needs to be enhanced by overtly Celtic performance or display, and secondly, a sense that Brittany and Ireland are the authentic homes of Celtic music and should, therefore, be emulated and deferred to.

However, as Kent demonstrates, in recent years the situation has changed somewhat. First of all, traditional Cornish music has found its own 'voice', no longer slavishly dependent on inter-Celtic models and more aware of its inherent worth and individuality. This, in turn, has meant less reliance on Celtic iconography and a move towards more recognizably 'Cornish' forms, together with a greater degree of independence and a sense of equality with performers elsewhere in the Celtic world. Moreover, this greater sophistication has been part of the broader development of popular music in Cornwall, where 'traditional' music has been able to construct links with the wider 'pop' world. This has been encouraged in part by the emergence of a distinctly 'Cornish' dimension in what is a globalized 'pop' industry, a shift that has been encouraged by venues and performers within Cornwall but which has reached an international audience through the success of artists such as Alex Parks (winner of BBC 1's *Fame Academy* in 2003) and the rock band Thirteen Senses. Here, says Kent, is a 'kool Kernow' in the making, where the fusionist strategies of different types of composers and performers are creating for Cornwall a higher profile and distinctive niche in the international world of popular music.

But as Kent also remarks, there has to date been relatively little research into this phenomenon, or into contemporary Cornish issues generally, and he sets his panoramic survey of the Cornish music scene within a more general call for greater work on popular culture in Cornwall. His plea finds an echo in John Dirring's article on 'Economic Theory and Cornwall', where, it is also inferred, the optimistic and catch-all rhetoric of 'New' Cornish Studies has yet to match reality. Despite heady claims for a 'New Cornish Social Science' (to match what is clearly a distinctive 'New Cornish Historiography'), there is – as Malcolm Williams pointed out in his review of social science research in *Cornish Studies: Ten* – a lack of theoretical sophistication in what is actually a fairly loose interdisciplinary entwining. Acknowledging that interdisciplinary contact is a very good thing, Dirring nonetheless echoes Williams's criticism, pointing out there have been very few instances of 'pure' applications of any of the individual social sciences to Cornish issues, and implying that little progress has been made in the half decade since 2002. In contrast to the great strides made in Cornish-language and Cornish-migration studies, social science in general – and economics in particular – has not received the attention it warrants.

Nonetheless, Dirring does detect the makings of a 'New Cornish Economics' (as he terms), returning to the earlier work of Ronald Perry to seek its origins, and pointing to an applied 'opposition' economics which sought to offer critiques of central, regional and local planning in relation to Cornwall. Building upon this inheritance, and comparing a range of economic theories (old and new), Dirring moves towards a theory of 'embedded choice', an analytical tool for dealing with the many oppositional tensions inherent in the Cornish experience – centre and periphery, for instance, or inward and outward migration. This, he hopes, will help point the way for a new methodological sophistication in 'New Cornish Economics', while retaining its practical utility and sense of historical perspective. Dirring has, in effect, opened-up a new discourse in Cornish Studies, and has issued a challenge to those economists and other social scientists with an interest in Cornwall's present and future. In the next half decade, perhaps, a new set of Cornish Studies practitioners will emerge to take forward this 'New Cornish Economics' and ensure its proper consideration within the multidisciplinary field in which we work.

Professor Philip Payton,
Director, Institute of Cornish Studies,
School of Humanities and Social Science,
University of Exeter, Cornwall Campus

I

The Cornish *Englyn*

Nicholas J. A. Williams

Introduction: Lhuyd's Cornish *Englyn*

Towards the end of his Cornish grammar Edward Lhuyd alludes to some Welsh *englynion* ('stanzas'); for example, *Englynion y Clyweit* 'the Stanzas of Hearing', *Englynion y Beddau* 'the Stanzas of the Graves' and the *Bidiau* (These are gnomic stanzas containing many examples of *Bid* 'Is wont to be'). He then tells us that he heard one *englyn* in Cornwall during his visit c.1700:

> *An lavar kôth yu lavar guîr,*
> *Bedh dorn rê ver, dhon tavaz rê hîr;*
> *Mez dên heb davaz a gollaz i dîr.*

> 'What's said of old, will always stand:
> Too long a tongue, too short a hand;
> But he that had no tongue, lost his land' (AB: 251c).

It is noteworthy that the word for 'short' in this *englyn* is *ber*. This word elsewhere in Middle Cornish occurs only in the fossilized phrases 1) *a ver spys* and 2) *a ver dermyn*, both of which mean 'in a short while, soon'. Here are some examples of the two expressions from the Middle Cornish texts:

> 1)
> *hep gul dyel **a ver speys** OM 947
> *yn certan hag **a ver spys** OM 1540
> *lauar thy'mmo **a ver spys** PC 509
> *the volungeth **a ver spys** PC 2053
> *ha crousyough ef **a ver spys** PC 2166

gura gueres thy'm a ver spys RD 1721
myr worto hag a ver spys RD 1729
arluth ker hag a ver spys RD 1785
ihesu gront dovyr a wur speys BM 668
the covs gena a fur spas BM 3979.

2)
me a'th kelm fast a ver termyn OM 1361–62
cous er the fyth a ver termyn OM 1441
rag the throg a ver dermyn OM 1601
ha kerenys a ver dermyn OM 2381
ny a thy a ver termyn PC 1654
leuereugh a ver termyn PC 1690
man gueller a ver termyn PC 1963
genevy a fur termyn BM 1741.

In Middle Cornish the ordinary word for 'short' is *cot*, as can be seen from the following examples:

na vo hyrre es am syn na byth **cotta** *war nep cor* 'that it be no longer than my mark nor any shorter in any way' OM 2511–12

re **got** *o a gevelyn* 'it was too short by a cubit' OM 2520

lemyn re **got** *ev a gevelyn da yn guyr* 'now it is too short by a good cubit truly' OM 2540–41

tres aral re **got** *in guyr* 'another time too short truly' OM 2549

cot yv the thythyow thegy 'short are your days' RD 2037

me a ra pur **cot** *y guyns* 'I will render his wind very short' BM 2253

an lesson **cut** *ma* 'this short lesson' TH 26

ha wosa an tyrmyn **cut** *a vethyn ny omma* 'and after the short time we will be here' TH 26

in kyth same lesson bean **cut** *ma* 'in this very same short lesson' TH 28a

an moar brase yn **cutt** *termyn adro thom tyre a vyth dreys* 'the great sea will be brought round my land in a short time' CW 88–9

in **cutt** *termyn ages negys cowsow y praya* 'in a short time tell your business, I pray' CW 592.

In the *englyn*, however, *ber* is used in the phrase *re ver* 'too short', and was apparently at the time of composition the ordinary word for 'short'. This would perhaps suggest that the *englyn* dates from the early Middle Cornish period, when *ber* (Welsh *byr*) was still the usual word for 'short.'

Lhuyd's cites his Cornish *englyn* in *Archæologia Britannica* of 1707. Two variant versions of it also occur in Pryce's *Archæologia Cornu-Britannica* of 1790. The first reads as follows:

> *An Lavor gôth ewe lavar gwîr*
> *Ne vedn nevera doas vas a tavas re hîr*
> *Bes den heb tavaz a gollas e dîr* (ACB: F f).

The second version cited by Pryce is from a letter printed by him but written by Edward Lhuyd. In the letter, which was written to T. Tonkin on March 16th, 1702/03, Lhuyd says he heard the stanza from the clerk of St Just. This version reads as follows:

> *An lavar koth yw lavar gwîr*
> *Na boz nevra dôz vâz an tavas re hîr*
> *Bez dên heb davaz a gollaz i dîr.*

This last version is from a letter of Lhuyd's and Pryce's first version with its *ô* and *î* circumflex also looks as though it has originally come from Lhuyd. It would seem then that all three variants come directly or indirectly from Lhuyd.

Lhuyd himself tells us that he heard the *englyn*, rather than read it in manuscript. It existed, moreover, in three slightly different versions. This would suggest that the *englyn* formed part of the Cornish oral tradition. Since, however, the language of the *englyn* is probably much older in origin than the eighteenth century, we should not be astonished to see that the original stanza has been reshaped by centuries of oral transmission. Even so, the underlying form is clear enough. We are dealing with a stanza of three lines of between eight and eleven syllables rhyming *aaa*. This is immediately reminiscent of the *englyn milwr* of Welsh, a form of *englyn* common in *Canu Llywarch Hen* and elsewhere. In the *englyn milwr* the syllable count is usually either seven syllables or more rarely eight syllables. There are sequences of *englynion milwr* in existence, however, in which the syllabic count is much less regular. Here are some examples:

> A)
> *Bid wlyb rhych; bid fynych mach;*
> *bid chwyrn colwyn, bid wenwyn gwrach;*
> *bid cwynfan claf, bid lawen iach.*
>
> *Bid chwyrniad colwyn, bid wenwyn neidr;*
> *bid nofiaw rhyd wrth beleidr;*
> *nid gwell yr odwr no'r lleidr.*

The furrow is usually wet; surety is often required;
a puppy is quick, a hag is venom,
the sick man is lamentation, happy is the healthy man.

The puppy snores, the snake is venom,
the ford rushes across sunbeams,
no better is the accomplice than the thief
(EWGP: 36).

B)
A glyweist di a gant y vronvreith
pan dramwych dros diffeith
na vit dy elin dy gedymdeith

Did you hear what the thrush sang?
When you travel through wild country,
let not your enemy be your companion
(BBCS iii (1927) 10).

In the first of the two *englynion* at A) above the syllabic count is 7, 8, 8 and
in the second it is 9, 7, 7. In stanza B) above the syllable count is 8, 6, 9.

Whatever the original length of the line in the Cornish *englyn*, I assume
that the metrical form of three lines rhyming *aaa* is a common inheritance
of Welsh and Cornish. It is probable also that in the early *englyn* from
which both the Welsh and the Cornish *englyn* derives, the syllable count was
considerably less regular than it later became in Welsh.

Until now the term *englyn* was exclusively known from Welsh but was
unattested in Cornish. The word now, however, appears in the recently
discovered Cornish play *Bewnans Ke*. In the second part of the drama King
Arthur and his court are at Caerleon upon Usk, where the king has just
received twelve legates from Lucius, emperor of Rome. Arthur says:

Dun ow amors ha'm cuvyon,
*gans solas hag **eglynnyon***
ha merth ha melody whek.
Th'agan palas gwel ew thyn
revertya gans cannow tek
ha predery, ren Austyn!
a'gen gwayow.

Come, my friends and my dear ones,
with entertainment and *englynion*

and mirth and sweet melody.
It is better for us
to return to our palace with sweet songs
and to consider, by St Augustine!
our moves (BK 2058–64).

The term *eglynnyon* in the second line of that passage is clearly the Cornish plural of **eglyn*. **englyn*, verse'. All our surviving Middle Cornish poetry has a religious background. It is perhaps interesting, therefore, that the metrical form **eglyn* in this passage in *Bewnans Ke* is associated with a courtly or royal *milieu* and is thus not expressly religious in context.

The term **eglyn* is only one of the correspondencies between Welsh and Cornish in metrical matters. There are others. It is noteworthy, for example, that the line in the Welsh *englyn milwr* is heptasyllabic as is the line of the common Welsh verse-form known as *cywydd*. This basic seven-syllable line is reminiscent of the seven syllables of the Cornish line of verse, seen, for example in *Pascon agan Arluth* and in the *Ordinalia*. The seven syllable line of Welsh and Cornish contrasts remarkably with the dominant line in Breton metrics, which has eight syllables.

In Welsh there are two words for 'poet', *prydydd* and *bardd*. *Prydydd* is the more elevated term of the two, deriving as it does from a Proto-Celtic form **kʷrutiyo-* 'maker, shaper'. *Bardd* on the other hand is identical with *barth* 'mime or jester' in OCV. Breton uses *barzh* exclusively for 'poet.' The Welsh term *prydydd* has its exact congener in Old Cornish *pridit* 'poeta' [poet]. It seems, moreover, that the word survived into the Middle Cornish period, since in *Bewnans Ke* a messenger addresses a Roman senator thus:

> *Beal syr du don vous bon ior,*
> *movn senior an* **prydyth** *mort* (BK 2496–97).

I take *an prydyth mort* here to be for *re'n prydyth mort* 'by the dead poet', a reference to Virgil, who was greatly revered in the Middle Ages. I would translate the whole: 'Fair sir, God give you good day, my lord, by the dead poet.' It would seem, then, that *prydyth* 'poet' was still known by the author of *Bewnans Ke* in the middle of the fifteenth century. I take it that *prydydd* ~ *prydyth* 'poet' was again part of the common inheritance of Welsh and Cornish.

The original form of Lhuyd's *Englyn*

It seems that the version cited by Lhuyd in *Archæologia Britannica* is the most archaic and probably therefore the most authentic of the three variants of the *englyn*. Since I believe that the *englyn* is in origin early Middle Cornish, I will respell it in a more traditional orthography:

> *An lavar coth yw lavar gwyr,*
> *byth dorn re ver the'n tavas re hyr;*
> *mes den hep davas a gollas y dyr.*

It is unmistakable that in the second line here the verb *byth* (Lhuyd's *Bedh*) is without preverbal particle. The absence of particle is a distinctive feature of Welsh gnomic poetry of this kind. Compare, for example, from the *Bidiau*:

> *Bit wenn gwylan, bit vann tonn;*
> *bit hyuagyl gwyar ar onn;*
> *bit lwyt rew; bit lew callonn*

> A gull is wont to be white, a wave is wont to be weak,
> blood is easily spattered upon a spear-shaft;
> frost is wont to be hoar; a heart is often broken.
>
> (EWGP: 34).

I would therefore suggest that the middle line of the Cornish may originally have read: **byth dorn re ver, byth tavas re hyr* 'a hand is wont to be too long; a tongue is wont to be too short'. I would tentatively reconstitute the whole *englyn* as follows:

> *An lavar coth yw lavar gwyr:*
> *byth dorn re ver, byth tavas re hyr;*
> *mes den hep davas a gollas y dyr.*

Here the syllabic count is 8, 8 and 10.

In two of our three examples of the stanza *hep* 'without' in the third line lenites the initial consonant of *tavas* 'tongue'. In the Middle Cornish texts *hep* lenites only *d* and *g* and even then only sporadically, for example, *hep thout* 'without doubt' OM 2668, *hep thanger* 'without hesitation' OM 1615, *hep wow* 'without a lie' OM 659, 2496, *hep worfen* 'without end' PC 1562. If the lenition in *hep davas* is authentic, the *englyn* quite possibly dates from a period when *hep* also lenited initial *t*. The phrase *hep davas* may thus be a further indication of the early date of the stanza.

The *englyn* must date from the Middle Cornish period, however, as can be seen from the internal rhyme between *davas* and *gollas*. The word for 'tongue' in Old Cornish was *tauot*, a form which would not have given rhyme with *collas* 'he lost'.

It is just possible, I think, that the final line represents a reshaping of the original syntax. Just as *byth* (Lhuyd's *bedh*) survives without preverbal particle in the second line, it may be that the verb in the last line stood originally at the head of its clause without particle. In which case the *englyn* may originally have been something like the following:

> *An lavar coth yw lavar gwyr:*
> *byth dorn re ver, byth tavas re hyr;*
> *mes collas den hep davas y dyr.*

If this version is correct, we have repetition in the first two lines: *lavar* x 2, *dorn* x 2; internal rhyme *collas* ~ *davas* and alliteration in *den: davas: dyr.*

The expression *kelly tyr* or *kelly y dyr* does not mean 'lose one's territory', but rather 'lose ground', 'fall back' or 'lose one's opportunity'. The poet is contrasting the disadvantage of too long a tongue when work is to be done with the advantage of being able to speak up for one's rights. I should translate the whole as follows: 'The old saying is a true saying: the hand is too short, the tongue is too long—but a man without speech loses his chance.'

A second Cornish *Englyn*

Pryce prints what is probably a second *englyn* of the same kind as follows:

> *Po rez deberra an bez, vidn heerath a seu; po res dal an vor, na oren pan*
> *a tu, Thuryan, houl Zethas, go Gleth, po Dihow*

This he translates:

> When thou comest into the world, length of sorrow follows; when thou beginnest the way, 'tis not known which side, East, West, to the North or South.   (ACB: opposite F f).

Notice also that Pryce prints the whole as continuous text, apparently not realising that it was a three line stanza. This in itself is no bad thing, because it is clear that Pryce has printed the item as he heard it, and has in consequence not edited it to any great degree. I would divide Pryce's text into lines as follows:

Po rez deberra an bez, vidn heerath a seu;
po res dal an vor, na oren pan a tu,
Thuryan, houl Zethas, go Gleth, po Dihow.

The original language of this *englyn* is unmistakably archaic. It is noteworthy, for example, that the word *houlzethas* is known otherwise only from Lhuyd, who gives *C[ornish] Houlzedhas* s.v. *Occasus* 'Sunsetting; the West' (AB: 104c). Usually in Cornish, however, the word for 'west' is *west*:

Yma oma yn penwyth nebes a **weyst** *the carnebre vn pronter ov cuthel guyth* 'There is here in Penwith a little to the west of Carnbrea a priest doing work' BM 783–85

Eugh thymo bys yn cambron a **west** *the carnbre dyson* 'Go for me to Camborne west of Carnbrea indeed' BM 965–66

Pan nowothou, pan guestlow us genough why a'n cost **west?** 'What news, what pledges have you from the west coast?' BK 2222–23

en pedden **West** *pow Densher* 'in the western part of Devonshire' BF: 27.

Here, however, it is certainly used to mean 'west' rather than 'sunset'. The usual word for 'north' in Cornish is *north*:

North *yst then chapel omma me a vyn mos the guandra* 'North-east of the chapel here I will go and wander' BM 664–65

golsowugh orth iubyter agis tassens a'n berth **north** 'hearken unto Jupiter, your patron saint from the north' BM 2327–28

agen tassens an barth **north** *re roys thynny pur guir y venedycconn* 'our patron saint from the north has given us his blessing' BM 3427–29

Ke souyth ha **north** 'Go south and north' BK 2350.

Gogleth 'north' is otherwise unknown, though it may occur in the toponym *Vounder Gogglas* (CPNE: 106). Its use here is unusual and probably archaic.

Dihow, dyhow in Middle Cornish invariably means 'right hand, right side' rather than 'south', for example in the following:

yn nef y feΔaff tregis an barth **dyghow** *gans am car* 'in heaven I shall dwell on the right hand of my Father' PA 93c

An lader an barth **dyghow** 'The robber on the right hand' PA 193a

gvlan ef re gollas an plas a'm lef **thyghyow** *a wrussen th'y wythe a'n geffo graas* 'he has quite lost the place I should have made on my right side to keep him had he had grace' OM 420–22

*theragoff sur disquethys ys guelys cleth ha **dyov*** 'displayed before me indeed
I saw them left and right' BM 1849–50

*A rag oll an golyov a thuk crist cleth ha **dyov** the vap den rag saluasconn*
'Ah, for all the wounds which Christ bore left and right for the
salvation of mankind' BM 3049–51.

The only place known to me in which the word *dyhow* means 'south' is in
the Old Cornish compound *dehoules* 'abrotanum' [southernwood].

The Cornish word *Thuryan* 'east' (cf. Welsh *dwyrain*) is otherwise
unknown, since the usual word for 'east' is *yst, est*:

*gwyth yn hans compas tha **yest*** 'keep yonder straight to the east' CW
1743

*a reege doaze teeze veer thor an **Est** tha Jerusalem* 'there came wise men
from the east to Jerusalem' RC 23: 194

*ha pel da **East** ev a Travaliaz* 'and far to the east he journeyed' BF: 15

*Wor duath Gra Gwenz Noor **East** wetha pell* 'At last let the north-east
wind blow afar' BF: 43.

From the point of view of vocabulary at least this *englyn* would thus seem
to be very archaic.

It is also apparent that the stanza as it stands is corrupt. Pryce takes *vidn
heerath a seu* to mean 'length of sorrow follows'. *Vidn* is a pre-occluded form
of *vin, vyn* 'will' used to express the future, but *vyn* is so used with a verbal
noun. Here the verb is *a seu* 'which follows' and is finite. I understand the
phrase *vidn heerath a seu* to be a corruption of an earlier **pyn hyr a'th sew* 'long
sorrow will follow thee'. The beginning of both the first and the second line
is *po res < pan wres* 'when thou wilt'. *Gwres* 'thou dost' for *gwreth* is a late
form, being first attested in the *Creation of the World* (1611):

*ganso **pan wres** comparya* 'when thou dost compare with him' CW
160

*pan **wres** ortha vy settya* 'when thou dost attack me' CW 214

*na **wres** na **wres** na barth dowte* 'thou shalt not, thou shalt not, fear
not' CW 218–19

*orthaf vy pan **wres** settya* 'when thou dost attack me' CW 232

*mara **gwrees** ow dyskevera* 'if thou dost expose me' CW 577.

It is, I think, unlikely that *gwres* stood in the orignal *englyn*. It is also highly
improbable that in such a terse verse form two lines would have begun in
the same way. It is more likely, I think, that in one case at least *po res/po rez*
is for **pan vo res* 'when it may be necessary'.

Pryce translates *pan rez dal an vor* as 'when thou beginnest the way', but it seems possible that this is a mistranslation, where *dal* has been understood as though for **dalleth*. I suggest that *dal* may be the verb < **dalgh* 'keep, hold to', not otherwise attested. **Dal* < ** dalgh* would be exactly parallel with Welsh *dal, dala* 'keep, hold' < ** dalg.* Compare also the Breton verb *derc'hel* 'to hold, resist', verbal adjective *dalc'het*; and also the lexicalised imperative *dal* 'tiens!, prends!' Although the verb **dal(gh)* is not otherwise attested in Cornish, the noun *dalhen* 'grasp' occurs in *syttyough dalhen scon ynno* 'seize (*literally* set a grasp in) him straightway' PC 976; and the verb *dalhenna* 'to grasp' occurs in *me a'n dalhen fest yn tyn* 'I will hold him very firmly' PC 1131. A Cornish verb **dalgh* would quite regularly have given **dal* in the same way that **calgh* 'penis' (cf. Breton *kalc'h* 'penis') has given *kal*, for example in *Komero 'vyth goz Kal* 'Take care of your cock' (BF: 58).

Pryce translates *Na oren pana tu* as ''tis not known' which side'. This is not strictly accurate; *na oren* must be for **na woryn* < *ny woryn* 'we know not', a late analogical form of *ny wothyn* 'we know not'; cf. *ny woryn pyscotter* 'we do not know how soon' TH 6a. Given that *na woryn* for *na wothyn* is late, the original verb here was probably not *oren* (< *woryn* < *wothyn*), but perhaps a phrase that looked and sounded superficially similar. I should suggest that instead of *na oren*, the *englyn* may have read *na fors* 'it matters not', which would originally have alliterated with *forth* 'road'. I would also suggest that *pan a tu* < *py ehen a tu* is a later corruption of an earlier *py du* 'which side'. I would tentatively reconstruct the original *englyn* as something like the following:

> *Pub dybarth y'n bys pyn hyr a'th sew*
> *pan vo res dal forth na fors py du,*
> *duryan, howlsethas, gogleth po dyhow.*

If we rearrange the four point of the compass in the third line we get:

> *Pub dybarth y'n bys pyn hyr a'th sew*
> *pan vo res dal forth na fors py du,*
> *howlsethas, gogleth, duryan po dyhow.*

Here there is internal rhyme with *howlsethas ~ gogleth* and alliteration with *duryan: dyhow.* The rhyme *sew* 'follows' ~ *du* 'side' is reminiscent of such rhymes as *a's pew* 'owns' ~ *a'y tu* 'on his side' PC 2858 & 2859 or *dew* 'God' ~ *tew* 'side' CW 138 & 139 and *tew* 'side' ~ *bew* 'alive' CW 1256 & 1258. The rhyme of *dyhow* with *sew* and *du* has no parallel elsewhere. It is certain that *sew* and *du* have the same diphthong, i.e. [ŷw]. It may be that *dyhow* is to be pronounced with a triphthong [dŷow], which was considered close enough to rhyme with *sew* and *du*. If so, we get three lines each with nine syllables. The simplest method for dealing with the awkward third line, however, is probably to omit *po* 'or' before *dyhow* 'south.' That would give us:

> *Pub dybarth y'n bys pyn hyr a'th sew*
> *pan vo res dal forth na fors py du,*
> *howlsethas, gogleth, duryan, dyhow.*

Here each line has nine syllables, and the final segment of *dyhow* [ow] may be considered an adequate rhyme for *sew* [sýw] and *du* [dýw]. I should translate:

> 'In every quarter of the world long tribulation will follow thee,
> when thou must hold to the road no matter which way,
> west, north, east, south.'

This *englyn*, like the first one we have discussed, is gnomic. It deals with the necessity of suffering in the world, whichever way one is compelled to travel. Its subject matter is similar to that of Lhuyd's *englyn* and it is equally archaic. Indeed it is even possible that both *englynion* come from the same collection of stanzas.

A third Cornish *Englyn*

Pryce cites a third stanza as follows:

> *Hithow gwrâ gen skians da:*
> *An gwîranath ew an gwella,*
> *En pob tra, trea, po pella* (ACB: two folios after F f 2).

This he translates:

> Act to-day with prudence good:
> The truth is the best,
> In every thing, at home, or far off.

Pryce implies that the *englyn* derives from William Gwavas. It is noteworthy, moreover, that a version of the second and third lines occurs in a stanza also by Gwavas, also quoted by Pryce, which deals with the verdict given by the jury in the case of Gwavas *v.* Kelynack (1728):

Pengelly Broaz, ha dowthack tíz,
Rag pusgaz dêk angy roz brez:
Fraga? Gwíranath yw an gwella
En pob tra trea po pella.
Ha nessa, Hale têg gen lavar fyr,
Ol poble gwrêz dho adzhan gwîr;
Hellier tubm e helfias reb pul:
Comyns skientek vye glan ol (ACB: obverse of folio after F f 2).

Kent and Saunders translate as follows:

Great Pengelly and twelve men
for fish tithe gave the word;
Why? Truth is best
in everything at home and far away.
And next, fair Hale with a wise saying
Help all people to know the truth,
A warm hunter chased by a pool:
Learned Comyns was all clean (LAM: 245)

That Gwavas uses two lines from the *englyn* in a second stanza seems to indicate that the *englyn* itself was proverbial, rather than an original composition of his own. Moreover, the syntax of the two lines is rather better than in much of the verse ascribed to Gwavas. I suspect, therefore, that he was not the author of the *englyn* nor of the two lines quoted from it in the stanza about the verdict. It is more likely, I think, that Gwavas had heard or read the *englyn* somewhere and not only wrote it out but also quoted part of it in one of his own compositions. If so, the original *englyn* was almost certainly in existence before the eighteenth century.

If we look at the 'Gwavas *englyn*' a little more closely, we notice that there are only six syllables in the first line. I suspect that the word *skians* was originally *conscyans* 'conscience'. If we assume that the *englyn* was older than the early eighteenth century and was in proverbial use, it is likely that it dates ultimately from the Middle Cornish period. I would therefore respell it in a more traditional orthography as follows:

Hethyw gwra gans conscyans da;
an gwyryoneth yw an gwella
yn pup tra tre bo pella.

I would translate:

Act today with a good conscience;
the truth is the best
in all things at home or abroad.

Although it may well have been medieval in origin, there is nothing in the *englyn* to suggest unequivocally that it is from early Middle Cornish period. It should be noted, however, that there is alliteration between *gwyryoneth* and *gwella* in the second line and between *tra* and *tre* in the third. This relatively high degree of metrical ornament may mean that this third, rather unproblematic *englyn*, is from the same period as the other two we have been discussing.

Englynion composed by Lhuyd and John Boson

Although Lhuyd himself tells us that the *englyn* beginning *An lavar coth yw lavar gwyr* was the only one he heard in Cornwall, it is possible, though perhaps unlikely, that Lhuyd had seen or read others in manuscript while he was there. It appears that he believed a series of *englynion* to be a natural enough metrical form in Cornish, since his lament for William III in 1703 was written in *englyn* metre and contained nineteen three-line *englynion* preceded by a stanza of five lines. Lhuyd prefaces his lament with the words:

In Obitum Regis Wilhelmi 3tii Carmen Britannicum Dialectu Cornubiensis: Ad Normam Poetarum Seculi Sexti

On the Death of King William III, a British poem in the Cornish dialect: in the manner of the the ˙oets of the sixth century. (LAM: 232).

By his allusion to the poets of the sixth century, Lhuyd is perhaps implying that he is imitating the Welsh *cynfeirdd* rather than following any tradition existing in Cornwall.

His lament is interesting in that the syllabic count of the lines is irregular. In the second stanza, for example, the lines have seven, seven and nine syllables:

Lavar lemmyn, genz ewhal lêv
Hannadzian down, ha garm krêv;
Golsowez d'ola pen perhen trêv

Speak now, with loud voice
Deep sighs, and strong cry;
Let the head of every household hear your weeping
(LAM: 232).

The tenth stanza, however, has ten, eleven and ten syllables in the line:

Sevowh a mann, ha sqwattyow goz dillaz,
Ha gwllow goz bolow genz dowr an lagaz;
Ha gwarrow goz pennow genz lidziw glâz

Arise, and scat your clothes,
And wash your cheeks with the water of the eye;
And cover your heads with grey ash (LAM: 232).

John Boson seems to have imitated Lhuyd's lament for William III. In a letter to William Gwavas dated 17th February 1712 Boson includes with translation his lament of four stanzas for James Jenkins of Alverton. It is in the same *englyn* metre as Lhuyd's lament. Most of the lines have ten syllables. The first stanza runs as follows:

En levra coth po vo Tour Babel gwres
Scriffas, Gomar mab Japhet vo en Beas
Ha Dotha Tavas Kornooack vo Res

Att building Babels Tower as Books doe tell
Did Gomer Grandson vnto Noah dwell
To whom the Ancient Cornish Language ffell (BF: 48).

It is noteworthy that the syntax of the whole is less than perfect. The English version would more naturally be rendered in Cornish as follows: *En levra coth po vo Tour Babel gwres/ Dell ew scriffas, yth era Gomer mab Japhet en Beas/ Ha dotha an Tavas Kornooack a vo Res*. The poor standard of John Boson's Cornish has been noted before now (see CT § 14.23). John Boson himself was almost certainly the author of this series of *englynion*.

Conclusion

Englynion, similar in form to the Welsh *englyn milwr*, were composed in Middle Cornish and three such *englynion* have survived. Unlike the stricter Welsh *englyn milwr*, the Cornish *englyn* could have a varied number of syllables in each line, from seven to ten, or perhaps even eleven. The Cornish *englyn* is certainly related to the Welsh *englyn* and it seems likely that the two are developments of the same British metrical form. The term *englyn* is now attested (in the plural *eglynnyon*) and it is likely that the Cornish word **eglyn* or **englyn* was used for the three-lined stanza we have been discussing.

The metres of the Cornish plays are very strict, where lines of seven and sometimes four syllables are the norm. The variable syllable count of the Cornish *englyn* might suggest one of two things: 1) that the inherited stanza tolerated a variable syllable-count or 2) that the Cornish *englyn* was a popular form, where the exact syllable count was less important than the number of stresses. Given that the two *englynion* beginning *An lavar kôth* and *Po rez deberra* are archaic in language, it seems likely that the traditional Cornish englyn was not a popular form at all, but a learned and ornate one. We must assume, then, that it could have a variable number of syllables in each line.

The relatively high degree of internal rhyme and alliteration in these two traditional *englynion* suggests that they were the work of specialist poets. The question then arises, who could have composed them? It is fairly certain that *Pascon agan Arluth* and the Cornish mystery plays were composed by educated clerics, many of whom learnt their craft in the college at Glasney. The Cornish *englyn* was probably in origin an aristocratic verse form, practised in the Cornish court before the loss of Cornish independence to the West Saxons in the tenth century. The term *prydyth* 'poet' now attested in *Bewnans Ke*, suggests that the speakers of Middle Cornish were familiar with the notion of professional poets and their poetry. Whether there were any poets in medieval Cornwall who were not also educated clerics is impossible to say with certainty. The absence of an independent royal court and native aristocracy makes it unlikely, in my view, that there were any wholly secular poets in Cornwall in the medieval period. In which case, it seems probable that the *englynion* beginning *An lavar kôth*, *Po rez deberra* and *Hithow gwrâ* were composed by educated clerics in the early Middle Cornish period.

References

AB Edward Lhuyd, *Archæologia Britannica* (London 1707; reprinted Shannon 1971)

ACB William Pryce, *Archæologia Cornu-Britannica* (Sherborne 1790; reprinted Menston, Yorkshire 1972)

BBCS *The Bulletin of the Board of Celtic Studies*

BF O. J. Padel, *The Cornish Writings of the Boson Family* (Redruth, 1975)

BK *Bewnans Ke* (text from the published edition of G. Thomas and N. Williams)

BM Whitley Stokes (ed.), *Beunans Meriasek: The Life of St Meriasek* (London, 1872)

CT Nicholas Williams, *Cornish Today* (3rd edn, Westport, Ireland, 2006)

CW Whitley Stokes (ed.), *Gwreans an Bys: the Creation of the World* (London, 1864; reprinted 1987)

EWGP Kenneth Jackson, *Early Welsh Gnomic Poems* (Cardiff, 1935)

LAM Alan M. Kent and Tim Saunders (eds), *Looking at the Mermaid: A Reader in Cornish Literature, 900–1900* (London, 2000)

OCV 'Old Cornish Vocabulary' (quoted from Norris, *The Ancient Cornish Drama* 1859, ii: 311–435)

OM 'Origo Mundi' in Norris, *The Ancient Cornish Drama* i–ii (London, 1859; reprinted New York 1968), i: 1–219

PC 'Passio Christi Nostri Jhesu Christi' in Norris, *The Ancient Cornish Drama* i–ii (London, 1859; reprinted New York 1968), i: 221–479

RD 'Resurrexio Domini Nostri Jhesu Christi' in Norris, *The Ancient Cornish Drama* i–ii (London, 1859; reprinted New York, 1968]), ii: 1–199

TH John Tregear, *Homelyes xiii in Cornysche* (British Library Additional MS 46, 397), text from a cyclostyled text published by Christopher Bice (no place, 1969).

2

Glasney's Parish Clergy and the Tregear Manuscript

D. H. Frost

Introduction

Until recently, the places of origin and ecclesiastical careers of John Tregear and Thomas Stephyn were largely unknown. Their names occur in the Tregear Manuscript,[1] two paper quarto Cornish texts dating from the second half of the sixteenth century, now bound together in one volume to form by far the longest piece of Cornish prose that survives. The well-known Gaelic scholar John Mackechnie reclassified the predominant language of the manuscript as Cornish, the Historical Manuscripts Commission in 1871 having first described it as Welsh.[2] It formerly belonged to the Pulestons of Emral in Flintshire, North Wales, who said that it had been confiscated from recusants – although I have previously suggested it may have come to them by marriage, from the Edwards family of Chirk Castle, near Wrexham.[3]

The manuscript has two main components. The first is a Cornish translation – usually attributed to a John Tregear whose name appears frequently throughout – of twelve of the Catholic homilies issued by Edmund Bonner, bishop of London in the reign of Mary I.[4] Although it was never printed, clearly someone considered it worthwhile to produce a fair copy of such a text in the Cornish language and may have imagined wider dissemination. It was presumably intended as part of some sort of Counter-Reformation programme of preaching or theological education in western Cornwall, and is most likely to date from some time between 1555 and 1558, although there is no incontestable internal evidence of this.[5] In the absence of a Bible[6] or Prayer Book, this translation of Bonner's Homilies, had it been more generally known, might have performed an important role in linguistic standardization – it is the longest surviving example of Cornish prose. (For students of Cornish, therefore, it could be important to know which part of Cornwall the translator might have come from, and where and when he worked.) The second component of the manuscript is a *catena* of eucharistic quotations in both Cornish and Latin compiled and added – in all likelihood – sometime after 1576.[7] (It is in a different hand to the first component, as are certain annotations and patristic references in the margins of homilies 11 and 12.) This *catena* draws heavily on the speeches of the Catholic divines in the 1554 eucharistic debates at Oxford, as recorded in John Foxe's *Acts and Monuments*.[8] It is no longer confused with the 'thirteenth homily' on the Blessed Sacrament printed in later editions of Bonner's Homilies, and so is best distinguished from the first twelve 'Tregear Homilies' (TH) with the title at the head of one of its folios, '*Sacrament an Alter*' (SA).[9]

The manuscript gives us the names not only of the original authors of Bonner's Homilies in English but also of certain others, unmentioned in any printed English edition. The original authors of the English homilies are well known, and their names are appended to the sections they wrote, even in the Cornish translation. They all held ecclesiastical office in Queen Mary's time. Edmund Bonner himself was bishop of London, John Harpsfield archdeacon of London, and Henry Pendleton one of the bishop's chaplains (who is remembered for being fired at whilst preaching at St Paul's Cross in 1554).[10] Some additional names are found at the end of some homilies, one of them in the hand in which later annotations are written. As will be seen, these names appear to be closely linked to the Cornish version.

There are two main hands in the Tregear Manuscript, each in two forms (although with a degree of overlap – see Appendix). The first (secretary hand A) is a clear, elegant hand of the sixteenth century, and it alternates with an italic version used for Latin quotations only (italic hand A). From the way the single pen is used on the paper, the thickness of the line and other distinctive features, it seems most likely that a single individual was responsible for all of this work, and therefore for both secretary hand A and italic hand A. Whether this hand belonged to the translator into Cornish, or to a scribe, or to someone making a fair copy at a later date, is difficult to determine from the textual evidence. There are few mistakes in this hand, and it is responsible for the first twelve homilies.

The second important hand in the manuscript (secretary hand B) uses a different pen and a great deal more ink, and shows signs of the sort of irregularity that often indicates someone of considerable age. Once again the convention is loosely adopted of using secretary hand for Cornish and an italic hand for Latin (italic hand B) but there is more confusion between the two. Both 'forms' exhibit many features that strongly suggest they belong to the same person. His work is confined to the latter parts of the manuscript, namely the eleventh and twelfth homilies (where it is only used for marginal notes and a name at the end) and the whole of the so-called 'thirteenth homily', *Sacrament an Alter.* The way in which the erratic additional marginal notes in secretary hand B (or its italic version) sometimes cross the original text or orderly marginal notes written in hand A – but always refer to them – indicates that they were written later.

It is in secretary hand A that, at the end of each of the first twelve homilies, the name John Tregear is written.[11] This name is usually followed by the word *clericus*, 'clerk', effectively meaning 'priest' in this context. At the ends of the two homilies (11 and 12) with the erratic additional marginal notes, a name is appended in secretary hand B – that of Thomas Stephyn, also *clericus*.[12] The 'thirteenth homily', *Sacrament an Alter*, is lacking its final page or pages, or is unfinished or damaged, and has no signature at the end. It is, however, also in secretary hand B, exhibiting features similar to those in the annotations and in Stephyn's name. Taken together, these textual considerations suggest to me that a John Tregear was in some particular way connected with the Cornish text of the first twelve homilies. Because they are simple translations, he is therefore commonly thought to be responsible for the work of translation itself, although the characteristic sixteenth century hand found throughout the first twelve homilies may or may not be his own. (The *quod* before the name perhaps suggests that while the words are Tregear's, they may have been set down by a scribe.)[13]

Because of their erratic and partly spontaneous nature, it seems very likely that the additional marginal notes to homilies 11 and 12 were all personally written by the Thomas Stephyn, who has clearly appended his name in the same hand (secretary hand B) to those particular sections. Since *Sacrament an Alter* is in exactly the same hand, it is also attributed to Stephyn. That two separate authors were responsible for the manuscript is no new discovery: it was suggested by Nance at the outset, and has for many years been the independent conclusion of others examining the texts, including Brian Murdoch, Matthew Spriggs, Charles Penglase, and myself.

A third name appears once only in the upper left margin of TH 12v.8–12, written at right angles to the text in hand C. It may read Richard Logan (as Nance thought), or possibly Logar, and is followed by a word which is difficult to make out, even in the original manuscript, but which may be *librarius*.[14] (In Tregear's time this would still have referred to a secretary or copyist rather than a librarian, but the name and particularly the appended word do not appear to be of the same period or in hand A or hand B.[15]) The word is so faint and short that it is difficult to be completely sure that it is in the same hand as the name, so it may in future need to be attributed to another (hand D). While it is possible that it identifies Tregear's scribe, one would have imagined that such a person's name would have been clearly appended in hand A – so it could indicate someone who had custody of the manuscript at another stage, perhaps even outside Cornwall.

It has been a common assumption among students of Middle and Tudor Cornish, that most of our surviving texts were collated and copied at the College of Our Lady and St Thomas of Canterbury, at Glasney in Penryn.[16] The College played a dominant role in mid-Cornish ecclesiastical life in the early sixteenth century, by which time it was responsible for the pastoral care of many local parishes and villages. It was a natural base for study and its residential canons (technically 'prebendaries') and vicars would have been influential. These factors alone make it a good starting place to look for Tregear and Stephyn, but the usual sources for clergy in residence during the period in question do not yield up their names.[17] It has been suggested several times, therefore, that Tregear and Stephyn may have been lowly chantry priests at the College, or even private chaplains to wealthy families associated with it.

There is no real foundation for either idea. If we cast the net wider than Glasney itself, to include the dispersed parish clergy only loosely associated with Glasney – especially vicars and curates in parishes where the College had appropriated the rectorial tithes – the search soon yields results. We find that both men were ordinary parish priests in western Cornwall. Both appear to have been ordained before the Reformation, yet continued in various ways to function after it. I believe that we can now show that their role in any Cornish Counter-Reformation was complex, tentative and above all parish-based. We shall see below that Tregear, far from being a formal recusant, appears to have remained in his parish under Henry VIII, Edward VI, Mary I and Elizabeth I – however Catholic his views may have been. He may have lived as a 'Church papist', helped by the remoteness of his parish and the fact that he died before the Elizabethan anti-Catholic measures got underway in earnest. Stephyn by contrast, appears to have been what we might call a 'Marian priest'[18] (though ordained long before, in Henry's time). The history of such clergy, in its nature, is surrounded by a good deal of fog. As it became steadily more dangerous to espouse Catholic views, it would have been foolhardy to create or leave behind much in the way of documentary evidence of illegal religious activity in the parishes. (As a result, we know far more of the centrally ordered Jesuits from continental seminaries, who began their mission from 1576 onwards, than we do of the older local clergy who sought to bridge the gap in the 16 years before those missionary priests began to arrive.)

In Cornwall there have long been folk-tales of the celebration of mass 'in the tin mines', although in practice it was more likely to have been in the vicarage parlour. A small number of recusant Catholic gentry – like the Arundells of Lanherne and the Tregians of Golden – were able to maintain chaplains for their own needs and those of the local populace. Less well documented is the thinking and strategy of the older traditional clergy who attempted to resist the reformed religion from inside the churches or by an itinerant preaching ministry. Although ultimately they failed, in the intriguing years between 1560 and 1580 the outcome often looked less sure. William Bradbridge sought to resign as bishop of Exeter in 1576, at least in part because his success had been so partial against such defaulters from the Elizabethan settlement.[19]

In order to understand the Tregear Manuscript, therefore, it is necessary to look in some detail at the parish careers of its authors in rural western Cornwall. Both priests (and possibly others about whom Cornish language scholars have been curious) are attested as being based in ordinary, local churches rather than in any college or religious community – although they may have been under the patronage of a particular canon before the dissolution. After the dissolution, of course, it was only out in the parishes that efforts to preserve traditional religion through the medium of Cornish could be made.

John Tregear, vicar of St Allen, 1544–1583

The Robert Morton Nance Bequest at the Courtney Library of the Royal Institution of Cornwall contains a number of notes gathered by Nance on the possible identity of Tregear. Among the most important of these is the information that the Revd G. C. Sara had found an entry in the parish register of St Newlyn East recording

> *John Tregear, clerk,*
> *bur[ied] the xxiv th day of march,*
> *the year [1583].*[20]

This raised a number of questions at the time. Sara told Nance that Tregear did not seem to have been the vicar or parish clerk of Newlyn[21] itself, as the names of these were known for the 1580s. Nor does the name Thomas Stephyn appear in this parish register. Sara was one of the first to suggest that one possible explanation might be that John Tregear and Thomas Stephyn held no benefices because of their Catholic views, and were perhaps private chaplains to a recusant household.[22]

A possibility that Nance and Sara appear to have overlooked, however, was that Tregear had been working elsewhere in the established church, and was for some particular reason either buried at Newlyn or recorded in the burial register there. The family name of Tregear has a long history in the parish, and there was a farm known as 'Tregair' there. He might have been brought home. Alternatively he might have held office in a neighbouring parish and been buried (in the absence of another) by the priest of Newlyn, who recorded the fact in his own register because it was unusual or held some other significance for him.[23]

It might be thought that a search for Tregear's will would resolve the question. Unfortunately, the Exeter ecclesiastical courts were moved from their former resting place in the Cathedral not long before the Second World War, to a new home nearby – the Exeter Probate Registry. This was comprehensively bombed in 1942. Almost nothing survived of the ancient wills of Cornwall and Devon at that time, unless they were proved or copied elsewhere. What has survived, because it was printed, is a full calendar or list of the wills that once existed. A printed survey of those proved in the court of the Archdeaconry of Cornwall, which gives notes and abstracts for some of them, contains references to two John Tregeeres – although these are of the wrong date.[24] (There are many Thomas Stephyns – a very common name, no doubt in some cases a simple patronymic.)[25] In the printed calendar of wills proved in the Bishop's Registry, however, there is a more relevant entry:

1583, Tregear, John, vicar of St Alin. 384 W.[26]

Fortunately, the Episcopal Registers for the Diocese have survived and it is possible to confirm the information given in the *Calendar of Wills*. The second entry for the 11 September 1583 in the Registers of Bishop Woolton[27] describes the institution of Christopher Colmer

de vic. perpetu. Sti. Aluni Exon. Dioc.
[as vicar of St Allen in the diocese of Exeter]

It is noted that it had become vacant

per mortem Johannis Tregeare.
[by the death of John Tregear][28]

This particular John Tregear had, therefore, been the vicar of St Allen until he died, and had naturally enough been buried by a priest from the neighbouring parish of Newlyn where he would have been well-known. Slight errors of transcription in *Hennessy's Incumbents*, a manuscript study of institutions from the Episcopal Registers,[29] have led in the past to confusion over Tregear's link with the parish.[30] Hennessy lists the appointment of 'Xfer Colmo'[31] to St Allen on the death of 'Jn Tregearn' [sic]. It has been imagined that this was another priest, but there is no John Tregearn in the manuscript sources of the period. Careful study of the entry in the Bishop's Register itself reveals that Hennessy should have recorded the spelling as 'Tregeare'.

St Allen church feels somewhat off the beaten track now: there is no large village around the church, the interior of which has been much altered since Tregear's day. In Tudor times, however, the parish was not without its wealthier dimension. The bishops of Exeter themselves had once had a chapel of St Martin and manor house at Lanner.[32] There were still Arundells of the Trerice branch at Gwarnick (a junior branch of the family founded in the fourteenth century when a younger son of the Lanherne branch married the heiress of Trerice).[33] John Leland visited Cornwall in 1533 and 1542; in his *Itinerary* he mentions staying in 'Alein' with John Arundell at Gwarnick rather than at Trerice (which the latter's mother may have held in dower at that time). He remarked on the 'very good corne' in the area.[34] Studies of the period have revealed a reasonably active church life and laity: there was a guild and store of St Anthony (and possibly also of St Allen) in the parish.[35] There were also close ties with Glasney and with the neighbouring parish of Newlyn East, where Trerice itself lay.

Having found a parish with a John Tregear as vicar, it is now a relatively easy matter to establish how long he served there. Hennessy, from his research in the Episcopal Registers, notes William Treruffe[36] as Tregear's predecessor, and the year he left office as 1544. It is therefore possible to return to the Registers – in this case of John Veysey – and look for the institution of Tregear himself. There, in an entry for the 28 July 1544 we find the appointment of

> *Johani Tregayre, presbitero*
> *vicarium p[er]petuam eccl[esi]e p[ar]ochialis de Alune*
> *in Cornub[ia].*[37]

> [John Tregear, priest,
> as vicar of the parish church of Allen
> in Cornwall.]

This indicates that while Tregear was being admitted to the cure of the parish, he would only be a 'vicar'; that is, only the vicarial tithes would be his and not the great tithes of corn. As in a good number of parishes in central and western Cornwall – including Budock, Gluvias, Feock, Mylor, Manaccan, St Just-in-Penwith, Zennor, Sithney, Kea and Kenwyn, St Goran, Colan, St Enoder and Mevagissey – these had long been assigned to Glasney College, as part of its considerable endowment, mostly accumulated between 1265 and 1288. (Mevagissey and St Just were added in the fourteenth century.) In other words, Glasney took the great tithes and Tregear, whose job was to be the parish priest, was responsible for raising his own income from the tithes and offerings which remained. This income was far from substantial.[38]

If this Tregear is the John Tregear of the Homilies (and, as we shall see, the only other contemporary references to a priest of this name are all identifiable with this man) then he is linked to Glasney as one of its rural parish priests. This is a fascinating piece of evidence of the possible ties between the college, its parish clergy and the production of Cornish texts. It has always been assumed before that the College's influence over the writing of these had taken place *in situ*. (Glasney is often glorified as some sort of 'proto-university' on this account.) In fact, Tregear's case raises the possibility that it was out in the parishes, within the College's wider orbit, that much of this work was done – and by the rural clergy rather than solely by scholarly residentiary canons. It is also an indication of the calibre of some of these country priests, even though (as we shall also see) many may not have been to university themselves.

Further references to Tregear at St Allen

It is of some importance that a John Tregear was still vicar of St Allen three years after Queen Mary's death, in December 1561, when Bishop Alley (it is assumed) ordered a survey of all the clergy of the Diocese for the records of Archbishop Parker.[39] In this we find a helpful entry for Allen:

> *Alene:*   *Dominus Johannes Tregeyre, vic[arius],*
> *non grad[uatus],*
> *pres[byter] non coni[ugatus] nec conc[ubinarius],*
> *satis doctus,*
> *residet, hospitalis, ibid[em] degens,*
> *non pred[ica]t, nisi in prop[rio] ben[eficio] nullum aliud.*

> [Allen: Sir[40] John Tregear, vicar,
> non-graduate,
> unmarried priest, not co-habiting,
> sufficiently educated,
> resident, hospitable, living in the same place,
> non-preaching unless in his own parish, no other.]

From this we learn that (1) Sir John Tregear was still at Allen, and still the vicar; (2) he had apparently never been to university; (3) he was still unmarried and a genuinely celibate priest; (4) he was well educated for a non-university man (and therefore had possibly gone to a grammar school, at

Glasney or elsewhere, or had otherwise been taught to read and write Latin – and, we may add, Cornish); (5) that he was not an absentee clergyman and was welcoming, hospitable and actually living in Allen when the survey took place; (6) that he at least claimed that he did not go about from parish to parish preaching, as some conservative clergy were reputed to do;[41] (7) he held no other parish.

The phrase *non predicat* – 'he does not preach' – perhaps needs some explanation. It should not be seen as an indictment, especially in the eyes of those compiling the survey. Many parish clergy did not claim to preach, and this was somewhat comforting to the authorities who increasingly held a dim view of those ordained before the Reformation, and many of those ordained after. Even before the Reformation pulpits were more likely to be used for 'bidding the bedes' than for sermons (although there are some indications that preaching had played an increasing role in some parishes).[42] Tregear is, therefore, among the small number of clergy in the survey who did acknowledge preaching in their own parishes (such as Christopher Trychay at Morebath).[43] Whereas in most cases *non predicat* may be taken fairly literally, in those cases with a qualifying phrase its import seems to be: 'he does not hold the bishop's licence to preach outside his parish and acknowledges that fact'. Very few indeed (only 6) were trusted with Bishop Alley's formal permission to preach more widely. Historically, the primary purpose of the general category of clergy without degrees was to celebrate the liturgy, offer pastoral care, give periodic spiritual and moral guidance (particularly through the sacrament of penance) and catechise the young in a straightforward manner. It is not that such clergy did not teach the faith, but rather that they did not generally do so from the pulpit. Although Tregear was something of an exception, and did acknowledge an ability to preach, he was careful to report what he did in a way that avoided official condemnation and removed all fears of any itinerant ministry.

Whatever the case, Cranmer's first *Book of Homilies* was meant to address the lack of adequate and acceptable preaching. (Bonner's *Homilies*, which Tregear translated, were meant to fulfil a similar role during Mary's brief restoration of Catholicism. It is fascinating that the two books have substantial portions in common.) The *Book of Homilies* came back into use under Elizabeth, in theory until her new bishops were able to ensure a sufficient supply of preachers of the reformed religion.

If we accept that Tregear was one of the few clergy noted in Alley's survey as preaching, the case is perhaps marginally stronger that his translation of the Homilies may have been intended for wider distribution: he was clearly capable of doing more than just reading a homily. On the other hand, since he only preached in his own parish it could still be argued that he made the translation for exclusive use there.

There is a number of indications, including those outlined by Julyan Holmes, that some Cornish was spoken in the area at this time.[44] Matthew Spriggs, building on crucial earlier studies by Holmes and others, places the parish of St Allen within an area where he believes Cornish was still spoken prior to 1600.[45] If Tregear had been writing in a parish where the language was extinct, it would have strengthened the case that his work was intended for general use. But even though he was not, it was still a considerable and meticulous labour, which, if helpful in St Allen, would be even more useful in many other parishes further west. It would be surprising if any Cornish-speaking clergy in Cornwall who knew of such a project (even without the bishop's involvement) did not view it as in some sense undertaken on their behalf, and may have harboured hopes to copy and use it.

We next hear of Tregear as a witness to the will of another priest, Lawrence Godfrey, on 12 September 1563.[46] Godfrey describes himself as the vicar of 'Saincte Piran in zandes', that is, Perranzabuloe, although Hennessy (who records Ralph Oldon as the incumbent from 1535, and William Howe from 1564) found no reference in the Registers to this incumbency between the two. (There was a John Godfrey in the parish in the 1569 Muster, but Lawrence Godfrey was dead by that time, as the date of the execution of his will – by Tregear – was 7 October 1564.)

Earlier in his life Godfrey appears to have been a chantry priest at Exeter Cathedral, and after the suppression he received a small pension and the sponsorship of a local farmer while he was based at Okehampton church. His pension was noted in a sheet found by Frances Rose-Troup in Portfolio 1 of the *Valor Ecclesiasticus* for Exeter, 1540–41, at the Public Record Office.[47] Rose-Troup records the entry as

In the Deanery of Okehampton.
In the parish church of Okehampton.
Mr Lawrence Godfrey,
employed by Thomas Hole, fermer.

In a document among the Exchequer Accounts dated 22 June 1548 concerning the pensions awarded to 'the Incumbents and Ministers of diverse late Colleges, Chantries and Free Chapels and to stipendary priests and other priests and to other persons'[48] there is a further reference to

Lawrence Godfrey. An Incumbent, Horseis. 100s

This shows that Godfrey originally held the Horsey Chantry in the Cathedral.[49] His life and career had therefore been considerably disrupted by the Reformation. Indeed his will gives some indications that he, like

Tregear and Stephyn, may have had traditionalist sympathies. His opening words are fairly conventional:

> *I bequeathe my soule to almightie god*
> *and my bodie to be buried in the Chancell of Sainct Piran aforesaide,*
> *where the highe alter stoode.*[50]

The mention of the old high altar, however, might just conceivably be significant. Whereas Christopher Trychay at Morebath seems to have desired burial between the old altar and the new table, Godfrey explicitly requires that he is laid to rest directly under the place where the high altar would have stood.[51] We cannot be sure, however, that this represents any nostalgia about the place where he offered mass in former years. Parish chancels were quite full of burials by the mid sixteenth century and removing the altar provided extra space, allowing a burial which might otherwise have had to have been elsewhere. (Nonetheless, similar considerations allow us to speculate on whether Tregear was buried in a similar way and may lie in a similar location within Newlyn church or even in his own parish church of St Allen.)

Godfrey's will goes on to leave two surplices, one to the church of St Piran, and one to St Agnes – as well as 'coverlets' (or palls) to be laid over the body at burial services, again a reminder of earlier customs and at the very least reflecting a concern for godly and decent order at a time when it was under threat. He also leaves many generous bequests to his godchildren, especially his godson Piran. Then he comes to John Tregear:

> *Item: to Sir John Tregeare clarke Vicar of Alune*
> *one stone of my beste wooll my ffrocke and my cassok ...*
>
> *... and I doe ordaine the saide vicar of Alune to be my superviser*
> *vppon this my laste will and testament*
> *and he to sell my corne and devide the value thereof*
> *as muche as is drye amonge the poore*
> *and in workes of charitie for the healthe of my soule.*
>
> *Item my bookes, to be devided amonge prestes*
> *to the saide vicar of Alunis discrecion.*[52]

It is perhaps pushing the evidence a little too far to detect a holy purpose and genuine kindness about this testament which may seem to come through the formal language. The same sentiments occur in hundreds of wills and clergy had a duty to leave surplus wealth for charitable purposes. Such bequests were more of an ethic than the personal sentiment they would be in our day. Nonetheless, there may be an echo of traditional theology in the notion that good works undertaken as a result of a bequest might ease the deceased soul's spiritual health. If so, it is well disguised. The Elizabethan authorities were increasingly on the lookout for 'one that prayeth for the dead'.[53] Whatever the significance of the individual bequests, John Tregear was clearly held in high regard by Lawrence Godfrey. One wonders what books might have been bequeathed, and where they eventually went. Once again there is a glimpse of some learning, and a valuing of it, among these Cornish country clergy.

A few years later, when another 'muster' of all those who could help in the defence of the country was conducted in Cornwall – the 1569 Muster Roll – Tregear's name appears again. All able-bodied men had to list the equipment they could be counted on to supply should it be needed in any war (although such muster rolls were really a thinly disguised way of establishing taxable values.) Under the entry for St Allen (where he was still the incumbent) we find:

John Tregear, bow, 12 arrows, jack.[54]

Archers customarily wore a jacket (jack) with a doublet beneath, and in addition to their longbow and arrows often carried a short sword or dagger for closer fighting if necessary.[55] It is fascinating to speculate on whether Tregear himself learned the use of his bow, perhaps in early youth, and to wonder whether he had been tempted to take up arms himself during the Western Rebellion in 1549. If he did, or if he had supported it in any other way, he had evidently managed to keep it quiet. (On the other hand, the muster may show no more than that he could supply these items as part of the militia stock.)

Tregear remained vicar of the parish from 1544 to 1583. He must, therefore, have been sufficiently discreet and adaptable to survive at least some of the ecclesiastical changes under Elizabeth, despite the rather Catholic views which his involvement in the translation of Bonner's Homilies might suggest. We do not have to suppose that he was some sort of early 'Vicar of Bray' on this account. Church life, in a remote Cornish parish, might have featured a number of compromises with tradition and delays to the innovations which would have been unthinkable in London. Initially, while the changes made under Henry VIII were far from insignificant, they did not strike at the central mystery of the mass, although the dissolution of the monasteries and the suppression of pilgrimages, shrines and venerated images must have been deeply felt. (There is some evidence, however – considered below in the section on Thomas Stephyn – that Stephyn and possibly Tregear defiantly continued with pilgrimages.) Then, like so many Cornish parishes, St Allen may have dragged its feet under Edward VI (and possibly even supplied some rebels at the Western Rising). The Edwardine period, while radical in its programme, was relatively short lived. What is often forgotten is that within four years of the introduction of the First Prayer Book (and only one year of the Second Prayer Book) Edward was dead, and his Catholic sister Mary I was on the throne. Where they had been destroyed, images, rood screens and all the accompaniments of the old liturgy were now ordered to be restored. In many cases the destruction and plunder may have been incomplete in the far west, like the introduction of the Second Prayer Book. (In Lancashire even Elizabethan visitations show altars, images, holy water, rosary beads and signs of the cross surviving long after they were abolished, although it was more fertile recusant territory.)[56] Bishops like Bonner and Exeter's own John Veysey were restored to their sees. Most of the clergy in Cornwall had not married and remained in post, with a few notable exceptions.[57]

At some point around 1555, in all probability, John Tregear began to translate Bonner's Homilies into the Cornish language. This surely reinforces the idea that he was one of the more traditional of priests, whether he undertook the task on his own initiative, or as part of a group, or on the specific request of authority. The importance of the translation can hardly be overstated in any estimation of Tregear's life and work. The episode has naturally attracted far more notice than the simple biographical matter which is the subject of this article,[58] and this is not the place to re-examine it in depth. It was a considerable achievement, and his diligence can still be seen in the manuscript, subsequently carefully bound, at the British Library in London. Whether the intention was to confine it to his parish, or copy it further, or even to print it in due course, another change of regime caused all such hopes to be swept away.

Thomas Stephyn, curate and vicar of St Newlyn East

Thomas Stephyn, the possible compiler of *Sacrament an Alter*, had a relatively common name so his footprint is much harder to trace than that of John Tregear, and we can never be wholly sure we have the right man. There were many Thomas Stephyns living in Exeter diocese around this time, and even more than one priest with the same or a similar name.[59] Furthermore, although the use of toponymics and other fixed surnames among Cornish speakers was well established, the earlier tradition of the patronymic still persisted.[60] Fortunately, we have both a *terminus post quem* and a *terminus ante quem* for Stephyn's literary work, and some of the other Thomas Stephyns are insufficiently close to Tregear in age, location, clerical status and faith to fit. Nor is it likely that a stranger would have been entrusted with so important and dangerous a manuscript, with all the risks that would involve to individuals, families and their reputations. It is also important to take into account the areas where Cornish was still spoken as a first language at the time. (The Thomas Stephyn we are looking for appears to be particularly fluent and natural in his use of the language, if allowances are made for 'late' usage, and he may have grown up surrounded by it.)

It therefore seems to me relatively secure to identify the man appointed in 1557 as vicar of St Newlyn East – the neighbouring parish to St Allen – with the Stephyn we are looking for.[61] This man appears not to have been an incumbent before and, at the very least, is unlikely to have been a committed Protestant, being appointed under James Turberville, Veysey's successor as bishop of Exeter. When Thomas Stephyn was instituted on 5 March 1557 – St Piran's Day – his job would have been to continue the business of restoring its Catholic practice in the typical Marian way, with masses, processions and even sermons to enrich joint pilgrimages with nearby parishes. (Perhaps for some of these – if they had not already been surrendered to Edward's meticulous men – the partly gilt silver chalice and the gilt pyx surmounted by a cross were used, that were given to the parish by John Snettisham, chancellor of the Cathedral, in 1447.)[62]

Fortunately, we have an almost contemporary account of a procession of relics to the chapel of St Nectan in this very parish at Rogationtide during the Marian years. Rogation processions were very popular and although banned under Edward, they were restored under Mary and even tolerated under Elizabeth. The account is included in Nicholas Roscarrock's *Lives of the Saints* and Roscarrock says he first heard it from a priest who had been present at the occasion – conceivably Stephyn himself:

> *Ther was a chapple in the parishe of Sct Newlan in Cornwall called Sct Neghtons of the saint to which it was dedicated, which chapple had a yard belonginge vnto it in which ther were foure stones on a little mount or hill at the Northwest corner wher the crosses and reliques of Sct Piran, Sct Crantocke, Sct Cuthbert, Sct Newlan were wont to bee placed in rogation weeke, at which time they vsed to meete ther [and had a] sermond made to the people, and the last was preached by persone Crane in Queene Maries tyme, as I haue bene credibly informed by a preist who had bene an eye witnesse.*[63]

Even if this procession took place before Stephyn became the incumbent, there are very good reasons for thinking he might well have been there. In addition to his spell as vicar, he seems to have been a curate in the parish – possibly for a considerable period – and trusted to run it during the previous incumbent's periods of residence elsewhere. This underlines what may have been a long association with the area and with Tregear. For evidence of his curacy at Newlyn we have to turn to a fascinating manuscript in the archives of the Dean and Chapter of Exeter, sometimes known as Bishop Veysey's *Valor*.[64] It takes the form of a paper book, torn, with the covering page missing, around 9" × 12" and with 36 folios. It is a sort of clerical subsidy for the diocese of Exeter, listing all the Cathedral dignitaries and personnel, and the rectors, vicars and – most useful of all – curates throughout the whole diocese by name, with the amount of their assessed contributions.

On 3 November 1534, parliament had passed the Act awarding to Henry VIII the first fruits (i.e. the first year's income) of all ecclesiastical offices and an annual pension of 10% of all church incomes.[65] The bishops in convocation, having accepted Henry's earlier criticisms and demands had, with hindsight, only whetted his appetite for more, and fines for clerical premunire and other supposed misdemeanours followed. The dating of this particular subsidy is, however, complex, and varies from place to place – possibly reflecting the time it took to compile. It was previously dated solely by the names of two Archdeacons – George Carew, who was not collated to the Archdeaconry of Totnes until April 1534, and Rowland Lee, who was elevated to the see of Lichfield in the same month. It was therefore assumed that early 1534 was a reasonably safe conjectural date.[66] However, Ralph Oldon was not appointed to Perranzabuloe until 1535, and the same is true of John Kenall's appointment to Wendron[67] – and both are in place by the time of the manuscript. More telling is the fact that it places John Rose at Maker and John Taylor at St Erme[68] – and they were both appointed in 1536. This brings us closer to the time of the official return from the diocese under the Act – made in early 1536, but not at first considered sufficiently detailed. A further return was required of Bishop Veysey, and was sent by him to the Crown on 3 November 1536.[69] It seems possible, therefore, that D&C 3688 was a draft of the more detailed information collected for this purpose, or even a revision compiled slightly later.[70] It may represent the last of three instalments of the fine that the clergy agreed to pay to Henry VIII for their breach of premunire. It is unlikely to have been compiled after 1537, as Simon Butler of St Clement (Moresk) died in that year, and such deaths were generally noted if they occurred before the document was finalised.

In any case, the manuscript clearly places Thomas Stephyn as the curate of Newlyn in the mid-1530s. Under the Deanery of Pydar on folio 33r we find:

Newlyn   *Mr Radulphus Trelobys Vic*
             d Thomas Stephyn cur

The use of 'Mr' (for *magister*) suggests that Ralph Trelobys, the vicar, may have held a degree or have been of a certain social standing (the title 'Mr' not being used indiscriminately for incumbents in the document.) The 'd' (for *dominus*) in the case of Thomas Stephyn tells us no more than that he was a priest. There is very little further information to be gleaned, but it seems likely that this is the same man who, in Mary's time, after the death of the vicar, was appointed as incumbent himself. We shall return to the question as to whether this service was continuous. (From the evidence presented so far it is much less clear than it was in the case of Tregear that Stephyn was in post during the Edwardine reformation, or whether he absented himself for a while and then returned with the restoration of Catholic order under Mary.)

One other reference to a 'Sir Thomas' as a 'parish priest of St Newlyn' occurs around this time, in fact in 1537.[71] Alexander Carvanell, a deputy to Peter Grisling a 'searcher' (or customs official) of Truro, wrote to the Council (i.e. to Cromwell) to record the occurrence of an unauthorized 'pope-holy' pilgrimage to Brittany. Carvanell and Grisling were effectively government spies in this regard, and on the lookout for illicit sea crossings. The ship concerned was the *Magdalen*, and the allegation was that, through the connivance of three priests it had set out to take people on pilgrimage to a Breton pardon at Treguier ('Lantregar') and had refused cooperation with the port authorities who wished to search it:

> *that is to saye, that the Mr of a certain Ship of the said poort of Trewrew called the Maudelyn … thorough the Counsaill of thre preste[s], faynyng a poope holly pilgrymage to a p[ar]donne in Brytayn, denyed not oonly the said deputie sercheor to s[e]rche the said ship, but also my deputie of thadmyraltie in those partes to doo his Office and duetie.[72]*

We already know from a number of sources (such as the Military Surveys) of the considerable number of Bretons living in Cornish parishes at this time. It is even more interesting to see this example of traffic the other way, apparently for religious reasons. If this could take place when all such expeditions were banned, what might have been going on before? (Although, perhaps, such 'pardons' were less of a draw when Cornwall had its own.) The greatest interest of this incident, however, lies in who the priests were who were behind it. The ringleader is described as 'parish priest of St Newlyn', and his name is given as Sir Thomas 'Trebilcock'. There is a long list of others involved, ending with the mention of 50 persons not formally listed:

> *These are the namys of the ry[t]tous p[er]sons hereafter following.*
> *Ffyrst Sr Thomas Trebilcok p[ar]yshe pryste of Saynt Newlyn.*
> *Sir Phillip … [space left blank] p[ar]ishe preste of Saynt Annys*

John Michell junior of Trewrew Captayn
Rychard Barrett m[er]chawnt of Trewrew.
Pascawe Trehar of Newlyn.
Richard Otes of Ffoweok of the said ship.
John Tradrack breton als spycer the masters mate.
John Loo brewton
John Hoskyn of Trewrew
John Hewitt brewton
Wyll[ya]m Mathewe
Wyll[ya]m Salpyn
Wyll[ya]m Carselyk w[i]t[h] other to the number of 1 p[er]sons.[73]

It is fairly clear that the names here are confused and even mangled. The priests and crew were far from cooperative, so may have given false names, and the list appears to be partly conjectural, and possibly second or third hand. 'Thomas Trebilcok' could therefore be a confusion, taking elements from both Thomas Stephyn and Ralph Trelobys. If so, it would be difficult to know which of them is meant, but it at least confirms that Newlyn was conservative in terms of its clergy at that time. Another possibility is that Thomas Stephyn was also known by an inherited family name – ultimately derived from the place-name Trebilcock in Roche. However, at the period in question there were also Trebilcocks at Stithians – a more likely origin for Thomas Stephyn, taking together his career, his clerical contacts, any possible early association with Glasney and his Cornish. (There were also tinners of the name even more widely dispersed, from Perranzabuloe to St Mewan.)

Of the other places mentioned, it is hard to resist identifying 'St Anne' with 'St Allen'. This would, however, presuppose a considerable mangling of the intelligence, and the priest's name is given as Sir Phillip, not Sir William.[74] (There must, of course, have been at least a degree of confusion, as the surname was not known, and one might suppose that the priests were reluctant to divulge their real names to Carvanell.) A more obvious link would be with St Agnes, often known at this time (and subsequently) as 'St Ann's', or possibly with Advent.[75]

Who the third priest was, we do not know, but the ship certainly gave Carvanell a run for his money.[76] He had attempted to board with two other men, Alexander Cock and John Bartholomew, but had initially been thrown overboard. Catching up with the vessel at St Mawes, they managed to arrest Richard Otes with four of his mariners, but in the end the crew would not let the ship be searched and carried Carvanell and his men out to sea. They put Cock and Bartholomew into a small boat about five miles outside Falmouth Haven, but Carvanell was carried all the way to Brittany, threatened continually with the fear of being cast overboard or towed at the stern. Once in Treguier similar rough sport continued, with the crew encouraging the Bretons to pick quarrels with him, 'shuldryng and buffeting him as though he had bene a turke or a Sarzin'.[77] Eventually he got home in another ship and filed his report. The case was to be examined by Godolphin, but we have no record of the outcome.

Possible further references to Stephyn in the diocese

Other references to a Thomas Stephyn, when collated, make it clear that there were in fact at least two priests of this name in the diocese in the mid sixteenth century. They occur in the same sources, with one always exercising a ministry in Cornish-speaking Cornwall, the other in Devon. Although we cannot be sure, it seems plausible to conclude that one was Cornish and the other was not. The first (who is easiest to identify with the Thomas Stephyn of Newlyn) was a curate of Mylor in 1522. The second (possibly Devon) man was only ordained in 1530 – although it is impossible to be completely sure beyond all doubt which is which in the subsequent references. Both require consideration in turn.

In the Glasney parish of Mylor – as well as the chapelry of Mabe – according to the Cornwall Military Survey of 1522, John Tregythyow was the vicar. But since he resided in Exeter, much fell upon his two curates, 'Thomas Stephyn, chaplain, curate of Mylor' and 'John Sampson, chaplain, curate of Lavabe' (Mabe). There is further information:

> *Thomas Stephyn, chaplain, curate there*
> *has in stipend £5.6.8, in goods £3.*[78]

This is revealing. It shows that in some parishes an absentee vicar might well provide a reasonable annual income for his curates, comparable to the stipend of a vicar in a poor parish. In consequence, a young priest might have both responsibility and security for a considerable period while never appearing in any list of incumbents. Effectively Stephyn was the parish priest, and the person that local people would have turned to for their spiritual and pastoral needs. Such an experienced pastor would then have been an ideal appointment for Newlyn, given the fact that Trelobys resided principally at Crowan. He would have known Stephyn from his links with Glasney.

Of course, it may be objected that the curate of Mylor must have been born too early to have written *Sacrament an Alter* as he would have been a very old man by 1576. Yet others had a similarly long career at the time. Ordained in 1516, John Tristeane[79] appears to have been a curate at Crowan (also under Ralph Trelobys, who held both Crowan and Newlyn) in 1522.[80] He may be

– allowing for a little mispelling – the 'd Joh⁽ᵉˢ⁾ Tresene' who was curate in charge at Perranarworthal in the mid-1530s.[81] Later in life Tristeane was one of Stephyn's successors at Newlyn (appointed 1573).[82] He died in December 1581, not long before John Tregear.[83] It was not impossible, then, for a rural parish priest – albeit in a modest way – to follow in the footsteps of a bishop like Veysey, who lived and worked into his late nineties.[84]

The second Thomas Stephyn did not begin his ministry until some eight years later than this reference to the curate of Mylor. On 11 June 1530, in the parish church of Colyton, the auxiliary (or 'suffragan') Thomas Chard, bishop of Solubria[85] confirmed a Thomas 'Stevyns'.[86] At the next ordination on 19 September in the Lady Chapel of the Cathedral, a Thomas 'Stephyns' is recorded as having been made subdeacon by Thomas Vyvyan, titular bishop of Megara.[87] After a very short interval for prayer and reflection, on 17 December 1530, this Thomas 'Stevyns' is made deacon – again by Vyvyan, in his Priory Church at Bodmin.[88] We would expect him to be priested the following year, but his name does not appear in the Bishop's Register – his final ordination may have been outside the diocese, as a number were.[89]

In the next likely reference to this man, D&C 3688 records a Thomas Stevyn as one of several clergy at the prebendal church of Cullompton around late 1536, at the same time as the 'Cornish' Thomas Stephyn was already at Newlyn. The more consistent use of 'v' in the references to the 'Devon' priest, as opposed to the consistent use of 'ph' with his counterpart, may also be a gentle pointer – although an unreliable one at a time when spelling was so variable. (Whether the 'Thomas Stevens' who accepted the rectory of Bickleigh in Devon on 13 August 1576 is the same as the Devon man is much less certain. According to Hennessy, the vicar of the parish from 1559 to 1577 was Hugo Foster, so this Stevens – not necessarily even a priest – may simply have held the great tithes and not in any way ministered in the parish.)

In any case, whether or not our Cornish-speaking Stephyn served some time at Mylor, he seems to have been both curate and vicar of Newlyn East before eventually disappearing from church life in the diocese in the time of Queen Elizabeth. No evidence has yet been found for his deprivation, ejection or resignation. He seems simply to disappear at some unidentified point after Elizabeth's accession. We know of many other deprivations in the diocese, including James Turberville, the bishop, Thomas Reynolds the dean, Thomas Nutcombe the sub-dean, John Blaxton the treasurer, 11 cathedral prebendaries (almost half the total), and around 30 incumbents, including some resignations.[90] These departures – not least among the senior diocesan staff – suggest that the Elizabethan Settlement was far from being a smooth transition in the west. John Rokeby, for example, Stephyn's neighbour at St Erme, who (like Stephyn) had been instituted in Mary's time, was soon ejected under Elizabeth. Manaccan, Creed, Roche and St Columb Major also lost their priests, but they were exceptional since on the whole the deprivations were in east Cornwall. The western clergy seem generally to have escaped censure at this point, and may have been too remote for immediate action. Of those diocesan clergy who did leave, some had outstanding recusant careers: Blaxton went on to be a thorn in the side of the bishop of Hereford, helping to establish a robust Catholic enclave in the Welsh borders, with clergy and laity moving in from elsewhere.[91] It is possible that Stephyn, although less well known to history, may have followed him in a similar career. Alternatively, he may have fled abroad for a time – like John Smart of Maker (one of the cathedral prebends) and Robert Yendall of Menheniot who boarded a boat and escaped to Brittany.[92] Perhaps most likely of all, he stayed in the Cornish-speaking area – at least initially – encouraging traditional Catholic belief and devotion while being sheltered by friends (the 'hospitable' Tregear perhaps among them).

No incumbent at all is recorded at Newlyn in Alley's survey, nor is any other Thomas Stephyn recorded as an incumbent in the diocese at that time.[93] Indeed, and rather curiously, only a 'capella' (possibly the chapel of St Nectan) is noted in the 1561 survey under the parish of 'Nulyn', with no incumbent given. It is possible that some information was missing – a few other parish entries are missing or defective such as Perranzabuloe, Padstow and Mevagissey – although it is intriguing to speculate whether Newlyn was left out for definite reasons. Against this speculation is the fact that the parish registers seem to have been well ordered from 1559 onwards, possibly completed under the direction of a neighbouring priest such as Tregear, of Stephyn himself, or of an immediate successor whose name has been lost.[94]

What we know of his later views – expressed indirectly by his collection of eucharistic quotations after 1576 (rather than the mid to late 1550s of Tregear's work) – might in any case have suggested that he was an unlikely candidate to remain in office under Elizabeth. His selection from Foxe's account of the 1554 eucharistic debates is thoroughly one-sided, and his marginal notes on Tregear's translation of Bonner's Homilies cite patristic sources in a Catholic sense. Inasmuch as we can judge from this editorial work, he appears to be completely 'Marian' in his approach to the eucharist.[95] That is to say, he valued the tradition and worked actively to ensure its survival and renewal, but his approach was underpinned by scholarship and he understood its complex implications.

Ralph Trelobys – a missing link?

The fact that Ralph Trelobys[96] was Tregear's neighbour at Newlyn, and employed both John Tristeane (Tregear's successor) and Thomas Stephyn, suggests that his career might shed light on the ecclesiastical world in which all these men worked. His connections with Glasney College add to the interest. By the time he died, Trelobys was typical of a successful Tudor clergyman in rural Cornwall, and until its dissolution had been a long-serving canon[97] of Glasney, with many links to its wider orbit of parishes. A number of interesting pieces of evidence have come to light which suggest that he may be pivotal in understanding the links between Tregear, Stephyn and the College.

Trelobys is a much rarer name than either Stephyn or Tregear, and in itself tells us quite a lot about him. There is only one place-name which coincides with the historical distribution of the surname. His birth (probably around 1488) could have been at Trelubbas just north of Helston (although by this date some toponymic surnames were being inherited).[98] The family seems confined to the close vicinity, rarely extending further than villages such as Breage, even later in the century.[99] This would locate Trelobys in one of the strongest Cornish-speaking areas. As with Tregear and Stephyn, we have no record of his formal education. I speculate below that he is likely to have been educated at Glasney, in view of his later connection, although this is far from certain. He may well have gone on to take a degree, since he was always described as *magister* by contemporaries. In all likelihood this was at Oxford, perhaps at Exeter College.[100]

Our first substantial evidence about his life, however, comes from the Bishops' Registers. On coming down from university the young Trelobys seems to have found a title (that of Bodmin Priory)[101] relatively easily, and we know a good deal about his ordination. On 15 February, 1505, he was priested in Exeter Cathedral by Thomas Cornish, titular bishop of Tenos, an auxiliary who worked in Bath & Wells, Exeter and throughout the South West.[102] This was during the first year of the pontificate of Hugh Oldham, bishop of Exeter,[103] but Oldham was being in no way negligent by the standards of the day. It was not generally expected that diocesan bishops would conduct many ordinations. Their state and religious duties often took them out of their dioceses more than modern bishops, frequently keeping them in London or sometimes even out of the country as ambassadors. In view of the constant stream of young men seeking a clerical career,[104] such ordinations – usually presided over by auxiliary bishops who represented a titular see *in partibus infidelium*[105] – were held regularly throughout the year, often in smaller churches and chapels and, like all ordinations at this time, were open to those of other dioceses who secured permission. Trelobys himself was made deacon at Ramsbury in Salisbury diocese.[106] It is unlikely that he actually 'served his title' at Bodmin. On the contrary, there is evidence from the Bishops' Registers that many young men secured titles from churches or monastic houses with which their links were tenuous to say the least.[107] It is even possible that money changed hands, despite the fact that ordination alone – without the prospect of a secure living – was by no means an automatic key to material prosperity. So many ordinations meant that some priests served for years conducting occasional offices, gathering stipends for requiems and assisting at high mass. Moderately fortunate young men might get a stipendiary curacy sponsored by an absentee vicar, but only the most able and well-connected became incumbents with any rapidity.

Trelobys – who seems to have had particularly strong connections with Glasney – was one of the exceptions to this rule. Within 8 years of his priesting he was appointed, on 1 December 1512, as vicar of Crowan.[108] While not formally a Glasney parish it lay between Sithney (which was) and Camborne (which had strong links with several provosts of Glasney). It was well within the College's sphere of influence. The St Aubyn family owned a great deal of land – and a house, Clowance – there, which gave it an important profile.

A few years later, on 16 April 1518, Trelobys was made vicar of Newlyn East.[109] This lay sandwiched between the Glasney parishes of St Allen, St Colan and St Enoder. Both his livings, therefore, may have helped the College to conveniently 'link up' areas where it already had a degree of control. Trelobys appears to have held both parishes in plurality until his death, probably residing more in Crowan than Newlyn. The Cornwall Military Survey of 1522 (masterminded by Cardinal Wolsey to finance the war with France) reminds us of a link between the two, through the Arundells of Trerice, landowners in both. It also records Trelobys as definitely resident at Crowan in 1522[110] as 'vicar of the parish church' and mentions possible relatives, John and Thomas Trelobys, in neighbouring Wendron.[111] Curiously a Ralph Trelobys is listed for his military equipment (a billhook) in the Tinners Muster Roll under Wendron, which may mean that the priest owned land in his home parish or that he had taken his name from his father or another relative.[112] In any case, it reinforces the notion that his family may have come from the Helston area.

The certain significance of Trelobys for the Tregear Manuscript is that Thomas Stephyn worked for him and he was an important local priest and a canon of Glasney. While Crowan and Newlyn were not the wealthiest of appointments (the rectorial tithes in the first case being held by Tewkesbury Abbey and in the second by Exeter Cathedral) they were certainly not among the poorest. According to the *Valor Ecclesiasticus*, Trelobys received £16 13s. 4d. per annum for his work as vicar of Newlyn, and £11 9s. 0½d. for Crowan.[113] To this should be added his income as a canon of Glasney (around £11 per annum at the dissolution)[114] giving a total of around £39. This was not a small income, compared with that of the poorest vicars – around

£6 per annum[115] – even though wealthier parishes such as St Columb Major yielded over £50 per annum and Warin Penhaluryk of Wendron and Stithians had an income of around £120.

Trelobys and Glasney College

Although the date of his prebendal institution has not yet been found, by 1534 Ralph Trelobys was already a canon of Glasney, since he subscribed to the King's supremacy on 17 August under the provostship of James Gentle.[116] Almost all the bishops and clergy did so at this stage, with some notable exceptions. (It was only after seeing the full extent of Edward VI's changes and the Counter-Reformation perspective under Mary I, that the bishops, at least, hardened their stance under Elizabeth and were almost all deprived or driven to resign.) According to Bishop Veysey's *Valor*, Trelobys was still in post as a prebendary of Glasney in late 1536, as well as continuing his work at Crowan and Newlyn.[117] Being a college of priests and to a large extent a chantry foundation, Glasney escaped the dissolution of the minor religious houses in 1536 as well as the final surrender of the greater houses in 1539.[118] We have already noted Trelobys's appearances in Bishop Alley's survey, and his possible involvement in the 'pope-holy pilgrimage' of 1537.

There is in existence a very interesting conveyance, preserved at the Courtney Library at Truro, which shows Trelobys in his social context (not least in relation to the St Aubyn family) and gives us an indication of the wider community involvement of Glasney canons at this period. It is dated 2 May 1541:

> *2 May 33 Henry VIII at Clewens [Clowance]. Conveyance from Tho. Sentaubyn [St Aubyn] esq. to Graynfylde, Whytyngton, Trelowbys, Blewett & Gayer of the Manor of Penpons etc. in accordance with the above agreement to be held by him for life paying £20 yearly to his son John Sentaubyn & Blanche his wife the dau. of Tho. Whittington & after his death to the s. [same] John & Blanche in tail with remainder to the grantors right heirs*[119]

As with so many transactions of this sort, the conveyance was in the end probably little more than a glorified way of 'keeping it in the family'. Yet Trelobys is clearly of some standing to be involved in this way. (His name is variously spelt on the document as Rd⁰ Trelowbys, Rad^us Trelowbys, Ralph Trelobes and even Richard Trelobes, which may be helpful in another context.)[120] The presence of a 'Gayer' – possibly one of a distinct family of gentry, based at Marazion and elsewhere – is also intriguing. But we do not have to clutch at half a name. There have long been important Tregears themselves at Crowan, the family being related to the Tregonwells.[121] It is an intriguing possibility that Ralph Trelobys, as well as employing Thomas Stephyn as his curate, may have known and encouraged the vocation of a young John Tregear for the priesthood – a speculation that I discuss in greater depth below.[122]

The dissolution of Glasney came at last in 1548, when Edward VI abolished the chantries.[123] Regrettably, only a few stones now survive above ground.[124] Penryn at that time was counted as having between 400 and 600 communicants and, as one of the Chantry Certificates makes plain, the College had a provost and 12 prebendaries, 7 additional assistant priests known as the vicars, and several others such as 3 chantry priests. There were also 4 boy choristers:[125]

> *The Towne of Peryn wherin ar[e] howselyng people cccc. The Colledge of Seynt Thomas of Glasney, standing in the said Towne, being the p[ar]ishe churche off the foundacon of Walter Goode sometyme Bisshoppe of Exceter to fynde a Provost & xij p[re]bendaryes wherof the said provost and vij of the said prebendaryes be now Resident and v not residente, vij vicars, a Chapell Clerke, a Bellrynger, iiij querysters and iij chantry prestes to celebrate in the said colledge.*[126]

Trelobys was 70 when the College was dissolved: it must have been a considerable wrench for him.[127] The reinforcing of the residency requirement for canons of Glasney may have reduced the time Trelobys could spend in Crowan, and the College had possibly become his home. His status there is mentioned several times in the Chantry Certificates.

> *Rauff Trelobbes of thage of lxx yeres hathe for his sallary in the said Colledge xij^{li} besides his promocions in other places vj^{li}.*[128]

Elsewhere his salary at Penryn is recorded as being just over £10 and his pension, to which he was entitled following the dissolution, somewhat less than this:

> *Raufe Trelobbes Prebendarye for his salary clere x^{li} ij^s ij^d.*
> *Pen. vj^{li} xiij^s iiij^d.*[129]

However, with at least £20 from his parish tithes alone he was still materially better off than many country clergy. Spiritually, they all faced the same depredations. With dubious legal authority in view of Henry VIII's will, the dissolution of the chantries was accompanied by other attempts at 'reform'

– decrees seeking to abolish Palm Sunday processions, images of the saints, requiem masses, the doctrine of purgatory, votive candles, the rood screen, the Easter sepulcre and parish guilds. Dr Simon Heynes, the notorious reforming dean of Exeter – at odds with most of the people and clergy of the diocese – demolished statues in the cathedral in front of his helpless canons. Veysey was retired and another leading reformer, Miles Coverdale, brought in as bishop. All this must have been difficult for the elderly Trelobys, as well as for Tregear and Stephyn.

Nonetheless, means seem to have been found, here and there, for going on as usual and even retaining some measure of control of the former Glasney estates, with the cooperation of landowners who received them in grant or bought them from the Crown. Another interesting conveyance, preserved at the Courtney Library, involves Ralph Trelobys in an arrangement for a good parcel of land from the former College, ensuring that it benefits the conveyor's wife:

> *Ralph Coche of Penryn, gen[tleman], conveys to Ric[hard] Gerves ... and Ralph Trelowbes all his lands in Penryn and Glasney and in the late dissolved College of Glasney and a lease of Penryn Mills from the B[isho]p of Exeter ... last of February 4 Edward VI [28th Feb 1550] ... to hold to the use of Thomasine, wife of [the] s[ai]d Ralph Coche ...*[130]

The mention of Coche's wife makes it clear that this was probably not the Rauf Cocke that was a non-resident canon at the time of the suppression, but rather the 'Rauff Coche' who was Chapel Clerk. John Nans, the former Provost of Glasney, also appears in the document as a witness. Things are once again being kept very much within the Glasney 'family'.

Mercifully, for him, Trelobys lived just long enough to see a partial and temporary restoration of traditional practice under Mary. Coverdale was deprived and Vesey got his old see back (although he spent most of his time after his restoration in the Midlands, developing charitable foundations in the town of his birth). The bishop was very old by this stage, and unable to travel long distances. Able assistants served him in Cornwall until, as the Registers record:

> *Dicesimo tertio die mensis octobris anno d[o]m[in]i*
> *mill[es]imo qui[n]gentesimo quinquagesimo quarto in manerio suo*
> *de More place infra pa[ro]chiam de Sutton Collfylld*
> *in Com[itatu] Warwick d[omi]n[u]s ab hac [vita] migravit*

[On the thirteenth day of the month of October in the year of our Lord one thousand five hundred and fifty-four, in his manor

of More Place within the parish of Sutton Coldfield,
in the County of Warwick, the Lord [Bishop] departed this life.][131]

He was in his hundredth year. Not long afterwards, Ralph Trelobys also died.
His will was proved in the court of the principal registry of the bishop of
Exeter in 1557, as that of 'Raff Trelobys, clerk, Crowen'.[132]

Some speculations

In some ways, it would be safest to end at this point. However, there are
a number of crucial questions which, although conclusive evidence may be
lacking, deserve an attempt at a provisional answer. These include the places
of birth of Tregear and Stephyn, their dates and places of ordination, their
role during the Western Rising, and their attitudes to the Elizabethan
church. I include them to give pointers for later researchers, who may at least
avoid repeating the less successful lines of inquiry.

Where was John Tregear born?

I have already suggested that it is possible that Tregear came from Crowan,
though the name is found in several places (including Newlyn) where it could
have arisen independently. There was certainly a family of note in Crowan
bearing the name. The Heraldic Visitation of 1620 traces a John Tregear (aged
9 in 1620) back through four generations to a John Tregear of Crowan who
married Amy, the third daughter of John Owry (one of the Tregonwells),
apparently in the early sixteenth century.[133] If this Tregear is something
to do with ours, he could conceivably be anything from his nephew to his
father or uncle. It is difficult to tell, as no dates are given for these members
of the family:
   The Tregears were well established in Crowan and continued to be
significant there for many generations. There is a good deal of evidence to
be explored, if the conjectural link between Tregear and Stephyn through
Trelobys could be established on a firmer footing.[134] A step in this direction
might be the fact that the two John Tregears who make an appearance in
the return for Crowan in the 1522 Military Survey are almost certainly of
this family.[135] Rated at £10, John Tregear apparently has a son, John Tregear
'junior', listed with him.[136] There is only one John Tregear noted, however,
by the time of the later surveys of 1544 and 1562. Of course, it is perfectly
possible that Tregear junior had married or moved away, or that Tregear
senior had died, but equally the translator of the Homilies would have moved
to St Allen by these dates. Could the young Tregear have been ordained soon

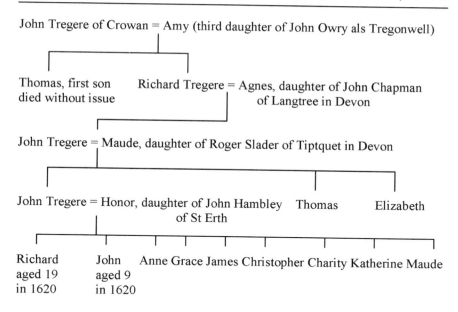

John Tregere of Crowan = Amy (third daughter of John Owry als Tregonwell)

Thomas, first son   Richard Tregere = Agnes, daughter of John Chapman
died without issue   of Langtree in Devon

John Tregere = Maude, daughter of Roger Slader of Tiptquet in Devon

John Tregere = Honor, daughter of John Hambley   Thomas   Elizabeth
                                  of St Erth

Richard   John   Anne Grace James Christopher Charity Katherine Maude
aged 19   aged 9
in 1620   in 1620

after the 1522 Survey, or even already been a priest at that point, spending some time serving as a chaplain informally in his home parish?[137]

In support of this idea, a 'John Tristene' appears in the same list as 'John Tregere, junior'. If this is the John Tristeane already noted, he was certainly already ordained at this point and may also have been acting as a sort of additional curate at Crowan. A 'John Treleigne, clerk' (recorded as owning some land) and a 'John Tregeyr' (recorded as contributing a loan of £5) are also listed for Sithney, the neighbouring parish.[138] If 'Treleigne' is an error or misreading for 'Tristeigne' (and I have come across no record of any other 'Treleignes' among the clergy of the time, while the spelling Tristeigne does occur for John Tristeane) it is possible to speculate that both Tristeane and Tregear were serving the two parishes in some way. It is no more than conjecture but, in view of the later connection between Tregear and Stephyn, it is interesting to wonder whether Trelobys was the man responsible for introducing the two authors of the Cornish Homilies: one his curate at Newlyn and the other a priest in his parish at Crowan (and possibly in Sithney).

We should not set too great a store by what is merely a possibility. There were many other Tregears throughout Tudor Cornwall – the name probably arose independently in several places named Tregear, the inherited toponymic then travelling to other areas. Tregear/Tregair has long been both a place name and family name in Newlyn East itself, although our John Tregear's connection with this parish where a name similar to his own flourished may be entirely coincidental.[139] The Parish Registers there show a James Morgan and Joan (Johan) Tregear marrying on 22 November 1569 (and, interestingly, an Oisburne Tresteane and Maude Polgreene marrying on 10 October in the same year).[140] Since we know for certain that Tregear was still unmarried and celibate as late as 1561, Joan is most unlikely to be his descendant. The contemporary spelling of these names, often Tregayre or Tregeyre, agrees well with that used for John Tregear's name in the ordination registers, though the scribe of the Homilies preferred Tregear. The variants have no particular significance. There were also Tregayres in nearby Cubert: Henderson cites the Chantry Certificates of 1549 stating on the oath of Henry Tregayre and Benedict Parker that John Body gave to the wardens of Cubert a parcel of land in the parish.[141] There is no Tregear found as a place name in the parish, however, so this is an instance of the surname travelling.

Place-names using both the elements of the name Tregear are, in any case, common throughout Cornwall.[142] Camborne and Stithians can be added to Crowan, Sithney, Newlyn and Cubert among the parishes that have families of the name Tregear at the period, and there are others elsewhere in Cornwall.[143] We may never be sure we have the right family. Variants such as Angeare and Geyre, presumably derived from places called *an ger*, often attract the eye in contemporary records, but should not be confused with Tregear.[144] Perhaps Tregear did become 'Gear occasionally in speech, as Tremaddock can become 'Mathick today, but there is little or no clear of evidence of this happening with surnames.[145] Our search for John Tregear does not then need to widen to include such men as John Geyre, an assistant priest in St Keverne in 1522. (This man had a stipend of £4.13s.4d., indicating that he was quite junior, possibly newly ordained.)[146] He is probably the John Geyre who was subdeaconed by Veysey in St Mary's Chapel in the Palace, 23 February 1519, deaconed by Thomas Vyvyan in the Lady Chapel of the Cathedral, 25 May 1520 (with Bodmin as his title) and priested by Thomas Chard also in the Lady Chapel, 21 September 1520.[147] A connection between our John Tregear and St Keverne would have been fascinating, in view of the support of the parish for the 1492 and 1549 rebellions, but there is no evidence here. John Geyre is almost certainly a different man.

Was Tregear ordained outside the diocese?

In the search for Tregear's ordination in the Exeter Registers there are other names -Tregates, Trekenes, Tregoyns, Geres and Treers – to lead our eye astray.[148] Several Johns are ordained without a surname of any sort. In addition, the secretary hand of some of the scribes can sometimes deteriorate to the point of being illegible, and the folios are not universally well preserved. The John 'Tregoyn' who was confirmed[149] by Thomas Chard on 17 December 1513 in St Mary Major in the precincts of the Cathedral, then made acolyte[150] the same day, at first looks promising (in view of later misreadings of Tregayre/Tregayne) but his subdeaconing as John 'Tregona' removes the confusion. In fact, I have failed to find an unambiguous John Tregear in any of the Exeter ordination registers so far.

The possibility of an ordination outside the diocese may resolve the impasse and is illustrated by the ecclesiastical careers of William Treruffe[151] and John Tristeane.[152] Treruffe was one of Tregear's predecessors at St Allen (1531–44)[153] after which he moved to Cubert as a near neighbour.[154] Tristeane, as has already been noted, was one of Stephyn's sucessors at Newlyn, also served at Manaccan, and knew Trelobys and his curates at Crowan. Both men were therefore clear contemporaries of Tregear and Stephyn. Both were confirmed and made acolyte by Thomas Chard, bishop of Solubria in the Lady Chapel of Exeter Cathedral on 22 December 1515.[155] On the following 16 February both were made subdeacon by the same bishop in the same place.[156] It is therefore most interesting that when Chard moved on to conduct an ordination in the Lady Chapel of Wells Cathedral on 8 March 1516, these two went with him. There, among others – including many monks of Glastonbury – he ordained Treruffe to the title of Launceston Priory, and Tristeane to the title of St John's Priory, Exeter.[157] Finally, on 22 March – barely a fortnight later – he ordained both to the priesthood in his Priory of St Peter and St Paul at Montacute.[158] The names are reasonably rare and do not otherwise appear in the ordination registers of either diocese. The men are specifically identified as Exeter ordinands. Thus, within the space of three months, Treruffe and Tristeane move from confirmation to the priesthood – all conducted by the same auxiliary bishop, partly in Exet   partly in Bath & Wells diocese. This surely gives quite a revealing picture of an aspect of Tudor church life not often appreciated. It also illustrates the difficulty of pinpointing Tregear's ordination, when so much of the Bath & Wells record is now lost.[159] We have seen already that ordinations could be even further afield: Ralph Trelobys, for example, was made a deacon in Ramsbury, in the diocese of Salisbury. There the registers are full of ordinands from a vast range of dioceses, including the nearer ones such as Bath & Wells, Exeter, Worcester, Hereford and Winchester, but almost as commonly from Carlisle, Coventry & Lichfield, Lincoln, London, Llandaff, St Asaph, Menevia (St David's) and York. Sometimes even Bangor, Rochester, Canterbury, Ely and Norwich appear. Even allowing for the remarkable elaboration of this practice in Salisbury diocese under Audley – a state of affairs that was already declining under his successor Cardinal Campeggio[160] – there is in theory almost no limit to the possible locations of Tregear's ordination. It may yet be found, although the registers from some of the likely dioceses and years are irretrievably lost. So far Exeter, Bath & Wells, Salisbury and Hereford have drawn a blank. In the case of Stephyn, the difficulty is compounded by the presence of so many others of that name among the clergy of the time.[161]

Were Tregear and Stephyn involved in the Western Rising of 1549?

There was much dragging of feet in Cornwall, when the introduction of the first Book of Common Prayer was attempted in 1549. Things had been building towards rebellion for a number of years. The Helston rioters had prepared the ground, and the execution of Martin Geoffrey, a priest of St Keverne, was fresh in people's minds. The removal of chalices, vestments and missals from Bodmin, Liskeard and many other places had caused deep offence. When the Prayer Book was introduced it met in many places with incomprehension and disapproval, and before long open rebellion broke out, with priests and parishes refusing the new service and comparing it to a 'Christmas game'. The demands of the rebels were clear and overwhelmingly religious, although there were also claims that many in Cornwall were monoglot Cornish speakers and could not understand English. The demands show what was already disappearing from Cornish church life: the Blessed Sacrament to be restored to the chancels; the faith of the Ecumenical Councils to be honoured and observed again; baptism and confirmation to be frequently celebrated as before; the use of palms on Palm Sunday, ashes on Ash Wednesday, and 'creeping to the cross' on Good Friday to be reintroduced; all statues to be set up again; prayers for the dead to be reinstated; Catholic priests in prison for their faith to be released; Reginald (later Cardinal) Pole to be brought back to England; some monasteries to be restored and, above all, the Prayer Book to be abolished and the mass to be reinstated. There are perhaps hints of a more reactionary tenor to this sweet reasonableness: while technically going no further than asking for a return to the Henrician *status quo*, the request for Pole to be brought into the King's Council seems to point in the direction of Rome.

One suspects that these are exactly the sorts of measures that Thomas Stephyn and John Tregear – who were apparently committed to the restoration of Catholicism under Mary – would have strongly supported. Unfortunately there is no direct evidence of their actions at the time, although Eamon Duffy's recent work on the parish of Morebath in northern Devon has raised the question of the extent to which normally law-abiding parishioners and traditionalist clergy may have been drawn into the 'commotions'.[162] The possibility that Morebath may have sent some men to 'sent davys down ys camppe' (the rebel camp outside Exeter at St David's Down)[163] inevitably makes us wonder if Tregear and Stephyn themselves joined the rebels or egged them on. If they did, when the Rising was eventually suppressed (with the help of foreign mercenaries, lack of cavalry on the rebel side, strategic errors and a measure of bad luck) they must have escaped any reprisals and, like a number of rebel priests, slipped back to their parishes.

The most actively involved clergy were not so fortunate. At least nine priests were executed, including the Cornishman Robert Welsh – from Penryn – who served at St Thomas the Martyr, Exeter. While sympathetic with the rebels' cause, he had in fact prevented them from burning Exeter and hardly deserved his terrible death: he was hanged from his own church tower in mass vestments, with his body left there for 4 years until Queen Mary's time. Others who were executed were William Alsa, once vicar of Gulval; Simon Moreton, vicar of Poundstock; Richard Bennett, vicar of St Veep and St Neot; Roger Barrett, who signed the Articles of the rebellion; John Thompson, Robert Bochym, John Barrow and John Woodcock.[164] Others may eventually have been executed, including Robert Boyse, vicar of St Cleer, who was attainted like Robert Rowe, the vicar of St Keverne, and Gabriel Morton of Uny Lelant.

There was a general rash of new incumbents at this time, in some cases, perhaps, replacing priests known to have been involved in the rising. Tregear was not replaced, however. It is true that, as we shall see, Stephyn seems to disappear from the surviving records around this time or even earlier. Even so, I have not found him mentioned among those being actively sought by the government for any part in the Rising.

We can only surmise, therefore, that Tregear and Stephyn played a relatively low-key role, if any – despite their enthusiastic support for the Marian reaction a few years later. Perhaps some in their parishes gave guarded support, as may have happened in Christopher Trychay's parish. The priests may even have visited some of the early camps themselves, along with colleagues and friends from the Newlyn area, although no record has been found of this. All we can say is that their part of Cornwall retained a reputation for harbouring small communities of unshakeable Catholic convictions well into the Elizabethan era, and Newlyn ultimately harboured a persistent recusant community very similar to those at Crantock and Mawgan.[165] It seems unlikely that such a community would have developed from priests and people who were neutral over the issues that lay behind the Rising.

Why did Tregear remain in his parish?

The suggestion of earlier scholars, that Tregear and Stephyn worked at Glasney itself and went into hiding once the Reformation got properly under way, assumes that as ardent supporters of the Catholic cause they had broken all ties with their parishes and dioceses as soon as the Reformation began.[166] This certainly did not happen with Tregear – nor with many other priests or even the loyal Catholic gentry. While traditionalists regretted the loss of the monasteries, many benefited from the sale of their lands. Families that were known later for their staunch Catholicism often bowed to the inevitable at the Dissolution and made sure of a good share of the spoils. Furthermore, despite the destruction of venerated images, and the undermining of papal allegiance, Cornish people had not yet experienced revolutionary changes in parish worship. By the time Tregear was offered St Allen, there had even been important reversals of the radical emphasis of earlier policy. The Act of the Six Articles in 1539 had caused the more committed Protestants like Latimer to resign, rather than have to enforce transubstantiation, private masses, confession and priestly celibacy – all now defended by the King. Cromwell, although ennobled early in 1540, was executed by that same summer – and a number of his supporters were subsequently hunted down. It would have seemed to conservative-minded clergy like Tregear that things were settling back in their old ways, and the Catholic cause was still reasonably secure.[167] The appearance of the King's Book in May 1543 further confirmed the importance of traditional ceremonies, and it was in this atmosphere perceived by some as a 'turning of the tide' that Tregear accepted his living. In any case, the changes in some of the remoter parts of the country had probably been less marked than in the larger towns. There had been martyrs, like Thomas More, John Fisher and the Carthusians, but others who would eventually take a staunchly Catholic stance (like Gardiner, Bonner and Tunstall) found themselves able to make concessions at this early stage. In July 1546, six months before his death, it has even been suggested that Henry was thinking of making overtures to Rome – however limited, indirect and insincere these might have been.[168]

So, while it is hard to see how Tregear could have survived as long as he did without some measure of compromise, we need not imagine that he ever thought of himself as anything other than a Catholic. Eamon Duffy, using the Churchwardens' Accounts of Morebath in the north east of Exeter Diocese, has comprehensively illustrated how a conservative, Catholic-minded priest could stay in office for many years after the Reformation, to some extent 'protecting' his people from its worst excesses, while gradually seeing some benefits in the English rites and new teachings.[169] We have evidence from Wales of devout Catholic families still attending the parish church on Sunday as late as the 1570s. The elderly and much respected Welsh exiles in Rome accepted this blending of loyalties since it was still common in parts of the country for the local vicar to say mass quietly and behind closed doors once the state imposed service was performed.[170] In Cornwall, there is scattered evidence that it was possible to resist conformity more comprehensively and for far longer than in many other areas. Such incidents as the vicar of Kilkhampton brazenly declaring in 1584 that he had 'never heard' of the new Prayer Book, and the reports of mass still being said at St Columb Major as late as 1590 make the point.[171] It is true that Cornwall was short of wealthy families willing and able to help the laity resist unwelcome reforms by bearing the burden of fines and supporting those priests who celebrated clandestine liturgies. But there were exceptions. Sir John Arundell of Lanherne was despatched to the tower for protecting and perpetuating the old religion in 1584, and Sir Francis Tregian provided sanctuary to the first Jesuits, including the Catholic martyr Cuthbert Mayne, from their arrival around 1576.[172] Until the end of the 1570s, a measure of clandestine Catholic activity was therefore going on. In April 1578, a 'Humphridus Hendye' was included among a list of recusants for daring to say that there was still 'holy brede, holy water, masse and mattens in Cornwall and that ytt shalbe every where shortlye' along with the hope that, ere long 'the Quene should be no bodye'.[173] Hendy was a harbour-master and therefore dangerous: he was soon indicted. In 1586, not long after Tregear's death, a list was made by the puritans of around 20 of Veysey's or Turberville's priests still in Cornish parishes working against the new religion to a greater or lesser extent – and a number more whose ordaining bishop is not given but who were also considered suspect.[174] In this overall context, therefore, it is possible to imagine Tregear remaining in his parish without abandoning cherished Catholic beliefs, but rather providing a sort of shelter, under which he could nourish the faith of his people while perhaps accepting some outward conformity. The undoubted compromises of such a position may have been balanced by a hefty degree of non-compliance. Had Tregear lived much longer, of course, there would have been little scope for any sense of continuing 'Church Catholicism' in his parish, and the only route left open would be that of the seminary priests like Cuthbert Mayne. As it is, he died before the storm gathered its full strength.

Was Thomas Stephyn a 'recusant priest'?

What happened to Thomas Stephyn in the years between the dissolution of Glasney and the accession of Queen Mary is something of a mystery. Of course, he may merely have remained at Newlyn under Trelobys for 25 years, before being eventually appointed to the living. We tend to imagine the passage of twenty or thirty years to be an inordinately long period of time to remain a curate, but for many clerics without a degree or wealthy patron it was quite possible. Some never attained livings of their own, but always served as junior clergy. Nonetheless, while Trelobys appears in various surveys and musters after Veysey's *Valor* of 1536, Stephyn seems to slip off the map. Could it be that he had to get out of the area after the Rising? Could he have left Cornwall even earlier, troubled by the religious changes under Henry and Edward? Throughout England and Wales there were several assistant clergy by the name of Thomas Stephyn who seem to have had a controversial relationship with traditional religion under the changes of Edward VI.

Of course, it is easy to be misled by the common occurrence of the name. The Thomas Stephyn helping Thomas Waryn in the parish of Cullompton after the dissolution is fairly obviously the Devon priest who was one of the clergy in the prebendal church there while our Thomas Stephyn was still at Newlyn.[175] The Chantry Certificate for Crantock's mention of a 'Thos. Stavern' on the College lands in Langurro might seem significant, but the name is probably better divided as Thomas Tavern, a form it takes in the same source.[176]

If we cast the net wider and look for Marian priests active in deathbed ministries or those in trouble with the government over religion, a number of Thomas Stephyns crop up. None of these is necessarily anything to do with the author of *Sacrament an Alter*, of course. I propose, however, to give an account of one or two of them because they shed some light on what priests of 'suspect' views may have been doing at various stages of the Reformation. There is an interesting priest at the deathbed of Sir Richard Gresham in London, on 21 February 1549, just before the formal introduction of the Book of Common Prayer. This is recorded in two separate legal depositions, of 27 – 31 July 1549 and 27 February – 17 March 1550, which have been discussed in depth recently by Danae Tankard.[177] Intriguingly, the prominent London citizen and former Mayor sends for one 'Sir Thomas Stephyn' to give him the last rites. This priest deposed that he was the

> *confessor and minystor of the holy com[m]unyon*
> *to S[i]r Richard Gresham ...*[178]
> *the daye that he deceassed*[179]

and that he had urged him

> *to make restytucyon to c[er]ten wydowes*
> *for c[er]ten iniuryes that he had doon them'*

This was not the first time that Thomas Stephyn had attended the sick man. He was

> *sundry tymes callyd to the said S[i]r Richard lying soore sicke to putte hym*
> *in the reme[m]braunce of the m[er]cy of god and the passion of Cryst*[180]

Yet Sir Richard had had his own chaplain for six years – a John Hall from All Saints, North Street in York (a church where the parishioners preserved much of its medieval beauty – sometimes, as at Abergavenny and Mawgan-in-Pydar, an indicator of enduring traditional religion in the area). Hall was also present at the deathbed, so it seems likely that there was an exceptional reason for wanting Stephyn to be there also. He is described as a 'chaplain resident in the parish of St Katherine Creechurch' – yet Sir Richard died in Bethnal Green and was buried in St Lawrence Jewry. Since the inexorable advance of Protestantism was now very much underway in London, it could be that the dying man wanted to be sure of a 'sound' Catholic-minded priest. Equally of course – and Tankard argues this – Sir Richard may have wanted to be sure of someone with more evangelical views. There was a 'Sir Stephen' reported as a curate of St Katherine Christ Church around this time, who was noted by Stow for opposing ancient May Day customs as idolatry, arguing for churches and the days of the week to be renamed, for Lent and other fast days to be kept freely at any time and not at the traditional time, preaching from an elm tree and singing high mass upon a stone tomb facing north.[181] These are far from being the actions of a stereotypical traditional Catholic. We may be dealing with two different men, and with another again in the 'Stevyns' of St Katherine's, Coleman's (the neighbouring parish) who appeared before the Privy Council in 1546 to answer charges that he had 'seduced' the Duke of Norfolk's servant 'towching opinion concerning the Most Blessed Sacrament'.[182] The Patent Rolls record other instances of the name in the parish.[183]

Of course, we cannot establish any real connection between these Stephyns and Cornwall, or even with each other. Nonetheless the deathbed of Sir Richard Gresham is a haunting image of a priest still reconciling penitents and administering viaticum, while holding no formal parish office, in the difficult years of Edward VI's reign. Wherever he was, our Thomas Stephyn might have been carrying on much the same ministry.[184]

If Stephyn had left the parish ministry in Edward's time, and only returned under Mary, he would certainly have had grave reservations concerning the accession of Elizabeth, and may have gone underground immediately. Already on 19 January 1559, it was clear that traditional religion was under attack. The bishop of Winchester had been under house arrest for 'such offenses as he committed in his sermon at the funeralles of the late Quene' and was discharged after being given 'a good admonicion' by the Lords of the Council.[185] By the 3 April 1559, the bishops of Chester, Coventry & Lichfield and Carlisle and Doctors Cole, Harpsfield and Chedsey were being required to report to the Privy Council daily.[186] Soon they were in prison. It is therefore of interest that in the Pardon Rolls of 1559, in the year after Elizabeth came to the throne, there is a decree for

Pardon for all treasons, felonies and other offences – fee to be 26s 8d only

with an exception made for serious offences such as conspiracy against Elizabeth in Queen Mary's time. The roll includes

Thomas Stephens, clerk, of
Wood Bevington, co. Warwick,
Alias of Baddisley Clynton, co. Warwick,
Alias of Glawdestre, co. Radnor.[187]

Baddesley Clinton is a well-known recusant house, now in the care of the National Trust. It appears to have been a Catholic centre throughout the religious changes, and harbours a number of priest-holes. Wood Bevington is less well known, but almost as interesting. The manor house is six miles north of Evesham and is a fourteenth century timber-framed building, with a chapel.[188] In 1531 the Augustinian canons of Kenilworth granted it to William Grey. His daughter Elizabeth married Edward Ferrers, second son of Sir Edward Ferrers of Baddesley Clinton; and their daughter, another Elizabeth, married Thomas Randolph of Codington, Bucks. Their son Ferrers Randolph took a 300-year lease of it from St John's College, Oxford, and was still there when Dugdale's Warwickshire was published in 1656, though in 1652 he had had to surrender the lease for defaulting on the rent.[189] Michael Hodgetts (who has made a comprehensive study of the recusant houses of the Midlands) has raised the question as to whether the lease or the surrender was a legal dodge to avoid sequestration. The suggestion is that it was very much a Catholic house. In 1656, Leo Randolph, St John Wall and other Franciscans from Douai returned to England, first making their way to Wood Bevington, which seems to have been Randolph's initial base, though it has been suggested that he later worked from Baddesley Clinton, as the Franciscans certainly did in the eighteenth century. There is a detailed inventory of 1578, when Edward Ferrers died,[190] which includes details of the 'chapel chamber' and mentions, 'in Mrs Ferrers' Chamber', 'one picture of Mary Magdalen, 12d'.[191]

Since Baddesley Clinton and Wood Bevington can be shown to have been Catholic centres in penal times, it is tempting to assume they had both taken on such a role at an early stage. If they had, it would seem likely that there was another safe house at Gladestry of much the same kind.[192] In that case, this particular 'Thomas Stephyns, clerk' would likely have held Catholic views, living as an itinerant 'Marian' priest, journeying between safe houses, early in the reign of Elizabeth and perhaps even under Edward. Gladestry is on the line of a chain of recusant centres from Monmouth right along the Welsh Borders up through Chirk to Holywell. (Apparently coincidentally, many of these centres appear along the line of Offa's Dyke). The eventual appearance of the Tregear Manuscript near Wrexham shows that at some point its custodian must have made similar journeys.

There are reasons for doubting, however, that the priest of Baddesley Clinton was the Cornish-speaking Thomas Stephyns. For one thing, the pardon seems early – his strident Catholicism in the previous reign was hardly criminal, and there had been little time for him to move and become active in Wales and Warwickshire in Elizabeth's first year. Although our Thomas Stephyn may indeed have later passed through Gladestry to Chirk, it is hard to believe that he left his parish so quickly before it became fully apparent that there was to be a return to a thoroughgoing Protestant policy under Elizabeth.

That the Privy Council was very interested in apprehending and personally interviewing a Thomas Stephens from Cornwall in 1564, however, is beyond doubt. Whether he was a priest, and whether religion was his crime, is less sure. From St James's Palace on 4 November 1564 they sent:

> *A letter to the Sheryf of Cornewall to take order that Thomas Stephens, Thomas Jenkins and John Coken, thonger, may be aprehended and good bandes be taken of them to appere before the Lords of the Queen's Majesties Pryvey Councell within such short tyme as they may convenientlye travaill hyther; and to use the like order with John Williams, Henry Otes, Rychard Boswall, Pyres Mychell and John Coken, thelder, remayninge in his warde.*[193]

Earlier, on 30 September 1564, Sir Peter Carew was ordered to apprehend a 'Stevins' of Falmouth among others for the 'victuallyng of pyrattes'.[194] This may explain the subsequent letter, and there may be no connection with the priest of Newlyn at all, though it is tempting to imagine the 'pyrattes' had Catholic sympathies, and were making the run to Brittany.

Much later on, another interesting 'Stephens' is the associate of Edmund Campion reported in the Acts of the Privy Council for 4 August 1581. We hear of Campion that:

> *he delivered a copie of his challenge to one Norice, a priest, commonlie remaining about London, and that he delivered it to one Pounde, then prisoner in the Marshallsey, who is thought to have dispersed the same abroade, and that one Stephens brought the said Pound to speak with Campion at Throgmorton House in London ...*[195]

Even if all these possible leads fail to afford us any solid proof of Stephyn's own recusancy, there remains the circumstantial evidence that Newlyn parish quickly became a stronghold of recusant Catholicism, which went on to survive there for several centuries. A key factor in this was the protection of the Borlases of Treluddra, who were faithful Catholics, but they in turn may have been strengthened by the earlier teaching and witness of Thomas Stephyn. These Newlyn Borlases remained Catholics throughout – unlike other branches of the family – rivalling the Arundells in their loyalty. The last of the line, Humphrey Borlase, was strongly supportive of King James II and awarded a peerage by him (after the King's exile, so it was never recognised by the authorities in Cornwall).[196] Henderson records, from a 1706 list of 'Popish Recusants' in Newlyn:

> *John Burlase [Borlase], John his son,*
> *James Lincolne & his wife, Nicholas James & his wife,*
> *Simon Trescowthick, Philip Oliver & his wife, and Alice Rowe.*

Again, under a slightly later date, he notes:

> *As at Mawgan there was a colony of Catholics in this parish centred upon Treluddra and they doubtless had a place of assembly in the mansion. In 1745 there were still 5 Catholic families (13 souls) in Newlyn.*[197]

Among documents and wills of the Borlase family there may yet be references to be found connecting them with Thomas Stephyn.

Where was Trelobys educated?

Trelobys would probably have been baptised at Wendron, and it seems likely (in view of his later history) that his education began early. We often forget that everyone in Tudor times knew someone who could read, if only the local priest, and promising boys who helped out at church might readily learn their alphabet.[198] Those lucky enough to live near Glasney itself might have had the bell ringer as a tutor from a young age:

> *John Pounde bell rynger there of thage of xxx yeres hathe for his salarye ther[e] xl[s] as well for teachynge of pore mens children there A.B.C. as for ryngynge the bells.*[199]

Of course, Trelobys himself probably did not live particularly close to Glasney at first. Nonetheless, in due course he could well have been schooled there, in view of his subsequent career. For promising local boys with the ability and interest to become 'clerks' and needing to learn their Latin it was an obvious place to start. Many colleges like Glasney, as well as monasteries and cathedrals, had schools of this sort right up to the period in question, catering mainly for altar-boys, choristers and novices.[200] Nonetheless, Nicholas Orme, in his recent survey of medieval and early modern education, draws our attention to the still wider range of potential schooling, for those who sought it and were able to access it. It is possible that Trelobys was first educated in a number of different ways. Oxford and Cambridge were both major centres for the teaching of schoolboys, as well as youths entering business and undergraduates. Youngsters could also be educated 'privately', by being placed in great houses or with local families that maintained a tutor and, as we have noted, they were increasingly commonly taught by a local priest. There were, of course, still the traditional monastic schools – at Tywardreath and Launceston in Cornwall, and at Buckland and Tavistock in Devon, among others.[201] There was also a boarding school at Week St Mary well-used by the Cornish gentry and, most significantly in the case of Trelobys, an important centre of education and church life at Bodmin Priory. He held his title from there when he was eventually ordained.[202]

Nonetheless, Glasney remains of prime interest for all of the clergy we are considering, in one way or another. There is no contemporary school roll from Trelobys's time, but we know something of the boys there later on, around 1547, from the Chantry Certificates, which recorded the abolition of the College. They had an annual income of 20 shillings each (and, presumably, bed and board).[203] They would probably have been taught by one of the 'vicars' who assisted the canons by taking responsibility (along with the humbler chantry priests) for many of the daily services at the College. One of these vicars certainly ran a more formal school:

> Memorand[um] a Scoole there one of the said vicars scolem[aste]r late deceased for the which the people maketh great lamentacione

Perhaps the most scholarly pursued further studies with the canons themselves and later might even be sent to university. Before going they would already have learned Latin reasonably well and perhaps the rudiments of other subjects such as rhetoric. Once there, they would have had the opportunity to progress rapidly. Like other young men from poor homes showing promise as scholars – Cardinal Wolsey himself rose from relatively humble beginnings as a butcher's son – Trelobys no doubt found that Church patronage was a great leveller.

Was 'Rad Ton' connected with Trelobys, Stephyn or Tregear?

Since we have strayed so far into the realm of speculation, we ought perhaps to end with one of the most elusive Cornish writer-priests of the early modern period, and ask whether he was, like Tregear and Stephyn, possibly connected with Glasney through Trelobys. At the end of *Beunans Meriasek*, one of two surviving medieval saint's plays in the Cornish language,[204] appear the words:

> *finit*[ur] *p[er] dnm Rad Ton*
> *anno domini m* [l] *v* [c[en]t] *iiij* [205]

> [finished by me, Sir Ralph Ton
> in the year of our Lord 1504]

The first part of the manuscript is in another hand – we may never know whose – but this mysterious 'Rad Ton' has been variously interpreted since the discovery of the play. Early suggestions failed to take account of *dominum/dompnum* usually requiring a Christian name, so Dominus Hadton or even Dominus Nadton were offered, but most scholars now accept that Charles Thomas is right that the safest reading is Rad (for Latin 'Radulphus', English 'Ralph) Ton.[206] *Dominus* would have become 'Sir' in English and, as we have noted before, this was the equivalent of the modern 'Father' when used of a priest. The date of 1504 is the most likely reading.[207]

As Charles Thomas notes, Ton is not unknown as a Cornish surname, but it is rare.[208] There appear to be no Tons among the parish clergy of the time to match the name appended to *Beunans Meriasek* apparently in 1504, with one glaring exception. Around 1536, according to D&C 3688, where we have already found Thomas Stephyn working for Ralph Trelobys, we find the following entry for Crowan:

> *Crowen*   *Mr Radullphus Trelobys Vic*
> *d Ricus Ton cur*

Because of the significance of Trelobys for Stephyn and possibly for Tregear, we are perhaps entitled to be excited. If some of those seeking to preserve the Cornish Catholic heritage through the medium of the Cornish language shortly afterwards were not at Glasney themselves, but were possibly influenced by a Glasney priest working out in the parishes, could the same be true of Ton? Of course, Ricardus/Richard Ton is not quite Radulphus/Ralph Ton. However, people have been looking for the elusive Ralph for a long time with little result. We have already seen that the abbreviation Rad seems occasionally to have been used (inaccurately) for Ricardus – as in the case of Trelobys.[209] While it is difficult for us to accept that a priest transcribing a document in 1504 could have been a curate thirty years later, we have also seen that Thomas Stephyn was likely to have been a curate from before 1522 and did not become an incumbent until 1557. All in all, and in the absence of other candidates despite repeated searching by many scholars, one is inclined to give more weight to Richard Ton as a candidate for 'Rad Ton' than would at first seem reasonable. Nance was well aware of the possibility, and mentions it in several places among his papers. Thomas also discusses it, and provides a fascinating reference for the death of 'Sir Ric. Tone, prest', buried at Camborne in 1547.[210] This firmly links Ton with Camborne, where *Beunans Meriasek* was presumably performed, and D&C 3688 establishes his connection with the College of Our Lady and St Thomas of Canterbury at Glasney, as a member of the parish clergy working with one of Glasney's canons, Ralph Trelobys. The common factor of the possible involvement of Trelobys with all three Cornish clerical writers adds weight to the supposition.

The absence of a Ralph Ton or even a Richard Ton from the ordination records of any of the reasonably near dioceses inevitably leads to speculation that Ton's name has been wrongly recorded by the notaries. It is difficult to believe, however, that a spoken Ton or Tonne could have been recorded as, say, Tom or Tomme – and it is only such names that we find. For example, in John Arundell's ordination on 6 March 1502 a certain Richard Tome [211] is made subdeacon, with Forde Abbey as his title. He is deaconed by Arundell as Richard Tomb at the next ordination, however, the implied pronunciation further undermining any possible identification with Ton.[212] (This may be the same Richard Tomb priested at St Mary Magdalene's, Taunton, on 23 March 1503 by the auxiliary Thomas Cornish, titular bishop of Tenos, during the *sede vacante* in Bath & Wells.[213] It is most unlikely that he is the Richard Thome at St Ives at the time of the 1522 Military Survey, since there is no mention of this man being a priest, and he is not grouped with the other clergy.) [214] A Richard Tonne (also Ton, Tonny or Tonnye) was admitted for the degree of BA at Oxford on 15 February 1534[215] – perhaps the same Richard Tonny to whom Master Richard Hilley bequeathed books on 19 November 1534.[216] But the spelling, dates and other circumstances make it highly unlikely that there is any connection with our Ton, although a John Arundell is also mentioned in Hilley's will.

Although Richard Ton is not an exact match with 'Rad Ton', it is perhaps helpful to indicate how much less of a match his potential rivals are. For example, Ton cannot be Rad Oldon who was not even ordained deacon until 1519, and it is even more unlikely that he was Richard Eston who was at Goran[217] in Alley's time, and certainly not Richard Down who was at Honeychurch, nor Rad Cols at Lanteglos by Fowey.[218] The 1522 Military Survey gives a 'Ralph Toll, chaplain', as the curate of Landewednack, under Richard Motton as rector, but Toll is not Ton.[219] Ralph John, on the other hand, sometime vicar of Perranzabuloe[220] and noted by Hennessy as Radulphus John 'als Treloy', does have a number of points in his favour. This

interesting clergyman spent some time in Wendron, after exchanging his
living in Salisbury diocese, and would have been a mature and experienced
priest in 1504.[221] The Cornwall Military Survey shows us that his name could
be written John or Jon. Nonetheless it seems unlikely that the unusual R for
Rad is matched by an even more unusual I/J for Jon. On balance, with the
growing circumstantial evidence of association (via Trelobys) with Glasney
and with others working on Cornish at a later date, Richard Ton seems the
most acceptable candidate for 'Rad Ton'.[222]

Conclusion

Leaving aside much of this speculation, we can now summarize what is
known about Tregear and Stephyn in a few paragraphs. The earlier search for
these authors among the residentiary canons of Glasney has been futile for a
reason. It appears that a good deal of the work to preserve traditional religion
through the medium of Cornish was done by the next tier down, or even
the tier below that – the humble parish clergy that ran the parishes in West
Cornwall from which Glasney drew its tithes. They may have been overseen
by one of the canons, Ralph Trelobys, although the evidence for this is merely
circumstantial. Of the greatest interest for students of the Cornish language
is the increasing likelihood that we can pinpoint the region where these men
grew up and learned to speak their native tongue. It appears to have been
an area on the borders of North Kerrier and East Penwith, around Crowan,
Camborne, Sithney, Wendron and Helston, although their area of operation
extended to Ewny Redruth, Mylor, St Allen and St Newlyn East.

John Tregear himself – possibly from Crowan – probably translated
Bonner's Homilies in the late 1550s when he was vicar of St Allen. He
remained in the parish ministering to his people until his death in 1583. At
some point his manuscript passed to Thomas Stephyn, who had been vicar
of the neighbouring Newlyn East in Queen Mary's time, and it was he who
added *Sacrament an Alter* (sometime after 1576). Stephyn had been curate of
Newlyn in 1537 under Ralph Trelobys (a canon of Glasney, and vicar of both
Crowan and Newlyn) and may have been curate of Mylor in 1522, at the
same time as Richard Ton was Trelobys's curate at Crowan. Ralph Trelobys
therefore knew all three men, and could be seen as a link with Glasney for
all of these parochial clergy. This link strengthens the case that Richard Ton
was 'Rad Ton'.

It seems clear that there was, in the era just prior to the Reformation,
and indeed after it, a concerted effort to preserve the treasury of Cornish
traditional religion through the medium of the language. This extended, in
Marian times, to the translation of Counter-Reformation texts, and thus

the Tregear Homilies were born. Such lengthy and detailed work, recorded in such a fair hand, may have been undertaken in the heady days of the Marian restoration with possible publication in mind, although this is far from certain. After the accession of Elizabeth, the manuscript must have been hidden away – it is hard to imagine Tregear writing it at this later time, when he conformed, at least outwardly, to the Elizabethan Settlement. Eventually – perhaps after Tregear's death, perhaps before – it passed to Stephyn. He compared its patristic quotations with other sources accessible to him – including the account of the Oxford Disputations in Foxe's Book of Martyrs. Compiling *Sacrament an Alter* from a highly selective and Catholic reading of that account, he perhaps intended it to be useful in teaching young Cornish Catholics that he hoped might enter the seminaries at a later date. It is hard to imagine any other *sitz im leben* that would account for such an extraordinary work. (Secrecy was clearly not the motive for writing it in Cornish, since virtually everything is repeated in Latin.)

Eventually the Tregear Manuscript – in the company of Stephyn or perhaps after his death with one of the missionary priests – began its journeys. It is impossible to be sure how far it may have gone before arriving in Flint. Cornish links with Brittany were stronger in the sixteenth century: many Cornish parishes played host to Breton workers and sometimes clergy during the pre-Reformation period, and though these ties atrophied after the Reformation, they did not disappear overnight. Ireland was also a frequent port of call for Cornish ships. In due course Cornish Catholics – men such as Richard Pentreath and Michael Penkevill – even made their way to the seminaries of the Iberian peninsula. There is no reason why the manuscript could not have travelled abroad, and certainly its signs of wear are very severe. It is fascinating how eucharistic vestments which once belonged to John Grandisson, bishop of Exeter, found a home in Ponta Del Gada Cathedral in the Azores, after first spending time in the Jesuit Missionary College at Terceira in the 18th century.[223]

In the end, however, the journey may have been a much simpler one, directly from Cornwall to Wales. Whether undertaken personally by Stephyn or by later priests, such a crossing was far from unusual. There was a bustling sea trade between Fowey and St Ives on the one hand and Neath and Milford Haven on the other throughout the Tudor period.[224] From South Wales a network of Catholic houses stretched up through the Marches to the traditionalist stronghold of Flint, where the manuscript came to rest.[225] There may, even at that late stage, have been thoughts of printing it, but if so, they came to nothing – despite the Mostyns sheltering a Catholic press in a sea cave, near the clandestine pilgrimage centre of Holywell. Eventually, as with all the important Cornish manuscripts in Wales, the dust began to settle, and their provenance was forgotten. Collections such as may have existed at centres like Raglan Castle were broken up, and the links with recusant houses obscured. What came to be seen as 'thirteen homilies in Welsh' ended up a long way from St Allen and St Newlyn East, where they had their origin.

Acknowledgements

I am grateful above all to Nicholas Orme for drawing my attention to important sources and offering much helpful advice; to Philip Payton of the Institute of Cornish Studies for constant encouragement; to Oliver Padel, Jo Mattingly and Michael Hodgetts for many useful suggestions; to Angela Doughty of the Exeter Cathedral Archives, Angela Broome at the RIC's Courtney Library and the staff at the British Library, the National Archives, the West Country Studies Library, the County Record Offices of Cornwall, Devon, Somerset and Wiltshire, the Bodleian Library, Cambridge University Library and the Library at Corpus Christi College, Cambridge, for invaluable assistance. Many errors have been averted due to the kindness of those who read earlier drafts and made suggestions, especially Oliver Padel and Nicholas Orme.

Notes and references

1. British Library (BL), Add MS 46397.
2. This is curious, since the work was even then headed with the title *Homelyes XIII in cornisch*. Cf. Appendix to 2nd report of Historical Manuscripts Commission, fol. 65: *'[the MS] contains thirteen homilies in Welsh ... nearly all ... transcribed or perhaps preached by John Tregear. The 12th and 13th are much tattered'.*
3. D. H. Frost, 'Sacrament an Alter – a Tudor Cornish patristic *catena* drawn from Foxe's account of the Oxford disputations of 1554', in Philip Payton (ed.), *Cornish Studies: Eleven* (Exeter, 2003), pp. 291–307.
4. Edmund Bonner (ed.), *Homelies sette for the [...]* (London, 1555) – although the precise edition used by Tregear is yet to be determined. I hope to do this as part of forthcoming work on an edition of SA.
5. It is possible that the project was undertaken at the request of church authorities charged with reforming Catholicism in the diocese of Exeter under its second Marian bishop James Turberville, but there is no firm evidence of this. Nonetheless, as diocesan bishops were charged with issuing homilies, and in practice all adopted Bonner's, it seems plausible to me that so complete a translation of a key Marian text could imply the involvement of authority, considering the remoteness of the area from London. The continual description of Harpsfield as Archdeacon of London (although this may be simply a copying of Bonner) may also suggest Mary's reign. So may the fact that in the mid-1550s the effort to spread these homilies was at its height. Furthermore, the earliest English editions did not include the

Aunswere to certayne obiections [...] (Bonner's '13th homily) perhaps also an indication of Tregear's work being early although it could, of course, have been done later from an early edition. Cumulatively, however, I feel all these factors tend to reinforce a 1555–58 date. (Incidentally, I do not believe SA to be in any way an imitation or representation of the *Aunswere*, although the subject – the Blessed Sacrament – is shared with it. Nor does SA appear to be an attempt to 'complete' TH, rather to identify its patristic material using Foxe as a source.)

6. Although Charles Penglase has argued for at least a partial translation. See Charles Penglase, 'La Bible en moyen-cornique', *Etudes Celtiques*, 33 (1997), pp. 233–43; but also the critique by Malte W. Tschirschky, 'The Medieval Cornish Bible' in Philip Payton (ed.), *Cornish Studies: Eleven* (Exeter, 2003), pp. 308–16.

7. Frost, D. H., *op. cit.* pp. 297–8.

8. John Foxe, *Acts and Monuments [...]*, The Variorum Edition [online] at http://hrionline.ac.uk/foxe [accessed: 29 December 2006] now supersedes the standard printed edition (S. Cattley and G. Townsend (eds), John Foxe, *Acts and Monuments* (London, 1841), VI, pp. 439, 531–2).

9. SA 60v.1. In giving formal references to the MS it was formerly customary to note recto sides with the plain folio number, and verso by adding an 'a', generally omiting line references altogether (eg. SA 60a). In my draft edition I note recto and verso sides of each folio with the usual 'r' and 'v', then the line number after a point (eg. TH 14r.3, SA 66v.9).

10. Brian Murdoch, *Cornish Literature* (Cambridge, 1993), p. 129.

11. Given as *Joh[ann]es Tregear* in TH on folios 11v, 16r, 26r, 54v, 58r and probably 51r (the page being slightly damaged), *Joh[ann]es Tregere* on fol. 35r, *JT* on folios 5v, 20r, 30r, 41r and 46r. In addition there is a monogram doodle at the foot of fol. 14r, which appears to involve the letter T.

12. *Thomas Stephyn, clericus* – in a different sixteenth-century hand in TH at the foot of folios 54r, 58r.

13. Ray Edwards has suggested that the scribe may even have read the English text to Tregear, on the basis of forms like '*narracion*' for 'an oration' – see Ray Edwards, *The Tregear Homilies with The Sacrament of the Altar* (Sutton Coldfield, 2004), p. viii, and TH 45r.5. The edition of SA in this work is based on my own reading of the MS.

14. This has tended to be overlooked by those using microfilm, photostats and photocopies. The reproduction in the Appendix is unfortunately from a such a photocopy and far from clear.

15. If the hand of the word *librarius* is the same as that of the name, it is possible that the name might be Logar or even Legar (conceivably representing Lodger or Ledger). The flexibility of spelling is illustrated by the name reported by Stoate as 'Richard Log.er' possibly being linked to the same family as a 'Nicholas Londyer' (in Callington in 1522 – cf. T. L. Stoate (ed.), *Cornwall Military Survey 1522, with the Loan Books and a Tinners Muster Roll c. 1535* (Bristol, 1987), p. 127).

16. Known after the Henrician reformation by the less politically contentious name of the College of Our Lady of Glasney. The best account is still Thurstan C. Peter, *The History of Glasney Collegiate Church, Cornwall* (Camborne, 1903). Another useful introduction is James Whetter, *The History of Glasney College* (Padstow, 1988).

17. Despite suggestive local place-names such as Tregaire in St Gerrans near Penryn – see Peter, *The History of Glasney Collegiate Church*, p. 47 and note.

18. The term usually refers not only to those ordained in Mary I's reign (and a few months after) but also to priests from earlier reigns, if they were ordained in the Catholic rite and worked overtly to uphold traditional religion in the early years of Elizabeth I. For an excellent introduction to the subject see Patrick McGrath and Joy Rowe, 'The Marian Priests under Elizabeth I', *Recusant History*, Catholic Record Society (CRS), vol. 17, no. 2 (October 1984), pp. 103–20.

19. R. J. E. Boggis, *A History of the Diocese of Exeter* (Exeter, 1922), p. 377.

20. *Nance Bequest*, Courtney Library (at the Royal Cornwall Museum) Box 7, Folder 22 (46). (It will be found among the opening notes placed with A. S. D. Smith's typescript of Nance's edition of Tregear. P. A. S. Pool's alternative numbering in brackets helpfully links the box to others containing relevant material.) Although Tregear died in March 1583, it is perhaps necessary to point out that this would have been reckoned as 1582 at the time, since the year did not change until Lady Day, on the eve of which he was buried. (I have amended all dates, however, as if the year began on 1 January.) The Newlyn registers are exceptionally complete and may be consulted on microfiche, along with excellent Victorian transcripts, at the Cornwall Record Office at Truro. The first volume contains Baptisms from 1560 and Marriages and Burials from 1559.

21. In Cornwall (as in the Cornish language) the prefix 'St' before parishes dedicated to Cornish saints is frequently omitted in speech and informal writing. Equally, the designation 'East' only became necessary in church documents when the parish of Newlyn St Peter near Penzance was created from part of the ancient parish of Paul in 1851.

22. *Nance Bequest*, Courtney Library, Box 7, Folder 22 (46). (At the foot of the typescript of 'Something New in Cornish').

23. It is also possible that Tregear may have been resident in Newlyn parish at the end of his life. This sort of 'neighbouring non-residence' became more common after the Reformation where vicarages had fallen into a poor state.

24. Cf. R. M. Glencross (ed.), *Calendar of Wills, Administrations and Accounts relating to the Counties of Cornwall and Devon, in the Archidiaconal Court of Cornwall, part I, 1569–1699* (London, 1929), p. 328. The John Tregeers died in Crowan, in 1614 and 1636 respectively. A Richard Tregear's will is recorded at both St Mawgan and Crowan for 1592, a Thomas Tregear at Crowan in 1601 and another Thomas at St Allen in 1609. Some of these could be related to John Tregear the priest.

25. Ibid., p. 309. For example, a Thomas Stephyns died in Zennor in 1578, in Uny Lelant in 1579, in Grade in 1586 (with an alias, Thomas Penick), in Madron in 1593, in Probus in 1602 and in St Columb Major in 1603, among others.

26. Edward Alexander Fry (ed.), *Calendar of Wills and Administrations relating to the Counties of Devon and Cornwall, proved in the Court of the Principal Registry of the Bishop of Exeter, 1559–1799 and, of Devon only, proved in the court of the Archdeaconry of Exeter 1540–1799*, vol. i (Plymouth, 1908), p. xxi in the Preface, correcting the misreading 'of St Olave' on p. 2. It is relatively easy to imagine how the cataloguers might at first have confused the form of a large initial 'a' in secretary hand with an 'ol' in italic, just as 'n' can also resemble a 'u'. Thus *Aluni*, 'of St Allen', might have been misread *Olaui*. This calendar (p. 183) also records the will of John Tristeane, vicar of the adjacent parish of Newlyn, who had died in 1581 – cf. also CRO, Parish Registers of St Newlyn East, first register, fol. 86.

27. *Episcopal Registers of John Woolton*, Devon Record Office (DRO) Chanter 21, fol. 11r. John Woolton was bishop of Exeter 1571–93.

28. I do not place any importance on the fact that the registrar, contrary to his usual practice, omits the word 'natural' in this case.

29. *Hennessy's Incumbents* in manuscript (along with a useful set of copies, with indices) is kept in the West Country Studies Library in Exeter. It consists of a record of beneficed clergy abstracted from the MS registers of the bishops of Exeter by the Revd G. L. Hennessy, rector of Monkokehampton. Hennessy drew up his lists – of incumbents only – by systematically working through the various inductions, collations and other appointments in the Episcopal Registers – sadly omitting any references to unbeneficed clergy and the ordination registers. His work – however incomplete and at times slightly inaccurate – is an invaluable form of index to the unpublished sixteenth-century registers.

30. The list of incumbents in St Allen parish church, for example, gives Hennessy's incorrect form.

31. Christopher Colmer, which may represent the modern name Colmore.

32. Charles Henderson, in his *Ecclesiastical History of the 109 Western Parishes of Cornwall*, *JRIC*, n.s., vol. ii, part 3 (1955), p. 12 suggests that the fifteenth-century stone altarpiece of this chapel may have been removed to the farmhouse garden at Tretherres, not far south-west of Allen church. The parish is also known for the poet Alexander Barclay, an earlier incumbent who, like Tregear and Stephyn, preserved Catholic views. *Letters and Papers Foreign & Domestic, Henry VIII*, arr. Gairdner, James, vol. xiii, pt ii (London, 1893). 'Frere Bartlow does much hurt in Cornwall and in Daynshire, both with open preaching and private comunication.' See also Rowse, *Tudor Cornwall*, pp. 152, 182–3.

33. Cf. H. S. A. Fox and O. J. Padel (eds), *The Cornish Lands of the Arundells of Lanherne, Fourteenth to Sixteenth Centuries*, Devon & Cornwall Record Society (DCRS), n.s. 41 (Exeter, 2000), p. xi; Bernard Deacon, *The Cornish Family* (2004), pp. 56–93; John Chynoweth, *Tudor Cornwall* (Stroud, 2002), p. 17.

34. Lucy Toulmin Smith (ed.), *The Itinerary of John Leland* (London, 1907), part iii, p. 185.

35. Joanna Mattingly, 'Going a-riding: Cornwall's late medieval guilds revisited', *Journal of the Royal Institution of Cornwall (JRIC)* (2005), p. 78 and Appendix 1, p. 88. The evidence for the guild of St Anthony is from Peter Bevill's will of 1511, National Archives (TNA), PROB 11/18, fol. 101v. See also, by the same author, 'The Medieval Parish Guilds of Cornwall'. *JRIC*, vol. x, part 3 (1989), pp. 290–329.

36. In some copies of Hennessy's work this is wrongly given as William 'Trerusse'.

37. *Episcopal Registers of John Veysey*, DRO, Chanter 14, fol. 113r. Tregear's appointment followed the resignation of William Treruffe. Treruffe (recorded as 'Tyrruffe') may well have been a curate at Ewny Lelant in 1522 during the incumbency of James Gentle, later provost of Glasney. Cf. T. L. Stoate (ed.), *Cornwall Military Survey 1522, with the Loan Books and a Tinners Muster Roll c. 1535* (*1522 Military Survey*) (Bristol, 1987), p. 7.

38. At the time of Henry VIII's *Valor Ecclesiasticus*, the priest of Allen would have received £8 13s. 4d. – perhaps a little more in Tregear's time. (See the printed edition of the *Valor Ecclesiasticus*, British Record Commission (London, 1821), vol. II, fol. 398.)

39. Parker Library, Corpus Christi College, Cambridge, MS 97, fol. 177r. There is an

excellent transcript of this – probably that made by A. J. Watson of the British Museum in 1927 – in the DRO (Z19/10/1b: fol. 54) along with photostats of the original (Z19/10/1a: fol. 44). Matthew Parker was consecrated Archbishop of Canterbury on the 17 December 1559 and he subsequently requested his bishops to compile a full list of clergy in their dioceses, indicating who were graduates, who were married, etc. William Alley's list for the diocese of Exeter, with an approximate date of Christmas 1561 from internal evidence, is the document fortunately preserved at Cambridge. See also *Devon & Cornwall Notes & Queries* (*DCNQ*), vol. xv (January 1928), no. 35, pp. 38–41.

40. The Latin title 'Dominus', abbreviated to 'Dom', was accorded at the time to any priest and translated into English as 'Sir' (with, of course, no implication of knighthood). 'Dom Johannes Tregear/Sir John Tregear' was simply the equivalent of the modern 'Fr John Tregear'. ('Magister/Master' tended to reflect academic or social standing, 'Doctor' almost always the former.)

41. For example Edward Scambler, bishop of Peterborough in 1564, complained of 'the straggling doctors and priests who have liberty to stray at their pleasure within this realm'. Cf. Mary Bateson (ed.), 'A Collection of Original Letters from the Bishops to the Privy Council, 1564', *The Camden Miscellany*, vol. ix (1893), p. 3. Before the Reformation travelling preachers, occasionally sent out by the religious orders or sometimes by the bishop, had sometimes had permission to tour parishes.

42. Eamon Duffy, *The Stripping of the Altars, Traditional Religion in England 1400 –1580* (2nd edn, New Haven and London, 2005), pp. 57–8.

43. Eamon Duffy, *The Voices of Morebath: Reformation and Rebellion in an English Village* (New Haven and London, 2001), p. 175. About 8 clergy in the diocese appear to have admitted to doing this.

44. Julyan Holmes, 'On the track of Cornish in a bilingual country', in Philip Payton (ed.), *Cornish Studies: Eleven* (Exeter, 2003), p. 271 points out that surnames in the parish such as 'Anvelyn' (the mill) recorded in the Consistory Court in 1554, suggest this, as does some place-name evidence east of the parish.

45. Matthew Spriggs, 'Where Cornish was spoken and when: a provisional synthesis', in Philip Payton (ed.), *Cornish Studies: Eleven* (Exeter, 2003), pp. 228–69 summarizes the range of evidence on the question, noting its complication by the question of sound changes and dialect, and citing in detail the important work of Holmes, George, Wakelin, Williams, Nance and others.

46. I am very grateful to Dr Joanna Mattingly for drawing my attention to this will, preserved in the Public Record Office and available online, ref. TNA, PROB/11/47.

47. Frances Rose-Troup, *DCNQ*, vol. xvii (Exeter, January 1932–October 1933), p. 192.

48. *DCNQ*, vol. xvii, pp. 334–6.

49. See Nicholas Orme, *The Minor Clergy of Exeter Cathedral, 1300–1548* (Exeter, 1980), p. 85. Orme notes that Godfrey was admitted to the chantry on 13 June 1545, and lost it at the dissolution, 1 April 1548. He gives the references to the chantry records (Exeter Cathedral Archive, D&C Exeter MS 3552, fol. 43v) and the pension records at the Public Record Office (PRO, E 101/75/9; E 301/80).

50. 'I bequeath my soul to Almighty God and my body to be buried in the chancel of Saint Piran aforesaid, where the high altar stood.'

51. Duffy, *Voices of Morebath*, p. 190.

52. 'Item: to Sir John Tregear, clerk, Vicar of Allen, one stone of my best wool, my frock and my cassock ... and I do ordain the said Vicar of Allen to be my supervisor upon this my last will and testament and he to sell my corn and divide the value thereof as much as is dry among the poor and in works of charity for the health of my soul. Item: my books, to be divided among priests to the said Vicar of Allen's discretion.'

53. Cf. McGrath and Rowe, 'The Marian Priests', p. 117, quoting A. Peel, *The Seconde Parte of a Register* (Cambridge, 1915), vol. ii, p. 83, with William Shaw at Baddesley Clinton described as 'a secret persuader of the simple to Popery, one that prayeth for the dead'.

54. H. L. Douch (ed.), *The Cornwall Muster Roll for 1569* (Bristol, 1984), p. 7.

55. Ibid., p. iii. (Introduction by T. L. Stoate).

56. Christopher Haigh, 'The Continuity of Catholicism in the English Reformation', *Past and Present*, 93 (November 1981), p. 40.

57. E.g. Nicholas Nicholls at St Kew.

58. See, among many others, Brian Murdoch, *Cornish Literature* (Cambridge 1993), pp. 129–30; Peter Berresford Ellis, *The Cornish Language and its Literature* (London), 1974, pp. 52–69; Robert Morton Nance, 'The Tregear Manuscript', *Old Cornwall* (1950), vol. iv, p. 11; *idem*, 'More About the Tregear Manuscript', *Old Cornwall* (1951), vol. v, p. 1; *idem*, 'Something new in Cornish', *JRIC* (1952), n.s. vol. 1, p. 2. See also the extensive correspondence between Nance and John Mackechnie and other papers on the Tregear MS in Box 8 of the Nance Bequest at the Courtney Library, Royal Cornwall Museum, Truro.

59. Priests with similar – and easily misread – names (such as the 'Thomas Screvyn' ordained in 1506 with Glasney as his title – presumably the Thomas Skrivan at St Teath in 1522) add to the confusing nature of the search. (Cf. *Episcopal Registers of Hugh Oldham*, DRO, Chanter 13, ff. 86v, 87v, 88r.)

60. O. J. Padel, 'Cornish Surnames in 1327', *Nomina*, 9 (1985), pp. 81–7; Fox and Padel, *The Cornish Lands of the Arundells*, pp. cxxiv–cxxxvii. Witness the Thomas Stephyn already mentioned, who was also known by the surname Penick (note 25 above).

61. *Episcopal Registers of James Turberville*, DRO, Chanter 18, fol. 15r. The impossibility of complete confidence with a priest of this name is illustrated by, for example, the Thomas Stephyns instituted to Llanstadwell in the diocese of Menevia (St David's) on 8 November 1554 (*Calendar of Patent Rolls* (*CPR*), *Philip and Mary*, vol. ii, London, 1936, pt xii) or the one appointed to the vicarage of Whitstable in the diocese of Canterbury on 9 July 1554 (*CPR, Philip and Mary*, vol. ii, pt xi, p. 214.) Even one of Wolsey's chaplains was called Thomas Stevyns.

62. Charles Henderson, *The Ecclesiastical History of the 109 Parishes of Western Cornwall (Ecclesiastical History)*, *JRIC*, n.s., vol. iii, part 2 (1958), p. 365.

63. 'There was a chapel in the parish of St Newlyn in Cornwall called St Nectan's (of the saint to which it was dedicated) which chapel had a yard belonging unto it, in which there were four stones on a little mount or hill at the north west corner where the crosses and relics of St Piran, St Crantock, St Cubert, St Newlyn were wont to be placed in the Rogation week, at which time they used to meet there [and had a] sermon made to the people, and the last was preached by Parson Crane in Queen Mary's time, as I have been credibly informed by a priest who had been an eye witness.' Cf. Nicholas Orme (ed.), *Nicholas Roscarrock's Lives of the Saints, Cornwall and Devon*, Devon and Cornwall Record Society, n.s., vol. 35 (Exeter, 1992), p. 94

(taken from Cambridge University Library, MS Add. 3041 C, fol. 327v). See also the useful notes on pp. 159–60. Henry Crane was the rector of Withiel and, in Orme's view, 'probably a moderate conservative'.

64. D&C Exeter MS 3688, Exeter Cathedral Archive, Exeter (D&C 3688). The information for the Archdeaconry of Cornwall begins on fol. 26. I am particularly indebted to Nicholas Orme for drawing my attention to this MS.

65. *Letters & Papers, Foreign & Domestic, Henry VIII* (London, 1883), vol. vii, 1377–85, pp. 523–7.

66. John Le Neve, *Fasti Ecclesiae Anglicanae, 1300–1541*, vol. ix, *Exeter Diocese* (revised by Joyce M. Horn) (London, 1964), p. 17. While Thomas Bedyll was collated to the Archdeaconry on 2 March and installed (by proxy) on 11 June 1535 he was dead by 1537 and Thomas Wynter was installed on 10 October 1537. Bedyll's short term may account for some of the confusion over the Archdeaconry.

67. Kenall was not even ordained priest until the vigil of Trinity, 22 May 1535.

68. D&C 3688, fol. 30r.

69. Peter, *The History of Glasney Collegiate Church*, p. 99.

70. For example, Robert Swimmer is shown (fol. 35r) at Minster, where Hennessy records he went on 30 October 1537. Perhaps the document is based on information gathered over a range of dates.

71. *Letters and Papers of Henry VIII*, vol. XII, pt 2 (London, 1891), p. 124 (n. 301) and p. 476 (n.1325). I am grateful to Nicholas Orme for pointing me to this reference. I have, however, worked principally from microfilms of the original documents (PRO/TNA, SP (Hen. VIII) 1/123, pp. 40–1, and SP 1/127, p. 183 – not 193 as in the PRO calendar).

72. TNA Hen. VIII SP 1/123/41 '... that is to say, that the Master of a certain ship of the said port of Truro called the Magdalen ... thorough the counsel of three priest[s], feigning a pope holy pilgrimage to a pardon in Brittany, denied not only the said deputy searcher to search the said ship, but also my deputy of the Admiralty in those parts to do his office and duty.'

73. TNA Hen. VIII SP 1/127/183. These are the names of the riotous persons hereafter following. First Sir Thomas Trebilcock parish priest of St Newlyn. Sir Phillip ... [space left blank] parish priest of St Ann's [?]. John Mitchell junior of Truro, Captain. Rychard Barrett, merchant of Truro. Pascow Trehar of Newlyn. Richard Otes (Otis?) of Feock (?) of the said ship. John Tradrack, Breton, alias Spicer the master's mate. John Loo, Breton, John Hoskyn of Truro, John Hewitt, Breton, William Matthew, William Salpyn, William Carselick, with other[s] to the number of 50 persons.

74. William Treruffe was the vicar at that time.

75. Oliver Padel has drawn my attention to 'Saynct Anne's hille' (= St Agnes Beacon) in Leland, I, 317, and for Advent see Orme, Nicholas, *English Church Dedications*, Exeter, 1996, p. 67. I have not had time to return to Exeter to examine the Bishops' Registers and D&C 3688 again for possible candidates for Sir Philip – further useful work could be done to identify him.

76. TNA Hen. VIII SP 1/123/41.

77. 'shouldering and buffeting him as though he had been a Turk or a Saracen.'

78. *Cornwall Military Survey 1522*, p. 34. John Sampson is also noted as having some land in Wendron and Gluvias parishes (pp. 29, 36).

79. He was made subdeacon by Thomas Chard, bishop of Solubria on 15 February

1515, deacon by the same bishop on 8 March 1516, and priest – again by Chard – on 22 March 1516. I give the references for these ordinations below (see notes 156, 157 and 158).

80. *Cornwall Military Survey, 1522*, p. 25. He may also – if there has been a slight misreading of the MS Survey – have been the John 'Treleigne' who held some land in Sithney parish at the same time (p. 32).

81. D&C Exeter MS 3688, Exeter Cathedral Archive, fol. 30v.

82. *Episcopal Registers of William Bradbridge*, DRO, Chanter 20, fol. 15v. Tristeane was appointed on 23 August 1573 – he was also vicar of Manaccan from 1572. Tristeane's immediate predecessor at Newlyn, Richard Martyn, resigned at this point, but it is not known when he himself was appointed.

83. CRO, The Parish Registers of Newlyn East, 1581, fol. 86.

84. The final absentee years of Veysey have sometimes been unfairly criticised for a form of ecclesiastical 'asset-stripping'. In fact, like many bishops under Henry VIII, he had little choice but to hand over manor after manor to the King's favourites. He did, however, seek to ensure some residual income during his lifetime for his charitable foundations in Sutton Coldfield.

85. I have preferred the term 'auxiliary' to avoid confusion with the various modern uses of the word 'suffragan' and the possible implication that these bishops served in one diocese only. Thomas Chard, titular bishop of Solubria, was active as an auxiliary bishop in both Exeter and Bath & Wells dioceses. His will is in the Public Record Office (PRO, Prerogative Court of Canterbury, Registered Copy Wills; prob/11/30) where he bequeaths his soul to 'Almighty God, Our Lady St Mary and all the Saints' in the traditional formula. He died in 1544. Cf. also Stubbs, William, ed. *Registrum Sacrum Anglicanum* (2nd edition, Oxford, 1897), p. 201.

86. *Episcopal Registers of John Veysey*, DRO, Chanter 14, fol. 171v. (The folios of the ordination register are not numbered, so this pagination is mine.) Stevyns, Stephyns, Stephens, Stephyn and Stevyn were all possible variants of the name at this time.

87. *Episcopal Registers of John Veysey*, DRO, Chanter 14, fol. 172v. Prior Vyvyan lived in state and was buried in a fine tomb at Bodmin, after his death on Whitsunday, 1 June 1533, 'just as the old order was changing' (Lawrence S. Snell, *The Suppression of the Religious Foundations of Devon and Cornwall* (Marazion, 1967), pp. 76–7). The house he built at Rialton, near Newquay, survives in part. A. L. Rowse evokes the scene in *Tudor Cornwall*, p. 148: 'From the large oriel window in his study, which he built for himself – the arms of the priory, the three fishes, with his initials, are still to be seen in the glass panes – he looked out upon the little courtyard with its holy well and into the orchards, fringed by the wind blown elms.' He was prior of Bodmin from 1508 so it is hard to believe that he was the Thomas Vyvyan of Bodmin Priory ordained outside Cornwall, at Ramsbury in Salisbury diocese – as deacon on 17 May 1517 (*Episcopal Registers of Edmund Audley*, WRO, D1, 2/14 fol. 31v of the ordination register) and as priest on 20 September 1517 (ibid. fol. 32r) – especially as the prior was made bishop that same year.

88. *Episcopal Registers of John Veysey*, DRO, Chanter 14, fol. 173r. Interestingly, Stevyn's title was the Collegiate Church of Our Lady at Ottery (where, in the previous century, another Thomas Stevens had been a famous Warden). On the same occasion, the bishop ordained Gerens John to the title of Glasney College as subdeacon. I have not been successful in finding the ordination of Thomas Stephyn

of Newlyn in the Exeter Registers, although both a Henry Stephyn and a John Stephyn were made deacon at the paschal vigil, 7 April 1520.

89. The practice was very common of attending a convenient ordination elsewhere with appropriate permission. An examination of the registers of neighbouring dioceses show frequent ordinations of Exeter clergy, even as far away as Wales. (See, for example R. F. Isaacson (ed.), *The Episcopal Registers of the Diocese of St David's, 1397–1518*, Cymmrodorion Record Series (1917–20), vol. II, pp. 702–6, where the many Exeter ordinands include John Tuell whose title was Launceston priory.) It was a two-way process. Exeter ordinations often included candidates from other dioceses – primarily Bath & Wells but also (for example) Salisbury, Worcester, Hereford and again even from Wales. (Two good examples would be a Meriadoc made subdeacon for St John the Baptist, Carmarthen in Menevia Diocese on 23 February 1519, and a Lewis ap Thomas made deacon for Neath Abbey in Llandaff Diocese on 2 June 1515.) There are also several years of missing ordinations in the Exeter registers.

90. C. W. Field, *The Province of Canterbury and the Elizabethan Settlement of Religion* (privately published, 1972), pp. 102–6, 108–9, 113–14.

91. *Calendar of State Papers Domestic*, Elizabeth I, Addenda, 1547–65, ed. Mary Anne Everett Green (London, 1870), p. 522. Bonner's own chaplains were 'wandering about seditiously', particularly one 'Morren' (or Morwyn) in Lancashire (p. 524).

92. Field, *The Province of Canterbury*, p. 109.

93. Corpus Christi College, Cambridge, MS 97 and transcription (Z19/10/1b) at the DRO. A 'chapel' (*capella*) is all that is noted, with no priest's name attached. Perranzabuloe is also missing.

94. Unless Richard Martyn began his ministry there as soon as Stephyn left.

95. See Lucy Wooding, *The Marian Restoration and the Mass*, in Eamon Duffy and David Loades (eds), *The Church of Mary Tudor* (Aldershot, 2006), pp. 227–57.

96. The surname varies in spelling from Trelobys, Trelabys, Treloves, Trelowbys, Treloubes, Trelobbes, Trelobes, Trelebs in the Tudor sources. In modern times it is Trelubbas or Trelubbis, the latter being the usual form for surnames, perpetuated as a modern street name in Helston. The Christian name is recorded as Ralph or Rauf, its Latin form being Radulphus.

97. I have used the term 'canon' somewhat freely – as indeed was done in Tudor times – formally, Trelobys was what we would now call a 'prebendary' of Glasney.

98. Trelubbas Wartha lies at SW 667296 near Coverack Bridges, near the boundary between the old Wendron and Sithney parishes. A Trelubbas Wolas is also attested in the sixteenth century.

99. W. P. W. Phillimore and Thomas Taylor (eds), *Cornwall Parish Registers: Marriages*, vol. v. (London, 1903), p. 6. Michell Trelobus (Michael Trelobys) and Elizabeth, dau. of William Lanion, Breage, 2 July 1581.

100. D&C 3688, fol. 33r. His name is not among the surviving lists of Oxford and Cambridge alumni in the reference works such as Emden, but inevitably many records have been lost.

101. A 'title', in this context, means a nominal position such as (what we would call) an assistant curacy, or the sponsorship of a religious community or a college like Glasney. No one could be ordained without being 'vouched for' in such a way, although it seems often to have been a formality at this period and not to require further association.

102. *Episcopal Registers of Hugh Oldham*, DRO, Chanter 13, fol. 83r. Cornish succeeded

the Augustinian canon John Valens as bishop of Tenos from 1486 till his death in 1513. (A. Hamilton Thompson, *The English Clergy (Ford Lectures for 1933)* (Oxford, 1947), p. 49 n.) He was closely identified with Ottery, a sometime Warden, and William Worcestre appears to have spent an evening talking and drinking with him there on 22 September 1478. (John H. Harvey (ed.), *William Worcestre: Itineraries* (Oxford, 1969), p. 39 and note 5.) See also A. L. Rowse, *Tudor Cornwall* (London, 1941; revised edition, 1969), p. 152.

103. As his name suggests, Bishop Oldham was a Lancashire man, although he had been Archdeacon of Exeter and a canon of the Cathedral for 12 years. Assigned to the see of Exeter by Pope Julius II in 1505, he also founded Manchester Grammar School and (with Bishop Foxe of Winchester) endowed Corpus Christi College, Oxford, to foster the education of the secular clergy.

104. As many as 300 a year on average in Exeter around this time – see Boggis, *Diocese of Exeter*, p. 325. This figure declined to an average of around 20 a year after 1534 – perhaps an indicator of the sea change in church life that was underway.

105. Usually in an area of the world that had once been Christian, but was now under Muslim rule. Some of these sees had once been famous Christian churches, such as that of Hippo in North Africa, where St Augustine had been bishop. After Thomas Cornish, the auxiliary bishops working in the diocese of Exeter leading up to the Reformation included, as we have seen, Thomas Vyvyan, prior of Bodmin from 1508 and bishop of Megara from 1517, and Thomas Chard, bishop of Solubria (Selymbria, in Thrace), the former prior of Montacute and Carswell and warden of Ottery. (A full list of the English bishops *in partibus* may be found in E. B. Fryde, D. E. Greenway, S. Porter and I. Roy (eds), *Handbook of British Chronology* (3rd edition, Cambridge, 1986), pp. 284–7.) Vyvyan assisted Hugh Oldham and Chard mostly John Veysey. Snell, *The Suppression of the Religious Foundations of Devon and Cornwall*, p. 44n. reminds us that Bishop Chard should not be confused, as is often done, with Thomas Chard the great last abbot of Forde. Eventually William Fawell of Cullompton, bishop of Hippo, succeeded Chard under Veysey. Fawell was the last prior of St Nicholas in Exeter, and held some ordinations in the priory chapel. (Boggis, *Diocese of Exeter*, pp. 66, 331.)

106. *Episcopal Registers of Edmund Audley*, Wiltshire and Swindon Record Office (WRO), D1, 2/14, fol. 186r (f.3r of the ordination register). Trelobys was deaconed on 21 September 1504 by the bishop of Salisbury himself, Edmund Audley, in the Lady Chapel of his manor at Ramsbury. 'Radulphus Treleboys' is clearly identified as coming from Exeter diocese, and his correct title (Bodmin Priory) is noted.

107. See Duffy, *The Voices of Morebath*, pp. 15–16. Christopher Trychay's title was from Frithelstock Priory, where he may have been educated, but where it is equally possible there may have been some other, looser arrangement.

108. *Episcopal Registers of Hugh Oldham*, DRO, Chanter 13, fol. 48r. (Transcribed as 'Trelovys' in *Hennessey's Incumbents* but in fact 'Trelobys'). He succeeded to the parish on the death of Richard Hooper.

109. *Episcopal Registers of Hugh Oldham*, DRO, Chanter 13, fol. 75v. 'Treloves' in *Hennessey's Incumbents*, but in fact 'Trelobes'. He succeeded to the 'parish of St Newlina' on the resignation of Robert Strangeways.

110. *Cornwall Military Survey, 1522*, pp. 24–5. Ralph 'Trelobis/Trelowbys' had £7 per annum from the living, and (p. 25) goods to the value of £16. Tewkesbury Abbey held the rectory.

111. *1522 Military Survey*, p. 30. There is also a Thomas Stephyn in the Tinner's Muster Roll for the nearby parish of St Michael's in Helston (p. 154).
112. *1522 Military Survey*, p. 153. There was a later Ralph Trelobys who died in the parish in 1580, and a Raw (i.e. Ralph) Trelobys who died in 1588. Cf. R. M. Glencross (ed.), *Calendar of Wills, part I, 1569–1699* (1929), p. 330. The name may have taken on a particular significance for the family.
113. *Valor Ecclesiasticus* (London, 1821), vol. II, fol. 400 (Newlyn) and fol. 395 (Crowan).
114. Lawrence S. Snell, *Documents towards a History of the Reformation in Cornwall: i, The Chantry Certificates for Cornwall* (Exeter, c.1953), pp. 36–40. Thurstan Peter, however, p. 99, gives only £1 6s. 0d. as Trelobys's prebendal income, from the further return of Bishop Veysey after the *Valor*, sent by him to the crown on 3 November 1536.
115. Around 10 marks (£6 13s. 4d.) was considered the fitting stipend of a vicar not in possession of the rectorial tithes and until Henry VIII clerical incomes below this level were rarely taxed.
116. Peter, *The History of Glasney Collegiate Church*, p. 80. Spelling 'Trelabys'.
117. This appears to be Peter's shorthand for D&C 3688. Spelling 'Trelebs'. He also cites the *State Papers of Henry VIII, Rolls Series*, vol. 5, 489.
118. Although Bishop Veysey found it in very bad condition in 1540, Leland described it as 'strongly walled and castellid' on his visit. See Peter, *The History of Glasney Collegiate Church*, p. 41. It was included among the chantries granted to the king by act of parliament, 37 Henry VIII, cap. 4, although the king later averred that he was not 'minded to deface any of his gret colleges'. On the accession of Edward VI, the remaining chantries were assigned to the Crown by act of Parliament, 1 Edward VI, cap. 14, including Glasney. Peter, pp. 100–1.
119. RIC, Courtney Library, St Aubyn Collection, HA/14/7 (Hend. Cal. 16 page 106, no. 225). I am very grateful to Angela Broome for helping me track down surviving Trelobys documents in the Library's collections.
120. There are also a few rare instances in the Bishops' Registers where 'Rad' alternates with Ric^{us} as an abbreviation for Richard, although it usually stands for Ralph (Radulphus).
121. J. L. Vyvyan and Henry H. Drake (eds), *The Visitation of the County of Cornwall in the year 1620* (London, 1874), pp. 225–7. Based on BL, Harl. MSS 1162 and 1164.
122. See footnotes 133 to 137 below, and associated text.
123. Although some colleges seem to have escaped notice at that time, including St Buryan and Crantock.
124. Throughout the country, the promised potential for education of the dissolution of the chantries fell short of early expectations. Only after 1550 did increasing complaints coincide with the foundation of the 'free grammar schools of King Edward VI'. Cf. Nicholas Orme, *Medieval Schools from Roman Britain to Renaissance England* (New Haven and London, 2006), pp. 324–7.
125. Chantry Certificate 9/1, printed in Snell, *Documents towards a History of the Reformation in Cornwall*, p. 36.
126. 'The town of Penryn wherein are houselling [i.e. communicant] people 400. The College of Saint Thomas of Glasney, standing in the said town, being the parish church of the foundation of Walter [Bronescombe, the] Good, sometime Bishop

of Exeter, to find a provost & 12 prebendaries whereof the said provost and 7 of the said prebendaries be now resident and 5 not resident, 7 vicars, a chapel clerk, a bellringer, 4 choristers and 3 chantry priests to celebrate in the said college.' Chantry Certificate 9/1, printed in Snell, *Documents towards a History of the Reformation in Cornwall*, p. 36. This seems to echo Leland's error over the bishop's name when he says 'One Water Good Bisschop of Excestre made yn a more caullid Glesnith in the botom of a park of his at Penrine a collegiate chirch with a provost, xij prebendaries, and other ministers'. (Toulmin Smith, *Itinerary of John Leland*, p. 197.)

127. The certificates list Mr John Libby, Provost; John Harrys LLB (80); Mr Ralf Trelabys (70); Mr Thomas Vivian (70); Mathew Newcombe (60), Matthew Broke (45); Gerens John (46) and Nicholas Nicholls (45). Non-resident were Henry Kyllyfree, Thomas/John Molesworthy and Rauf/Philip Couch. in addition there were 5 vicars, 4 choristers, 3 chantry priests a chapel clerk and a bellringer.

128. 'Ralph Trelobys of the age of 70 years hath for his salary in the said college £12 besides his promotions in other places £6.' Snell, *Documents towards a History of the Reformation in Cornwall*, p. 37.

129. 'Ralph Trelobys, prebendary, for his salary clear £10 2s. 2d. Pension £6 13s. 4d.' Chantry Certificate 10/1, Snell, *Documents towards a History of the Reformation in Cornwall*, p. 39.

130. I have expanded the contractions. RIC, Courtney Library, Bassett Collection, HB/1/1 (Hend. Cal. 5 page 145, no. 587). Ralph Couch was 50, with a salary of £6 12s. at the dissolution. Perhaps one of the choirboys, Henry Couch, may have been his son, or grandson (cf. Snell, *Documents towards a History of the Reformation in Cornwall*, pp. 37–8.)

131. *Episcopal Registers of John Veysey*, DRO, Chanter 16, fol. 31v.

132. Edward Alexander Fry (ed.), *Calendar of Wills and Administrations relating to the Counties of Devon and Cornwall, proved in the Consistory Court of the Bishop of Exeter, 1532–1800*, vol. II (Plymouth, 1914), p. 206.

133. J. L. Vivian, *The Visitations of Cornwall, comprising the Heralds' Visitations of 1530, 1573 & 1620* (Exeter, 1887), pp. 469–70 (from the original 1620 Visitation, Harl. MS. 1162). The Visitations are now online at http://www.uk-genealogy.org.uk/england/Cornwall/visitations/imgs/p469.jpg (accessed 29/08/2006). Of course, there may be mistakes or omissions – deliberate or otherwise – in the pedigree. As for the Thomas Tregear who died without issue, H. L. Douch (ed.), *The Cornwall Muster Roll for 1569* (Bristol, 1984), p. 29 includes a 'Thomas Tregayre' at St Mawgan, possibly connected with the recusant centre at Lanherne. It is intriguing to speculate whether this could this be a member of the same family, perhaps also a cleric and a Catholic. The same roll records a Thomas Stephen at St Columb Major (p. 33) – largely owned by the Arundells of Lanherne, who would have encouraged traditional religion there – and another at Cubert (p. 36).

134. Wills that have survived outside Devon and Cornwall would no doubt be a fruitful area for investigation. Of the later fortunes of the family, the parish registers of the seventeenth century are a good witness. For example, Maude Tregear, 'daughter of John Tregear of Crowan, gent. deceased', married a 'Richard Mountstephen of Michaelstow, gent.' on 31 January 1655, and may be found with many other Tregears in W. P. W. Phillimore and Thomas Taylor (eds), *Cornwall Parish Registers: Marriages*, vol. i (London, 1900), p. 87. H. Miles Brown, *What to look for in Cornish Churches* (Newton Abbot, 1973), p. 76 describes a slate headstone to Richard

Tregeare in 1668 in the tower vestry at Crowan with 'a curious inscription', which I have not seen.

135. *1522 Military Survey*, p. 25, spelt 'Tregere'.

136. Both are likely to have lived at the farmstead of Tregear, which, as its name suggests, lies adjacent to an ancient fort or 'round' at SW 640343.

137. *1522 Military Survey*, p. 25.

138. *1522 Military Survey*, p. 34. They may have owned property in their own right in both places.

139. CRO, Parish Registers of Newlyn East. Cf. also Charles Henderson's manuscript *Materials for a History of the Parish of Newlyn, Part II: Subsidies* (February 1924) in the Courtney Library, which quotes examples of the name (in the form Tregayr) from the Lay Subsidy of 1327.

140. W. P. W. Phillimore, Thomas Taylor and William J. Stephens (eds), *Cornwall Parish Registers: Marriages*, vol. xvi. (London, 1909), p. 67.

141. Charles Henderson, *Ecclesiastical History*, in *JRIC*, n.s. vol. ii, part 4 (1956), p.134, quoting PRO 6/36.

142. The name comes from the Cornish words *tre*, 'farmstead' and **ker*, 'round, fort' – see O. J. Padel, *Cornish Place-Name Elements*, English Place-Name Society, vols LVI, LVII (Nottingham, 1985), pp. 50–4.

143. *1522 Military Survey*, Camborne (p. 3), Stithians (p. 151) and Sithney (p. 34, already noted, and p. 154). In later surveys Tregears are found in Gwinnear and Ladock, as far west as St Just in Penwith and as far east as the Tamar (again demonstrating the portability of toponymic surnames at the period).

144. W. P. W. Phillimore, Thomas Taylor and W. J. Stephens (eds), *Cornwall Parish Registers: Marriages*, vol. xviii (London, 1910), pp. 114–15 has both Angeare and Tregear as a surname in close historical proximity at Crowan, though well after the period we are considering. The solitary instance of Angeare in the seventeenth-century registers – a Richard Angeare marrying Katherine his wife on 30 June 1683 – is matched by large numbers Tregears over several generations.

145. I am grateful to Oliver Padel for sorting out my thinking on this matter, and pointing out that place names of the form Gayr/Geere run in parallel with those of the form Tregear in the parish from the thirteenth century at least. They may represent two separate place names, or at least separate families.

146. *1522 Military Survey*, p. 48.

147. *Episcopal Registers of John Veysey*, DRO, Chanter 14, 147r, 147v, 148v. However the John Gayre of the conveyance, if he is a cleric, could be another, older priest, John Gere/Geere (cf. *Episcopal Registers of Richard Fox*, DRO, Chanter 12 II: fol. 155r, 1st series, shows his priesting at Tavistock).

148. *1522 Military Survey*, p. 123: 'John Treer, chaplain, in stipend £4, in gods £2.10.0d': serving with John Havell, curate, under Thomas Basely, the Rector of Northill parish in East hundred.

149. *Episcopal Registers of Hugh Oldham*, DRO, Chanter 13, fol. 114r.

150. Ibid., fol. 114v.

151. Hennessy sometimes reads the name as Trerusse in the Exeter registers, although is more clearly Treruffe elsewhere. I have taken it as the latter as in two places it is written Treruth.

152. The name is written variously as Tristeane, Tresteane, Trysteyn, Tristeyne, Tristeigne, Trystayne.

153. *Episcopal Registers of John Veysey*, DRO, Chanter 14, fol. 55r. Treruffe was appointed on 7 September, 1531.
154. At Cubert in 1558 according to *Hennessy's Incumbents*.
155. Tristeane's surname is spelled 'Trystayne' in this instance, and the ordination took place in the Lady Chapel of Exeter Cathedral; DRO Chanter 13, fol. 122v.
156. *Episcopal Registers of Hugh Oldham*, DRO Chanter 13, fol. 123v. Again in the Lady Chapel, with Tristeane spelled as 'Tristayn'.
157. *Episcopal Registers of Cardinal Hadrian de Castello*, bishop of Bath & Wells and cardinal priest of St Chrysostom, *Somerset Record Office (SRO), D/D/breg/10, fol. 157v.*
158. Episcopal Registers of Cardinal Hadrian de Castello, SRO, D/D/breg/10, fol. 158r. Treruffe is clearly spelled 'Treruffe' here, and Tristeane as 'Tristeyne'. Apparently there was a short-lived attempt to restore Montacute under Mary I. (J. H. Bettey, *The Suppression of the Monasteries* (Gloucester, 1989), p. 118.)
159. All records of the ordinations between 1526 and 1547, for example, are now lost.
160. Campeggio, an eminent lawyer and a married man with five children, was ordained after his wife's death and rose rapidly in the hierarchy. Originally sent to England to enlist Henry VIII's aid in a crusade, he made a favourable impression and soon became bishop of Salisbury. Later, judging Henry's divorce case alongside Cardinal Wolsey, he resolutely followed papal guidance in not coming to any conclusion. The fall in ordinations during his time at Salisbury was probably less to do with zeal to reform abuses (since he was effectively an absentee bishop) than part of a general trend across the whole of England, reflecting the changing status of the church.
161. For example, the Thomas Stephyn ordained priest by John Pinnock, bishop of Syene (and auxiliary to Campeggio) on 19 December 1528 in Salisbury Cathedral. (*Episcopal Register of Cardinal Campeggio*, WRO, D1, 2/15 fol. 64v.) This particular Stephyn is most unlikely to have any connection with Cornwall, however. He was a monk (of Farleigh) and was in any case ordained after the Mylor curate.
162. Duffy, *The Voices of Morebath*, pp. 118–41.
163. Ibid. p. 135.
164. Philip Caraman SJ, *The Western Rising, 1549* (Tiverton, 1994), p. 105, citing Hooker and Holinshed.
165. Charles Henderson, *Ecclesiastical History*, in *JRIC* n.s. vol. iii, part 2 (1958), p. 367. In Newlyn East the Borlases of Treluddra remained Catholics for a long time, like the Arundells of Lanherne – those at Trerice conformed.
166. It also underplays the relationship of the College with its wider network of parishes.
167. Duffy, *The Stripping of the Altars*, pp. 424–30. For a different view see G. W. Bernard, *The King's Reformation* (New Haven and London), 2005.
168. Caraman, *The Western Rising*, p. 5.
169. Duffy, *The Voices of Morebath*.
170. D. J. Mullins, 'St Francis Xavier College', unpublished lecture given to the Wales and Marches Catholic History Society, June 2006. I am grateful to Bishop Mullins for lending me his notes for this lecture. The evidence comes from a long letter written to his family by Robert Gwyn of Bangor diocese, who entered Douai College in 1571 and was ordained in 1575. Gwyn argues in this letter against attending the established church services in future.
171. Philip Payton, *Cornwall, A History* (2nd edition, Fowey, 2004), pp. 126–7.

172. See P. A. Boylan and G. R. Lamb, *Francis Tregian, Cornish Recusant* (London and New York, 1955), p. 47 for a list of others implicated with Cuthbert Mayne including Nicholas Roscarrock of St Endellion, Francis Ermin of Newlyn and Richard Tremayne of Tregonnan – all of whom suffered years in prison for their faith. To these may be added the Becketts of Cartuther near Liskeard, the Hores of Trenowth, the Penkevells of St Minver, the Kempes of Lavethan and the Williamses of Treworgy in Probus. The main sources for Tregian's life are: Oscott MS 545 (1593) printed in J. Morris, *The Troubles of our Catholic Forefathers* (London, 1872), and F. Plunket, *Heroum Speculum* (Lisbon, 1655) reprinted by the Catholic Record Society, vol. lxxxii. (Boylan and Lamb also cite BL, Add MS 24489, fol. 296; 21, 203; Cotton MSS, Titus B.7, fol. 46; John Roche Dasent (ed.), *Acts of the Privy Council*, n.s. vol. ix, 1575–77 (1894), p. 390 and vol. x, p. 29.) Tregian eventually died in Lisbon, and his reputedly incorrupt body is buried in St Roche's church there. For Rowse's perspective – unjustly negative in my view – see Rowse, *Tudor Cornwall*, pp. 344–75.
173. CRS, vol. liii, Clare Talbot (ed.), *Miscellanea: Recusant Records*, p. 115. This is a transcript from the Cecil Papers, 9/112 (cf. Historical Manuscripts Commission II, p. 177).
174. Albert Peel (ed.), *The Seconde Parte of a Register, being a calendar of Manuscripts under that title intended for publication by the Puritans about 1593, and now in Dr Williams' Library, London*, vol. ii (Cambridge, 1915), pp. 98–110. The suspect priests may in some cases have been harshly judged as 'mass-men' simply because they were ordained under the old rite, but others were clearly working against the prevailing stream in religion. Still others appear who seem also to have been Marian priests but about whom less was known by the compilers: often their integrity is criticized.
175. *Devon and Cornwall Notes and Queries (DCNQ)*, vol. XVII, January 1932–October 1933, p. 88. Frances Rose-Troup has abstracted from the Valor Ecclesiasticus, the Exchequer Accounts and the records of Special Commissions in the PRO the fate of many Cornish and Devon religious after the dissolution in her lists in this volume (pp. 81ff, 143ff, 191ff, 238ff, 285ff, 334ff, 381ff.)
176. Charles Henderson, *Ecclesiastical History*, in *JRIC*, n.s. vol. ii, part 4 (1956), p.116, quoting PRO 6/36. Oliver Padel has suggested to me the original form might have been Scovern – common in the area at the time – and therefore nothing to do with Thomas Stephyn.
177. Danae Tankard, 'The Reformation of the deathbed in mid-sixteenth-century England', *Mortality*, vol. viii, no. 3 (August 2003). To this article I am indebted for descriptions of Sir Richard's death, the references in notes 179 and 180, and to the insight that in a time of such religious volatility deponents may have been cautious in giving too much away about their ministry at the deathbed. I am not, however, fully convinced by the interesting argument that we are witnessing a 'reformed' deathbed.
178. It should be remembered that, while Sir Richard holds his title as a knight, the 'Sir' in the case of Thomas Stephyns is by contrast a simple title of address for priests, as we would say 'Father' today.
179. PRO/C24/16.
180. PRO/C24/25.
181. John Stow, *A Survey of London (written in the year 1598)*, ed. Antonia Fraser (Stroud, 2005), pp. 135–6.

182. Tankard, 'The Reformation of the deathbed'. Tankard credits S. Brigden, *London and the Reformation* (Oxford, 1989) with the link between the two.

183. *CPR*, Elizabeth I, vol. iii (London, 1960), p. 355 (8 Elizabeth, 17 November 1565–16 November 1566, Part I, C.66/1019, no. 1977.)

184. There were Greshams in Cornwall, however: a Thomas Gresham was the incumbent at St Mabyn from 1534 to 1558, when John Kenall replaced him.

185. *Acts of the Privy Council*, vol. vii, p. 45.

186. Ibid., p. 79.

187. *CPR, Elizabeth I*, vol. i (London, 1939), p. 217 (*Pardon Roll*, 1 Elizabeth (1559) – part 2. Supplementary Patent Roll 68, MS fol. 19.)

188. The village is now little more than a row of houses, along a single track at SP 056538.

189. *Victoria County History: Warwick*, vol. iii (London, 1945), p. 160.

190. H. S. Gunn, *History of the Old Manor House of Wood Bevington* (privately published), 1911), pp. v–xvi.

191. Michael Hodgetts, personal communication. The whole of this paragraph is based on research undertaken by Mr Hodgetts.

192. Gladestry – in Welsh *Llanfair Llethonw* – had an ancient house known as the *Cwrt*, which belonged to Sir Gylla Meyric who, in Elizabeth's time, was attainted for high treason, condemned and executed.

193. John Roche Dasent (ed.), *Acts of the Privy Council* (London, 1893), n.s. vol. vii, 1558–70, p. 156.

194. *Acts of the Privy Council*, vol. vii, p. 153.

195. John Roche Dasent (ed.), *Acts of the Privy Council* (1896), n.s. vol. xiii, 1581–82, p. 153.

196. Charles Henderson, *Materials for a History of the Parish of Newlyn, Part II, Subsidies* (1924).

197. Charles Henderson, *Ecclesiastical History*, in *JRIC*, n.s., vol. iii, part 2 (1958), p. 367.

198. Nicholas Orme, *Medieval Children* (New Haven and London, 2001), pp. 238–46.

199. Chantry Certificate 9/1: printed in Snell, *Documents towards a History of the Reformation in Cornwall*, Penryn, 35a (p. 38).

200. Orme, *Medieval Children*, p. 240.

201. Orme, *Medieval Schools*, especially pp. 244–53, 283–7, 309–11. In one delightful remembered scene recorded in the sixteenth century church courts (p. 162), one elderly man looked back on his schooldays at Tywardreath Priory, where he used to guard the fish as it dried in the sun.

202. Ibid., especially pp. 240, 299, 371.

203. Chantry Certificate 15/79: Snell, *Documents towards a History of the Reformation in Cornwall*, p. 40.

204. National Library of Wales (NLW), Peniarth MS 105B. The other saint's play, an edition of which is in preparation by Graham Thomas and Nicholas Williams, is *Beunans Ke*, NLW MS 23849D.

205. When I studied the manuscript itself, I at first thought it possible that a faint 'x'-shape before the 'iiij' (and an even fainter 'v'-shape after my 'x') were significant. I suspected we would have to revise the date upwards. (Very good digital images of this area of fol. 92r may be selected and viewed at: http://digidol.llgc.org.uk/METS/BMK00001/frames?div=0&subdiv=0&locale=en&mode=thumbnail.) However, at

my request, the National Library of Wales kindly agreed to look again at the date. Dr Maredudd ap Huw, the Manuscript Librarian, re-examined it under ultra-violet light but still believes 1504 is the best interpretation. The 'x' and 'v' are probably colour variations in the paper.

206. Charles Thomas, *The Christian Antiquities of Camborne* (St Austell, 1967), p. 25.

207. See note 205. A pity, since (say) 1518 would have accorded well with Ton being part of Treloby's project.

208. Thomas, *Christian Antiquities*, p. 25. The Ton family was, however, established nearby around this time according to the *1522 Military Survey*. There is a William Tonne in Sithney (p. 33) and a Peter Ton in Mabe near Glasney (p. 33). Also the *Cornwall Subsidies in the reign of Henry VIII, 1524 and 1543 and the Benevolence of 1545*, ed. T. L. Stoate (Bristol, 1985), p. 23 (Mabe) and p. 41 (Sithney) reports Tons though none of these sources mentions a Ralph or Richard.

209. Cf. note 120 and associated text. Even where names were otherwise established as distinct, they could be colloquially interchangeable in some circumstances. S. Schoenbaum, in *Shakespeare's Lives* (Oxford, 1993) – apropos Anne Hathaway – notes that many women in Shakespeare's day were interchangeably called Anne or Agnes. He gives the example of the wife of Philip Henshawe, the theatrical entrepreneur – referred to as Agnes in Henshawe's will, but as Anne in the funeral records. This may not be a fair parallel, however, as Oliver Padel has raised the question with me as to whether the scribes were far less accurate in recording women's names than men's throughout the medieval period (as they certainly were in the fourteenth century court rolls of Dyffryn Clwyd).

210. Thomas, *Christian Antiquities*, quoting T. Tapley-Soper (ed.), *The Registers of ... the parish of Camborne, 1538–1837*, 2 vols, DCRS (Exeter, 1945).

211. *Episcopal Registers of John Arundell*, DRO, Chanter 12 II, fol. 13v (3rd series). The name could easily be mistaken here for Tonne, but for the spelling Tomb at subsequent ordinations.

212. *Episcopal Registers of John Arundell*, DRO, Chanter 12 II, fol. 14r (3rd series).

213. *Episcopal Registers of Bath & Wells: Sede Vacante 1503–4*, SRO, fol. 7r. Note that the otherwise admirable printed editions of these registers omit the detailed ordination lists, which can only be consulted in the manuscript original registers.

214. *1522 Military Survey*, p. 9.

215. A. B. Emden, *A Biographical Register of the University of Oxford, 1501–1540* (Oxford, 1974).

216. PRO, prob/11/25: Will of Richard Hilley, clerk, of St Dunstan in the East, London, 1534.

217. DRO, Z19/10/1b, fol. 53 (and fol. 35 – at Idesforde in the Deanery of Moreton).

218. DRO, Z19/10/1b, fol. 28 and fol. 43.

219. *1522 Military Survey*, p. 52.

220. *Episcopal Registers of John Arundell*, DRO, Chanter 12 II, 3rd series, fol. 7v, 29 November 1502.

221. *Episcopal Registers of John Booth*, DRO, Chanter 12 II, 1st series, fol. 32r – where, on 29 April 1475, the exchange between Mr Michael Carvanell (or Carbinell – perhaps a relative of the Alexander Carvanell who crossed swords with the 'pope holy pilgrimage') of Wendron and Radulphus John of All Saints Farnborough is recorded. Wendron, like Stithians, was held by Rewley Abbey near Oxford.

222. Cf. Oliver Padel, 'Oral and literary culture in medieval Cornwall', in Helen Fulton

(ed.), *Medieval Celtic Literature and Society* (Dublin, 2005), p. 98 for possible links between Glasney and the Cornish medieval texts. Padel points out that Doble in 1929 (*Four Saints of the Fal*, pp. 17–18) and 1935 (*St Meriadoc*, pp. 6, 30) had already given reasons for connecting *Beunans Meriasek* with the College in some way, and had postulated a 'missing link' which may have turned up in *Bewnans Ke*.

223. I am most grateful to Angela Doughty at the Exeter Cathedral Archives for drawing my attention to these. Photographs in the possession of the Archives (ED 53) clearly show Grandisson's arms.

224. Cf. E. A. Lewis, *Welsh Port Books, 1550–1603*, Cymmrodorion Record Series XII (London, 1927).

225. The uncanny similarity between the recycled remains of a cope found in the South Hams and the sumptuous pre-Reformation vestments at Abergavenny may bear testimony to lines of communication now forgotten, although the Welsh vestments have clearer royal and episcopal connections. Cf. Devon & Cornwall Notes and Queries, vol. 18 (1933), no. 26, p. 50: 'Old Church needlework at Malborough, near Kingsbridge' and Peter Lord (with John Morgan-Guy), *The Visual Culture of Wales: Medieval Vision* (Cardiff, 2003), pp. 200–1, 271. On the other hand, the similarities may simply be coincidental or the result of a pattern-book.

Appendix

TH 13r.6-9, right side of folio, showing secretary and italic hand A:

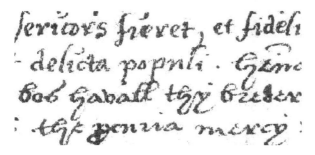

SA 63v.14-19, right side of folio, showing secretary and italic hand B:

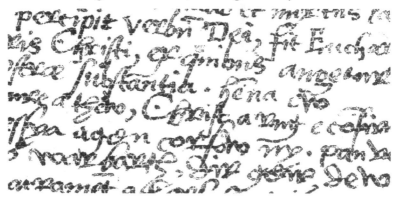

Upper left margin of TH 12v.4-12, showing name in hand C:

Upper left margin of TH 12v.4-12: word (in hand D?) conjecturally restored

Signature and date from Beunans Meriasek, folio 92r:

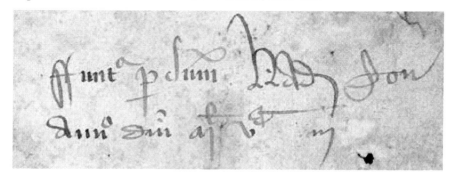

Signature and date from folio 92r, with suggested faint numerals drawn in:

3

'We don't travel much, only to South Africa'

Reconstructing Nineteenth-century Cornish Migration Patterns

Bernard Deacon

Introduction

Dudley Baines poses a key question about nineteenth-century migration: 'why did some places produce relatively more migrants than others which were outwardly similar?'[1] Yet pursuing an answer to this question is problematic in two ways. First, there is no agreed consensus on the scale to be adopted. In Britain most demographic data available to the historian of nineteenth-century migration is organized at regional, county or at registration district (RD) level. The average size of the latter units were around 20,000 people. Although this enables investigation at a sub-county level, meeting Baines' point that neither regional nor county scale is sufficiently sensitive to answer the relative migration question, it does not allow for easy testing of his further suggestion that the appropriate migration unit might be at the much smaller village or local community level. But the fluid process of immigration may need to be approached more flexibly. Charles Tilly has argued that the 'effective units of migration were (and are) neither individuals nor households but sets of people linked by acquaintance, kinship and work experience'.[2] Transferring attention in this way from spatial units to neighbourhood, family or occupational networks tends to emphasize one of the broad approaches put forward by migration historians to explain the propensity to migrate, the existence of information networks, the other being economic conditions.[3]

The existence of information networks linking kin and community groups is seen as playing a particularly important role in the international migration that gathered pace in the nineteenth century.[4] But widening migration fields after 1800 and the rise of mass overseas emigration from Europe also produce a second problem by creating a sub-division of migration history between studies of overseas emigration on the one hand and the explanation of internal migration (within the British Isles) on the other.[5] But what if the question faced by potential migrants in the nineteenth century was not so much 'where shall I/we move' but 'shall I/we move'? If this was the principal issue facing would-be migrants then a merely geographical division between emigration studies and studies of internal migration would seem untenable. We can go further; this epistemological divide may actually distort our understanding of the migration process in the nineteenth century by focusing attention on one or other types of destination to the exclusion of viewing migration as a holistic process common to the majority of individuals. In one of the few works that encompass both processes, Baines concludes that there was no transparent trade-off between emigration and internal migration in England and Wales, at least at the county level.[6] However, this conclusion does not preclude a trade-off at local or community levels. In order to test for this relationship he proposes that a 'fruitful area of research' might be the 'very detailed micro-analysis of areas where internal and overseas migration overlapped'.[7]

One such area is of course Cornwall. Cornish migration has attracted a voluminous literature, much of this a direct result of the pull of the 'great' emigration on perceptions of Cornwall's modern history. The enthusiastic and dramatic, even heroic, participation of thousands of Cornish people in the movement to the frontiers of the 'British world' in North America, Australasia and South Africa, and elsewhere to South America, has caught the imagination of late twentieth-century Cornish historians. This has led to a raft of studies on Cornish emigration. Over the past decade there has been a determined attempt to move beyond the earlier classics of Cornish emigration that focused on the description of discrete migration streams.[8] Philip Payton has synthesized this work and provided an overview of the process of emigration from Cornwall, connecting its disparate parts and linking it back to conditions in Cornwall itself. Other work by Payton highlights the role of the 'emigration trade' and the activity of emigration agents who stimulated and directed streams of migrants overseas.[9] In a robust critique of the state of Cornish migration studies Sharron Schwartz added to the emergent revisionism by emphasizing the dynamic nature of Cornish migration, making up a global circuit with multiple settings. She proposed that this is best understood by borrowing the concept of transnationalism from contemporary migration studies. At the same time, with Ronald Perry, she has re-assessed the feedback effect of migration on communities in Cornwall, revising an overly pessimistic picture of remittances and return migration.[10]

Yet revisionist writings on Cornish migration continue to exhibit three more traditional aspects. First, their focus remains resolutely fixed on overseas migration, with the considerable migration streams to the rest of the UK receiving much less attention.[11] Second, they focus on either a Cornwall-wide scale or the individual level rather than on intermediate levels. And finally, they prioritize the issue of the production and reproduction of the Cornish identity.[12] In contrast, in this article I wish to supplement this traditional paradigm in three ways. My first contention is that we need to break down the wall that divides overseas emigration from Cornish migration to other parts of Britain and within Cornwall itself if we are to evolve a generally applicable model of migration in nineteenth-century Cornwall. Second, I delve beyond a simple Cornwall-wide level in order to identify migration patterns at lower levels of analysis.[13] Finally, much has been written on Cornish emigration but the quantitative basis for this is, on inspection, extremely sketchy. Analysis of the processes of migration has tended to be based on surprising uncertainty about the precise patterns of that migration and conclusions are drawn on the basis of general historical knowledge rather than quantitative evidence. Therefore, I intend to focus here on measuring the patterns of Cornish migration, beginning the task of establishing surer empirical grounds for the discussion of migration processes.[14]

In the remainder of this contribution I start not with emigration but with the migration process in general, and not with models of contemporary migration but with a survey of actual historical migration. After setting the context by briefly reviewing patterns of western European migration in the nineteenth century, I use three different sources of nineteenth-century data to bring together what is known about movement from Cornwall, both overseas and to other parts of Britain. I provide some preliminary answers to two questions. First, how many migrated, of what age and from which parts of Cornwall? Second, where did they go? After establishing the patterns of Cornish migration I return in the final section of the article to the processes of Cornish migration, comparing them with other migrations and identifying why many migrants left some places in Cornwall while few migrants left other places.

A typology of migration[15]

Three types of migration were present in Europe around 1800. First, there were short-distance moves responding to local land, labour and marriage markets. This migration was closely related to the life cycle, including the migration of young people for service, and was directionless, sometimes described as circular. Second, we can discern a more purposefully directed migration stream from the countryside to towns. Peter Clark has divided this into betterment and subsistence migration.[16] The former, which could also be termed career migration, relied on kin support, was relatively short-distance (although movement to capital cities was an exception) and respectable. Grounded in social networks, it was an early example of chain migration. The other kind of movement to towns has been characterized as subsistence migration: nomadic, longer-distance, not reliant on kin and less respectable. Finally, there was another form of circular migration but this time temporary and involving the regular return of the migrant. This was seasonal migration of people from economically marginal regions in search of work. This labour migration had become a part of life for many, particularly in upland regions in western Europe and was usually highly selective by sex, having a major impact on gender relations, child rearing and the household economy.

In eighteenth-century Cornwall all these were occurring. Seasonal, or more properly temporary migration (as it might have involved several years), was especially associated with the mining industry as miners began to be sought out for mining developments elsewhere in Britain.[17] Labour migration of miners was joined in the new century by a further variant, international or overseas migration. For example, by the 1820s Cornish miners were being recruited on a three year contract to work at mines in Mexico.[18] Brettell notes how in the early modern period the most common migration was local and circular but that rural to urban migration grew in the later eighteenth and nineteenth centuries with the rise of industry and then longer-distance international migration became increasingly common in the mid and late nineteenth century. Emigration, she claims, was paradoxical in its effects. Broadly, it acted as a safety valve, allowing peasant owners of land to sustain their way of life and maintain standards of living as family members emigrated and sent remittances home. But this conservative aspect combined with changing the lives of those who left, especially those who never returned.[19] Work on Cornish emigration, often prefixed by the descriptor 'great', would suggest that the phenomenon of mass emigration occurred early and strongly in Cornwall.

When did they go?

From the aggregate population numbers in Cornwall we can fairly accurately pinpoint the beginnings of mass emigration. Before the 1830s, population grew at a mean 16 per cent a decade, exactly the same rate as that of England and Wales. During the 1830s the Cornish growth rate slowed but was still within one per cent of that of England and Wales. Then growth slowed abruptly in the 1841–51 period to just 3.9 per cent, compared with 12.7 per cent in England and Wales. Massive net out-migration had set in during the 1840s, probably in response to the economically depressed years and bad harvests of 1846–48. Once begun, out-migration proceeded at a vigorous rate.

We know this from Baines' county level analysis of migration within and beyond the boundaries of England and Wales.[20] Cornish migration historians have made much of this. Yet they have also misread Baines' work in a number of particulars. The most important error has been to confuse his results for net emigration flows from the UK with net emigration from Cornwall. In fact, Baines' study gives him a global figure for the net migration of all Cornish-born, irrespective of place of residence. Thus it includes those Cornish-born who emigrated from Cumberland as well as from Cornwall. As a result, a table published in 1998 that has served as the basis for overall estimates of gross migration flows needs to be revised, using new estimates of native net migration flows direct from Cornwall (for the method see below) and combining these with Baines' results for migration of all Cornish-born. This is done in Table 1.[21]

Table 1.   Migration from Cornwall, 1851–1901
(percentage of mean native population)

	Net Cornish-born migration to counties in England and Wales		Net Cornish-born emigration direct from Cornwall		Net Cornish-born emigration from other places in England and Wales		Total net Cornish-born out-migration	
1851–61	18400	(4.8)	25100	(6.6)			43500	(11.4)
1861–71	26200	(6.7)	27800	(7.1)	10300	(2.6)	64300	(16.4)
1871–81	40800	(10.4)	32400	(8.3)	3300	(0.8)	76500	(19.6)
1881–91	18100	(4.7)	18900	(4.9)	11100	(2.9)	48100	(12.5)
1891–1901	24000	(6.3)	13000	(3.4)	1800	(0.5)	38800	(10.2)
Total	127500		115200		28500		271200	

Source: Deacon, 2007; Baines, 1985, 289; 1851–61 calculated from published Census (BPP 1852–53 [1631] LXXXV; 1863 [3221] LIII) and *Registrar General's Annual Reports*, BPP 1852–62.

The effect of this revision is to reduce the decadal flow of net emigration direct from Cornwall (and incidentally re-emphasize the importance of net flows to England and Wales). Nonetheless, Baines' point that Cornwall was unique in that more people eventually went overseas than went to England and Wales stands. In fact, Cornish men had a higher relative propensity to emigrate than any group at county level in England or Wales.[22] Overall, migration out of Cornwall gathered pace from the 1840s to peak in the 1870s and then fell back in the final two decades of the century. Net overseas emigration ran strongly from the 1840s to peak in the 1860s and 70s, but fell away rapidly in the 1890s. (Although the fall in the 1890s may mask an increase in returns.) Migration to English and Welsh counties was more volatile. Only in the crisis decade of the 1870s, when plummeting copper and lead prices and seriously depressed tin prices led to a widespread contraction of the mining industry, and in the final decade of the nineteenth century, did migration across the Tamar exceed that of Cornish-born overseas. But many migrants to England and Wales in the 1870s later moved overseas from other places in Britain. This reinforces the point that in some decades overseas emigration and internal migration were clearly interrelated.

Who went?

How far did net migration rates vary by age and sex? Andrew Hinde has proposed a method of calculating net native and non-native migration for small areas by age, deriving survival probabilities from age-specific death rates.[23] To make use of this, we need to know the number of births by sex and deaths by age in any particular decade as well as the age structure of natives and non-natives at the beginning and end of each decade. Fertility and mortality data were published for Registration Districts for the 1850s, 1860s and 1880s in the decennial supplements to the *Annual Reports* of the Registrar General of Births, Deaths and Marriages while the gap in the 1870s can be filled from the *Annual Reports* themselves. Meanwhile the age structure is available in the published census reports although not broken down between natives and non-natives.[24] However, the proportions of natives and non-natives in the population at each census date can be derived from the census enumerators' books (CEBs). Because of the time involved in extracting the CEB data Hinde restricted his method to individual parishes, assuming the death rate of the RD of which they were a part applied to them. This is of course only an acceptable method if the parish is representative of the RD and is best reserved for occupationally homogenous RDs. However, in the Cornish case, we can derive the age structure of natives and non-natives by RD relatively easily by making use of the computerised databases of the

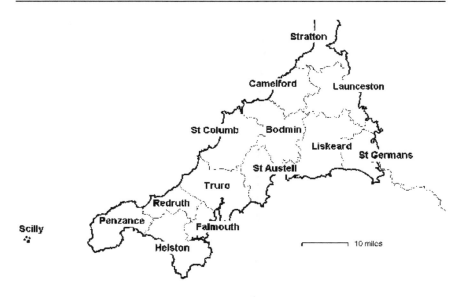

Map 1.   Cornish Registration Districts

nineteenth century censuses supplied by the Cornwall Family History Society (CFHS).[25]

A second and more subtle qualification of Cornish migration historians' readings of Baines' work can be made in relation to his discussion of the age structure of emigration flows. Payton and Schwartz both report Baines' conclusion that 'Cornwall lost [overseas] (net of returns) 44.7 per cent of the male population at risk (15–24) but only 29.7 per cent to other English and Welsh counties, 26.2 per cent of the female population at risk went overseas compared with 35.4 per cent who moved internally'.[26] But their statements could give rise to the potential misunderstanding that in every decade between 1861 and 1900 in Cornwall 45 per cent of men and 26 per cent of women aged 15–24 emigrated. This is not the case. Baines' calculation was obtained by dividing the total number of natives aged 15–24 in the whole period 1861–1900 by the estimated number of emigrants (net of returns).[27] This tells us that total emigration of Cornish born in the later nineteenth century was *equivalent to* 44.7 per cent of the male population aged 15–24 over the whole period from 1861 to 1900. This is not the same as saying that 44.7 per cent of all men aged 15–24 emigrated in any one decade. That would only be so if all emigrants had been aged 15–24. Although this was indeed the age group that was most likely to migrate, the calculations of age-specific net native migration from Cornwall in this period would suggest that they accounted for at most 60 per cent of all migration net of returns. Therefore, it would be more accurate to say that an average 26–27 per cent of those men aged 15–24 in any one decade may have emigrated, net of returns, still a very large proportion. That for women was lower, at round 10 per cent.[28]

How do these estimates of the more global net migration of natives compare with evidence for the age and sex composition of net native migration flows out of Cornwall's thirteen mainland RDs?[29] The quantitative evidence reinforces the impression that migrants were overwhelmingly young. In all RDs and in all decades the 15–24 age group dominated net native male out-migration. In the 1870s in the mining districts of Redruth, Truro and Liskeard net out-migration of this age group was over 50 per cent of those present in 1871, indicating that well over half of young men left those districts in that decade. Together, the 15–24 and 25–34 age groups supplied over two thirds of male net out-migration, reinforcing the view that most migrants were young adults. The exception was the 1870s when young men aged 15–34 accounted for only 60 per cent of male native migration net of returns, evidence for a greater level of migration by families in this crisis decade. The pattern of female migration was however significantly different. The total net native migration rate for women was consistently lower than for men, at almost two thirds of the male level, although the two rates converged during the 1870s. Furthermore, women in the 15–24 age group accounted for a lower proportion of net female out-migration and young women aged from 15–34 made up only 56–57 per cent of female native net migration. However, the distribution of female migration by age shows the same changes as that of men in the 1870s, implying the structural conditions of that decade affected both sexes in the same manner.

While there was little difference in male native net migration rates by age group across Cornwall, the female pattern betrayed an interesting difference between east and west Cornwall. In the 1850s east of Truro RD the highest female net native out-migration occurred in the 15–24 age group, as for men. But in west Cornwall net native out-migration was significantly lower in this age group, with net migration actually peaking in the older 24–35 age band. This may be evidence for the greater job opportunities for young women as surface workers in mining and the presence of the larger towns of Penzance, Camborne, Redruth, Falmouth and Truro which kept them within their RD. By the 1880s this difference in the female migration pattern was restricted to Penzance and Redruth RDs, suggesting it was related to the mining sector, possibly to overseas migration, as women followed men overseas, but with a lag of a few years.

From where did they go? Net out-migration from Cornwall

Birth data by sex and death data by age are unfortunately only available at RD level. This means that calculating the more sophisticated age specific net migration rates for natives and non-natives is only possible for relatively large units. However, an alternative and much simpler measure is that of overall net-migration. To understand this we need to appreciate that population change is caused by changes in three components: fertility, mortality and migration. This relationship can be seen in the basic demographic accounting equation, which can be stated as:

P1 + births P1 to P2 − deaths P1 to P2 + net migration P1 to P2 (in-migrants − out-migrants) = P2

where P1 is the population at a particular census date and P2 the population at the succeeding census.[30]

If we apply this equation to Cornwall, we obtain the following figures for net migration out of Cornwall as a whole.

Table 2.   Net migration, Cornwall, 1841–91

	Net migration	% of mean population
1841–51	−31650	−9.1
1851–61	−35466	−9.8
1861–71	−53827	−14.7
1871–81	−65560	−18.9
1881–91	−39140	−12.0

Sources: Population Census (BPP 1841 Session 2 [52] II; 1852–53 [1631] LXXXV; 1863 [3221] LIII; 1872 [C.676] LXVI; 1883 [C.3563] LXXIX; 1893–94 [C.6948–1] CV); Registrar General's supplement to twenty-fifth annual report, BPP 1865 XIII, 216–25; Registrar General's thirty-fifth annual report: supplement, BPP 1875 XVIII, 220–9; Registrar General's supplement to fifty-fifth annual report, Part 1, BPP 1895 XXIII, 386–99; Registrar General's Annual Reports, BPP, 1841–62 and 1873–82.

This simpler net migration measure consistently repeats the pattern seen in Table 1. This suggests that we can make use of the net migration statistic to uncover the relative picture at lower levels of analysis. The net migration rates for the Cornish RDs in each decade from 1851 to 1891 were as shown in Table 3.

Table 3.   Net migration: Registration Districts, 1851–91
(% of mean population)

	1851–61	1861–71	1871–81	1881–91
Stratton	–16.3	–15.7	–18.4	–15.3
Camelford	–23.6	–7.8	–23.4	–18.1
Launceston	–21.2	–13.4	–19.6	–13.0
St Germans	–4.4	–9.3	–17.0	–1.0
Liskeard	–1.2	–15.1	–29.7	–18.8
Bodmin	–15.7	–9.7	–12.4	–12.8
St Columb	–18.6	–13.0	–15.6	–16.4
St Austell	–9.9	–19.1	–18.8	–9.2
Truro	–10.0	–13.8	–22.0	–14.2
Falmouth	–3.0	–1.9	–6.6	–11.6
Helston	–7.2	–19.6	–26.1	–15.3
Redruth	–6.7	–19.4	–24.3	–4.2
Penzance	–11.0	–13.6	–17.1	–14.7

Source: As for Table 2.

While every Cornish RD lost people through migration in every decade there was considerable variation, both across the RDs in any single decade and to an even greater extent in individual RDs over time.[31] In the former case the greatest variation occurred in the 1850s. In that decade out-migration was highest in the rural and farming districts of east and mid Cornwall but low in Liskeard RD, where the mines near Liskeard and Callington were expanding rapidly, and in the maritime districts of St Germans and Falmouth. Net out-migration peaked generally in the 1870s, with the highest rates in that decade being experienced in the districts of Camelford, Liskeard, Truro, Helston and Redruth, districts where rural mining and quarrying industries were seriously hit by economic depression. These also tended to be the districts that experienced the greatest variation over time. Meanwhile the lowest variations were seen in Stratton, with a net out-migration rate that was consistently high, in Bodmin and St Columb RDs in mid-Cornwall and, perhaps more surprisingly, as it was a RD with a high proportion of its people engaged in the more volatile mining activities, in Penzance.

Hinde states that for small groups of parishes or for individual parishes 'civil registration data or decadal rates of births and deaths are not normally available'.[32] While the decennial supplements to the *Annual Reports* of the Registrar General do not include registration sub-districts (SDs) (which were comprised of parishes or groups of parishes) these statistics can be found – although less conveniently for the researcher – in the individual *Annual Reports* from the 1850s to the 1880s. These annual birth and death data were extracted for the 54 Cornish mainland SDs and their net migration rates calculated.[33] At this level there was an even greater variation across districts, with the largest differences occurring in the 1870s. Again, those SDs with the highest differences over time usually had occupational structures dominated by mining, such as Callington, Liskeard, Fowey (including the mining parishes of Tywardreath and St Blazey), St Agnes, Kea, Wendron, Breage, Crowan, Gwennap, Redruth, Phillack, Marazion and St Just-in-Penwith. Indeed, the very high overall net migration experienced in the 1870s in Breage and St Just in Penwith SDs, at around 44 per cent of the mean population, implies that gross out-migration of young men must have been well over 60 per cent in that decade, a major migration flow by any standards. Large differences over time were also seen in the urban districts of Launceston and Antony in east Cornwall, although the latter is the result of movements of military personnel in and out of barracks and of movements of naval vessels. The geographical pattern of out-migration at the SD level can be illustrated by two maps of the net migration rates in the 1850s and 1870s.

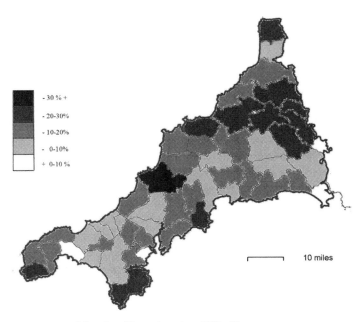

- 30 % +

- 20-30%

- 10-20%

- 0-10%

+ 0-10 %

10 miles

Map 2.   Net migration 1851–60

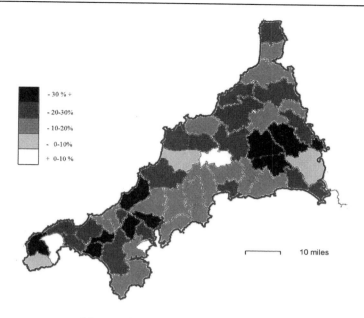

Map 3.   Net migration 1871–80

Comparing these maps clearly demonstrates how the districts with the highest out-migration were mainly found in east Cornwall in the 1850s – with a noticeable arc of districts with high out-migration north and east of Bodmin Moor – but in rural mining districts in west Cornwall and to the south of Bodmin Moor in the 1870s.

Where did they go?

What were the destinations of migrants in the second half of the nineteenth century? And how far did this vary across Cornwall? We might begin to answer these questions by reviewing some preliminary analysis of the database of emigrants amassed by the Cornish Global Migration Programme (CGMP), based at Murdoch House, Redruth. This database contains records of over 36,000 Cornish emigrants. However, many of these lack critical data about parish of origin or are imprecise about the date of migration. Nevertheless, there are such details for almost 3,000 women and over 6,000 men who emigrated to the United States, the most popular destination for Cornish emigrants, from the 1830s to the 1900s.[34]

As Map 4 shows, in the 1830s and 1840s two distinct districts within Cornwall supplied higher than average gross outflows to America, more than

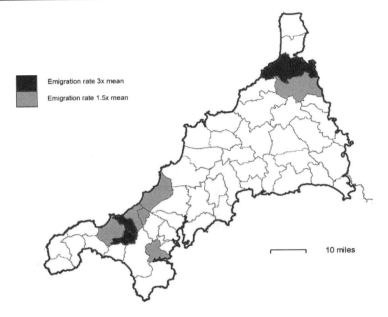

Map 4.   Emigration to USA, 1831–50

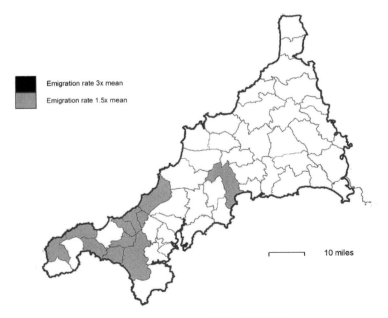

Map 5.   Emigration to USA, 1891–1910

half of these emigrants going to Wisconsin. One was the farming district comprising Whitstone and North Petherwin in north Cornwall while the other was the mining area centred on Camborne and Crowan in the west. By the end of the century the rate of emigration from the north of Cornwall had fallen away and those districts with more than the average number of migrants leaving for the States (by this time around half were homing in on the state of Michigan) were clearly correlated with depopulating mining districts. But was there a more general relationship at SD level between the overall net migration rate and emigration? The correlation coefficient between net out-migration and overseas emigration to North America at the SD level is shown in Table 4.

Table 4.   Pearsons product moment correlation coefficient:
net out-migration and emigration to North America at SD level

1851–61	+0.190
1861–71	+0.520
1871–81	+0.533
1881–91	+0.108

Source: *Registrar-General's Annual Reports*, 1852–92; published *Census Reports*, 1851–1891 and CGMP database.

There is indeed a weak correlation at the beginning and end of the period studied here but it is not significant at the 99 per cent confidence level. However, the relationship in the 1860s and 1870s is significant at that level, indicating that in those decades those SDs that lost most people through migration were also the districts from which people were more likely to leave for the USA. This might seem to suggest that the process of emigration, at least in the 1860s and 1870s, was produced by the same factors causing general out-migration, whether overseas or internally within the UK. Conversely, it implies that emigration and internal migration were conceptually more differentiated and perhaps complementary processes in the 1850s and 1880s.

   In the final exercise discussed here the aggregate demographic data provided by the Census and the Registrar General's statistics, which produce native net migration for Cornwall and RD levels and net migration rates for SD level, and the Cornish Global Migration Programme's database, which allows us to establish the migration streams across the Atlantic at SD level, are supplemented by a third source, the census enumerators' books.

   The use of CEB data has been confined in the past in local population studies in Britain to the study of in-migration, largely because of the time it would take to trace out-migrants.[35] However, the availability of computerised databases of the census books now allows for more rapid searches. Two possibilities open up. First, individuals can be traced across censuses even if they had moved from one end of the country to the other.[36] This is, however, still a lengthy process that demands a considerable input of time and an amount of lateral thinking in coping with the normal variation and drift in the details of name spellings, ages, and place of birth that any family historian soon realises were common practices amongst their forebears. The second potential method is to use the CEB databases to search for aggregate numbers of people rather than specific individuals. This second method was used here. The objective of the research was to seek the location in 1891 of anyone born in Cornwall in the decade from 1851 to 1860. By 1891 this age cohort would have been aged 31–40. As we have already seen, the majority of net migration took place in the 15–34 age groups. Work collated by Mills indicates that the native born proportion of nineteenth century communities stabilised after age 34, suggesting that individuals were less likely to move after their mid-30s. Moreover, James Jackson, making use of much fuller migration data for Duisburg in Germany, also concludes that the typical male migrant in the 1800s may have moved as many as 15 times, the majority of these moves taking place when aged under 30.[37] Therefore, identifying the geographical location of the 31–40-year-old age cohort in 1891 would hopefully capture the moves they had made in their 20s and early 30s, the ages when migration was most likely.

The age-specific death rates calculated for the RD level and the survival probabilities deduced from these were applied to the birth cohort. This provides a rough estimate of the number of those born in the 1850s that might be expected to have survived to 1891. Of course, as soon as someone migrated then they would have been subject to a different set of structural variables producing a different death rate. For the purposes of this exercise however, it had to be assumed that those who travelled to healthier districts were balanced out by those who travelled to less healthy districts. By finding all survivors resident in England and Wales in 1891 then, logically, the residual number (i.e. the number of expected survivors minus those actually identified in the census) will include all overseas emigrants. This residual might therefore provide a surrogate for the numbers emigrating overseas.

With this in mind, two databases were systematically searched for those born in Cornish parishes. First, the Cornwall Family History Society census database for 1891 was searched for those in this age cohort still resident in Cornwall. Second, the online database provided by ancestry.co.uk was searched by parish of birth. While the logic of this method is straightforward its efficacy is clearly dependent on the robustness of the data. There are three potential problems in this respect. First, some people in the nineteenth century forgot or otherwise changed their place of birth details from one census to another. From other work tracing individuals across censuses it has become clear that there was a noticeable tendency for migrants to change their place of birth, either to the place they had moved, especially if they had married a native of that place and had lived there for a few decades, or from a village in Cornwall to a nearby town, for example from Mabe to nearby Falmouth. The former problem was minimized by the fact that most in this age cohort in 1891 had only relatively recently moved. However, the latter problem will affect the data. This practice seemed most common for those who moved long distances and to cities. The result of this is to exaggerate the apparent number of long-distance migrants born in Cornish towns and diminish the number born in rural parishes. With this in mind, the method is therefore best reserved for at least SD scale where districts will often, although not always, combine a market town with some of its surrounding parishes. Its effect is minimized even further by restricting analysis to the RD scale and that is the scale focused on here.

The second and more insurmountable problem is presented by transcription error. Not only did nineteenth century enumerators (and heads of households) make mistakes in spelling placenames but this has been exacerbated by the process of digitising the CEBs. This latter does not seem to be a serious problem for the CFHS database where 'native' knowledge has been used to correct misspelt places of birth. But it is a major issue for the ancestry database. Misreadings of the original census page are common, for example Camborne appears frequently as Lamborne and the letters <a> and <o> are commonly transposed. Furthermore, what presumably involved a computerized scan as part of the process has resulted in many people whose place of birth was entered as 'Cornwall' followed by a parish appearing in the ancestry database as born in 'Cork'. A sample of Cornish places of birth revealed that about 25 per cent are misspelt in the ancestry database. However, many of these misspellings occur at the end of words and thus can be surmounted by computer wildcard searches and resort to the original page of the enumerators' book. In addition, local knowledge of placenames and dialect reduced indecipherable placenames to a much more manageable proportion of just over two per cent.

The third problem is that an unknown number of persons gave a place within a parish as their place of birth rather than a parish. Therefore, searching for parishes alone misses these people. In consequence all the sub-parochial entries that appeared under the place of birth column in the CFHS database were listed and these searched for separately in the ancestry database. Furthermore, to minimise the problem of misspellings each parish name was searched using spelling variants and a liberal use of wild cards. While these methods hopefully reduced those not found, the precise proportion in our age cohort who were actually present in the 1891 census but remain undiscovered remains unknown. A further group of people gave no parish of birth at all in the 1891 census but the entry would read just 'Cornwall' or variants of 'Cornwall, not known'. The numbers of these amounted to 8.9 per cent of the total Cornish born males and 9.2 per cent of the females. If the parish of birth of these people were known it would therefore reduce the residual by up to ten per cent.

With all these caveats in mind what does the exercise reveal? Where was the Cornish age cohort born in the 1850s living in 1891?

If we look first at the differences in the residual (the difference between the expected number of survivors and the actual numbers of the cohort located in 1891) for men we find that four of the RDs had a distinctly higher residual – Camelford, Liskeard, St Austell and Redruth (see Table 5). This implies that a larger proportion of men had emigrated from these districts than from the others. Conversely, these four districts spread across Cornwall also had the smallest proportions of their male cohorts still present in Cornwall. Three of these districts (the exception being Camelford) were also among those with the largest percentage of natives living in 1891 in the north of England. However, there were distinct differences in the actual places in which they were found. Men from Liskeard RD were more likely to have moved to Durham whereas natives of Redruth RD were most concentrated in Lancashire. And there two destinations dominated. The first was Burnley, whose attraction is well known from the qualitative literature; in the 1860s families from Camborne and Redruth were reported as being recruited for the cotton mills of Lancashire, while Cornish miners were being brought into Burnley as strike breakers in 1873.[38] This migration stream to Burnley was a well-established one and still strong twenty years later. The second destination – Rochdale – has not received such prominence hitherto. Presumably for similar reasons as Burnley, the possibility of employment for men in coal mining and women in the textile factories, people from Redruth were moving in considerable numbers to Rochdale during the 1870s and 1880s. In contrast, movement to the north of England from St Austell RD was more dispersed across Lancashire, Cumberland, Yorkshire and Durham.

The problems of Cornish mining in the 1870s and 1880s clearly explain this pattern, with those RDs with higher numbers of migrants to the north of England also being the districts with a larger proportion engaged in mining. The opposite is also the case. Men from districts with an insignificant or non-existent mining sector were more likely to end up in the south of England. St Germans, Bodmin and Falmouth – agricultural or maritime districts – supplied the highest proportions of migrants to the south of England. These were also the RDs with the lowest male residuals, implying lower overseas emigration rates. To an extent, therefore, the density of migration

Table 5.   Location of 1850s Cornish birth cohort by RD in 1891

	Number of expected survivors	Cornwall (% of survivors)	Devon (% of survivors)	Other southern England (% of survivors)	Northern England (% of survivors)	Wales (% of survivors)	Percentage of survivors not found
Men							
Stratton	740	43.4	17.0	6.6	1.3	2.6	27.6
Camelford	863	38.1	4.1	5.8	1.9	0.6	48.8
Launceston	1581	41.2	10.9	9.6	4.4	0.9	32.6
St Germans	1526	38.7	15.7	11.1	3.1	1.0	23.8
Liskeard	4088	30.4	7.5	6.6	8.3	0.8	44.9
Bodmin	1830	48.1	7.0	11.9	2.9	2.0	25.7
St Columb	1634	49.6	4.5	10.7	2.1	1.4	29.9
St Austell	3255	38.2	4.1	6.0	4.1	1.2	43.7
Truro	3457	41.2	4.2	10.3	4.4	2.1	36.4
Falmouth	1577	44.1	6.0	16.2	6.2	2.7	21.8
Helston	2506	50.5	2.0	4.9	3.2	1.3	37.6
Redruth	1669	39.5	2.0	5.5	5.9	2.2	44.4
Penzance	2080	48.5	2.0	7.0	5.0	2.5	33.5
Women							
Stratton	798	46.0	17.7	10.1	1.1	1.3	23.8
Camelford	730	52.7	10.7	9.1	3.2	0.5	23.6
Launceston	1640	41.8	15.6	11.4	2.9	1.3	27.1
St Germans	1575	40.0	20.7	12.6	3.6	0.5	22.5
Liskeard	4211	40.6	13.7	8.3	7.5	0.9	29.0
Bodmin	1745	57.3	11.5	15.4	3.8	1.4	10.5
St Columb	1641	60.9	6.2	13.5	1.8	0.7	16.9
St Austell	3172	52.6	7.9	12.0	5.0	1.2	21.2
Truro	3462	62.6	6.2	14.1	5.1	2.2	9.6
Falmouth	1655	57.4	7.8	18.9	6.3	2.2	7.5
Helston	2594	68.5	3.7	7.9	3.1	0.9	16.0
Redruth	4384	61.4	4.5	8.8	7.5	2.1	15.8
Penzance	4181	67.0	3.9	11.9	6.1	2.4	8.7

Source: Census enumerators' books, 1891: The National Archives RG12 (accessed via Cornwall Family History Society transcription and www.ancestry.co.uk)

flows to the north of England at this period may act as a surrogate for the relative frequency of overseas emigration at RD and SD level. Yet men from Falmouth RD were also amongst the most likely to move to the north of England. Here again the overall pattern of regional destinations hides a distinct migration stream as Falmouth men were more likely to move to Liverpool, the third focus for Cornish migrants in Lancashire, alongside Burnley and Rochdale.

There is more than a hint that cities such as Liverpool attracted proportionally greater numbers of migrants from urban places within Cornwall. The biggest city in Victorian Britain by far was London, and Falmouth was one of the RDs with the highest number of men found in London in 1891, the others being Bodmin and Truro. The other RD supplying a relatively high number of migrants to London – St Germans – was less urban, but its proximity to Plymouth and convenient rail links to the metropolis by the 1880s may have increased movement to the capital. At SD level all those districts from which more than ten per cent of the identified cohort were found living in London were urban – Launceston, Truro, Falmouth and Helston for men and Launceston, Truro, Falmouth and Bodmin for women.

For women generally, the untraced residual was much lower (only in some agricultural districts in east Cornwall was this figure close to that of men). This reinforces the conclusions drawn from native net migration data that women were about half as likely to emigrate as were men. Those RDs with a large difference between male and female residuals (Camelford, Truro, Redruth and Penzance) may also have been the districts with larger sex-specific migration flows overseas. Yet the residual figures for women present an unexpected pattern. This time there is no relationship between a high residual and the presence of mining. Instead, the residual was generally significantly higher in east than in west Cornwall.[39] Why over 20 per cent of the women were untraced in this age cohort in 1891 in east Cornwall and yet fewer than ten per cent in the west is difficult to explain. It is unlikely this is a result of higher rates of overseas emigration from east Cornwall, unless the pattern of origin of emigrants from Cornwall varied dramatically between the sexes, something that the CGMP database does not suggest. Such a variation would also be at odds with the general pattern of movement to England, which for women was similar to that for men; women from Falmouth, Bodmin and Truro RDs were more likely to move to southern England and women from Redruth, Liskeard and Falmouth to the north, Perhaps it suggests that greater numbers of women born in east Cornwall changed their place of birth or were otherwise unidentifiable from the census records in 1891.

From patterns to processes

What has the quantitative evidence told us? Calculations of both net native migration and the less sophisticated net migration rates reveal an out-migration at its height in the period from 1861 to 1891. The economically depressed 1870s stand out not only as the decade with highest net out-migration but for other reasons. This was the only decade before the 1890s when net migration to counties in England and Wales exceeded the net native overseas migration of Cornish-born people and it was during this decade that the usual preponderance of young people in the migration stream was weakest …

Within Cornwall, net out-migration was highest in the 1850s from the more marginal agricultural sub-districts as well as districts with specific economic problems, such as Newlyn East SD, where output from one of Cornwall's most productive lead mines in the 1830s and 1840s – East Wheal Rose – fell by three quarters during the decade.[40] Unpredictable variations in the productivity of mining help to explain some of those SDs that were experiencing net in-migration or very low out-migration at mid-century, such as Marazion, Breage and Camborne in the west or Callington and Liskeard in the newer mining districts of the east. By the 1870s and 1880s the generalized difficulties of mining meant that many of these same districts were by now seeing the largest losses from net out-migration, whereas net migration from agricultural sub-districts such as Kilkhampton or Altarnun in north Cornwall remained more consistent.

Table 6.   Pearsons product moment correlation coefficient: net migration and occupational structure, Cornish SDs, 1851–91

	% of men employed in mining and net migration	% of men employed in agriculture and net migration
1851–91	+0.255	+0.233
1851–61	−0.344	+0.552
1861–71	+0.431	−0.030
1871–81	+0.590	−0.128
1881–91	−0.089	+0.434

Source: As for Table 2 and Census enumerators' books, 1891: The National Archives RG12 (accessed via Cornwall Family History Society transcription).

This can be stated with more certainty by measuring the correlation between the occupational structure and the net out-migration rates at SD level as in Table 6. Over the whole of the period 1851–91 there was a positive correlation of out-migration with both mining and agricultural sectors. This means that those SDs with higher numbers either of miners or of farmers/agricultural labourers in their occupational structures were both likely to experience higher net out-migration. However, when this broad correlation is broken down into decades, it can be seen that it disguizes a more complex picture.

Two patterns co-exist. At mid-century those SDs dominated by mining were actually less likely to lose people through net out-migration than were SDs with relatively few miners. In contrast, there was a strong and more significant correlation between SDs dominated by farming and net out-migration. This is evidence not for the absence of out-migration from mining districts in the 1850s but for the strength of natural population growth in those districts, which offset the levels of gross migration, and the strong net out-migration flows from agricultural districts in this decade. However, in the 1860s and 70s this correlation reversed and a strong relationship appears between the mining industry and net out-migration, while that between farming and net out-migration disappears. In the 1880s the relationship between mining and out-migration is not so clear. (The weak positive correlation is not a significant one.) Yet the positive relationship between farming SDs and net out-migration re-appears and is almost as strong as at mid-century.

To some extent the pattern of overseas emigration, at least to North America, reflected these changes. In the 1830s and 1840s some of the marginal agricultural districts of north Cornwall were, relatively, amongst the most important exporters of people to North America, along with mining districts in the west, which had well-established networks reaching across the Atlantic. However, by the final decades of the century those districts with the highest relative number of emigrants to North America were all rural mining districts and the migration chains linking parts of north Cornwall to North America had snapped. It appears that emigration flows became more structured over the century as a result of the vicissitudes of the mining industry. In this sense the criticism that Cornwall's emigration history has been too 'minocentric' might be overplayed.[41] On the contrary, the geography of the declining Cornish mining industry became a more important variable explaining the pattern of overseas migration as the nineteenth century proceeded (although not internal migration after the 1870s). Of course, the emigration flows from those districts could well have included large numbers, even a majority, of non-miners.

Finally, the destination of men in the age cohort born in the 1850s (and aged in their 20s and 30s in the 1880s) also displays a pattern clearly linked to the occupational structures of Cornish RDs. Migration streams to the north of England were predominantly from mining districts; those to the south were more likely to be from non-mining districts. The proportion of the age cohort that was not found in the 1891 census enumeration books implies high rates of overseas migration, at least for men. For women, while the regional pattern within England parallels that of the men the higher residual number is not easily explained. It suggests the need to refine this method further and test it on other age cohorts and other censuses.[42]

Work on tracing individuals longitudinally across censuses may also shed light on the numerical differences between men and women. Indeed, research based on life histories is required to complement the aggregate approach adopted here. It is significant that this aggregate, quantitative investigation has resulted in a stress on economic conditions and the occupational structure as a prime explanatory variable in migration from Cornwall at a district level. This echoes the conclusions of those who have employed similar data to study migration at RD, county or national levels.[43] But it may overestimate the more easily measurable economic factors and underestimate the less quantifiable information flows that structured migration and help to explain why districts with similar economic structures had different rates of migration. For example, Kilkhampton and Whitstone SDs in north Cornwall had very similar proportions of men employed in farming. But the flow of emigrants from Whitstone to the USA in the 1850s was considerable while that from Kilkhampton was negligible, despite a higher total net out-migration from the latter district.

Local variations in migration such as these can only be explained by life history research, both qualitatively and quantitatively, through making interconnections between movement and particular life events. The preliminary results of research on individuals' movement from contrasting communities in mid-Cornwall bears out Baines' conclusion that the most appropriate emigration unit may be the locality or community rather than the county or the intermediate levels such as the registration districts and sub-districts analysed here. However, this research also strongly hints that the migration unit may more usefully be viewed as family and neighbourhood networks rather than locality or parish.[44]

Conclusions

This survey of some of the quantitative evidence available to us confirms the broad parameters of the migration patterns on which we might reconstruct the processes of the Cornish migration system of the mid to late nineteenth century. At mid-century that system involved three types of migration familiar from the general pattern of migration in Europe. First, the circulating, short-distance moves common to all regions occurred in Cornwall. These were triggered by local occupational opportunities, marriage and changing household income and expenditure. Second, such moves co-existed with rural to small town and small town to city movement up the settlement hierarchy. These involved a balance of career moves, either individually or in family groups, responding to the greater market opportunities of larger settlements, and more desperate tramping in search of work. Finally, long-distance migration occurred, including to destinations overseas. This depended on levels of savings amassed in periods of relatively high earnings, plus the activities of emigration agents and the existence of assistance schemes that both diverted existing migration streams and created new ones. Long distance migration was sex-specific, involving more men than women, although a considerable though at present unknown proportion took place within family groups.

This system was disrupted in the later 1860s and the 1870s by the economic crisis induced by the sudden contraction of mining. The problems of mining injected additional push factors into the migration system, leading to a temporary surge in the movement of those in middle age and of family groups. Much of this was long-distance movement but it was more likely to be directed towards other more buoyant UK industrial regions rather than overseas because of the lack of financial reserves. Some of the extra push migration of the 1860s and 1870s was directed to large towns and cities but this was restricted by the preference on the part of miners for geographical over occupational mobility.[45] Those who might in earlier times have emigrated often used the industrial regions of Britain as stepping-stones to mining frontiers overseas once sufficient funds were amassed.

By the 1890s the importance of overseas migration was waning, partly because of the reduction in the demographic base remaining in those mining communities that had disproportionately fed this movement but also because of the greater attraction of internal migration. There is also a strong suggestion that net migration overseas fell back considerably in this decade partly as a result of a change in the composition of overseas migration flows. This was now more likely to be dominated by young single men as family migration fell away. Short stays overseas and higher rates of return migration became more common, related to the rise of the South African gold mining districts as a destination option.[46] International, transcontinental migration had by the end of the century come to resemble more closely the earlier common European pattern of seasonal labour migration, with a high rate of return and more sex-specific flows. It also fulfilled a similar function as did emigration for peasant communities in Europe, enabling families to maintain their cottages and smallholdings at home and sustaining this way of life up to the end of the century.[47]

This was a system within which people decided to migrate or stay, that decision being taken in response not just to rational (or irrational) assumptions about prospective earnings elsewhere and current prospects at home but to cultural sub-systems such as chapel and community attitudes towards migration, to state policies and to marketing activities both in Britain and elsewhere.[48] But the final decision whether to go or to stay and where to go was often structured by existing family and kin networks and to the information supplied by return migrants and letters from overseas as well as the resources provided by remittances. It was a system which was fluid and changing, where economic changes encouraged new and expanded old migration streams but where pre-existing migration chains and established networks led to recognizable continuity in the pattern of movement across generations.

Notes and references

1. Dudley Baines, 'European Emigration, 1851–1930: Looking at the Emigration Decision Again', *Economic History Review* 47.3 (1994), p. 540.
2. Charles Tilly, 'Transplanted Networks', in Virginia Yans-McLaughlin (ed.), *Immigration Reconsidered: History, Sociology and Politics* (Oxford, 1990), p. 84.
3. Baines, 'European Emigration, 1851–1930'.
4. Caroline Brettell, 'Migration', in David Kertzer and Marzio Barbagli (eds), *Family Life in the Long Nineteenth Century, 1789–1913* (Yale, 2002), p. 244.
5. For the former see Eric Richards, *Britannia's Children: Emigration from England, Scotland, Wales and Ireland since 1600* (London, 2004); Carl Bridge and Kent Fedorowich (eds), *The British World: Diaspora, Culture and Identity* (London, 2003). For the latter see Colin Pooley and Jean Turnbull, *Migration and Mobility in Britain since the Eighteenth Century* (London, 1998); Dennis Mills and Kevin Schürer (eds), *Local Communities in the Victorian Census Enumerators' Books* (Oxford, 1996).
6. Dudley Baines, *Migration in a Mature Economy: Emigration and Internal Migration in England and Wales, 1861–1900* (Cambridge, 1985), pp. 213–49.
7. Baines, 'European Emigration, 1851–1930', p. 540.
8. Among the classic works on Cornish emigration are A. L. Rowse, *The Cornish in America* (London, 1969); John Rowe, *The Hard Rock Men: Cornish Immigrants and the North American Mining Frontier* (Liverpool, 1974); and Philip Payton, *The Cornish Miner in Australia: Cousin Jack Down Under* (Redruth, 1984).
9. Philip Payton, *The Cornish Overseas* (Fowey, 1999; second edition 2005) and '"Reforming Thirties" and "Hungry Forties": The Genesis of Cornwall's Emigration Trade', in Philip Payton (ed.), *Cornish Studies: Four* (Exeter, 1996), pp. 107–27.
10. Sharron Schwartz, 'Cornish Migration Studies: An Epistemological and Paradigmatic Critique', in Philip Payton (ed.), *Cornish Studies: Ten* (Exeter, 2002), pp. 136–65; Ronald Perry and Sharron Schwartz, 'James Hicks, Architect of Regeneration in Victorian Redruth', *Journal of the Royal Institution of Cornwall* (2001), pp. 64–77. For a solidly based quantitative assessment of the role of remittances see Gary Magee and

Andrew Thompson, "'Lines of Credit, Debts of Obligation': Migrant Remittances to Britain, *c.*1875–1913', *Economic History Review* 59.3 (2006), pp. 539–77, and 'The global and the Local: Explaining Migrant Remittance Flows in the English-speaking world, 1880–1914', *Journal of Economic History* 66.1 (2006), pp. 177–202.

11. For the latter see Bernard Deacon, 'A Forgotten Migration Stream: The Cornish Movement to England and Wales in the Nineteenth Century' in Philip Payton (ed.), *Cornish Studies: Six* (Exeter, 1998), pp. 96–117.

12. For the latest examples of this see Bernard Deacon and Sharron Schwartz, 'Cornish Identities and Migration: A Multi-scalar Approach', *Global Networks* 7.3 (2007), pp. 289ff.; Philip Payton, *Making Moonta: The Invention of 'Australia's Little Cornwall'* (Exeter, 2007).

13. This builds on my earlier call to move from analysing Cornwall to analysing 'Cornwalls'. See Bernard Deacon, 'In Search of the Missing "Turn": The Spatial Dimension and Cornish Studies', in Philip Payton (ed.), *Cornish Studies: Eight* (Exeter, 2000), pp. 213–30.

14. On the distinction between pattern and process in migration studies see W. T. R. Pryce, 'A Migration Typology and Some Topics for the Research Agenda', *Family & Community History* 3.1 (2000), pp. 65–80.

15. The following section is based on the discussion in Brettell, 2002, pp. 229–47.

16. Peter Clark, 'The Migrant in Kentish Towns, 1580–1640' in Peter Clark and Paul Slack (eds), *Crisis and Order in English Towns 1500–1700: Essays in Urban History*, London, 1972, pp. 117–63.

17. Fishing after the 1810s could be viewed as another example of seasonal migration – see John Rule, 'The South Western Deep Sea Fisheries and their Markets in the Nineteenth Century', *Southern History* 22, 2000, pp. 168–88.

18. *West Briton*, 26 March 1824 and 1 April 1825.

19. Brettell, 'Migration', p. 246.

20. Baines, *Migration in a Mature Economy*, p. 159.

21. The table appeared in Deacon, 'A Forgotten Migration Stream', p. 100. As net native migration of Cornish-born to counties in England and Wales is the same as net native migration from Cornwall to those counties, the difference in the figures for native net migration from Cornwall and net native emigration of Cornish born must be equal to the number emigrating direct from Cornwall. (It is not possible to break down the emigration figure for the 1850s because of lack of data on the location of Cornish-born in England and Wales in 1851.) Confusion between net native migration from Cornwall and net migration of Cornish-born from England and Wales also underlies the apparent anomaly between Baines' results and my calculations of net native migration reported in Bernard Deacon, 'Reconstructing a Regional Migration System: Net Migration in Cornwall', *Local Population Studies* 78 (2007), pp. 28–46.

22. Unfortunately, while calling for more quantitative evidence of migration flows, Schwartz ('Cornish Migration Studies', p. 136) confuses absolute and relative migration rates. She states that the Cornish male was 'by far the largest group of native emigrants to leave the shores of England and Wales', this being 'all the more remarkable given that Cornwall's population never exceeded half a million'. Cornish men were not the largest group to emigrate and for the reason she cites – their relatively small numbers.

23. Andrew Hinde, 'The Use of Nineteenth-century Census Data to Investigate Local

Migration', *Local Population Studies* 73 (2004), pp. 8–28.

24. *Registrar General's supplement to twenty-fifth annual report*, BPP 1865 XIII, 216–25; *Registrar General's thirty-fifth annual report: supplement*, BPP 1875 XVIII, 220–29; *Registrar General's supplement to fifty-fifth annual report, Part 1*, BPP 1895 XXIII, 386–99; *Registrar General's Annual Reports*, BPP, 1873–82. These were obtained from the online database of Parliamentary Papers at http://parlipapers.chadwyck. co.uk/home. The Decennial Supplements are also available from the UK Data Archive at the University of Essex (http://data-archive.ac.uk).

25. The Cornwall Family History Society has transcribed the CEBs for Cornwall into relational microsoft access databases. These provide an invaluable resource for anyone working on the demographic history of nineteenth century Cornwall.

26. Baines, *Migration in a Mature Economy*, p. 159; Payton, *The Cornish Overseas*, p. 42; Schwartz, 'Cornish Migration Studies', p. 137.

27. Baines, *Migration in a Mature Economy*, pp. 122–3.

28. These calculations assume that the age distribution of overseas emigrants and migrants to England and Wales were the same. This is probably unlikely.

29. For an expanded discussion of age-specific net native migration at RD level see Deacon and Schwartz, 'Cornish Identities and Migration' (2007). For the full dataset of native net migration at RD level by age and sex see www.projects.ex.ac. uk/cornishcom/workingpapers.htm.

30. For an explanation of the method see Andrew Hinde, 'The Components of Population Change', *Local Population Studies* 76 (2006), pp. 90–5.

31. This can be measured by the standard deviation of the net migration rates, varying from a high of 7.1% in the 18590s to a low of 5.1% in the 1860s and from 11.8% in Liskeard RD over this period to just 1.4% in Stratton.

32. Hinde, 'The Components of Population Change'.

33. For the full dataset see www.projects.ex.ac.uk/cornishcom/workingpapers.htm.

34. A full dataset of destinations and origins of these migrants is available at www. projects.ex.ac.uk/cornishcom/workingpapers.htm.

35. Mills and Schürer, *Local Communities in the Victorian Census Enumerators' Books*, pp. 217–77.

36. Kevin Schürer, 'Victorian Panel Study', *Local Population Studies* 73 (2004), pp. 73–7.

37. Dennis Mills and Kevin Schürer, 'Migration and Population Turnover', in Mills and Schürer, *Local Communities in the Victorian Census Enumerators' Books*, p. 225; James Jackson, 'Migration in Duisburg, 1867–1890: Occupational and Familial Contexts', *Journal of Urban History* 8 (1982), pp. 250–1.

38. *West Briton*, 25 January 1867, 25 September 1873.

39. This difference is far too high to be explained by any difference in age-specific death rates across the districts.

40. Roger Burt, Peter Waite and Ray Burnley, *Cornish Mines: Metalliferous and Associated Minerals, 1845–19130* (Exeter, 1987), p. 419.

41. Schwartz, 'Cornish Migration Studies', pp. 138, 156–8.

42. Although the absence of fertility and mortality data at the RD level before the 1850s makes this difficult.

43. George Boyer and Timothy Hatton, 'Migration and Labour Market Integration in Late Nineteenth-century England and Wales', *Economic History Review* 50.4 (1997), pp. 697–734; Dov Friedlander, 'Occupational Structure, Wages, and Migration in

Late Nineteenth-century England and Wales', *Economic Development and Cultural Change* 40.2 (1992), pp. 295–318. This is also noted by Paul Hudson: 'English Emigration to New Zealand, 1839–1850: Information Diffusion and Marketing a New World', *Economic History Review*, 54.4 (2001), p. 680.

44. Bernard Deacon, 'Communities, Families and Migration: Some Evidence from Cornwall', *Family & Community History* 10.1 (2007), pp. 49–60.

45. Roger Burt and Sandra Kippen, 'Rational Choice and a Lifetime in Metal Mining: Employment Decisions by Nineteenth-century Cornish miners', *International Review of Social History* 46.1 (2001), pp. 45–75.

46. Payton, *The Cornish Overseas*, pp. 344–69.

47. Damaris Rose, 'Home Ownership, Subsistence and Historical Change: The Mining District of West Cornwall in the Late Nineteenth Century' in Nigel Thrift and Peter Williams (eds), *Class and Space: The Making of an Urban Society* (London, 1987), pp. 108–53.

48. For the advantages in adopting a systems approach to the study of past migrations see James H. Jackson and Leslie Page Moch, 'Migration and the Social History of Modern Europe', *Historical Methods* 22.1 (1989), pp. 27–36 and James Fawcett, 'Networks, Linkages and Migration Systems', *International Migration Review*, 23.3 (1989), pp. 671–80.

4

From St Just to St Just Point

Cornish Migration to Nineteenth-century Victoria

Charles Fahey

Introduction

Since the publication of Oswald Pryor's *Australia's little Cornwall* in 1962, South Australia has been seen by historians as the main destination for Cornish miners to the Australian colonies in the nineteenth century. Although he acknowledged the presence of Cornish in Victoria, the 'myth' of Australia's Little Cornwall was perpetuated by Geoffrey Blainey in his history of Australian mining – *The Rush that Never Ended*. The copper mining towns of Moonta and Kadina 'were possibly the largest Cornish communities beyond Land's End'. Here the miners

> built their cottages from the sun-dried bricks with low streamlined chimneys above the wide Cornish hearth. At Christmas they whitewashed the cottages until they glared in the sun. Inside Cornish pasties were cooking on the oven and saffron cake for Sunday, and the tub of warm water awaited the miner home from his shift with his billycan and white calico bag which carried his pasty.[1]

At New Year carnivals the game, Blainey writes, was Cornish wrestling and the towns celebrated Midsummer Eve in their new southern home on 22 June. For a generation the mines gave the men a holiday on 'Midsummer Eve', and deliberately ignored the Queen's birthday.

Blainey's depiction of the copper triangle of South Australia as the largest Cornish communities beyond Land's End ignores the significant streams of

Cornish migration to the United States. Yet there is no doubt from the work of Philip Payton that the 'Middle Colony' was an important destination for Cornish migrants. From shipping lists he has demonstrated that of the 162,853 immigrants who arrived in South Australia by ship between 1836 and 1886 some 12,967, or 8 per cent, were from Cornwall. Although the lists are often fragmentary and provide an incomplete record of occupation, miners were the largest group of Cornish immigrants, amounting to 57.5 per cent of those for whom occupations were recorded. All told miners, agricultural labourers and general labourers made up almost ninety per cent of male Cornish immigrants to South Australia. Once in the colony, Payton argues, these Cornish men made the back bone of the mining workforce, first at Burra and Kapunda and later in the copper triangle of Moonta, Kadina and Wallaroo. From here they played a substantial part in the agricultural settlement of the Central Hill country and the Yorke Peninsula.[2]

Both Blainey and Payton recognized the influence of the Cornish in Victoria but have left the detailed telling of the story of the Victorian Cornish to dedicated amateur historians. The champion of the Victorian Cornish is undoubtedly Ruth Hopkins. A descendent of Cornish settlers, Ruth Hopkins in *Where Now Cousin Jack?*, has compiled a wealth biographical data on the Cornish who settled in Bendigo. Keen to restore the Cornish to a place of importance in the history of Bendigo, she describes their impact on the cultural and religious life of Bendigo. She writes of Cornish sports, of Cornish choirs, of religious revivals and temperance and, most importantly, of the place of the Methodist churches in Bendigo. Miners play a large part in her story of the Cornish in Bendigo and she emphasizes the part they played in the formation of trade unions. In a later book she has also traced the Cornish beyond Bendigo and explored the part they played in the general development of nineteenth-century Victoria.[3]

These accounts leave us in no doubt that the Cornish played a major part in the settlement of the mining districts of both South Australia and Victoria. Yet many questions remain. Reading much of the South Australian literature, one could be forgiven for thinking that mining in Moonta was an exclusive Cornish occupation. Philip Payton can tell us how many Cornish came to South Australia; a more difficult task is to show precisely what proportion of the mining workforce they were. In her zeal to restore the Cornish to their rightful place in Victoria, Ruth Hopkins relies on lists on names and at times is given to wild exaggeration. We are told for example that the Scots and the Irish were outnumbered in Bendigo by the Cornish.[4] But was this the case? One of the great problems investigating the Cornish contribution to both South Australia and Victoria is the simple fact that in all districts the printed census aggregated the Cornish with English settlers. And in Australia there are no census manuscripts. However, as Ruth Hopkins realized, the Victorian records of the registration of Birth, Deaths and Marriages often give detailed information about places of birth and a wealth of other information about nineteenth-century migrants. Using these in a systematic way, we can learn much about Cornish and other migrants.

This article examines the Cornish in regional Victoria. From the Registers of Births full certificates have been taken from goldfields registration districts for 1861, 1871, 1881, 1891 and 1901, that is at each census year. In 1861 the main focus of investigation is the two major goldfields – Bendigo and Ballarat. For 1871 the sample was extended to include all the major goldfields towns and districts of central Victoria – from Heathcote in the east to Stawell in the west. In 1881 the focus was further extended to include the agricultural lands that were settled under the 1869 Land Act – the Wimmera and Northern plains. The Victorian birth certificate listed the age and place of birth of parents (often down to the level of a village), the date and place of their marriage, the number of children (both living and deceased) at the time of the current registration and the occupation of the father. In addition, more detailed data has been compiled from the birth and marriage returns of one major Cornish destination – Bendigo. Like the birth certificate, the Victorian death certificate contains a wealth of social information including place of birth, years in the colony, occupation of the deceased and his or her father's occupation. Death certificates have also been collected for the Northern Counties of Bendigo, Gunbower and Rodney for six years at the end of the century and have been linked to probate inventories.[5]

Victorian goldmining

Gold was discovered in Victoria in 1^^1 and was mined intensively until the Great War. This industry had a number of key phases. The early 1850s were the years of the great alluvial rushes. In these years little technology and capital was required, and these were the halcyon days for the independent prospector. By the mid-1850s gold diggers on Ballarat had moved to a more difficult resource – deep leads. At the same time crude horse-driven machinery, known as puddling machines, were introduced on other fields – most importantly at Bendigo. Requiring little more than timber and a horse, puddling enabled the prospector to survive on Bendigo, even if precariously, for another decade. But from at least the mid-1850s prospectors began to tackle the difficult task of winning gold from quartz reefs. Quartz reefing and deep leads transformed the social and economic structure of the goldfields. Both required capital and signalled the demise of the independent prospector. And both forms of mining were largely exploited after the great collapse of Cornish copper mining in the mid-1860s.

Of the two forms of mining, quartz reefing would have been most familiar in its technology to Cornish miners. Deep leads were essentially ancient rivers containing alluvial deposits of gold that had been covered by ancient volcanic eruptions. To mine the deep leads shafts had to be sunk below the ancient river. Once below the river, drives were tunnelled under the ancient river and rises were driven into the alluvium to drain the stream. When this had been completed miners entered the ancient river beds and 'blocked out' the alluvial dirt, a combination of sands, clays, river pebbles and, hopefully, gold. Working the alluvium was similar to longwall coal mining. Miners worked back from the extremity of the alluvium to the shaft. Their workplaces were supported by massive amounts of timber, and the abandoned areas were allowed to collapse after the alluvial soil had been removed. For the Cornish migrant the most familiar feature of this mining was the Cornish boiler houses that were erected to drain the old leads, and which can still be seen in many parts of Victoria. Blocking out the wash dirt was foreign to traditional Cornish mining but Cornish skills were essential in sinking shafts and driving tunnels.

The Cornish migrant would have been more at home in the hard rock of quartz reefing. Although a number of early quartz reefers on Bendigo brought German experience to colonial mining, Cornish methods and language – stulls, stopes and so on – were quickly adopted in Victoria. Deep leads were worked in Ballarat from the mid-1850s but the great days of deep lead alluvial mining were from the mid-1860s to the early 1870s. Deep leads were later worked at Maryborough, Creswick, Clunes and Talbot in central Victoria and in at Chiltern in the North East. Quartz reefs were eventually exploited at Ballarat in the late 1870s and 1880s. Although quartz reefing occurred across the central goldfields, the major field was Bendigo, with Stawell and Maldon also having important reef deposits. Reefs were eventually worked to over 3000 feet below the surface.[6]

Cornish migrants

In her brief study of the Cornish diaspora in the nineteenth century, Gill Burke suggested that there were two kinds of migrants: 'The first was that of the "single roving miner" who, if married, left wife and family in Cornwall and who (married or single) returned as often as possible to Cornwall either to work or en route for somewhere else. The second type was emigration pure and simple, with the miner and his family never to return'.[7] This second type characterized the period of depression in Cornwall from the mid-1860s.

The first phase of Victorian mining undoubtedly attracted a fair proportion of single roving men looking to rapidly make their fortunes. Sometime in the 1880s John Bartlett Davies recalled that,[8]

> in common with many others of my station, I got dissatisfied with my prospects at home and determined to try my fortune in Australia. After some difficulty in getting the needful outfit for the voyage owing to my father being unwilling to part with me (he having suddenly discovered that I was useful on the farm) I found myself starting for the golden land with something over forty pounds in my pocket.

Davies left Cornwall in 1857 and arrived in Bendigo in early 1858. On his arrival he observed the extent of worked over alluvial mining ground and obtained his first job working for a party of Irish prospectors operating a puddling machine. Giving up this job after only a week, he was much surprised to be paid in paper currency, the first he had seen in his life and a strange sight in the 'cradle of gold sovereigns'.

Although a Cornishman, Davies did not have a mining background and this was probably the norm among during the first wave of alluvial prospectors. In the late 1850s mining on both Bendigo and Ballarat was undertaken by all nationalities (Table 1). Yet even at this early date the Cornish were a significant proportion of the mining population. On Ballarat, where deep lead mining had already made significant progress, they were a quarter of all miners. Bendigo mining at this date was still very much dominated by shallow alluvial mining – particularly puddling – and the Cornish were 17 per cent of miners. Puddling was very little different from navvying; it required brawn to remove the alluvial top soil, an acquaintance with horses and little knowledge of mining. For these reasons the Irish could often, as Davies found out, turn to puddling.

However, as early as 1861 there were indications that the Cornish were a distinctive type of gold-seeker. It has long been recognized that the Victorian gold rush generation were generally young – between the ages of 20 and 45 – and unmarried. In the second half of the 1850s the Colonial Government, concerned about a nation of footloose bachelors, decided to sponsor assisted migration for single women. At the same time, many single men called for the fiancés to join them in the colony. And by the early 1860s the goldfields had an extremely high marriage rate for women and high rates of marital fertility. The Cornish, like other migrant groups, participated in this process of colonial family formation. For the Cornish, however, family formation was more frequently commenced before migration than other gold seekers. Among the sample of births for Ballarat and Bendigo in 1861 the proportion of Cornish men married at home was about a 57 per cent; for all other fathers it was only about a third. The respective proportions for mothers

Table 1.   Places of birth of miners who registered a birth in Bendigo
and Ballarat, 1861

	Bendigo	Ballarat	Total
Australian colonies	1.3	2.4	1.8
Scotland undefined	1.3	0.3	0.8
Highland counties	2.1	3.8	2.9
Lowland counties	8.4	10.0	9.1
Ireland undefined	0.3	0.3	0.8
Connaught	1.6	0.9	1.2
Leinster	3.7	2.6	3.2
Ulster	3.9	2.9	3.5
Munster	10.5	10.6	10.5
England undefined	0.5	0.3	0.4
London	6.5	4.7	5.7
Midlands	2.9	1.2	2.1
North	11.8	10.6	11.2
East	4.2	2.6	3.5
South-East	6.3	4.4	5.4
South-West	6.3	5.9	6.1
Cornwall	17.3	25.6	21.2
Wales	0.8	3.5	2.1
Channel Isles	0.3	0.6	0.4
North America	0.8	1.5	1.1
Germany	7.1	3.5	5.4
Other Europe	1.8	1.2	1.5
China	0	0.3	0.1
Other Countries	0.5	0.3	0.4
Number	**764**	**680**	**1,444**

Source: Birth Records for Bendigo and Ballarat, 1861. This table grossly under-reports
the proportion of Chinese involved in mining as few Chinese travelled with their
families or married on the goldfields.

were two thirds and a fifth. It would appear that Gill Burke's family leaving Cornwall, never to return, may have been established in the 1850s. This trend was undoubtedly strengthened in the 1860s as the crisis in Cornish copper mines intensified and new capitalist mining in Victoria called for specialized skills.[9]

Within days of settling in Bendigo, John Bartlett Davies found childhood friends who had travelled before him to the golden colony. Using the last of his savings and borrowing from a mate he invested with colleagues in a carting business. From the late 1850s he carted timber to the new emerging quartz reefs and carried quartz from the mines to the crushing batteries. He thus became well acquainted with the fortunes of the new quartz mines and invested the profits from carting in buying shares in mining companies. By 1871, when the Bendigo mines boomed, he retired from carting and lived the life of a gentleman investor. Such mobility, as we shall see, was rare, and the typical Cornish migrant to the Victorian goldfields worked as a proletarian miner.[10]

Richard Pope arrived in Melbourne almost a decade later than John Bartlett Davies, in February 1868. Unlike Davies, Pope was not alone and he travelled with his wife Mary Ann and their six children, aged from seven to one year. Pope did not tarry in Melbourne and within a day caught the train to the mining city of Ballarat. Pope was keen to avoid the costs of a hotel, and 'after much trouble' they rented a four roomed house in the suburb of Soldier's Hill at '13 shillings per week'. During his first two days in Ballarat, Pope struggled to find employment. When he did at last succeed in getting work at the Inkerman and Durham claim he summed the chances of a migrant:

> It seems fresh arrivals or New Chums as they are called stand but a poor show of getting work in this country when there are plenty of old hands about, unless they have some one to speak for them. The pay here is seven shillings and sixpence per shift of eight hours and the claims are kept in full work from Sunday night twelve o'clock to Saturday night twelve o'clock, and in many of the claims there is a gang of men on every Sunday repairing Drives, Roads etc. The work is very hard and dangerous and fatal accidents being of frequent occurrence and though animal food is very cheap a great many things, which are absolutely necessary in a family, are so dear that it is quite impossible to save much money, and taking every thing into consideration it appears to me that the poor man does not improve his position by emigrating.[11]

Pope's reservations about the wisdom of migrating were given added weight when his youngest son, Richard Wearne Pope, 'was snatched from them by the grim monster death'.

Pope was born at Breage in 1834. At the age of twenty one he joined the army of footloose Cornish miners seeking better wages in the United States. He worked in the Virginian coal mines and the copper mines of the Midwest before returning to Cornwall where he married in 1858. Within days of his marriage he returned briefly to the US and then joined his father, who managed a mine in Ireland. When his father died he decided join his brother, Joseph, who had migrated to Victoria. Pope worked for 18 years in Victoria and in 1886 he migrated once again, to Broken Hill in New South Wales. In his sixties he briefly attempted to obtain work in the Transvaal. He died in Broken Hill in 1900. Throughout his life Pope was unusual in that he kept detailed journals, but he was absolutely typical of the majority Cornish migrants to Victoria who came not to win their fortunes from prospecting but to support their families through waged work.

In 1851 mining was the major source of employment in the communities of western Cornwall. In the parishes of Camborne and St Just-in-Penwith almost two thirds of men were employed in mining, and in Redruth the proportion was about 45 per cent. Yet Cornwall had few large towns and mining was often located in rural districts. In 1851 about a tenth of the male population of St Just were engaged in agriculture.[12] The majority of the Cornish who came to Victoria were brought up in families where the copper and tin industries were the main sources of employment for their fathers. Victorian death certificates included a question on the occupation of the deceased's father. In many cases children and others filling out the death certificate were in the colony and had little contact with family at home. Nonetheless, this question was answered sufficiently well enough for us to explore the social origins of Cornish settlers. Table 2 examines the occupations listed on death certificates from Bendigo from 1897–99 and compares the Cornish with another distinctive ethnic group, the Irish. The Cornish who migrated to Bendigo came largely from mining backgrounds; over 60 per cent were either the sons of miners or mine mangers. And the proportion with fathers engaged in and around mines was probably even higher for the category of skilled artisans included jobs associated with mining such as engine drivers and blacksmiths. Few of the Cornish migrants had middle class backgrounds. In his study of the Welsh in Ballarat, Robert Tyler examined similar records for Ballarat. Here the Cornish also had mining backgrounds and his analysis of death certificates for 1853 to 1891 showed that over half (52.%) of the Cornish had fathers who were miners.[13] The comparison with the Irish is also instructive, with a majority of Irish coming from farming backgrounds. In northern and central Victoria this difference in background had, as we shall see, a major impact on the way migrants took up economic opportunities.

Table 2. Occupations of the fathers of the Bendigo Cornish and Irish

	Cornish	*Irish*
Miner	55.8	1.2
Mine manager	5.8	–
Farming and fishing	10.5	57.5
Skilled artisans	13.9	21.2
Professionals/white collar	3.5	2.4
Unskilled	7.0	16.2
Commercial	3.4	1.2
Number	**86**	**80**

Source: Manuscript Death Registers, Bendigo 1897–99

The story of the collapse of the Cornish copper mines has been told many times and there is no reason to repeat it here.[14] The critical point is that this depression occurred at the very time when the Victorian gold mines were moving from shallow alluvial to deep lead alluvial and quartz reefing, and the Cornish miner became absolutely essential in opening up these resources. Analysis of death certificates indicates that over half of Cornish migrants arrived in Victoria after 1860, when deep lead and quartz reefing were replacing alluvial prospecting.[15] By 1871 the area covered by the central goldfields had been opened up to land settlement and in the gold towns themselves stable mining communities had given opportunities for migrants to diversify out of mining; by 1871 just under 40 per cent of fathers who registered a birth worked as miners. And of this birth cohort 12.6 per cent of fathers and 10.3 per cent of mothers were born in Cornwall.[16] The Cornish proportion varied from community to community but was strongest in areas where mining was the predominant industry. By 1871 the proportion of fathers who were Cornish in Ballarat was only 12.7, a clear indication of the collapse of the deep leads mines. As a consequence, miners had been forced to migrate to more prosperous fields. Richard Pope, for example, left Ballarat for Bendigo at the end of 1870. Extrapolating from birth registrations to the total population recorded in the census of 1871, there were probably in excess of 15,000 Cousin Jacks and Cousin Jennys on the central goldfields at this date. By 1881 a large number of native born Australians had begun to appear as mothers and fathers in goldfields registration returns. Yet the Cornish presence was still high in the major quartz reefing and deep lead towns and cities (Table 3).

Table 3.   Proportion of fathers who were Cornish in selected mining communities

	Total population 1871	Cornish fathers 1871 (%)	Total population 1881	Cornish fathers 1881 (%)
Talbot	2,878	18.3	2,318	21.4
Ballarat	47,201	12.7	39,758	11.8
Bendigo	28,577	20.4	35,515	22.5
Castlemaine	6,935	5.6	5,597	6.1
Chewton	2,387	18.2	1,692	21.4
Clunes	1,261	39.3	5,670	34.7
Creswick	3,969	15.8	3,717	22.5
Daylesford	1,082	25.0	4,152	6.0
Dunnolly	1,553	6.9	1,733	8.0
Maldon	3,817	27.1	2,962	27.3
Maryborough	2,935	6.3	3,469	9.8
Stawell	5,166	8.2	7,187	17.8

Source: Manuscript Birth Certificates, Victorian Registry of Births, Deaths and Marriages and Census of Victoria. Most of the above communities had mines located beyond Municipal boundaries.

A significant part of most mining towns and cities, the Cornish were particularly prominent in the mining sector of these communities. This can be clearly seen in the case of Bendigo, Victoria's major quartz reefing city. From 1861 to 1881 the proportion of Cornish fathers who were miners rose from under a fifth to two fifths. And while the Cornish never made up a majority of the mining workforce, the overwhelming majority of Cornishmen were miners. And having joined the mining workforce of towns such as Bendigo it would appear that most of the Cornish who remained in these towns continued to work in mining throughout their working lives. Among a sample of Cornish settlers who died in Bendigo in the late nineteenth century, almost two thirds were recorded as miners. And if we add in mine managers, engine drivers and others employed in ancillary trades around the mines, perhaps seven in every ten Cornishmen remained in the mining industry.[17] This 'loyalty' to mining had important consequences for the way the Cornish experienced life in Victoria.

Local Cornish communities

Mining produced very distinctive communities in the cities and towns of the gold fields. This can be readily seen in the case of Bendigo. In the 1850s alluvial gold spread prospectors over a wide area, and areas that were to become the business centre of the city were mined in the early 1850s. The development of quartz mining, however, concentrated the industry on the western side of the city in the suburbs of Golden Square, Sutton, Long Gully and California Gully (See Map 1). Miners dominated these districts and as a result they also had a particularly strong Cornish presence. In each of this districts over a third of fathers who registered a birth in 1881 were born in Cornwall, and in Long Gully – the heart of the mining industry – the proportion was almost half. The Cornish were under-represented in the centre of the city – in Sandhurst Central, Barkly, Darling and Quarry Hill. These areas were dominated by commercial, professional, white collar, and craft workers. The Cornish character of the west was also strengthened by the tendency of Cousin Jacks to marry Cousin Jennys. In over half the Cornish-headed households, both partners were born in Cornwall.

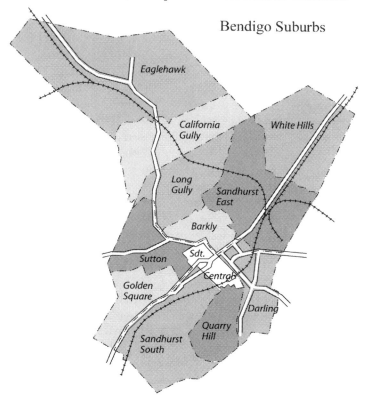

Bendigo Suburbs

Living under the shadow of mullock heaps and mining plant gave the Cornish ready access to employment. Just as importantly, these mining areas provided access to cheap land known as miners' residence areas. Rather than alienate potentially auriferous land the Victorian government made available lots of up to a quarter of an acre at the derisory rent of 5s. per year. On these residence areas the Cornish were able to continue their tradition of owner-building. In the major mining towns of Cornwall speculative builders built terrace housing to accommodate the mining population. Much mining, however, was conducted in semi-rural settings and here a different pattern of housing was found. In rural parishes cottages were erected on small acreages on a leasehold basis of three lives. The annual rent was 5s. per year and the tenant was expected to clear and enclose his plot and build a cottage. At the end of three lives the lease could be re-negotiated by the payment of a capital sum of £30. These blocks produced a small income from waste land, and the food produced by miners supplemented their meagre incomes. These houses generally had thatched roofs and walls were of cob (clay and straw) or stone and sometimes slag from the mines. The houses were often erected on the sides of hills, with three built walls. They were generally no bigger than around 12 foot squared. In Victoria the miner's residence area permitted Cornish settlers to continue this practice owner-building.[18]

In his history of Ballarat, *Lucky City*, Weston Bate trumpeted the apparent high levels of home ownership as firm evidence of the egalitarianism of the goldfields. In the City of Ballarat West his analysis of rate books revealed that 69 per cent of houses were owner occupied in 1870, and 89 per cent of miners owned the house they occupied. However, Ballarat rate books did not distinguish freehold from miner's residence areas, and much the high apparent levels of home ownership was due to the occupation of crown land. In 1873, at Long Gully in the heart of Bendigo's mining district, over 90 per cent of miners' houses were erected on residence areas. The existence of this cheap land enabled the erection of very cheap houses to meet the rapid influx of population.[19] In May 1868 Richard Pope purchased a house in Ballarat for £58 with a further £4 4s. 0d. to obtain a title.[20] But cheap housing also carried risks. When he moved out of Ballarat Pope could only sell his property for £40.

Migrating to Bendigo in 1870, Pope initially rented an unfinished two-room house at Long Gully for 5s. 6d. per week. Into these cramped quarters he moved his wife and five young children in September 1870. Yet cramped conditions were only one of Pope's concerns; more important was the need to stop rent payments. Late in January 1871 Richard Pope used the provisions on the miner's residence area clause of the Lands Act to select a piece of crown land at St Just Point in Long Gully. In anticipation of the sale of his Ballarat house, Pope immediately employed a carpenter to put up the shell

Table 4.   Cornish miners on Ballarat and Bendigo, 1861–81

| | % of miners who were Cornish | | % of Cornish who were miners | |
	Ballarat	Bendigo	Ballarat	Bendigo
1861	25.6	17.3	78.4	77.6
1871	21.4	31.3	75.0	83.3
1881	19.6	40.4	51.4	76.8

Source: Manuscript Birth Certificates

of a four room house – 22 feet long by 20 feet deep with nine feet high walls. The labour for the shell was quoted at £7 10s. 0d., and he purchased the timber on account for £25. In February he received a draft for £40 for the sale of his Ballarat house. Although he had trouble cashing this cheque, he paid the timber merchant, gave the carpenter £5 on account and outlaid a further 30s. for a chimney. On 4 February he moved into his unfinished house, 'to save the rent'. The following Monday his wife gave birth to their seventh child, and for less than £40 their humble cottage was home to two adults and six children.[21]

Pictures of the mining suburbs of Bendigo in the 1870s show bleak, treeless surroundings. Until the early twentieth century few streets were formally laid out. Rate books often refer to houses being 'off' Victoria Street or other main roads. In the 1860s shafts were sunk literally everywhere in these districts and by the late 1860s and early 1870s abandoned shafts were an ever present threat. Most vegetation had been removed by prospectors in the 1850s and hot summer winds carried dust from the tailings heaps into houses. In winter, if it rained, back yards became quagmires. Most houses were made of weatherboards and were lined internally with Hessian and paper. In the 1870s tin roofs, a necessity for catching water, replaced shingles. The blistering heat of summer days and the icy cold of winter nights easily penetrated these humble residences. In mining communities across the Great Dividing Range securing water was a problem until municipal reservoirs were constructed in the 1860s. For Bendigo, Castlemaine and Chewton more reliable water supply was secured by 1877 through aqueducts which brought water north from better watered southern areas. It was not until well into the twentieth century that the mining suburbs were sewered.

In Ballarat, with a relatively high rainfall, infant death rates were lower than in the drier communities north of the divide. In 1861 Bendigo had an infant death rate of 225 deaths per 1000 births. A more secure water supply reduced this to 151 by 1881. The respective rates for Ballarat were 153 infant deaths in 1861 and 133 in 1881. The difficulties of living in mining suburbs fell heavily on Cousin Jennys. It was they who had to wash children and clothes with limited water supplies. They confronted the swirling summer dust storms which covered household furniture in dust. And they faced a heavy burden of child bearing and rearing. In 1881 the marital fertility of Cornish wives was 9.1 children.[22]

By the early 1880s the mining suburbs had lost some of their raw, frontier appearance. Through political action miners secured greater security of tenure over residence areas and virtually obtained freehold in 1881. From this date improvements on residence areas could be freely transferred and bequeathed to heirs. While house prices remained low, mining families made significant improvements to their houses; extra gables were added and verandahs provided summer shade. With more secure water, gardens were developed and generous blocks permitted miners to grow vegetables and fruit trees.[23] And there were no weekly payments to landlords. The humble miner's cottage provided a measure of security in rapidly deteriorating labour market.

The growth of unemployment

Gold mines, like the copper mines from which the Cornish had fled, were wasting assets and all goldfields faced the inevitable depletion of their reserves. In the cases of deep leads this could come very rapidly. The buried alluvial gold was found in discrete locations. It took time to sink shafts and drain the ancient rivers but once found the resource was quickly worked out. On central Ballarat the early 1860s were a period of exploration. When gold was found miners, like Richard Pope, poured into the community. Yet from the late 1860s it was clear that all was not well and in the early 1870s unemployment became widespread. Arriving in 1868, Pope missed the great days of Ballarat's alluvial deep leads, and his years in the Ballarat district were characterized by a constant need to change jobs and search for employment. Richard Pope arrived in Ballarat in February 1868 and worked in Ballarat and district mines until the beginning of August 1870. In this period of about 31 months he worked in no fewer than 14 mines. On a number of occasions Pope voluntarily left his position – on one occasion he had made a bad contract, tendering to drive a tunnel, and on another he felt nauseous from the decaying vegetable matter in the deep lead. In the end the underlying cause of his insecure work was the exhaustion of the leads.[24]

Like hundreds of other miners, Pope migrated internally to Bendigo in the early 1870s. Here he quickly found work. However, even on this booming field work could be insecure. There were a number of reasons for this. First, far too many claims were floated during the boom of 1869–71. Many simply closed up when gold was not found. Second, Victorian mines suffered from a chronic lack of capital. Mines were floated as limited liability or later no liability companies. When gold was found dividends were paid recklessly and mines were left without capital to finance exploration. When yields declined, labour was laid off. Over the course of the nineteenth century Bendigo quartz reefs experienced a number of recurring crises – in the mid-1860s, in the late 1870s and again in the late 1880s – as mining companies searched deeper and deeper for the famous saddle reefs. Bendigo was the premier quartz field in Victoria and the problems of raising capital were more difficult on smaller, less wealthy fields.

Pope arrived in Bendigo in 1870 and worked as an underground miner until 1879. From his journal we have detailed information on his employment and earnings from 1870 through until 1878. When he first arrived on Bendigo he worked in a number of speculative companies and work was insecure. From August 1870 to August 1872 he worked in six mines. For the next two years Pope worked in the Old Chum mine. In March 1874 he observed in his journal that mining on Bendigo was 'looking dull', many mines were 'stopped' and all were 'reducing hands'. By July the Old Chum mine was shaft sinking, looking for a new reef. Initially Pope undertook this shaft sinking on wages, but when this proved expensive, the mine management offered this work on contract in September 1874. Although Pope tendered at £5 10s. 0d. per foot, a more desperate party put in a bid for £3 3s. 0d. per foot. Pope ruefully noted that he was forced to take his clothes from the change house after two years and one month of work.[25]

In the second half of the 1870s many Bendigo mines were forced to undertake exploration work and unemployment rose. From September 1874 to December 1878 Pope worked in seven mines. In the late 1870s employment was particularly insecure and a strike from August to November left Pope unemployed. At the termination of the strike he left Bendigo and worked away from his family in the Victorian high country. Pope returned to Bendigo in August 1880 and secured work as a miner in the Johnsons Reef Extended mine. In the early 1880s the introduction of mechanical rock borers improved exploration and the mines experienced a new period of prosperity. Pope continued to work as a miner until January 1882 when he replaced his ill boss as mine manager. However, by the late 1880s Bendigo faced another period of crisis and Pope was dismissed. He left Bendigo for the new silver mines of Broken Hill.[26]

When he first arrived on Ballarat in 1868 Pope initially questioned the benefit of emigrating. Over the course of his 18 years on the Victorian goldfields such questioning may have continued each time he was forced to look for a new job. Yet there is no doubt he was better off materially in Victoria than he would have been in Cornwall. For most of the 1870s the weekly wage rate for a miner on Bendigo was 45s. Due to unemployment Pope seldom made full wages, and from 1870 to 1878 his average earnings were 43s. 4d. per week. In money terms this was more than double the wage a miner earned in Cornwall. Even allowing for difference in the cost of living, a factor Pope was aware of, his move to Australia gave him a bonus of 80 per cent over Cornish wages. And there were no forced deductions for barbers or doctors and wages were paid weekly and not monthly in arrears.[27]

From 1882 to 1886 Richard Pope enjoyed years of stable employment and as a mine manager he was a respected member of the local Cornish community. In these years he played a major part in the running of the Long Gully Bible Christian Chapel and he was prominent in a local self-improvement society. Yet being a mine manager did not protect him from the down turn in the mining industry, and from the late 1880s Cornish migrants found a more difficult working environment. On Bendigo, the most prosperous field, unemployment rose dramatically from around an annual rate of 8 per cent per annum in the mid-1880s to 15 per cent in 1889. As yields declined mine owners attempted to reduce costs, and to achieve this they adopted the Cornish systems of tribute and tutwork, the former with a novel colonial twist. Much of the development work in mines – shaft sinking and driving, for example – was carried out by contractors, similar to Cornish tutworkers. From the late 1880s desperate miners engaged in cut throat competition to win contracts.[28] More insidious was the colonial take on tributing.

Under Victorian mining legislation claim holders were obliged to enter into labour covenants, and agree to employ a specified number of working miners. When claims were paying this was not a problem. In all mines the largest cost, apart from dividends, was the wage bill. When development work was required the labour covenants became a drain on the resources of owners and share holders. One option was to cease working and watch what was happening in adjoining mines. This was given the pejorative term of 'shepherding'. This led to protests from miners. To avoid the loss of their leases mine owners and companies used tributers.

Under the Victorian tribute system the mine owners offered to employ labour on limited tenure for an agreed share of the gold won. The percentage varied from 15 to 30 per cent of the gross yield of gold, but the miner had to pay the company for hauling and crushing the quartz. The miner also provided timber, candles and other mining materials. On the Bendigo field there was an alternative form of tributing known as the 'halves system'. Under the halves system the miner received only half the gross yield of gold, and the company paid for hauling, carting, crushing and provided timber. Tributes were let for specific periods, usually six to twelve months. However, the miner had no security of tenure and if he or his party came across paying gold they could have their agreement terminated. A return by the Mines

Department in 1889 indicates that 25 per cent of all miners were employed as tributers. Gold mining was in aggregate profitable in the 1890s but tributing remained a feature of the poorer claims. In 1893 one union official estimated that a quarter of union members were employed as tributers and in 1898 the proportion was still estimated at around one fifth. Few tributers made the full wage rate.[29]

Cornish Unionists

The dominant view of the Cornish miner as a chapel-going, thrifty and sober individual who avoided collective action has been challenged by Bernard Deacon. Deacon has demonstrated that Cornish metal miners attempted to form trade unions in 1866. In 1872–74 they protested against the five week month.[30] At much the same time their brothers and cousins who had migrated to Victoria took part in attempts to win the eight hour day and resist attempts to reduce wage rates. The initial drive towards trade unionism took place at Bendigo under the leadership of Robert Clark, the son of a Durham pitman. In 1865–66 he campaigned to win an eight hour day and in 1872 he resisted attempts to reduce wages. Out of the impetus gained from this later battle a Victorian union was formed. This fell into abeyance and was revived in August 1879 to once again resist wage reductions. The union vanished when the crisis had passed. Many miners believed that Clark simply used the union to advance his own political ambitions to win a seat in the Victorian Legislative Assembly. A more enduring union was formed by W. G. Spence, a Scot by birth, in 1884. Through the use of friendly society accident benefits Spence was able to create an enduring union and this body was extended from Creswick to all other Victorian mining fields.

Although they were not the founding figure heads of the Amalgamated Miners Association, Cornish miners were critical in forming and running this union at the local level. For most of the 1880s the committee men of the Bendigo branch were Cornish and the long-term secretary Peter Phillips was born at Stithians. These Cornish activists were prepared to engage in industrial action in the 1860s and 1870s and in 1888 the Bendigo miners' union enforced a closed shop. In the 1890s the union took up the fight to reform the tribute system and won political support for a select committee investigation. Cornish unionists John Praed (born Marazion) and George Hawke (born St Just) were prominent in this campaign. In the late 1890s high levels of unemployment made industrial action difficult and in these bitter years the Bendigo union was wracked by deep personal divisions. The main protagonists were invariably Cornish. At the turn of the century Cornish unionists fought over the affiliation of the miners' union with the new Labor Party. Peter

Phillips led the fight to maintain separation from the Labor Party, while Hawke supported amalgamation and stood as a Labor candidate at the new party's lowest point in 1900. In the early twentieth century Cornish miners and the sons of Cornish miners, often radicalized by working at new fields such as Broken Hill, led the fight to win wage justice through the Victorian Wages Boards and later through the Commonwealth Arbitration Court. Cornishmen were prominent in giving evidence to this Court in 1915.[31]

Working away from the mines

In the 1850s goldmining offered migrants from Britain the prospect of rapidly making their fortunes. By the early 1860s this dream was rapidly receding, and mining had become fields of employment for wage earning proletarians. This type of mining rapidly transformed the economic base of the goldfields and expanded the sources of employment. Capitalist mining encouraged the growth of metal works and a relatively stable population provided a market for local manufacturing, commerce and services. As alluvial mining declined diggers called for the opening up of crown land in the goldfields districts and land sales were held from the mid-1850s. In 1860 the first of a series of land acts was passed to enable settlement on the public estate. In the 1870s and 1880s settlers moved out of the goldfields and onto the plains across the Great Dividing Range.[32]

In 1854 Joseph Chapple, a Cornish agricultural labourer, left his native Cornwall for Victoria. He carried with him a reference from his employer, Thomas Laity. Laity wrote: 'This is to certify that Joseph Chapel [sic] worked with me for upwards of five years. I always found him a most steady, honest and industrious young man. And I very much regret his leaving this country as I know his equal I shall not be able to get.' Unlike most of his fellow Cornishmen, it appears that Joseph Chapple did not work as a miner and for his first two decades in the colony he worked as a quarryman near Geelong, on the coast. However, when the free selection act came into operation in February 1870, he joined the rush across the divide and took up land in the parish of Terrick Terrick, 50 miles north of Bendigo. Under the 1869 land act settlers faced a daunting task carving farms out of the bush. Under the act, settlers could take up to 320 acres on credit. In the first three years they had they had had to cultivate a tenth of the property, build a permanent home, enclose the property with a boundary fence and generally improve the property to the value £1 per acre. Payment of the property could be made over ten years at 2s. per acre. In Northern Victoria the amount of work required to build a farm varied according to the area settled. On the grasslands of the Wimmera plains there was little clearing, while on the Northern plains open woodlands interspersed with open grasslands were encountered. It was in this later environment that Joseph Chapple took up land.

Chapple proved to be a highly successful farmer. With the aid of his sons he was able to select more than the statutory 320 acres and he also brought out several of his less successful neighbours. By the end of the century he had acquired a farm of 1522 acres, and when he died in 1914 his estate was probated at £7,660.[33] Chapple was not alone among his fellow Cornish migrants in moving onto the land and by 1881 around a tenth of the Cornish in Northern Victoria had either purchased or selected land (Table 5). Yet as a group the Cornish were under-represented among the farming population. The Irish on the other hand were over-represented among the farmers of Northern Victoria.

The Victorian Cornish frequently came from semi-rural districts – the Parish of St Just-in-Penwith was the most frequently recorded place of birth on vital records. This familiarity with rural environments did not induce most of them to take up land in Victoria and it may also have inhibited their ability to participate in urban occupations. The Cornish, despite their background in mining, were not among the major mining investors of the gold fields. Nor were they major urban land investors. A clear exception to this pattern was the experience of Thomas Hawkey. The son of a farmer, Hawkey arrived in Victoria from Cornwall in 1854 and established a store. The profits of store keeping were reinvested in land in Bendigo and Melbourne. He also dabbled in mining shares. By the mid-1880s he had an annual income of over £1,200 and he left a net estate of £48,724.[34] . The Cornish were underrepresented in business and the professions in regional Victoria (Table 5). A small minority did exceptionally well in mining related trades. John Robert Hoskins, the son of a mining agent, rose from a working miner in the 1860s to one of Bendigo's major timber merchants. He left an estate of £14,043 in 1905. Abraham Roberts turned a humble blacksmith's shop into one of the larger foundries on the goldfields,[35] and John Goyne joined the ranks of the colonial wealthy elite from the manufacture of metal grates for quartz crushing batteries. He left an estate of £61,436 when he died in 1907.[36] Successful mine management could lead to modest but very comfortable wealth. Samuel Remfrey, the son of a St Agnes miner, was himself a miner in 1875. Promoted to manage a mine for George Lansell, the Victorian 'Quartz King', he later managed public companies and left an estate of £2,363 in 1888.

These successful men managed to acquire wealth that could only be dreamed of in their native home. They were, however, the exceptions and most Cornish migrants acquired only modest property, if any. To measure the success of Cornish settlers, death certificates for selected years in the late nineteenth century have been matched to probate inventories for three northern Victorian counties – Bendigo, Rodney and Gunbower. This study

Table 5. The occupations of fathers in Northern Victoria, 1881

	Cornish (%)	Irish (%)	All birth places (%)
Farmers	12.4	43.6	29.7
Business	5.0	5.8	7.5
Gentlemen	0	0.2	0.2
Professional	1.4	3.6	2.9
White collar/clerical	1.8	6.8	3.8
Skilled trades	12.4	5.3	14.5
Unskilled and semiskilled	3.2	8.0	8.6
Labourers	1.1	12.4	8.0
Miners	62.6	14.1	24.7
Number	261	411	2,519

Source: One in four sample of births registered in the counties of Lown, Borung, Kara Kara, Gladstone, Tatchera, Gunbower, Bendigo, Rodney and Moira, 1881.

indicates that most Cornish settlers did not leave estates that were probated. From a sample of 238 Cornish male deaths only 70 per cent left a probated estate and average value of all estates was £242 (median £0). It is possible that some property was missed by the probate court. We have seen that the institution of the miner's residence area provided cheap housing on the goldfields. It is likely that in many cases these residence areas passed from husbands to wives and from parents to children without relatives seeking a formal grant of probate. Nonetheless these were generally of little capital value, often only £50–£75, and if we assume that most of the non-probated Cornish left a residence area then the median estate may have risen from £0 to a modest sum of around £60. The key to acquiring property in rural Victoria was moving out of mining and onto the land. Among the minority of Cornish who died as farmers the average estate was £1,249.[37]

The End

By the last two decades of the nineteenth century, Victorian goldmining was in decline, and the stream of Cornish migrants dried up. By the 1890s the young Cornish migrant looked to new fields – most importantly

South Africa – to work his traditional occupation.[38] Yet their influence in mining undoubtedly endured long after their raw numbers declined. By the late nineteenth century Victorian mining had become almost a hereditary occupation and young miners who entered the industry had grown up among the Cornish-mining communities of central Victoria. Among a sample of miners who married in Victoria in 1896 to 1899, two-thirds were the sons of miners. For those Cornish and their descendants who remained on the gold fields, employment opportunities contracted dramatically in the years leading up to the Great War. When the Federal Government forbade the export of gold during the war years the mining industry collapsed, and the gold fields town and cities sunk deeper into depression. For most of the inter-war years the Victorian goldfields towns languished economically and lost population. Hundreds of Cornish families packed up and left for other mining fields interstate or moved to Melbourne. Humble miners' cottages were loaded onto drays and moved to the expanding wheat fields of the Victorian Mallee. The once proud Bible Christian, Primitive Methodist, and Wesleyan chapels lost most of their congregations; the cottages that remained fell into disrepair amid the dusty mining detritus of former Cornish communities such as Long Gully or Maldon. And for over fifty years the proud part played by the Cornish in the creation of Victorian mining industry was forgotten. South Australia, meanwhile, usurped the title of 'Australia's Little Cornwall'.[39]

Notes and references

1. Oswald Pryor, *Australia's Little Cornwall* (Adelaide, 1962); Geoffrey Blainey, *The Rush the Never Ended: A History of Australian Mining* (Melbourne, 1963), p. 119.

2. See Philp Payton, *The Cornish Miner in Australia (Cousin Jack Down Under)* (Penryn, 1984), and *The Cornish Farmer in Australia or Australian Adventure: Cornish Colonists and the Expansion of Adelaide and the South Australian Agricultural Frontier* (Redruth, 1987). This second book contains detailed analysis of the South Australian shipping lists in appendices 1–3. See also the entry by Philip Payton in James Jupp (ed.), *The Australian People: An Encyclopedia of the Nation, Its People and Their Origins* (Cambridge 2001), see pp. 227–34.

3. Ruth Hopkins, *Where Now Cousin Jack* (Bendigo, 1988), and *Cousin Jack, Man For the Times: A History of the Cornish People in Victoria* (Bendigo, 1994).

4. Hopkins, *Where Now Cousin Jack*, p. 124.

5. I would like to thank Anne Fullarton from the Victorian Registry of Births, Deaths and Marriages for making these records available to me for statistical research. Limited information is available through the indexes of these records, but in the absence of census manuscripts full certificates are necessary for detailed research. I am grateful for access to these records without the usual fee. Victorian probate inventories can be located at the Victorian Public Records Office, VPRS 28. There is a project under way to digitize these records and make them available on the

internet.

6. The best source for understanding Victorian goldmining is the *Quarterly Reports of the Mining Surveyors and Registrars*, 1863–91. The local newspapers also carried a wealth of detail. See also Ralph Winter Birrell, 'The Development of Mining Technolgy in Australia, 1801–1945, unpublished Ph.D. thesis, University of Melbourne, 2005. Birrell's thesis has an excellent appendix on ore extraction methods, see pp. 351–75. This thesis also includes useful information on the structure of Victorian public mines describing the evolution from the Cornish Book system to the no liability companies. See pp. 87–92.

7. Gill Burke, 'The Cornish Diaspora of the Nineteenth Century', in Shula Marks and Peter Richardson (eds), *International Labour Migration: Historical Perspectives* (London, 1984), p. 62.

8. The Journal of John Bartlett Davies, p. 1. This journal is held by the University of Melbourne Archives. It appears to have been compiled by Davies sometime in the 1880s from journals.

9. The information on marriage and fertility has been compiled as part of a larger study by the author on families and community on the Victorian goldfields.

10. Davies journal ends in the 1880s. I suspect he may have hit rough times later in the century and the value of his investments may have declined substantially. Although he worked as a broker in the early twentieth century, I have not been able to find a probate file for him.

11. Diary of Richard Pope, Australian Manuscripts Collection, Ms. 11918, State Library of Victoria, 18 February 1868.

12. For the demography of Cornwall in the nineteenth century see Mark Brayshay, 'The Demography of Three West Cornwall Mining Communities, 1851–1871', unpublished Ph.D thesis, University of Exeter, 1977. For occupations in the parishes of St Just, Camborne and Redruth, see p. 279.

13. See Robert Llewellyn Tyler, 'A Handful of Interesting and Exemplary People from a Country called Wales: Identity and Cultural Maintenance: the Welsh in Ballarat and Sebastopol in the Second Half of the Nineteenth century', unpublished Ph.D. thesis, Melbourne 2000, p. 39. Although about the Welsh, Tyler's thesis has important information on other groups.

14. For a brief summary of the demographic impact of the collapse of copper see Mark Brayshay, 'Depopulation and Changing Household Structure in the Mining Communities of West Cornwall, 1851–1871', *Local Population Studies* (Autumn, 1980), pp. 28–41. More detail can be found in his unpublished thesis, 'The Demography of Three West Cornwall Mining Communities, 1851–1871', University of Exeter, 1977.

15. Based on an analysis of the entry 'number of years in the colony' listed on death certificates.

16. The 1871 data was taken from an area which covered the Census mining districts of Ararat, Ballarat, Castlemaine, Maryborough and Sandhurst (Bendigo). This area included both mining and agricultural areas and had a total population of 237,810.

17. This sample is described below.

18. My understanding of Cornish houses is derived from Brayshay, 'The Demography of Three West Cornwall Mining Communities', pp. 49–52.

19. For Bate's analysis of home ownership on Ballarat see Weston Bate, *Lucky City*

(Melbourne, 1978) p. 190. The Ballarat Rate Books do not distinguish freehold from crown land. For Bendigo Rate Assessment Books, the working documents used to compile rate books, survive and list residence areas.

20. Pope, Diary, 12 May 1868.
21. Pope, Diary, 18 December 1870, 4 January 1871, 4 February 1871.
22. These demographic statistics were calculated from manuscript birth and death registers, Registry of Births, Deaths and Marriages.
23. Changes in housing conditions can be seen in the changes in rate valuations and in probate inventories. Sadly these houses do not appeal to heritage architects and they have little protection. Yet it is still possible to see the later additions of gables and verandahs, and a handful of miners' gardens survive.
24. Pope, Diary, 14 February to 4 August 1870. Pope it must be admitted never really enjoyed working in deep leads. He was uncomfortable with the dank air and never trusted the timber work required to make work places safe. See 4 July, 16 July and 29 July 1870.
25. Pope, Diary, 14 and 28 March 1874, 1 August 1874 and 29 August 1874.
26. For Pope's experience as a mine manager see his diary for January 1882 to May 1886. Pope played a major part in a strike in 1879 and was a member of a deputation to the major mine owner, George Lansell. This may have been his reason for leaving Bendigo. His job was secured by Robert Clark, the leader on the union.
27. Pope gave very detailed accounts of his earnings from 1870 to 1878. Nominal wage rates were published annually in *Mineral Statistics*. For Cornish wages at the beginning of the 1880s see the South Crofty Pay Books, DD/SC/14, Cornwall County Records Office. I have attempted a preliminary examination of relative retail prices using Australian newspapers and prices reported in the *Cornubian* and the *Royal Cornwall Gazette*. Relative estimates of house prices are derived from Australian rate books and the Redruth Poor Law Rate Book, DC/CR/178 Cornwall County Records Office.
28. From 1884 to 1891 the *Annual Report of the Minister for Mines* printed unemployment statistics provided by the miners' union.
29. The evidence on the problems of tributing was raised constantly in the press and was brought up in a Royal Commission on Gold Mining in 1891. The problems of tributers were investigated by parliamentary select committee in 1893.
30. See Bernard Deacon, 'Attempts at Unionism by Cornish Metal Miners in 1866', *Cornish Studies* 10 (1983), pp. 27–36, and 'Heroic Individualists? The Cornish Miners and the Five Week Month, 1872–74', *Cornish Studies* 14 (1986), pp. 39–53.
31. For a more detailed account of mining unionism see Charles Fahey, 'Labour and Trade Unionism in Victorian Goldmining; Bendigo, 1861–1915', in Iain McCalman, Alexander Cook and Andrew Reeves (eds), *Gold. Forgotten Histories and Lost Objects of Australia* (Cambridge University Press: Melbourne, 2001).
32. For the best account of the economic diversification of goldfields communities see Bate, *Lucky City*, pp. 207–19. For the Victorian land acts see J. M. Powell, *The Public Lands of Australia Felix: Settlement and land Appraisal in Victoria 1834–91 with Special Reference to the Western Plains* (Melbourne, 1970).
33. Probate file 138/434. I was kindly given access to the Chapple papers by Margery Brisbane of Mooroopna, Victoria.
34. Probate file 31–492 and Bendigo City Rate Books.
35. Roberts left an estate of £6,565 in 1897, probate inventory 97-7877. On his death

certificate his father was described as a gentleman. This may have been an inflation of his background by his children.

36. Probate inventory 104/259. In 1907 Goyne had an annual income of almost £1,800 from his bank deposits and mortgages. I have not been able to determine the occupation of his father.

37. Death certificates were matched to probate inventories for 1889, 1890, 1891, 1897, 1898 and 1899.

38. By the 1890s a Cornish place a birth was rare among parents registering births on the Victorian goldfields. See also *Report of the Secretary of State for the Home Department on the Health of Cornish Miners*, Cd paper 2091, 1904. The detailed appendix listing the deaths of tin miners in the district of Redruth for 1900, 1901 and 1902 reveals that few had traveled and worked in Australia.

39. See Philip Payton, *Making Moonta: The Invention of 'Australia's Little Cornwall'* (Exeter, 2007).

5

Home Away From Home

Cornish Immigrants in Nineteenth-century Nevada

Ronald M. James

Introduction

In 1994 my article in *Cornish Studies: Two* examined the nature of ethnicity among the Cornish who in the second half of the nineteenth century came to Virginia City, Nevada, and its Comstock Lode, one of the richest gold and silver deposits ever found. Employing the 1880 manuscript census for the mining district, it was possible, for example, to compare the Cornish with Irish and (non-Cornish) English immigrants. The Cornish were not as numerous as the Irish, but nearly a thousand of them lived in the mining district that year.[1] Primary sources strongly indicate the Cornish chose to express their ethnicity as a strategy to counter Irish solidarity and the latter's domination of the mining district through superior numbers and organization. The analysis of the Comstock in 1880 concluded that those identified by surname as 'possibly Cornish' were statistically similar to those likely to be Cornish, and they were distinct from the English with non-Cornish surnames. The article contrasted average age, the number of children, and the percentage of immigrants involved in mining. It concluded that the use of surnames (even the more ambiguous ones) as indicators successfully pointed to Cornish ethnicity, at least when it came to a mining district like the Comstock.

Over the intervening fourteen years since the article appeared in *Cornish Studies*, Nevada has emerged as the only state in the USA with all its federal manuscript census records encoded in a fully searchable database.[2] This online tool offers an opportunity to conduct a wide range of studies, from the genealogical to the demographic. Where restrictions in available data limited the earlier *Cornish Studies* article, analysis can now be conducted for anywhere in Nevada using the census database from 1860 to 1920. The following article focuses on 1860, 1870, and 1880.[3]

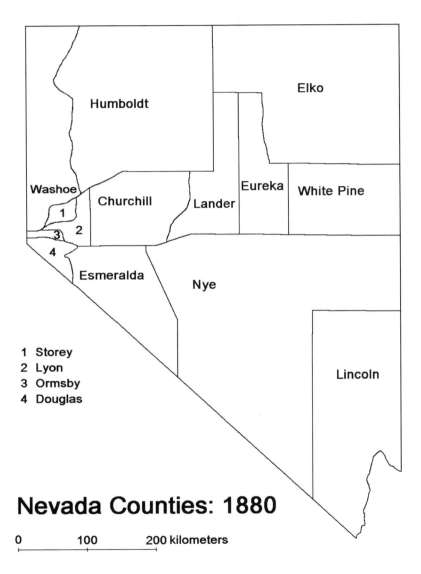

Nevada Counties: 1880

1 Storey
2 Lyon
3 Ormsby
4 Douglas

0   100   200 kilometers

Map 1.   Nevada counties, 1880

Problems in identifying Cornish immigrants

An examination of Cornish immigrants using census data is still beset with the difficulties encountered during the 1994 effort. Those who have dealt with some of the maddening problems associated with Cornish immigration know that census enumerators usually identified those from Cornwall as natives of England. Only twenty-one immigrants in Nevada between 1870 and 1910 identified themselves as being from Cornwall, and yet there were certainly thousands who came from that Celtic country. There were two likely reasons for this. Some immigrants may have tired of explaining where Cornwall was and became in the habit of saying merely that they were from England. Others may have felt the distinction was significant enough to declare but, in all but the tiny number of instances noted above, the enumerators 'corrected' the information and listed England rather than Cornwall as place of birth. A similar situation can be found among some Manx immigrants to Nevada, who declared the Isle of Man as a place of birth in 1870 and then appear with English nativity in 1880.[4] Ultimately, explaining these variations can only be a matter of speculation. The important fact is that Cornish immigrants are almost always identified as English, and the challenge is to otherwise recognize these people so that their patterns can be understood.

The familiar rhyme, 'By Tre-, Lan-, Ross-, Car-, Pol-, Pen-; you may know the most of the Cornishmen', served as a useful way for western settlers to identify their Cornish neighbours.[5] Modern historians must use a similar means to identify these immigrants, although it is recognized that a great many other Cornish possessed patronymic surnames such as Williams, Thomas and Richards. The concentration on 'Tre, Pol and Pen' surnames, therefore, may well identify trends but overall numbers are likely to be on the conservative side. Nonetheless, searching the 1870 Nevada census for men identified as being 'born in England' and having surnames beginning in 'Tre' reveals a good cross-section of the Cornish. Twenty-eight individuals emerge, all of whom were apparently Cornish and involved in the mining industry. Besides twenty-six miners, there was also an engineer and a mill employee. Twenty-one lived in Virginia City or nearby Gold Hill, within the Comstock Mining District. This survey is unscientific but its results are indicative of what it was to be Cornish in Nevada in the nineteenth century. Unfortunately, not all Cornish surnames are so easily isolated. Any attempt to identify and understand all the Cornish in the census will result in some mistakes.[6]

A specific example of the problem with using surnames as ethnic indicators is provided by the example of R. E. Kelly, who appeared in the 1870 census with English nativity, then living in Carson City and working as a clothing store clerk. Kelly, that most Irish of surnames, can also appear in Cornwall.

Two Cornish immigrants with a patrynomic surname: William; father and son.

There is consequently the question as to whether this person was Cornish or was, perhaps, the descendent of Irish immigrants who had settled for a generation or more somewhere in England before moving to North America. At the risk of applying a reverse logic to the problem, Kelly was not a miner and he was living in a community not noted for its Cornish immigrants. Not all Cornish immigrants were miners, but a 'Kelly from England' who was a miner in a mining district would seem more Cornish than this clerk from Carson City. There may be a universal standard to avoid prejudicing the results, but on a subjective level it seems that possible Cornish immigrants to non-mining areas in Nevada invariably have ambiguous surnames that could be from elsewhere. In 1870, for example, there were no 'Tres, Pols, or Pens' in Carson City, s settlement which relied on state government, not mining, for its economy.[7]

Then there is the larger problem of identifying Cornish women when using the census. It is generally assumed that fewer women than men emigrated from Cornwall.[8] Beyond that, identifying these women is even more problematic than working with the men, making conclusions about this part of the group elusive. The problem is that only a handful of potential Cornish women among their already limited numbers emigrated without being married. Some conclusions are possible, but because women surrendered their maiden names in marriage, they represent a challenge when dealing with census records.

The 1860 census

Having acknowledged the frustration of working with an American census in attempting to understand the Cornish, it is nonetheless possible to identify likely immigrants from Cornwall in order to examine them as a group and understand something of their experience in the American West. The story begins in 1860 before Congress created Nevada. For this year, the census database includes that part of the western Great Basin that would become Nevada in less than a year.[9]

An earlier analysis of the region's Cornish in 1860 concluded that these immigrants were slow to arrive on the Comstock. This was true even though the mining district had claimed international headlines for thirteen months by the time the enumerators documented those living there. The famed 'Rush to Washoe', which began in the summer of 1859, had attracted thousands of fortune seekers by the time enumerators recorded the mining district in August 1860. Although there were a few Cornish, it appears others of these immigrants were reluctant to relocate to a boomtown, perhaps being aware that these places too often burned brightly but briefly. Based on the Comstock example, one might conclude the Cornish preferred to wait to make certain a mining district was a 'sure thing' before relocating. For most people, arriving early was the only chance to exploit the best opportunities, but a Cornish miner with his ethnicity's well-known reputation for underground expertise could arrive at his leisure and still expect the choicest employment.[10]

A large percentage of (non-Cornish) English lived in Carson Valley in 1860, a lush agricultural area at the eastern base of the Sierra Nevada mountains and settled by then for a decade. While other Europeans had few representatives outside the Comstock that year, the English were more widely distributed, but most were probably not Cornish. This suggests that English immigrants, unlike most other Europeans, had been arriving throughout the 1850s before the Comstock mineral discoveries.[11]

The 1870 census

In 1861 the Nevada Territory organized its own government, and then three years later became a state. By 1870, Nevada boasted thirteen counties and a total population of almost 42,000. Of these, the census recorded 2,691 residents as having English nativity, while enumerators specifically identified only seven as coming from Cornwall. An examination of surnames indicates that perhaps as many as 963 of the 2,217 English men and boys were actually Cornish. The Cornish were unevenly distributed, preferring mining communities over places with economies based on other industries. The story of the distribution of these immigrants reveals a great deal about the choices they made in the years leading up to 1870.[12]

The Nevada story of the Cornish begins with the Comstock in the western part of the Great Basin. By 1870, the district's hard-rock mining had thrived for eleven years, following a previous decade of placer mining. Because of the prosperity of the mines and thanks to being the first location of organized mining labour in the West, underground work earned a miner a minimum of four dollars for an eight hour shift, making him the best paid industrial worker in North America, if not the world. More experienced miners could earn six dollars a day. Not surprisingly, the Comstock was internationally attractive for miners, and Storey and Lyon Counties, which shared the Comstock, had stable economies with a mature, skilled labour force.[13]

Dayton, established in 1850, became the seat of government for Lyon County in 1861. Although it was the home base for placer miners working north along Gold Canyon throughout the 1850s, the Comstock discoveries of 1859 eclipsed the older settlement. Virginia City and Gold Hill grew into larger communities, but Dayton continued to serve a valuable function.

Table 1. 1870 counties without a dominant mining industry
(English males indicated the group without those identified as Cornish)

Place	Total males	Total miners	# Irish males	# Irish miners	# English males	# English miners	#Cornish males	#Cornish miners
Churchill	144	0	4	0	3	0	0	0
Douglas	889	0	41	0	32	0	11	0
Ormsby	2,791	28	183	5	75	1	28	1
Washoe*	2,299	12	151	0	56	1	20	2
Total	**6,123**	**40**	**379**	**5**	**166**	**2**	**59**	**3**

* This includes figures from Roop County, which was never incorporated and became part of Washoe County.

Rodda House, Gold Hill: home to the Rodda family from Cornwall.

Situated on the Carson River, Daytonites were able to use the ample supply of water to mill ore taken from the underground mines in the mountain to the north. Also founded in 1859, Lyon County's Silver City, half way between Gold Hill and Dayton, had modest mines supporting stable but limited production. By 1870, Dayton and Silver City, one a twenty-year-old settlement with mills and the other a younger, decade-old mining town, had left their boomtown phase behind them.

Of the 99 'Englishmen' identified in Lyon County, 34, or roughly a third, were apparently Cornish. Nearly half of these were involved directly in mining while only 10, or 15 per cent, of the other English found a career in the excavation of ore. As a point of comparison, only 21, or 13 per cent, of the 168 Irishmen in Lyon County were miners. Almost half of the (non-Cornish) Englishmen – 27 to be precise – found employment in milling and the related foundries compared to seven, or roughly a fifth of the Cornish. Although milling was closely related to mining, most Cornish immigrants apparently shunned processing ore for work underground. In addition to the mines, agriculture thrived in Lyon County's well-watered valleys. Not surprisingly, farming provided an opportunity for others of English nativity but generally the Cornish looked elsewhere. It is a pattern echoed repeatedly throughout the state in 1870.

Storey County, home of the internationally famous mining capital of Virginia City and its neighbour, Gold Hill, was the leading population centre for the state from 1860 through the 1890 census.[14] Like Dayton and Silver City, these places had grown past the volatile boomtown phase years before, but a dependence on mining meant the economy could still change rapidly. Two slumps occurred in the 1860s. Coincidental discoveries in central Nevada, founding Austin, and in White Pine County to the east in Treasure Hill and Hamilton, inspired many to abandon the Comstock when it seemed fortune would shift elsewhere. Nevertheless, Comstock miners always seemed to find the next *bonanza*, using the popular Spanish term for a profitable ore body, and Virginia City and Gold Hill retained the title of Nevada's pre-eminent centre of mining throughout the 1860s and 1870s.

While the Cornish had initially been slow to settle on the Comstock, ten years later they were a prominent part of the mining labour force. The Storey County part of the Comstock, where all of the spectacular mines existed, boasted hundreds of Cornish. Although the Cornish represented a minority of those with 'English' nativity statewide, in Storey County the pattern was reversed. Of the 768 males with 'English' nativity, 495 were apparently Cornish in the 1870 census. Separating the 10 school-age boys from the men and adding the 21 Cornish pursing other mining-related occupations, reveals that 89 per cent of these immigrants worked in the retrieval of gold and silver. This is nearly the entire male Cornish population in Storey County, leaving only a few remaining men pursuing a variety of other occupations.

Austin, the capital of an important mining district in central Nevada, was a magnet for immigrants just as the Comstock was, though on a smaller scale. In 1862, William Talcott discovered silver ore in Pony Canyon, a pass through central Nevada's Toiyabe Mountains. The strike attracted newcomers who established Austin further up the canyon. Because of the growing population, legislators created Lander County in December 1862. Austin boomed the following year. A temporarily depressed Virginia City even contributed its International Hotel to the new rush, businessmen moving the substantial building the 274 kilometers east to the new mining district. Before the end of the year, Austin became the seat of Lander County. Profits peaked during the late 1860s and early 1870s, just when census enumerators were documenting the community.[15]

The 1870 census identified 151 males of 'English' nativity in Austin with 195 in all of Lander County. Mineral Hill, an emerging mining district, was part of Elko County, but within a few years the legislature would remove this part of Elko County to be placed elsewhere. In fact, Mineral Hill was a satellite community of Austin in 1870. Its population should, consequently, be considered here, increasing the number of Lander County males from 'England' to 214. Of these, it is possible to identify 114 Cornish. Their distribution tells a great deal about migration patterns and what these men sought as they settled in a mining district. Austin served as a hub for a large

Table 2.   1870 counties dominated by mining
(English males indicated the group without those identified as Cornish)

Place	Total males	Total miners	# Irish males	# Irish miners	# English males	# English miners	# Cornish males	# Cornish miners
Elko*	2,780	729	166	49	79	12	11	1
Esmeralda	1,257	370	124	71	38	16	16	15
Humboldt	1,549	352†	148	32	87	49	88	82
Lander‡	2,216	1,013	234	162	100	72	114	86
Lincoln	1,687	533	215	117	81	17	26	17
Lyon	1,383	149	168	21	65	10	34	16
Nye	888	287	74	54	25	9	12	6
Storey	7,817	2,603	1,426	864	273	152	495	410
White Pine	6,190	2,369	906	521	341	180	108	62
Total	25,767	8,405	3,486	1,906	1,089	517	904	695
Total all counties	31,890	8,445	3,865	1,911	1,255	519	963	698

* These statistics are for the county without the Mineral Hill population.
† Humboldt County lists miners as 'Quartz Miner', which changes totals if one were to search exclusively for miners.
‡ These statistics include the Mineral Hill population, removed from Elko County.

network of lesser mining districts that burst into existence and survived for shorter or longer periods. By 1870, Austin, like the Comstock, had a proven track record, and 86 Cornish claimed it as home.[16]

The presence of Cornish immigrants in Austin is not surprising, given the supposition that these miners preferred to relocate to stable districts. The remaining 28 Cornish in Lander County are of more interest. The majority – 25 of the Cornish – worked either in Mineral Hill or the Eureka Mining District. These two satellites of Austin were the sites of new mining, so the question arises as to why the Cornish chose to settle there and not in more established camps. A census is a demographic snapshot, which does not indicate how people came and went during the intervening years. Mining towns blossomed and faded throughout the 1860s, and the census is silent on those who passed through during the decade between the times when enumerators completed their work.

While Eureka would eventually become a stable mining town and the seat of a new county carved from Lander County, Mineral Hill had a less promising future. Entrepreneurs founded the Mineral Hill district after discoveries in 1868 and 1869. Both of these areas of mining presented those living in central Nevada with new opportunities at the time of the 1870 census. It is easy to imagine a group of Cornish miners setting off to develop nearby excavations, having already settled in Austin to work in its established industry. All eleven immigrants who appear to be Cornish in Mineral Hill were miners, representing roughly a tenth of that occupation in the district. By 1870, there were only 212 people living there, a place where women and children were rare.[17]

The Cornish who settled in Eureka and Mineral Hill could not know if their new homes would have longevity, so the question remains as to why these immigrants relocated to these places. The answer seems to rest in the proximity of Austin and in its stability. The Cornish avoided coming to the Great Basin immediately after the 1859 discovery of the Comstock Lode, presumably because its long-term prosperity was uncertain and it was a long way from any established mining districts where they might have been working. In all likelihood, they were initially slow to settle in Lander County for similar reasons, but once Austin, the county's seat of government, demonstrated that its mines would produce for years, the Cornish arrived. Satellite camps near Austin did not call for the sort of expense needed to relocate to another region, so the Cornish could choose which opportunities to exploit. They were not evenly distributed among all the peripheral mining camps in 1870. Other towns were devoid of a Cornish presence. The immigrants apparently relocated as teams for mutual support, this ethnic solidarity guaranteeing their status in the new places they selected. There was no reason to believe any of the peripheral districts would survive for long, but from the perspective of the Cornish working nearby, there was little risk by moving to the next valley to exploit the new opportunity for as long as it lasted.

Counties without much of a mining presence in 1870 exhibited other patterns with regard to Cornish immigration. Elko County, in Nevada's northeast corner, has always been far removed from the western clusters of settlements, and is in many ways more connected to its Utah neighbour than to the rest of Nevada. The 1870 census identified 109 men of 'English nativity', 26 of whom are possibly Cornish, but most of these lived in Mineral Hill. This mining district, as discussed above, is best considered in the context of Lander County. Removing Mineral Hill with its Cornish cluster leaves Elko County with 90 'English-born' males and 11 from Cornwall. At the time, Elko depended as much on ranching and the railroad as on mining. Since the transcontinental railroad had arrived just two years before, the local economy was only beginning to show the diversity it would later develop.[18]

While some Elko County mining districts were established early, others were just starting to emerge in 1870. By then, nothing in the county achieved the notoriety or wealth of the Comstock far to the west, the Austin area in Lander County to the southwest, or the newly discovered mines in the Treasure Hill and Hamilton area to the south. Consequently, Elko County did not attract many Cornish immigrants, its mines being either too remote or not sufficiently promising. In contrast, Irish labour managed to find Elko's mining districts.

The story of the Cornish in the western non-mining counties of Washoe, Douglas, Churchill, and Ormsby, home to Carson City, Nevada's capital, repeats what can be observed in Elko County in 1870. These places had scattered immigrants who may have been Cornish, but most men with 'English' nativity appear to have been from elsewhere. Washoe County had a limited mining economy employing three 'English-born' men with solidly Cornish surnames, but this sort of representation was the exception. Taken together, the other counties also had a handful of Cornish miners, but most of those identified as possibly from Cornwall had ambiguous surnames and were removed from the mining industry.

For the most part, the Nevada economy in 1870 relied on mining, scattered across the state, to open development and secure prosperity. Besides those in Storey, Lyon, and Lander Counties, other mining districts exhibited various degrees of success, but their existence was often brief and unremarkable. Humboldt County was largely dependent on mining, and its English and Cornish population followed the pattern described for Lander County. Of the 175 'English-born' males in 1870 in Humboldt County, 88 were likely to have been Cornish. Over half were in Unionville, the county seat and an established centre of mining, and nearly all of the Cornish in the county were involved in mining.

Esmeralda, Nye, and Lincoln Counties, constituting the southern part Nevada, were just opening up as ' stinations for mining in 1870. The combined counties constituted 114,706 square kilometers, or slightly less than the size of England. The total population of these three counties in 1870 was 4,838, which included a few people who had settled at a natural spring known as Las Vegas. There were almost 24 square kilometers per person, but in this sagebrush ocean the inhabited islands were small, scattered communities typically founded on mining.[19] Of those living in this expanse of real estate, only 198 appeared in the 1870 census as 'English-born' males, and 54 of them were possibly Cornish. It was a slim representation of the immigrants for a mining-based region. Some communities in the region were a decade old while others were newer and showing some promise, but regardless of their nature, most towns failed to attract many Cornish. Exceptions included Lincoln County's newly established Pioche, where 18 of the Cornish lived. Esmeralda County's Pine Grove had 11 Cornish in 1870, and Nye County's Silver Peak had 5 of these immigrants, for a total of 34 of the 54 Cornish in three counties. Other Cornish in this expanse were even more thinly distributed among the dozens of mining and agricultural settlements in the region.

Miners established Pine Grove after a discovery in 1866. The town reached its peak in the early 1870s at the time of the census, which recorded a population of 783.[20] Silver Peak also dates to the mid-1860s and had a brief period of prosperity, spanning the 1870s census, which documented 355 residents.[21] Both these places had intermittent prosperity throughout the nineteenth and twentieth centuries but in 1870 it was not possible to determine if they would thrive. The most important of the three communities was Pioche, which was founded in 1869 and in 1872 became the seat of government for Lincoln County. A rush ensued with the earliest discoveries, and the census only a year after the community sprang into existence identified 1,298 residents, roughly a quarter of those living in the three southern counties. Ultimately, Pioche was destined to have decades of mining productivity, but in 1870 that could not have been apparent.[22] The sparse Cornish population in these counties suggests the region's immigrants did not recognize sufficient potential there to justify the move. By 1880, the Cornish would have more of a presence in Pioche, but true to the nature of these miners, they waited to see if relocation to this remote outback was worth the effort.

In 1870, Nevada's outstanding success story was the White Pine Mining District at the eastern edge of the state, which was booming in response to discoveries in the late 1860s. During the 1870 census, Hamilton, Treasure Hill, Shermantown, and several other communities were the heart of the district and the newly created White Pine County, which already boasted 7,189 residents.[23] These included 449 'English-born' males of whom as many as 108 were likely to be Cornish. While this was an impressive number of immigrants, the Cornish represent a lower percentage of 'English born' than in some of the more established mining districts.

The rush to White Pine was one of the great mineral excitements in nineteenth-century North America. It coincided with a brief period of depression on the Comstock and also in Lander County. Contemporary observers noted that people were leaving those mining districts to exploit the new opportunity presented by the silver strikes in the eastern part of Nevada.[24] The Cornish who responded to this rush arrived in numbers greater than those who had come to the 1859 Rush to Washoe, but they were still fewer than elsewhere. For example, the Cornish were half or more of the 'English-born' in Storey, Humboldt, and Lander Counties, which had established mines, while they were less than a quarter of the 'English-born' males of White Pine County. For the most part, the Cornish failed to respond to the White Pine Mining District's initial excitement. It is tempting to regard those who did arrive as following a group decision not unlike the process that apparently populated Mineral Hill and Eureka. Indeed, this new mining district was not far from Austin, the source of so many other mining expeditions, and it is possible that this was their point of origin.

It seems clear that the White Pine example reinforces the conclusion that Cornish miners were generally slow to respond to gold and silver rushes. Most would wait, and in this case, they were prudent. The White Pine Mining District produced a great deal of wealth in a short time, but then it failed for want of extensive ore bodies. Those who did travel to this new opportunity likely found the effort of relocation from depressed Nevada mining districts not so onerous to discourage the effort because of proximity. While relocating from California or elsewhere to the Comstock in 1859 inspired caution, the White Pine Mining District was close enough to established mining districts for over a hundred Cornish to make the move.

The Irish of 1870 offer an opportunity for comparison because they were so numerous and, like the Cornish, they came from United Kingdom. With nearly 4,000 Irish males counted in the 1870 census, this ethnic group was one of the largest in the state. Sheer numbers meant the Irish were likely to be important in every Nevada county. Although many Irish miners had worked in the underground operations of the Bere Peninsula, County Cork and then came to the western United States to market their trade, not all immigrants from Ireland worked in the industry. Only about half the Irishmen sought mining as an occupation. Whether miners or not, these immigrants were quick to respond to new mining districts. The allure of a gold or silver rush was enough to persuade the Irish to follow at a much higher rate than the Cornish. For them, it appears the best strategy was to arrive early, perhaps because if the Irish were late arrivals, there was no guarantee of good employment.[25]

The 1880 census

By 1880, Nevada's mining-based economy was in distress. Still, overall its population had increased, and its economy was beginning to diversify. The state was, nevertheless, dependent on mining, and there were signs the astute could read that indicated a magnificent chapter was about to close. Enumerators recorded 3,009 'English males' living in Nevada, and of these it is possible to identify 1,626 Cornish. Again, Cornish women remain elusive when dealing with census records, so focusing on the men is the only alternative with these data.

While the 1870 census documented a region experiencing the growth of the mining economy, by 1880 the industry was beginning a long painful decline. Numerous anecdotal accounts tell of the Cornish eventually giving up on Nevada during this depression and moving to other states and territories where new mines thrived.[26] The 1880 census provides an opportunity to understand how immigrants responded to the first phase of the failure of the economy.

Many Nevada residents assumed the declining output of gold and silver was temporary as most were unable to perceive that this was actually part of a long downward slide. During the mid-1870s, the Comstock mines had thrived with the discovery of the internationally famous 'Big Bonanza'. Elsewhere in Nevada, mines had also done well, and optimism ran high throughout the region. Nevertheless, by 1880 discoveries of new ore bodies were rare, and the demonetization of silver had begun the process of devaluing one of the state's most plentiful precious metals. The increased number of Cornish in 1880 reflects the prosperity of the 1870s that attracted miners and continued to lure many with the promise of employment.

Although Nevada mining was faltering, diversification in the state's economy created new ways to make a living. Indeed, the population of the state increased considerably, but the number of miners declined from 8,455 in 1870 to 5,964 ten years later. Part of this was due to more specialized terms used by the industry. In 1880, there were far more industry-related workers labeled as 'working in mine' or as 'laborer', but the reality of a declining mining economy was clearly having an effect.

Overall, the number of Cornish men nearly doubled since 1870, and Cornish miners increased from roughly 8 per cent of all those identified in the Nevada census with that occupation to nearly 17 per cent. Mines were closing, and unemployed workers either left Nevada or found other ways to make a living. Still, the presence or absence of Cornish immigrants in the state serves as a map of the economic fortunes of mining districts. A well-paying job could be more important than the long-term health of a mine. The fact that Nevada employed far more Cornish miners in 1880 when the industry was faltering than in 1870 when it was ascending speaks volumes about the strategies of these immigrants. By way of comparison, Irish immigrants in Nevada declined in number and percentage, representing over 12 per cent of the men in 1870, but only 8 per cent in 1880. Furthermore, the Irish were leaving the mines, decreasing from 1,911 miners in 1870 to 1,195 ten years later. So it is reasonable to ask why the number of Cornish increased. The question is answered in part when considering where specifically they lived and worked.

The 59 Cornish men in the non-mining communities of Nevada's agricultural, western valleys represented only about a quarter of the 'English' population living there in 1880 and continued to be of little note numerically. The southern swath of Lincoln, Nye, and Esmeralda Counties included

Table 3.   1880 counties without a dominant mining industry
(English males indicated the group without those identified as Cornish)

Place	Total males	Total miners	# Irish males	# Irish miners	# English males	# English miners	# Cornish males	# Cornish miners
Churchill	349	21	10	2	3	0	1	0
Douglas	1,127	27	40	3	26	0	4	0
Ormsby	3,489	20	147	5	59	0	25	2
Washoe*	3,871	67	139	8	79	2	29	1
Total	8,836	135	336	18	167	2	59	3

* This includes figures from Roop County, which was never incorporated and became part of Washoe County.

Table 4.   1880 counties dominated by mining
(English males indicated the group without those identified as Cornish)

Place	Total males	Total miners	# Irish males	# Irish miners	# English males	# English miners	# Cornish males	# Cornish miners
Elko	3,922	442	174	41	117	32	102	63
Esmeralda	2,470	654	232	143	91	48	76	65
Eureka	5,527	1,228	434	191	318	211	320	263
Humboldt	2,622	299	100	21	72	31	49	43
Lander	2,563	264	250	21	104	16	209	51
Lincoln	1,809	288	106	48	77	26	66	51
Lyon	1,747	212	191	52	48	18	54	32
Nye	1,358	369	105	77	39	17	25	14
Storey	9,228	1,636	1,334	520	291	93	610	374
White Pine	1,963	439	114	64	59	24	56	45
Total	33,209	5,831	3,039	1,177	1,216	516	1,567	1001
Total all counties	42,045	5,966	3,376	1,196	1,383	518	1,626	1004

Cornish Row, above the Divide.

mining communities that had not performed as well as they might have. The overall population grew over the intervening decade from fewer than 5,000 to 7,702 people in 1880. Although the number of Cornish tripled to 167, they were still so few and scattered that they were also of little consequence statistically. Clusters of Cornish lived in places like Lincoln County's Pioche, with its on-going prosperity, but the remoteness of the region apparently combined with the lack of opulence in failing to attract Cornish workers in significant numbers. Ironically, this area would witness the last great gold rush in the continental United States, with the turn-of-the-century strikes at Tonopah and Goldfield, but miners in 1880 could not peer into the future and recognize the region's potential.

Declining prosperity in the White Pine Mining District after its short-lived boom resulted in a precipitous fall in the number of miners by 1880. Most of White Pine County's statistics related to various groups as well as overall population declined by two thirds or more. While the number of Cornish immigrants was halved, miners from Cornwall showed only a slight reduction. The mines may have failed, but sufficient work remained to employ 439 miners, and the Cornish apparently were able to keep their jobs longer than others.

Reflecting the downward trend in the industry, the number of miners working in Lander County's Austin shrank from 1,013 to 264 in 1880. This is in part because the 1880 census enumerator counted many working in the mines as 'laborers', but even if all of the 507 laborers were working underground, there was still a decrease in those employed by the industry. In spite of the loss of employment, the number of Cornish men doubled, and most found employment in the mines.[27] It is possible that some had left in the 1870s, but those who remained were able to do better than others in the mining industry. The presence of Irish men in Lander County, for example, increased over the decade, but number of Irish miners declined dramatically.

Mining also suffered a depression in Humboldt and Elko Counties at the northern end of the state. In the case of Humboldt County, the failure of the industry drove off most of the Cornish who had been there in 1870: those there in 1880 only numbered half of those ten years earlier. In Elko County, however, a reduction in the size of the mining labor force overall was not reflected in fewer Cornish, whose miners increased from one in 1870 to 63 in 1880, representing a significant part of the otherwise shrinking workforce. The 1880 statistics for the two counties tell a story of declining fortunes. Many of Humboldt County's mines had passed below a point where they could be reasonably productive, and so most Cornish left. Fortunes declined in Elko County, but enough employment remained for Cornish miners to linger, and because they could command the best or even the last of the jobs, they were content to stay.

To understand most of the Cornish in 1880, one must consider the Comstock and the newly created county of Eureka. By 1880, the Comstock was twenty-one years old, and for many it still seemed promising. Insiders recognized that discoveries of new ore bodies were scarce and the profitability of the mines was slipping. Over 5,000 miners worked in Storey County's industry in 1875.[28] Their number had declined to 1,636 in 1880, but that does not reflect the many alternative titles employed by the census enumerator for underground work. Still, the work force in the industry had declined by half over the previous five years and by roughly a thousand since 1870. The Irish, who dominated Virginia City, nevertheless saw their numbers fall away in the mines and overall. In spite of this trend, the number of Cornish actually increased over the decade since 1870. As in the case of the mines in Elko County, the Cornish were able to solidify their position as leaders in the industry and become a larger part of the labor force.

It is important to recognize that immigrants from the United Kingdom were critical to the labor force working on the Comstock in 1880. Taken together, they represent a clear majority of the miners. More Irish may have left the industry, but more Cornish arrived, and taken together, labour from the United Kingdom dominated the work underground.

In 1860, a distinction had already begun to emerge that was turning Virginia City Irish and Gold Hill English – and eventually Cornish. The Irish were 9.5 per cent of the entire region's population, but they represented almost 12 per cent of the people living in Virginia City. While there is little evidence of Cornish in the western Great Basin in 1860, the English were 4.3 per cent of region but only 4 per cent of the Virginia City population. In Gold Hill, however, the trend is reversed: the number of Irish declined to roughly 8 per cent while the 'English' population increased to 6.2 per cent.[29]

Understanding the degree of the distinction between a 'Cornish' Gold Hill and an 'Irish' Virginia City is made difficult by the fact that many Cornish eventually lived in an area known as the Divide, which straddled the border between the two communities. Most of the Divide was technically part of Virginia City, and so the spillover of Cornish living there would appear as Virginia City residents. In reality, the Cornish neighborhood ran from Gold Hill, up and over the Divide to the southern part of Virginia City. One street in particular, perched on the hill above the Divide, was known as Cornish Row, but its residents appear in the census as living in Virginia City.[30] The Irish homes were to the north and east, maintaining largely distinct neighbuorhoods. The strength of the Cornish population in Gold Hill is demonstrated by the fact that in 1880, 90 per cent of those with 'English' nativity born in Virginia City City's southern neighbour can be identified as Cornish. The 'English-born' of the Divide follow a similar pattern, leaving the majority of the (non-Cornish) English living in Virginia City proper.

While many Comstockers still saw promise in their industry during the 1880 census, the dramatic success story in Nevada mining at the time was in the Eureka Mining District. Silver ore there was extensive though obnoxiously bound with lead and other minerals. Once millers learned the secret of processing the ore, miners could work ample deposits for years of productivity. Fortunately for Nevada and its workers, Eureka opened up just as other areas were collapsing. As a result of this turn of events, the mining district was the only place in Nevada to show a dramatic increase in the number of miners. Not surprisingly, it attracted the attention of many Cornish looking for new opportunities.[31] Many would eventually leave the state as the depression of the 1880 deepened in the 1890s, but while there were good industry jobs available, the Cornish were usually at the head of the queue.

Conclusion

This analysis of the Cornish in Nevada's federal census records from 1860 to 1880 offers an opportunity to understand choices immigrants were making. It appears the earlier supposition, that Cornish miners were slow to participate in mineral rushes, is supported by evidence collected from the online Nevada census database. The example of the California Gold Rush beginning in 1849 would presumably confirm this conclusion if that state had a similar database. It is unlikely that many Cornish miners were attracted to the opportunity to work for placer gold during the earliest phase of the Californian phenomenon. Once hard rock gold mining began in places like Grass Valley, California, the Cornish arrived in large numbers.[32] There is the possibility that the Nevada pattern of slow participation in mineral rushes was echoed in other western states and perhaps internationally. Testing this idea remains an avenue for future research, but without the data encoded so researchers can easily search census manuscript pages from other states, the question is likely to linger unanswered.

The nineteenth-century census data for Nevada also provide the chance to examine some of the choices immigrants made on the local level. Mineral Hill, Eureka, Treasure Hill, and other places inspired Cornish participation, while many other mining districts did not. Immigrants appear to have employed centres of mining such as Austin as home bases from which they could decide to avoid or pursue new discoveries as circumstances dictated, and it seems they tended to make choices as groups. Perhaps in this observation, it is possible to recognize the basis for the name 'Cousin Jack'. According to at least one popular explanation, neighbours referred to the Cornish with this term because the immigrants always seemed to have a relative they could summon to exploit any given opportunity. The census gives statistical reinforcement to the subjective nineteenth-century observation that the Cornish arrived for work in teams.[33]

That the Cornish were following a distinctive pattern is underscored by comparing them with other groups from the United Kingdom. The Irish and the (non-Cornish) English arrived early and scattered everywhere. The Scots and Welsh, who came to Nevada in fewer numbers, exhibited a similar profile. Although immigrants from the Isle of Man were relatively scarce, they appear to have followed the Cornish pattern. Most Manx were single miners who selected a few mining districts to exploit in groups. When the mines failed, they left, presumably for other opportunities on the international mining frontier.[34]

Ultimately, to understand the nineteenth-century Cornish in Nevada fully, we need to return to other treatments of the Cornish immigrants. Cold census statistics do not give us a comprehensive view of the people. There are inherent flaws in linking surnames and ethnicity. A Cornish surname does not mean the bearer considered himself to be Cornish. Someone with a Cornish surname may have descended from ancestors who had lived for generations someplace other than Cornwall. People and their surnames move, and perspectives change.[35] A presumably Cornish miner raised in Devon becomes the subject of this analysis while his Devonian neighbors are regarded as English. Yet a clear pattern emerges when considering Nevada's census data from 1860 to 1880. The Cornish fill a demographic profile different from that of their (non-Cornish) English counterparts. Within that conclusion – that the Cornish made distinct choices about where to settle and work – is powerful evidence that they were a discrete, relatively cohesive group among those listed in the census as having 'England' as a place of birth.

Notes and references

1. Ronald M. James, 'Defining the Group: Nineteenth-century Cornish on the North American Mining Frontier', in P. Payton (ed.), *Cornish Studies: Two* (Exeter, 1994). Statistics presented in the earlier article do not match those presented here exactly because women and American-born children in Cornish families were included in the earlier discussion. In addition, the previous method of identifying Cornish was more inclusive, allowing for more non-Cornish to be added to the population. Figures presented here should be regarded as more reliable.

2. The database is online at www.nevadaculture.org

3. The database consists of nearly 310,000 files, and it can be searched using each of the data fields in any combination. One can, for example, search for all married, English-born miners in a particular county. The possibilities are only limited by the number of fields in the census. Each census asked different questions, so there can be limitations in making comparison from census to census. Because of a warehouse fire in Washington, D.C. most of the 1890 census data does not exist for the entire nation. This is not, consequently, part of the database.

4. Ronald M. James, 'The Manx in Nevada: Leaving "The Dear Little Isle of Man"', *Nevada Historical Society Quarterly* (accepted for publication; date TBA); as a point of clarification, no one in Nevada appears in the 1860 or 1920 census with place of birth listed as Cornwall.

5. A version of the poem appears in Robert M. Neal, 'Pendarvis, Trelawny, and Polperro: Shake Rag's Cornish Houses', *Wisconsin Magazine of History*, 29 June 1946. Many variations exist.

6. Cornish surnames employed for this exercise came from G. Pawley White, *A Handbook of Cornish Surnames: Enlarged Edition* (Exeter, 1981), from http://freepages.history.rootsweb.com/~kernow/ consulted 2005–06, and from previous work identifying Cornish immigrants to the Comstock conducted with the assistance of Moira Tangye, formally of the Murdoch House/Institute of Cornish Studies 'Cornish American Connection'. Ms Tangye continues to have the author's gratitude for her assistance.

7. That is to say, there are no surnames beginning with these prefixes that seem Cornish. There are no 'Pols' and only a few surnames beginning with 'Pen' or 'Tre', but these people were not born in England and seem to be of other ethnicities. Similar to an Irish Kelly born in England, there is the problem of a Welsh Evans born in England or descendents of Cornish immigrants who had settled in Devon or elsewhere for generations. Cornish-like surnames do not necessarily mean Cornish background or that the bearer thought of himself as a Cornishman. See Bernard Deacon, 'A Forgotten Migration Stream: The Cornish Movement to England and Wales in the Nineteenth Century', in P. Payton (ed.), *Cornish Studies: Six* (Exeter, 1998).

8. James, 'Defining the Group', p. 38; Ronald M. James and C. Elizabeth Raymond, *Comstock Women: The Making of a Mining Community* (Reno, Nevada, 1998), pp. 255–6. For excellent overviews of Cornish immigration see Arthur Cecil Todd, *The Cornish Miner in America: The contributions to the Mining History of the United States by Emigrant Cornish Miners – The Men Called Cousin Jacks* (Spokane, Washington, 1995, reprint; originally 1967); A. L. Rowse, *The Cornish in America* (London, 1969); Philip Payton, *The Cornish Overseas* (Fowey, 1999); and Sharron P. Schwartz, 'Cornish Migrations Studies: An Epistemological and Paradigmatic Critique', in P. Payton (ed.), *Cornish Studies: Ten* (Exeter, 2002). References to women are scattered throughout, but a comprehensive portrait of gender and the Cornish immigrant is as elusive as the women themselves, but for an excellent look at Cornish families, see Shirley Ewart, *Cornish Mining Families of Grass Valley, California* (New York, 1989).

9. See an analysis of the 1860 census for the western Great Basin in Ronald M. James, 'A Tale of Two Wests: A New Census Report for Nevada in 1860', *Nevada Historical Society Quarterly* (accepted for publication; date TBA).

10. The subject of the Cornish and the 1860 census is discussed by the author in *The Roar and the Silence: A History of Virginia City and the Comstock Lode* (Reno, Nevada, 1998) pp. 30–1. Cornish migration was heightened by the failure of mines in Cornwall during the mid-1860s, but there were ample immigrants in the region who could have responded to the first phase of the development of the Comstock.

11. James, 'A Tale of Two Wests'.

12. A search for males with English nativity unfortunately also captures boys, but these are generally rare as the majority of the Cornish in Nevada were not living with families. The 1870 enumerators identified seven people with Cornish nativity, listing them with a place of birth of 'Cornwall' or 'Cornwall England'.

13. See James, *The Roar and the Silence*, pp. 140–2; and Eliot Lord, *Comstock Mining and Miners* (Washington, DC, 1883) pp. 266–7.

14. Although the 1890 manuscript census burned, the census report survives allowing for county-by-county summaries.

15. Donald R. Abbe, *Austin and the Reese River Mining District* (Reno, NV, 1985); Oscar Lewis, *The Town that Died Laughing: The Story of Austin, Nevada, Rambunctious Early-Day Mining Camp and of its Renowned Newspaper, The Reese River Reveille* (Reno, NV, 1986, reprint).

16. It is worth noting that the Cornish were unevenly distributed among Austin's neighbourhoods: they dominated the fourth ward political subdivision and the neighbourhood known as Yankee Blade. This clustering represents evidence of the

Cornish awareness of their specific place of origin as they chose to live together. For the history related to the 1875–77 transference of Mineral Hill from Elko County to the newly created Eureka County (formerly part of Lander County), see Dean Heller, *Political History of Nevada: 2006* (Carson City, NV, 2006, eleventh edition) 125.

17. On the Eureka Mining District and Mineral Hill see Lambert Molinelli and Company, *Eureka and its Resources: a complete history of Eureka County, Nevada, containing the United States mining laws, the mining laws of the district, bullion product and other statistics for 1878, and a list of county officers* (Reno, NV, reprint, 1982) and Shawn Hall, *Romancing Nevada's Past: Ghost Towns and Historic Sites of Eureka, Lander, and White Pine Counties* (Reno, NV, 1994).

18. For Elko County and its mining camps see Shawn Hall, *Old Heart of Nevada: Ghost Towns and Mining Camps of Elko County* (Reno, NV, 1998) and see Myron Angel (ed.), *History of Nevada, 1881* (Oakland, CA, 1881) pp. 384–401.

19. The term 'sagebrush ocean' was used as the title of Stephen Trimble's *The Sagebrush Ocean: A Natural History of the Great Basin* (Reno, NV, 1989).

20. Pine Grove is now part of neighboring Lyon County. Angel, *History of Nevada*, p. 417; Stanley W. Paher, *Nevada Ghost Towns and Mining Camps* (Berkeley, CA, 1970), pp. 81–5; Heller, *Political History of Nevada: 2006*, p. 125.

21. Hugh A. Shamberger, *Silver Peak* (Carson City, NV, 1976); Paher, *Nevada Ghost Towns*, p. 424. A later boundary adjustment identified Silver Peak as part of Esmeralda County.

22. James W. Hulse, *Lincoln County, Nevada: 1864–1909* (Reno, NV, 1971); Angel, *History of Nevada*, p. 487.

23. For a substantial look at the mining district, see W. Turrentine Jackson, *Treasure Hill: Portrait of a Silver Mining Camp* (Tucson, AZ, 1963).

24. James, *The Roar and the Silence*, pp. 78–80.

25. Enumerators recorded 5,046 men, women, and children from Ireland in 1870. For the Irish and Nevada mining see James, 'Ethnicity Defined', and also by the author, 'Timothy Francis McCarthy: An Irish Immigrant Life on the Comstock', *Nevada Historical Society Quarterly* 39:4 (Winter 1996) and 'Erin's Daughters on the Comstock: Building Community', in James and Raymond (eds), *Comstock Women*. And for comparison, see David M. Emmons, *The Butte Irish: Class and Ethnicity in an American Mining Town, 1875–1925* (Urbana, IL, 1989).

26. Numerous sources document the Cornish leaving Nevada. See, for example, Todd, *The Cornish Miner in America*, pp. 203ff; and for the fluidity of the Cornish on the international mining frontier, see Payton, *The Cornish Overseas*, pp. 296–338 and throughout.

27. Many of the Cornish miners are listed in Lander County as laborers.

28. A state census in 1875 documented the state during a mid-decade peak in population. Standards for recordation were low, and this document has not been encoded as part of the database, but it is nevertheless of some use.

29. James, 'A Tale of Two Wests'.

30. This was South Howard Street, now abandoned and little more than a series of archaeological sites. *Gold Hill Daily News*, 24 February 1880, 3:2.

31. Molinelli and Company, *Eureka and its Resources*.

32. Todd, *The Cornish Miner in America*, pp. 54 ff; and see Ewart, *Cornish Mining Families of Grass Valley, California*.

33. Todd, *The Cornish Miner in America*, p. 22; and see Archie Green, 'Single Jack: Double Jack: Craft and Celebration', in Roger D. Abrahams, Kenneth S. Goldstein, and Wayland Hand (eds), *By Land and By Sea: Studies in the Folklore of Work and Leisure Honoring Horace P. Beck* (Hatboro, 1985) pp. 97–100.

34. James, 'The Manx in Nevada'.

35. See, for example, the excellent article on Cornish immigrants with less motivation to perpetuate ethnicity: Dorothy Mindenhall, 'Choosing the Group: Nineteenth-century Non-Mining Cornish in British Columbia', in P. Payton (ed.), *Cornish Studies: Eight* (Exeter, 2000).

6

Representing the Duchy

Francis Acland and Cornish Politics, 1910–1922

Garry Tregidga

Introduction

The first quarter of the twentieth century was a time of rapid change in British politics. Before the First World War the Liberals were the dominant force at Westminster, following their historic landslide victory in 1906 over the Conservatives and their Liberal Unionist allies. By 1924, however, a new order had been created, with Labour and the Conservatives competing for a now declining Liberal vote in order to become the principal party of government. Less obvious were the changes taking place in 'Celtic' Britain. By the outbreak of the First World War the stimulus of the 'Irish question' had led to a renewed interest in Scottish and Welsh concerns over issues like devolution and Anglican disestablishment. Growing disenchantment with Westminster was to culminate in the formation of Plaid Cymru and the National Party of Scotland in the 1920s. The implications for the future were significant since nationalist movements operating outside of the London-based parties had finally been established during a crucial period of realignment for Britain as a whole.

There has been a tendency in Cornish Studies to emphasise the contrasting theme of continuity west of the Tamar. In the first place, economic and social stagnation enabled the Cornish Liberals to survive the early 1920s, a period which Chris Cook termed the Age of Alignment, leaving the old-style radicals firmly secure as the principal alternative to the Conservatives with Labour unable to win even a single seat until 1945.[1] This produced a distinctive pattern of party politics in Cornwall that essentially endures to the present day. One might add that in terms of nationalist politics it was not until the launch of Mebyon Kernow (Sons of Cornwall) in 1951 that a Cornish political movement even existed. Scholars have focused on the non-political stance of early Revivalists like Henry Jenner and the continuing appeal of antiquarianism for organisations like Cowethas Kelto-Kernuak (Celtic Cornish Society) in 1901 and the Old Cornwall movement.[2] Yet by the late 1990s there were indications that both interpretations were starting to be modified in the light of new research. In the immediate aftermath of the First World War, Cornwall was briefly at the forefront in the rise of Labour, with the party's share of the vote in 1918 comparing favourably with other regions destined to become Labour strongholds.[3] Similarly, there has been some consideration of the political dimension to Cornish identity ranging from Jenner's right-wing sympathies to the impact of the Celtic Revival on party politics.[4] Nonetheless, it is surprising that there has been no major study of this critical period in Cornish political history. In particular there is a clear need for an approach that can usefully draw together both avenues of inquiry by placing Cornwall within a wider British context.

This article seeks to initiate further debate through a case study of the early political career of Francis Acland. In December 1910 he was selected to fight the radical stronghold of Camborne and his subsequent twelve years as a Cornish MP coincide with the process of transition taking place in British politics, since by 1922 Labour had already emerged as the national opposition to the Conservatives. After outlining Acland's neglected achievements at Westminster, the article moves to a thematic consideration with his personal experiences analysed in relation to Labour's challenge to Liberalism in a regional framework. His strategy for dealing with this situation, notably through the advocacy of a more meaningful post-war relationship between the Liberal and Labour parties, offers further insight into the history of progressive politics at this time. Biographical studies of individual politicians can also highlight the political dynamics of the provinces. In the case of Acland, the article will focus on the challenge of the Labour movement, the early rise of anti-metropolitanism, and his personal perspectives on Cornwall and the Cornish.

The forgotten Liberal: locating Acland in relation to British and Cornish politics

An article based on a study of Francis Acland (1874–1939) might seem surprising given his virtual invisibility in historical studies of the twentieth century. Although a junior government minister at the War Office and the Foreign Office during the years leading up to the First World War, there are few references to his activities at these key government departments. In 1998 he was not even included in the standard *Dictionary of Liberal Biography*. Although this volume covered the biographies of over 200 individuals associated with British Liberalism, since Acland had not been a party leader, served as a cabinet minister or been recognised as a leading intellectual thinker, he simply did not meet the relevant criteria. In contrast there was a biographical note dedicated to Sir Richard Acland, his more famous son, who had resigned from the party in 1942 after a brief career as MP for the Devon seat of Barnstaple to establish the Common Wealth movement.[5] There has been a similar lack of interest in regard to his place in Cornwall's political history. Philip Payton rightly notes that the 'towering figure of Cornish Liberalism in this period was Isaac Foot'.[6] Indeed, the ability of Foot to personify the regional interests of Cornwall established a model that was to be embraced later in the century by popular and charismatic politicians from Harold Hayman for Labour to David Penhaligon for the Liberals. Significantly, all three politicians are still fondly remembered in oral history recordings relating to Cornwall. By contrast, Acland found it difficult to develop a similar appeal that could enable his parliamentary career to pass into cultural memory.[7] Even at the time there were individuals who dismissed him as merely 'an academic politician' from the aristocratic elite who could not truly understand the daily struggle of his constituents.[8]

But the evidence suggests that Acland's contribution deserves greater recognition. He was the heir to a baronetcy and the extensive Killerton estates across the South West of Britain, including 5,000 acres in Cornwall alone.[9] The Aclands were accustomed to playing a prominent role in provincial affairs, with Francis boasting in his election address in December 1910 that in 'each of the last three centuries members of my family have had the honour of representing Cornish seats in the House of Commons. It will be my constant endeavour that in this century also I may be found no less worthy than they of the trust and friendship of Cornishmen'.[10] During the final years of Herbert Asquith's government he seemed destined to 'go far in the counsels of the nation'.[11] After serving at the Foreign Office he was appointed as Financial Secretary to the Treasury in 1915 and became a member of the Privy Council a year later. Acland also played a key role in the pre-war campaign for women's suffrage, with Jo Vellacott portraying him as the most sympathetic member of Asquith's government.[12] Following the disastrous performance of the Liberals in 1918, Acland briefly emerged as a potential leader of the parliamentary party and a leading advocate of a rejuvenated Liberal-Labour alliance. In the mid-1920s his defection to the David Lloyd George camp resulted in a new role in the party's ongoing policy review. He became a key member of the former wartime leader's inner council alongside more famous individuals like John Maynard Keynes who was responsible for producing the party's radical programme to reduce unemployment entitled *Britain's Industrial Future*, the so-called *Yellow Book*, in 1928. Acland's reputation as a progressive landowner meant that in his case he became the leading figure associated with the party's parallel land reform programme, the *Green Book*.[13] But his subsequent reputation was undermined by his failure to return to the House of Commons – for a lengthy period of eight years – following his defeat in 1924 at Tiverton. When Acland finally managed to win a seat following his narrow victory at the North Cornwall by-election in 1932, the *Liberal Women's New* was lavish in its praise for his parliamentary abilities:

> From every aspect – character, intelligence, experience, tradition – Sir Francis is eminently a parliamentarian; his place should always be among those who help to govern, but owing to the workings of our electoral system and the party's ill luck at [elections] Westminster has missed his front-bench mind for many years.[14]

However, Acland had returned to parliament at a time when the Liberals were once more moving into the political wilderness. In the previous year the other Liberal MPs for Cornwall had been able to strengthen their political reputations by receiving ministerial posts in the National government. Both Walter Runciman at St Ives and Sir Donald Maclean in North Cornwall became members of the cabinet, while Isaac Foot was appointed as the Minister for Mines. In 1933, however, the independent Liberals withdrew their support from the government, and Acland remained out of office for the remaining period up until his death in 1939. Paradoxically, while Acland's absence from parliament came at a critical time in regard to his own political career, it should be acknowledged that he represented constituencies in Cornwall for a longer period than any other Liberal in the twentieth century. His record of nineteen years as MP for Camborne and North Cornwall compares favourably to more well-known individuals like Thomas Agar Robartes (1906, 1908–15), Isaac Foot (1922–24, 1929–35), John Pardoe (1966–79). Paul Tyler (1974, 1992–2005) and David Penhaligon (1974–86).[15] Moreover, his parliamentary victories assisted the survival of Cornish Liberalism at critical times in the party's history. In both 1918 and 1935 he was the only Liberal to be returned for Cornwall and without his success, albeit by narrow majorities, the regional party might well have lost all credibility. A Labour victory in the earlier election could easily have been the catalyst that the socialists required in order to sustain their initial breakthrough. Similarly, success at North Cornwall in the 1930s helped to sustain Liberal traditions during the difficult middle decades of the century when the party appeared to be in a state of permanent decline.

Acland also provides an interesting example of a politician trying to define his position in connection to the conflicting worlds of high and low politics. In retrospect, he was one of the last rising stars in the Liberal Party who could still aspire to high office. The *Cornish Post* described him in 1917 as 'an able and conscious specimen of the cultured and trained' class of parliamentary officials and administrators that had traditionally dominated British politics.[16] By the early 1930s, however, a new generation of Liberals were calling on the party to adjust to the fact that it was no longer able to meet its traditional goal of forming the next government.[17] This was particularly the case in Cornwall where the party was to reposition itself after the Second World War as the anti-metropolitan alternative to the other parties. By studying a particular individual we can obtain further insight into the early stages of political change. The next section will analyse the impact of political change in Cornwall through reference to Acland's own experiences.

Cornwall in transition?

Historians have been divided for many years in their search for a convincing explanation for the rise of Labour and the decline of the Liberals. The view that the social foundations of Liberalism were being undermined by the emergence of Labour even before 1914 has proved very popular. Advocates of this approach, such as Keith Laybourn and Michael Childs, argue that the demise of the old order was only to be expected given the rise of class politics, particularly amongst the younger generation.[18] But other historians have challenged this interpretation. Trevor Wilson claimed that it was the political and social consequences of the First World War that were really responsible, and Duncan Tanner subsequently developed this perspective when he stressed the significance of the wartime collapse of the Progressive Alliance between Labour and the Liberals.[19]

The complex nature of realignment has been essential in maintaining a sense of debate over the reasons for Labour's breakthrough. Yet by the late 1990s scholars were starting to claim that this was also the very reason why the discussion should move to a balanced consideration of the subject. A good example was Andrew Thorpe, who concluded that rival interpretations of the potential of the pre-war Labour Party were often too simplistic considering that there was no 'clear pattern to the movement of events'.[20] Similarly, David Dutton argues the case for a 'multi-dimensional' approach based on a careful and sensitive consideration of the subject that covers both high and low politics. As he puts it, 'whatever the precise truth, it seems improbable that any monocausal explanation will suffice'. Despite the sense of inevitability that was associated with Labour's breakthrough, there is a need to 'accord more importance to the clashes of personality, the accidents of history and ... the individuality of the voter'.[21] Such a view highlights the need to explore realignment from a multiple voices perspective by analysing the careers of individual politicians, recognising the existence of regional variations and exploring counterfactual possibilities.

All three avenues of inquiry can be applied to a case study of Acland's early years in Cornwall. In the first place, his personal story of realignment needs to be located within the micro political environment of Camborne politics. Local studies of the rise of Labour tend to concentrate on those industrial and urban areas of Britain where the party was able to make an early and sustained breakthrough.[22] Although Camborne was essentially an industrial constituency, there was little evidence of a direct parliamentary threat from Labour before the war. Working-class voters in the area still identified with Liberalism rather than Labour and in 1906 a Social Democratic Federation candidate had polled a derisory 1.5 per cent of the vote. Election issues in December 1910 simply echoed the debates of the previous century. Despite references to social reform in Acland's election address, his supporters concentrated on religious concerns like temperance and Welsh disestablishment.[23] The issue of Irish Home Rule was particularly controversial because of the anti-Catholic sentiments associated with Cornish Methodism. Following the Liberal split of 1886 it was the breakaway Liberal Unionists that emerged as the dominant political force in Cornwall and they had survived as the largest political force until 1900. In December 1910 the Unionist candidate for Camborne attempted to shift the focus of the campaign away from House of Lords reform to Irish Home Rule. He argued that 'it would be an everlasting disgrace to the Nonconformists here if they put in a man who voted in favour of ... putting the Nonconformists in the North of Ireland under the heels of a majority ruled by the Catholic priests'.[24] Acland was forced to recognise that many voters had been 'thoroughly worked up by religious bigotry against Home Rule' for Ireland.[25] Nonetheless, the critical factor was that at the local level the Liberal versus Unionist cleavage was still firmly established.

By 1918 there had been a dramatic change in the nature of party politics in Camborne. Labour was able to mount a credible challenge to Acland with George Nicholls, the party's candidate, coming remarkably close to success with 48 per cent of the vote in a straight fight. Acland admitted to Asquith that 'my return was rather a fluke for though I beat a good Labour man in a straight fight, I should not have won if the Tory candidate, ... had been put forward'.[26] The regional weakness of Labour before the war makes its early breakthrough appear even more surprising. One possibility is that the tensions generated as a result of the 1913 China Clay strike in mid-Cornwall had a radicalising effect on the Labour movement throughout the region.

The eventual defeat of the strikers following their bitter campaign for union recognition and a minimum wage of 25 shillings a week is still remembered today. But a recent study by Ronald Perry and Charles Thurlow casts doubt on the long-term importance of the strike. In their view the reality of the conflict was that the clay strikers were isolated from the wider community with 'half the workforce ... reluctant to join in'. More significant for the local Labour movement after the First World War was the impact of wider trends in British industrial relations. Perry and Thurlow conclude that it was only to be expected that Cornwall would be influenced by a rapid expansion in trade union membership throughout the United Kingdom that 'shifted the balance to workers' at the expense of the employers. 'Even without the 1913 strike, and the powerful intervention of the Workers' Union, labour strength in the clay industry would probably have grown'.[27]

This interpretation underestimates the scale of the Labour advance in Cornwall. It was mentioned earlier that in regard to party politics the region was actually leading, not copying, the rise of the British Labour movement by the end of the First World War. Underlying these developments on the electoral front was a growing confidence on the part of the trade unions in industrial areas like the Clay Country and the mining districts further west.[28] Whatever the actual realities of the dispute, it perhaps took on added significance because of the absence of a trade union tradition in Cornwall. With the decline of the mining industry the Clay Country was 'left as the isolated rump of extractive production in an otherwise de-industrialising economy'.[29] In these circumstances the 1913 strike provided a rare symbolic event that could define and articulate the values of the Cornish Labour movement. Although no Labour candidate actually stood in 1918, partly because the abolition of the old St Austell division meant that the Clay Country became part of the much larger seat of Penryn & Falmouth, it became the only major area in Cornwall in which the party made steady progress throughout the inter-war period. Although further research is required in order to conclude if there was a specific relationship between the strike and these subsequent developments, letters written to Acland in 1913 indicate that the strike did have a profound impact on the political culture of the time. J. F. Williams, a solicitor from Gorran Haven, remarked on 2 September that police tactics were making the strikers feel 'outcasts, with all society fighting against them':

> I went round most of the clay district this afternoon in a motor. There were policemen everywhere. The whole place had a Russian appearance. Groups of men were on the peaks of the St Austell Alps like the chamois in Cook's pictures of Switzerland. The district is quiet – terrorised into quiet. But the whole countryside is full of rumours;

this morning in our little fishing village – and we have no connection with the strikers – over 11 miles away – there was a rumour that a man and a little girl had been killed by the Welsh strike-breakers – and things were said not pleasant for a Liberal to hear.[30]

Acland's private correspondence also gives particular prominence to the impact of the Asquith-Lloyd George split of December 1916. Just at the very moment when a more confident Labour movement was emerging in Cornwall, the Liberals were distracted by events at Westminster. A few months after the formation of Lloyd George's wartime coalition Acland was already warning of the rise of socialism and the demise of his own party. In May 1917 he remarked that Camborne was 'going Labour as fast as it can' and a month later expressed doubts that there was even 'going to be a Tory and Liberal party anymore'.[31] With Lloyd George, the former champion of radical Liberalism, now in alliance with the Conservatives, such views were to be expected. Moreover, Acland was frustrated by the failure of Asquith to mount a real challenge to the government. Writing towards the end of 1917 he claimed that the former Prime Minister was 'too much of a gentleman to hit hard'. The party was also failing to develop a post-war reconstruction programme and he was critical of the 'ex-Cabinet ministers [who] might have done more than they have done in working out policies on social questions'. Acland concluded that 'I really think the Liberal party is dead & that one will simply have to think of men & policies after the war – not of parties'.[32] Such comments tend to support the view that it was internal divisions that created a negative mindset amongst radical Liberals. This sense of a party in a state of imminent demise is evident in the following letter written to Acland in August 1918 by C. A. Millman, the Liberal agent for Bodmin:

No one can deny that our position as a party is being gradually undermined and our power for usefulness destroyed. We look for a lead in the House of Commons and in the country but we look in vain. Meanwhile the Tories, accustomed to underhand methods, and the Labour party with a courage and purpose I admire and should much like to emulate, are preparing for the struggle which cannot long be delayed. We are daily losing supporters because we refuse to formulate a well-conceived programme. Never in our political history has a great political party been content to allow judgement to go against it by default.[33]

Within a year such views were to lead Millman to defect to Labour. His personal transition from radicalism to socialism was symbolic of similar decisions being taken by many other erstwhile Liberals. Yet it also suggests that the rise of Labour was far from an inevitable process. What was crucial was the existence of an independent Labour party at this time that could offer an alternative home for those radicals who were disillusioned by the actions of Lloyd George and the inactivity of Asquith. In May 1919 Charles Trevelyan, a former junior minister in Asquith's government, remarked to Eleanor, the wife of Francis, that parties were 'only methods of combining for political purposes'. He justified his defection to Labour on the grounds that it offered an alternative vehicle for progressive politics. Since the Liberals had now lost their reputation for moral and intellectual leadership, it was time for Radicals to look elsewhere. He added that he did not 'expect much from the Labour party except that it will manage to evolve the organisation which will pretty soon get hold of the government, probably to make a horrid mess of it'. What was important was that it offered 'a new conscience and policy' that contrasted markedly with the timidity of the Asquithian leadership.[34] In that sense his views echoed Acland's belief that the post-war order would be based on 'men & policies' rather than parties.

With hindsight it can be said that realignment actually resulted in rigid electoral polarization based on powerful party machines, rather than loose and competing programmes reflecting principles and ideas. Yet a consideration of developments in Cornwall indicates that we should avoid assumptions of inevitability in relation to the process of realignment. For example, it was mentioned earlier that the career of Isaac Foot, the founder of a political dynasty that was to include a future leader of the Labour Party, is synonymous with the survival of Cornish Liberalism. In early 1918 this seemed a remote possibility since Foot wanted to retire prematurely from active politics in order to devote more time to a young family and growing business commitments. A plan was arranged for Acland to withdraw from Camborne in order to contest Bodmin, and it was only shortly before the 1918 election, probably due to Acland's decision that the honourable course of action was to defend his own seat, that Foot agreed to fight Bodmin.[35] It is worth speculating on the long-term implications. The Foot tradition was to become central to the cultural memory of Cornish Liberalism following his by-election victory at Bodmin in 1922. This symbolic event, which sustained the party's traditions at the very moment when the Liberals were under threat at the micro level, was vital in paving the way for subsequent regional victories in 1923 and 1929.[36] One might add that the strength of Cornish Liberalism down to the present day can be traced back to the inspirational stimulus of the Foot era. Yet in reality this particular course of events was far from inevitable in the closing months of the war.

Just as likely at the time, perhaps, was Acland's own vision of a new progressive force. He believed that an opportunity now existed for 'an entirely new division of parties' that could bring about a revival in progressive politics based on an equal partnership between Labour and the independent Liberals.[37] Rather than the demise of organized Liberalism he envisaged a natural extension of the pre-war Lib-Lab pact, which had been responsible for the early expansion of Labour as a parliamentary force. Cornwall was to be in the forefront of collaboration with Acland's move to Bodmin paving the way for a regional pact in which Labour would be offered the opportunity for a straight fight against the Conservatives in Camborne and possibly another Cornish seat. In return the Liberals would be able to make their 'position absolutely safe and sure with regard to the remaining three seats'.[38] The proposal demonstrated the decline of morale amongst the Liberals since their historic victory in all seven Cornish constituencies in 1906. It also led to a serious bid by Acland to transform the cause of progressive politics throughout Britain. Following Asquith's defeat in 1918 he was to present himself as the 'Radical' contender for the chairmanship of the parliamentary party with the aim of forming a close alliance with Labour. It could be argued that the failure of his challenge had serious implications for the subsequent development of British politics as a whole. Yet the significance for Cornwall is that it challenges assumptions that the survival of Liberalism was inevitable just in the same way that it has been suggested that change was guaranteed elsewhere. In reality the period immediately before and after the end of the First World War was characterised by fluidity rather than political continuity.

The Cornish Question

The subject of political realignment should not be restricted to the established debate surrounding the rise of Labour. By the 1920s there were indications that British politics was moving in a variety of directions, ranging from a strengthening of the rural-urban divide to the emergence of territorial parties in the 'Celtic fringe'. Taking rural politics momentarily as an example, it could be argued that the ability of the Liberals to make significant gains from the Conservatives in agricultural constituencies in the early 1920s demonstrated that the potential for realignment went further than just the core process of Labour replacing the Liberals. By establishing a secure bloc of rural seats, some Liberal strategists concluded that their party would then be in a credible position to present itself as the real alternative to Labour.[39] Even in the early 1930s Acland believed that the key to a Liberal revival was the party's ability to 'wrest control of the countryside from the Conservatives'.[40] Indeed, it is no coincidence that the survival of Cornish Liberalism after the Second World War was more evident in rural Bodmin and North Cornwall, rather than in the industrial areas further west. However, the main purpose of this particular section is to focus on the growing impact of territorial politics in Acland's Cornwall. It will examine the fusion of Celtic rhetoric and anti-metropolitanism in the region's political culture, with a view to developing a wider picture of the Cornish Celtic Revival. The implications of this process for Cornwall's subsequent political alignment are then considered.

Before returning to Acland it is necessary to briefly review the historiography of the Revival. It was noted earlier that the emergence of the Celto-Cornish movement in the late nineteenth and early twentieth centuries has been seen as an essentially cultural phenomenon. Bernard Deacon in the 1980s remarked that 'The Cornish Revivalists, more than their Celtic colleagues, positively wallowed in the un-reason of Romanticism'.[41] Its central concern was with the restoration of the Cornish language along with the creation of new cultural institutions such as Gorseth Kernow (the Cornish Gorsedd) in 1928. Payton points out that there 'were, predictably, no corresponding political or economic aims'.[42] Leading figures like the Rev. W. S. Lach Szyrma and Thurstan Peter were unable to embrace the cause of Cornish Home Rule due to their personal support of the Conservative and Liberal Unionist parties. In any case, the Revivalists themselves admitted that their activities had 'scarcely touched the lives of the common people in Cornwall'.[43] Amy Hale, writing in 1997, asserted that in the early 1900s 'Celtic status was not then a burning issue in Cornwall itself'. Cowethas Kelto-Kernuak's campaign to persuade the pan-Celtic Celtic Association to recognise the Duchy as a Celtic nation was hardly popular since 'the press was at best ambivalent ... and the issue drew virtually no response from the public'.[44] The general consensus, then, is that the early Cornish Revivalists were an apolitical and marginal force that was unable to engage with wider trends in society at the very moment when their counterparts in Scotland and Wales were laying the foundations of separate nationalist parties.

But when it comes to the politics of Cornish identity, there is a need to reassess the wider influence of the Revival. A useful starting point is Acland's own election campaign at Camborne in December 1910, which provides some revealing insights into the way in which a popular sense of 'Celticity' was already starting to make an impact on political debate. For example, when Acland declared his support for Irish Home Rule at his adoption meeting he added that this move could then be followed by devolution for Scotland, Wales, England and Cornwall.[45] Local newspapers referred to the Celtic character of the Cornish electorate with the *Cornubian* comparing Acland to other 'great Parliamentary speakers [that] have come into Cornwall to find that their eloquence is foreign to the locality, for Cornishmen have a Celtic love of fervid speech'.[46] An 'outsider' whose debating skills did prove popular with Cornish voters was George Hay Morgan, Liberal MP for the adjacent constituency of Truro from 1906 to 1918. Truro had been a Unionist seat since 1886 but Morgan, a Baptist preacher and a former member of the Welsh nationalist movement Cymru Fydd, went out of his way to attract the Methodist vote by preaching in the principal chapels in his constituency. Even in December 1910 when the Unionist champion was Charles Williams, the son of a popular local landlord, the Liberals were able to retain the seat. Significantly, Morgan justified his right to represent a Cornish seat on the grounds that he was a fellow Celt. In an election speech he expressed his admiration for 'Mr Williams because he was a Cornishman, a Celt, and he (Mr Morgan) was that. They all belonged to the same stock, of the same blood and line but the ancestors of one went to Mid Wales and of the other to West Wales ... They were all Welshmen'.[47]

Experienced politicians like Morgan were unlikely to make such statements if a general sense of Cornwall's Celtic identity was not understood in relation to the popular culture of the time. A possible catalyst for this emerging Celtic discourse during the years leading up to the First World War was Cornwall's eventual acceptance as a 'Celtic nation' at the 1904 Celtic Congress. Despite the ambivalence of some local newspapers, the fact that the campaign was reported at all was significant since it appears to have encouraged a greater public use of the word 'Celtic' in relation to Cornwall's political and religious culture in subsequent years.[48] References to Cornwall's 'Celtic passion for liberty' or the 'Celtic fervour' of Cornish Methodism could in any case be understood through a popular understanding of the region's past. It is recognized today that 'much earlier in the eighteenth and early nineteenth centuries, the Cornish intelligentsia had already constructed its own ethnic history' through the writings of individuals like William Borlase and Samuel Drew.[49] Moreover, political activists in the Liberal Party, in contrast perhaps to the Celtic Revivalists themselves, were able to make an instinctive connection between cultural and nationalist politics. A good example was Alfred Browning Lyne, editor of the *Cornish Guardian* and a future chairman of Bodmin Liberal Association. In 1912 he expressed his support for Cornish Home Rule after making the logical assumption that the antiquarian agenda of Cowethas Kelto-Kernuak would inevitably lead to calls for regional autonomy:

There is another Home Rule movement on the horizon. Self-government for Cornwall will be the next move. There has been a remarkable revival in the pan-Celtic movement, particularly in Brittany. 'Bretons will not be satisfied', we read, 'until they have reinstated their native land as a federal state under the French flag, but with as much independence as the ... German States. They want Home Rule'. In these seditious ideas, Cornishmen appear to be sharing ... It is true that the programme sketched out for the [Cornish] Association at present is simply 'the

study and discussion of Celtic relics, literary, artistic, and legendary'.
But who can doubt that it means 'separation'?[50]

Lyne's interpretation of the Revival also reflects the importance of pan-Celtic issues in pre-war British politics. The campaign for Irish Home Rule was increasingly linked to a wider agenda that included the disestablishment of the Anglican Church in nonconformist Wales and the creation of a federal system of government for the British Isles. For the Cornish Liberals the Duchy's official recognition in 1904 as a Celtic nation had been timely. The opposition was campaigning on a pro-English and anti-Celtic platform that criticized Asquith's government for neglecting the national interest in favour, as Acland's Unionist opponent in Camborne put it, of 'Ireland for the Irish, Scotland for the Scottish, Wales for the Welsh and England for the foreigner'.[51] By presenting their policies in a pan-Celtic context the Liberals attempted to deflect these attacks by appealing to Cornish patriotism. A space for nationalist politics was created in the process, with a 'Cornish question' now starting to be posed alongside the more established 'Irish question'. In terms of practical policies there is evidence that an anti-metropolitan agenda was starting to emerge at this time based on policies ranging from Acland's own concern for the local issue of leasehold enfranchisement to calls for greater financial assistance from the state to support the Duchy's farming and fishing interests.[52]

It was the issue of Anglican disestablishment that raised the prospect of some form of separate constitutional accommodation for Cornwall. The Cornish Celtic Revival has been portrayed as a 'quest to rebuild a pre-industrial Celtic-Catholic culture in Cornwall' that was unable to 'address [its] aspirations to the Methodist majority'.[53] It was certainly the case that key figures in the early days of the Revival like Jenner, Louis Duncombe Jewell and Lach Szyrma were either High Anglicans or Roman Catholics. But this did not mean that the nonconformists were unreceptive to the cultural discourse of the Celtic Revival. Even Jenner remarked in 1904 that 'a very large proportion' of the support for his Cornish language work came from 'the classes of hard-working clerks, small business men, shopkeepers, and artisans, the classes that form the backbone of Cornish Methodism – a very different sort of people from the same classes in a non-Celtic country'.[54] Comparisons were also made with the nationalist campaign for Anglican disestablishment in nonconformist Wales. Advocates on both sides of the debate acknowledged that Cornwall's Celtic identity could be used to justify its independence from the jurisdiction of the established Church of England.[55] A revealing insight can be seen in the comments of Mr T. J. Bennetto, the headmaster of Mevagissey Council School, who gave a talk on Cornwall's Celtic identity to the congregation of Mount Charles United Methodist Chapel in March 1912.

Bennetto concluded that Cornwall's ability to maintain 'its independence for so long differentiated [it] from every county in England. With regard to the Christian religion it could be said of Cornwall, as Mr Lloyd George had said of Wales, that the Established religion was an imposition'.[56] Once again there is a need to look beyond the beliefs and activities of Cowethas Kelto-Kernuak in order to understand the full impact of the Revival on Liberal-Nonconformist Cornwall.

However, the failure of the Liberals to support the Cornish anti-redistribution campaign during the First World War highlights the limitations to that party's ability to act as a surrogate nationalist movement. In 1917 there was widespread opposition across the political spectrum to the recommendations of the boundary commission for a reduction in Cornwall's parliamentary representation from seven to five seats. A petition was organised by local councils, trade unionists and political activists in favour of a compromise measure of six seats that would allow for the historical link to continue between parliamentary divisions and local industries.[57] The latter concern was of particular importance to St Austell, with its china clay interests, and Camborne, which was popularly known as the 'Mining Division'. Interestingly, it was Acland who emerged as the principal opponent of the campaign. Although the Liberals had been the 'pioneers of the six-seat scheme', the member for Camborne undermined the chances of an all-party alliance by publicly declaring that the 'Liberals were honourably bound not to try to disturb the redistribution proposals'.[58] With Cornwall's other Liberal MPs generally loyal to the new Lloyd George Coalition the anti-redistributionists required Acland's support to mount an effective challenge. In the event Cornwall's representation was reduced to just five seats as a result of the changes implemented by the 1918 Representation of the People Act.

What was significant about the campaign was the way in which it appealed to regionalist sentiment. The official petition document called on central government 'to grant them a one and undivided Cornwall which will satisfy all local interests, aspirations and feelings'.[59] This concern for the region's territorial integrity was to become the cultural pivot, as Deacon suggests, for ethnic mobilization in Cornwall in the second half of the twentieth century.[60] Moreover, the anti-redistributionists consciously adopted the model advocated in connection to the 'Irish Question' in order to justify separate accommodation for Cornwall. Gladstone in 1885 had defended the principle of greater representation for Ireland on the grounds that the more remote parts of the United Kingdom required special treatment since they were so far from London. The anti-redistributionists now argued that this precedent should be applied to Cornwall. Intriguingly, the *Cornish Post*, which supported the campaign, now promoted the views of Reginald F. Reynolds, a member of Cowethas Kelto-Kernuak in the early 1900s. Reynolds claimed that the real problem for the Revivalists was that they had been 'struggling to find expressions of their views' until the emergence of the threat to Cornwall's parliamentary representation. He added that 'Home Rule reigns in the heart of the Cornish' and saw the anti-redistribution campaign as a unique opportunity to 'put the Cornish case' to Westminster.[61] Acland was forced on the defensive by newspaper criticism of his stance. He claimed that extra seats for Cornwall could not come at the expense of those urban areas that had 'grown enormously since the last redistribution' and denied the claim 'that this can be dealt with solely as a Cornish question' since the national interest had to take priority:

> I am quite aware that I might become the most popular man in the Duchy by running a campaign that Cornwall is of such special importance that there must be no reduction of the present membership. But this is not a time for bothering about personal popularity. It's a time for facing up to facts, and the facts are that we must either accept the present proposals or work out a new system more likely to be generally approved.[62]

These comments underline the fact that the absence of effective parliamentary support was a serious problem for the embryonic cause of Cornish nationalism. Despite occasional appeals to Celtic and regionalist sentiment on the part of the Duchy's Liberal MPs, there was no individual prepared to take on the mantle of leadership, in contrast to Ireland and Wales. This certainly applied to Acland who preferred to focus on the great issues of state. A good example of his lack of interest in low politics can be seen in a letter written to his wife Eleanor in November 1917 when he revealed his true feelings on the subject of redistribution. Writing from the House of Commons he remarked that he had to remain in London 'in case we reach Cornwall in the Schedules to the Reform Bill – not that there's anything much I want to say but that if every other Cornish member says something I must'.[63] Although placing great emphasis in public on his duty and responsibilities in representing the interests of his constituency, he preferred to focus his energies on securing the core goals of female suffrage and proportional representation under the terms of the 1918 Act.

Acland's growing disenchantment with Cornwall was another factor. His letters to Eleanor express his frustration with the nonconformist sentiments of a community that, as he saw it, seemed to believe in the 'sinfulness of feeling happy'.[64] The impact of war appeared to strengthen the fundamentalist beliefs of the hard core of Cornish Methodism, resulting in the refusal of many nonconformist farmers to work on the Sabbath, public criticism of sexual immorality in the armed services, and a popular campaign for the total prohibition of alcohol.[65] It was the latter concern that caused particular problems for Acland, since his moderate policy of simply controlling the liquor trade was not acceptable to his local party activists. He claimed that 'the good citizens of St Day, Lanner & St Agnes' were only interested in the 'Drink question' rather than the wider issues of foreign affairs and post-war reconstruction.[66] Indeed, he portrayed wartime Cornwall as a parochial and insular society, with his constituents opposing the presence of 'outsiders' and critical of his wartime absence from Camborne. Acland's frustration with the Cornish increasingly took on racial overtones during the war. This included patronizing comments about 'their present state of development' and the claim that 'it was quite impossible to judge what they were thinking of, if anything'.[67] One might add that Acland was not alone in expressing racist remarks about the Cornish. Before the First World War Lyne wrote of his annoyance at the tendency for 'outsiders' to dismiss Cornwall as an uncivilised place where 'perhaps it is thought the natives eat a missionary now and then'.[68] In the case of Acland, we have an example of an individual who could only relate to Cornwall through an appreciation of its landscape rather than any sense of affinity with its inhabitants:

> After the Redruth meeting I've had a regular Cornish time. Utterly unable to find any sign that the people regard themselves as citizens or have any sort of duties in connection with carrying on the war ... We had a jolly time this morning at Tehidy and on the north cliffs. There was a fair sea on & hundreds of gulls resting on the rocks and flying up and filling the air whenever we looked over. They were pairing but not nesting yet, and a raven, & flocks of jackdaws flying higher than the gulls. And all the gulls screamed. It started a drizzly day but gradually cleared and a good cold wind got up and I really like it ... I slept all the afternoon and that was pleasant but that and the cliffs were the only things I've liked.[69]

Acland's frustration was to lead to his retirement from Camborne in 1922. Yet his preference for high politics was to be repeated by other Liberal candidates. During the 1920s Cornwall's reputation as one of the party's few remaining strongholds meant that it attracted the attention of national politicians in search of a safe seat. The classic example was in 1929 when three out of the five Cornish MPs had previously served as government ministers under Asquith or Lloyd George.[70] Isaac Foot's personal popularity in Cornwall perhaps reflected the fact that he was a rare example of a Liberal MP who was able to build a political career through his personal efforts at the community level. Even his son John, who was to contest Bodmin for the Liberals after the Second World War, was to declare in 1950 that there 'were too many MPs already who were more concerned with the welfare of their own constituencies than with the wider and more important national and international issues'.[71] Paradoxically, such sentiments ran parallel to continuing attempts to portray Liberalism as the peninsula's natural ideology, with claims in the inter-war period that 'Cornishmen had always been Liberals' and only Liberals could 'understand Cornish folk'.[72] Preliminary oral history research suggests that it was this regionalist dimension to the party's identity in Cornwall that passed into cultural memory. A recorded group discussion in 2000 found that interviewees tended to make sense of their political memories through reference to stories about 'local' Liberals like Robartes and Foot. One individual even summed up political alignment before the Second World War by claiming that 'If you wasn't Methodist and Liberal you weren't Cornish'.[73]

These conflicting agendas influenced the subsequent development of electoral politics. The popular perception that the Liberals were Cornwall's traditional party helped them to compete effectively against Labour and the Conservatives. On the other hand the party's electoral position might well have been weakened in the long term by the perception that its MPs simply regarded Cornwall as a way of returning to Westminster. In 1935 a party activist in Camborne complained that 'We have had Liberal members in this division whom we have never seen nor heard of after they have been elected'.[74] Acland was undoubtedly one of those individuals since he had been criticised by his own supporters for this very reason. The problem was that inter-war Cornwall was no longer a Liberal stronghold. All of the seats won by the party in three-cornered contests in this period were held by relatively slender majorities. This meant that it was essential for sitting members to address local concerns in order to retain vital votes. It was a point recognized by a series of Conservative MPs like Peter Agnew (Camborne, 1931–50) and Douglas Marshall (Bodmin, 1951–64) who gradually consolidated their party's supremacy at the local level during the middle decades. Whilst there is an understandable tendency to focus on the myth of Liberal Cornwall, given the party's survival as an effective force, consideration should also be given to the failure to retain its traditional strongholds in contrast, for example, to rural Wales. Part of the answer may well have been the general absence in Cornwall of Liberal candidates who could identify with their constituencies. There were also implications for nationalist politics. The emergence of a 'Cornish Question' in the pre-war period had suggested that the Duchy was moving in the same direction as the other Celtic nations. Yet there were no effective agencies to sustain this interest into the 1920s. In the same decade that nationalist parties were formed in Scotland and Wales the Cornish Revivalists could only attempt to attract public opinion by creating cultural institutions. The Cornish Liberals, now lacking the external stimulus of pan-Celtic causes like Welsh disestablishment, and with a parliamentary leadership looking to Westminster, were unable to fill the void by building on pre-war developments and reinventing themselves as a consistent anti-metropolitan force.

Conclusion

Acland represented Camborne at a critical period in Cornwall's political history. The early appeal of Labour, combined with the impact of the Cornish Celtic Revival on popular culture, appeared to be leading to a realignment of Cornish politics in line with developments elsewhere in Britain. By the early 1920s, however, there was to be a return to the old order. To some extent social and economic conditions in Cornwall were not really conducive to political change. The lack of a trade union tradition, following the decline of mining in the previous century, along with the strength of small family businesses in sectors like agriculture, certainly presented obstacles to Labour. A similar weakness could be seen in regard to the antiquarian nature of the Celtic movement in Cornwall. Yet this study suggests that we should recognize the part that individuals and events can play at a time of transition. Acland's failure to lead the anti-redistribution campaign in 1917 came at a time when the 'Cornish question' had been placed firmly on the political agenda. It could also be argued that his decision to fight Camborne rather than Bodmin in 1918 indirectly led to Foot emerging as the champion of traditional radical nonconformity in the early 1920s. By examining the actions and beliefs of a forgotten Liberal we can, therefore, gain greater insight into the history of twentieth-century Cornish politics as a whole.

Notes and references

1. C. Cook, *The Age of Alignment: Electoral Politics in Britain, 1922–1929* (London, 1975). For an emphasis on continuity in Cornish politics see G. Tregidga, 'The Survival of Cornish Liberalism, 1918–45', *Journal of the Royal Institution of Cornwall*, n.s. II, Vol. 1, Part 2 (1992), pp. 211–32; P. Payton, *The Making of Modern Cornwall: Historical Experience and the Persistence of 'Difference'* (Redruth, 1992), pp. 156–9; P. Payton, 'Labour Failure and Liberal Tenacity: Radical Politics and Cornish Political Culture, 1880–1939', in P. Payton (ed.), *Cornish Studies: Two* (Exeter, 1994), pp. 83–95.
2. For examples see Payton, *Making of Modern Cornwall*, pp. 128–35; A. Hale, 'Genesis of the Celto-Cornish Revival? L. C. Duncombe-Jewell and the Cowethas Kelto-Kernuak', in P. Payton (ed.), *Cornish Studies: Five* (Exeter, 1997), pp. 100–11.
3. G. Tregidga, 'Socialism and the Old Left: The Labour Party in Cornwall during the

Inter-War Period' in P. Payton (ed.), *Cornish Studies: Seven* (Exeter, 1999), pp. 74–94. See also T. Crago, "'Play the Game as Men Play It'": Women in Politics during the Era of the "Cornish Proto-Alignment", 1918–1922', in P. Payton (ed.), *Cornish Studies: Eight* (Exeter, 2000), pp. 213–30.

4. S. Lowena, "'*Noscitur A Sociis*'": Jenner, Duncombe-Jewell and their Milieu', in P. Payton (ed.), *Cornish Studies: Twelve* (Exeter, 2004), pp. 61–87; 'G. Tregidga, 'The Politics of the Celto-Cornish Revival, 1886–1939', in P. Payton (ed.), *Cornish Studies: Five* (Exeter, 1997), pp. 125–50.

5. D. Brack (ed.), *Dictionary of Liberal Biography* (Politicos, London, 1998), p. 3.

6. Payton, *The Making of Modern Cornwall*, p. 157.

7. For examples of oral history recordings on this subject see Cornish Audio Visual archive (CAVA hereafter), AV1/165, interview with H. Beswetherick, 17 May 2002; CAVA, AV1/176, interview with I. Sowell, 30 July 2002; CAVA, AV1/464, interview with G. Pawley White, 5 May 2004. See also Rescorla Centre Collection, RA/1/1, group recording, 4 December 2000.

8. *Cornish Post*, 23 November 1918.

9. For a study of the Acland family see A. Acland, *A Devon Family: The Story of the Aclands* (Chichester, 1981). See also G. Tregidga (ed.), *Killerton, Camborne and Westminster: The Political Correspondence of Sir Francis and Lady Acland, 1910–29* (Exeter, 2006).

10. National Liberal Club collection of election addresses, University of Bristol Library, DM 668, election address of Francis Acland in December 1910.

11. *West Briton*, 22 December 1910.

12. J. Vellacott, *From Liberal to Labour with Women's Suffrage: The Story of Catherine Marshall* (Montreal, 1993), pp. 267, 279.

13. For a discussion of Acland's career from 1918 to 1928 see Tregidga, *Killerton, Camborne and Westminster*, pp. 12–17, 27–30.

14. *Liberal Women's News*, September 1932, p. 804.

15. Acland's record has only recently been overtaken by Matthew Taylor, MP for Truro and St Austell since 1987.

16. *Cornish Post*, 5 July 1917.

17. D. Foot, 'The Liberal Crisis', *Contemporary Review*, Vol. 139 (May 1931), pp. 582–8.

18. H. Pelling, *Popular Politics and Society in Late Victorian Britain* (London, 1968); K. Laybourn, *The Rise of Labour: The British Labour Party, 1890–1979* (London, 1988); K. Laybourn, 'The Rise of Labour and the Decline of Liberalism: The State of the Debate', *History*, vol. 80 (1995), pp. 207–26; M. Childs, 'Labour Grows Up: The Electoral System, Political Generations, and British Politics, 1890–1929', *20th-Century British History*, vol. 6 (1995), pp. 123–44.

19. T. Wilson, *The Downfall of the Liberal Party, 1914–1935* (London, 1966); D. Tanner, *Political Change and the Labour Party, 1900–1918* (Cambridge, 1990).

20. A. Thorpe, *A History of the British Labour Party* (London, 1997), p. 31.

21. D. Dutton, *A History of the Liberal Party in the Twentieth Century* (Basingstoke, 2004), pp. 2–3.

22. Examples include D. Clark, *Colne Valley: Radicalism to Socialism* (London, 1981); I. McLean, *The Legend of Red Clydeside* (Edinburgh, 1983); K. Laybourn and D. James (eds), *The Rising Sun of Socialism* (Wakefield, 1991); D. Tanner, C. Williams and D. Hopkin (eds), *The Labour Party in Wales, 1900–2000* (Cardiff, 2000).

23. *Cornubian*, 1 December 1910.
24. *Royal Cornwall Gazette*, 1 and 8 December 1910.
25. *Cornubian*, 1 December 1910; Acland papers, Devon Record Office, 1148 M 14/516, F. Acland to E. Acland, December 1910.
26. Asquith papers, Bodleian Library, MS. Asquith 33, fol. 34, F. Acland to H. Asquith, 29 December 1918.
27. R. Perry and C. Thurlow, 'The 1913 China Clay Dispute: "One and All" or "One–That's All"?' in P. Payton (ed.), *Cornish Studies: Fourteen* (Exeter, 2006) pp. 187–203.
28. Acland papers, 1148 M/667, F. Acland to E. Acland, late 1917. *Cornish Guardian*, 21 February 1918. *Western Morning News*, 2, 5, 12 and 16 December 1918.
29. Payton, *Making of Modern Cornwall*, p. 145.
30. National Archives, Kew, HO 45/10710/24202, J. F. Williams to F. Acland, 2 September 1913.
31. Acland papers, 1148 M 14/667, F. Acland to E. Acland, 28 May 1917; 1148 M/669, F. Acland to E. Acland, 3 June 1917.
32. Ibid., 1148 M 14/687, F. Acland to E. Acland, ? November 1917; 1148 M 14/698, F. Acland to E. Acland, ? December 1917.
33. Bodmin Liberal Association papers, Liskeard Liberal Democrat Office, C. A. Millman to Francis Acland, 20 August 1918.
34. Acland papers, 1148 M 14/889, C. Trevelyan to E. Acland, 24 May 1919.
35. Bodmin Liberal papers, C. A. Millman to F. Acland, 21 February and 20 August 1918.
36. See Tregidga, 'Socialism and the Old Left', p. 81.
37. *Cornish Post*, 5 July 1917.
38. Bodmin Liberal papers, C. A. Millman to E. C. Perry, 13 August 1918.
39. M. Kinnear, *The British Voter: An Atlas and Survey since 1885* (London, 1968), p. 120. See also A. M. Dawson, 'Politics in Devon and Cornwall, 1900–31, Ph.D. thesis, University of London, 1991.
40. G. J. De Groot, *Liberal Crusader: The Life of Sir Archibald Sinclair* (London, 1993), p. 98.
41. B. Deacon, 'The Cornish Revival: Ar Analysis', unpublished paper, 1985, p. 8.
42. Payton, *Making of Modern Cornwall*, p. 134.
43. Ibid., p. 135.
44. Hale, 'Genesis of the Celto-Cornish Revival?', p. 105.
45. *Cornubian*, 1 December 1910.
46. Ibid.
47. *Royal Cornwall Gazette*, 8 December 1910.
48. For examples of the 'Celtic' nature of Cornwall's political and religious culture see *Cornish Guardian*, 16 December 1910 and 20 February 1914, *West Briton*, 7 and 13 January 1910; *The Times*, 28 October 1912.
49. B. Deacon, D. Cole and G. Tregidga, *Mebyon Kernow and Cornish Nationalism* (Cardiff, 2003), p. 7.
50. *Cornish Guardian*, 6 September 1912.
51. *Royal Cornwall Gazette*, 29 February 1912.
52. Acland papers, 11 48 M/512, Francis Acland to Eleanor Acland, 27 November 1910. *Cornish Guardian*, 26 January and 19 July 1912.
53. Payton, *Making of Modern Cornwall*, p. 132. P. Payton, 'Paralysis and Revival: The

Reconstruction of Celto-Catholic Cornwall 1890–1945', in E. Westland (ed.), *Cornwall: The Cultural Construction of Place* (Penzance, 1997), pp. 25–39. See also D. Everett, 'Celtic Revival and the Anglican Church in Cornwall, 1870–1930', in P. Payton, *Cornish Studies: Eleven* (Exeter, 2003), pp. 192–219.

54. Quoted in D. R. Williams (ed.), *Henry and Katharine Jenner: A Celebration of Cornwall's Culture, Language and Identity* (London, 2004), p. 69.

55. *Royal Cornwall Gazette*, 21 February 1910 and 29 February 1912.

56. *Cornish Guardian*, 15 March 1912.

57. *Cornish Post*, 14, 21, 28 June and 12 July 1917.

58. Ibid., 5, 12 and 26 July 1917.

59. Ibid., 12 July 1917.

60. B. Deacon, 'And Shall Trelawny Die? The Cornish Identity', in P. Payton (ed.), *Cornwall Since the War: The Contemporary History of a European Region* (Redruth, 1993), p. 213.

61. *Cornish Post*, 14 June and 12 July 1917.

62. Ibid., 5 July 1917.

63. Acland papers, 11 48 M/682, F. Acland to E. Acland, 17 November 1917.

64. Ibid., 11 48 M/669, F. Acland to E. Acland, 3 June 1917.

65. *Cornish Post*, 22 March and 12 April 1917; *West Briton*, 28 March 1918; *Royal Cornwall Gazette*, 17 January 1918.

66. Acland papers, 11 48 M/668, F. Acland to E. Acland, 31 May 1917.

67. Ibid., 11 48 M/777, 9 October 1917; 11 48 M/760, ? February 1918.

68. *Cornish Guardian*, 20 September 1912.

69. Acland papers, 11 48 M/760, F. Acland to E. Acland, ? February 1918.

70. Leif Jones, another Liberal MP returned in 1929, should also be regarded as a leading politician at the national level. Jones, who had replaced Acland as the party's candidate for Camborne, was president of the United Kingdom Alliance, a leading temperance organisation, and a former MP.

71. *Western Morning News*, 31 January and 22 February 1950.

72. *Cornish Guardian*, 16 February 1923 and 9 January 1930; *West Briton*, 31 October 1935.

73. Rescorla Centre Collection, RA/1/1, group recording, 4 December 2000.

74. *West Briton*, 31 October 1935.

7

John Betjeman and the Holy Grail
One Man's Celtic Quest

Philip Payton

Introduction

John Betjeman (1906–84) was, in the eyes of his countless devotees, quintessentially English: in manner, outlook, humour, and in his own sentimental pre-occupations as well as in his many anxieties. Moreover, Betjeman has been celebrated routinely as perhaps the most successful twentieth-century purveyor of nostalgic constructions of England and Englishness, evidenced in a life-time's corpus of work as poet (he was England's Poet Laureate from 1972 until his death), author, journalist, broadcaster, and public speaker and performer.[1] And yet, John Betjeman was never confident of his English credentials, his supposedly 'Dutch' surname – anglicized from Betjema*nn* – only thinly disguising his family's German's origins, leading among other things to the school-boy taunts ('Betjeman's a German spy') that tormented him during the Great War. He was, he decided, 'an alien', though his mother rushed to reassure him that 'you're English on your mother's side' ('Thank God').[2] But, much as he loved his mother, in this as in other things he did not quite trust her judgement or opinions, and remained convinced that at root he was an outsider in England.

If John Betjeman was an outsider in England, then he was doubly so in Cornwall. He was, he admitted freely, a 'foreigner' in Cornwall, just like the other well-to-do up-country 'visitors' who, in the Edwardian period when he was a small boy, had begun to acquire second homes in picturesque Cornish locations. His contemporary and sometime friend, A. L. Rowse, always alive to the contested boundaries of Cornishness and Englishness, poured scorn on any suggestion that Betjeman might be considered 'Cornish' – or could even become Cornish by adoption – and protested that only an idiot could possibly mistake 'Betjeman' for a Cornish name.[3] Coming on top of existing doubts about his hereditary right to be called 'English', such discouragement in Cornwall – where he was so clearly 'not one o' we' – might have served to deter him completely. Yet, like his father, Ernest Betjemann, John yearned to make a claim upon Cornwall, to find common cause with Cornwall and the Cornish. When Betjeman wrote of his father's wistful longing for Cornish credentials, he was also expressing his own predicament:

> My father's sad grey eyes in gathering dusk
> Saw Roughtor and Brown Willy hide the view
> Of that bold coast-line where he was not born –
> Not born but would he had been, would he had
> More right than just the price of them to wear.[4]

This is a predicament that many early twenty-first century in-migrants or second-home owners in Cornwall would still recognize, and to that extent the experience of John Betjeman is an exemplar or case study of a much wider phenomenon: the intense desire of those outsiders who have 'fallen in love with Cornwall' to construct conduits of legitimacy and belonging. These might be Cornish twigs somewhere distant in a family tree, or some other long-established connection with Cornwall, or even a sense – like Marion Bowman's 'cardiac Celts' – that somehow deep in one's heart one feels profoundly 'Cornish'.[5]

The Betjemann family seemed to nurture such sentiment, for even before Ernest Betjemann's acquisition of a holiday home on the North Cornish coast, an earlier forbear – Gilbert H. Betjemann (1840–1921) – had alighted upon Hawker's famous Cornish ballad 'Trelawny', composing a cantata, 'The Song of the Western Men', for the Highbury Athenaeum. Musician-in-Ordinary to both Queen Victoria and Edward VII, Gilbert H. Betjemann was in his day a noted violinist, composer and conductor. He was a cousin of John Betjeman's grandfather, and when a small boy young John was taken to see this elderly relation in Camden Town. Young Betjeman was an intensely sensitive child, in those early years forming impressions and opinions that stayed with him for life.[6] It cannot be entirely coincidental that John Betjeman developed a lasting enthusiasm and affection for the life and work of Robert Stephen Hawker (1803–75), who was vicar of Morwenstow (on Betjeman's beloved North Cornwall coast) for forty years until his death in 1875. There was an intimate and enduring connection between the holy man and that wild Cornish coast, Betjeman thought: 'Stormy nights, and a sea mountains high, and the thunder on the shore, heard three miles inland – those are the times', wrote Betjeman, 'when I like to think of Parson Hawker, the Cornish mystic and poet'.[7] It was, perhaps, in his family blood.

Or, at the very least, John Betjeman had inherited his family's enthusiasm for Cornwall, an enthusiasm that in his life time he was to develop into something close to an obsession, forging a relationship with Cornwall which was for Betjeman fundamental to who he was and how he imagined his destiny.

Part of the problem?

But for all the sense that the Betjemann family had, through several generations, forged its own special links with Cornwall, there was for John the uneasy, ever-present discomfort that he was somehow 'part of the problem'. For all his celebration of things Cornish, he fretted, he was still an interloper, part of a class that was by its presence and through its activities already 'ruining' Cornwall, his own work popularizing hitherto little known Cornish spots and encouraging their despoilation through the creation of mass tourism. Again, this is a predicament that remains familiar in early twenty-first century Cornwall, where those who trumpet the charms of Cornwall run the risk of colluding in its exploitation. Once more, Betjeman's personal experience points to a wider phenomenon in modern Cornwall. As Betjeman expressed it, capturing the sense of complicity and personal responsibility: 'The visitors have come to Cornwall. "Visitors", "foreigners" we're called by the Cornish. We litter the cliffs with our houses. We litter the cliffs with our shacks. When I was a boy all this was open fields'.[8] Yet he wanted to share the wonders of Cornwall with the like-minded, those who would also be stirred to a sensitive appreciation of place and people. In a wireless broadcast in February 1949, for example, he could not resist singing the praises of Padstow – another of his favourite places on the North Cornish coast – but in the same breath he offered his apologies to the town for spilling its precious beans: 'Farewell, Padstow! Forgive me, a stranger, for telling some of your secrets outside your little streets. I have known them and loved them so long, I want others to enjoy, as I have done, your ancientness and beauty'.[9]

Earlier, in a broadcast in May 1938, Betjeman had played cat-and-mouse with his listeners, extolling the attractions of hidden coves and picturesque harbours, though taking care not to reveal their identities too closely: 'I shan't tell you where all the lovely places are: I want them for myself. But I'll let you know where to look: between Falmouth and St Ives, between Pentire and Tintagel, and right up in the north beyond Bude where Cornwall thins out into Devon and Hartland stretches on into the Atlantic'.[10] Put like this, it sounded rather like a harmless topographical game. But beneath the fun there were, as Betjeman had pointed out already, far more serious concerns.

As well as the despoilation of place, there was also the deleterious effect of intrusive mass tourism on the indigenous Cornish. As Betjeman explained:

> fishermen have become stage fishermen, who lounge on the quay to tell apocryphal tales of King Arthur and John Wesley at half a crown apiece or take out London businessmen and make them seasick at ten bob an hour ... The avariceness which is the least charming thing in simple people has been exploited [in Cornwall] to the full. It's not their fault that this has happened: it's the fault of the visitors who have corrupted and uprooted them.[11]

At times, Betjeman was aware of the latent – and occasionally not-so-latent – hostility of the locals in Cornwall:

> 'Come away, Henry, from those common little children. They're only visitors'.
> 'Don't have anything to do with those people, Bertie – they think they own the place'.[12]

Betjeman was convinced that it was his generation that had done the damage in Cornwall: 'it was not the Victorian but our own age that ruined the wild west coast with bungalows and ... littered the roadside with shacks and hoardings, [and] turned old inns into glittering pretension'.[13] However, Betjeman also believed that all was not yet lost. He had a deeper faith in Cornwall and its ability to endure, a faith quite literally, as it turned out, of religious intensity and proportion. Cornwall was still, he argued, despite all those recent depredations, 'like another country within our island, as yet not quite suburbanized, not quite given over to the chain store and the farming syndicate, the local-government official and his ally in Whitehall'.[14]

'Cornwall is a Duchy. It is separated from England'

Like 'Q' – Sir Arthur Quiller Couch – and other writers of the era, Betjeman used the term 'Duchy' to emphasize this distinctiveness and to suggest Cornwall's cultural and constitutional distance from England. Ignoring the tedious legal pedantry which worried over whether 'Duchy' was territorially coterminous with 'County', and why the Duchy as an institution owned more land outside Cornwall than within, Betjeman understood that the term was a badge of 'difference'. 'Cornwall is a Duchy', he wrote, 'It is separated from England by the picturesque Tamar Valley, and has more sea coast than anywhere else in Britain'.[15]

In common with other 'outsiders', Betjeman was drawn to land- and seascapes – the 'picturesque Tamar Valley', the 'sea coast', and the fact that 'the Celtic field system makes the Duchy look different from England'[16] – but, more unusually, he was interested in the people too. As he explained, 'The Cornish are the same sort of Celts as the Welsh and Bretons',[17] which made them fascinating as well as different. Yet Betjeman stopped short of painting the Cornish as an exotic 'other', as those who deigned to mention them at all did usually, and instead he claimed common cause with the locals among whom he holidayed regularly. This was partly because, as we have seen, the Betjemann family already felt a strong affinity with Cornwall – an affinity which John Betjeman would do much to strengthen and enhance – but it also mirrored his early childhood experiences on the north coast at Trebetherick, St Enodoc and Polzeath. In those days, he reflected years later, 'there were many Cornish still resident' in the area: 'Charlie Mably who collected golf balls on the course and lived at the oldest house; Tom Buse, who, with his wife and daughters ran the Haven Boarding House at which first we stayed, and drove the jingle to take us to the station'. There was the 'old farm at the top of the hill owned by Francis Mably and another one, lower down, farmed by Tom Blake'.[18] They co-existed with the holidaymakers who visited year-on-year, and with those who had moved down to settle permanently in Cornwall. 'We were a family', Betjeman insisted, 'though not related. We were all equal, and the Cornish inhabitants – the Buses, the Mablys, the Coxes, the Males, the Champions, the Camps and many others in the shops and farms were all part of us'.[19] Here was the other side of the coin to the hostility that Betjeman had sometimes detected, though in his darker moments he continued to regret that Trebetherick was really 'a suburb by the sea and for all our crabbing, fishing and bathing, nothing to do with the real Cornish who regarded us as the foreigners we still are'.[20]

Betjeman was glad that in the winter months the majority of visitors went home, leaving Cornwall in peace. Now the Cornish could regain what was properly theirs, while the more sensitive, better informed type of visitor might creep in unannounced and 'out of season' to see what Cornwall and the Cornish were really like: 'The Duchy becomes its native self in winter, and that is the time to see it'.[21] Similarly, Betjeman was pleased that the majority of summer visitors was attracted to the coastline, leaving the interior relatively untouched. 'Inland, Cornwall is mercifully considered dull', he wrote, so that the tourist hordes did not yet know that 'The wooded inland valleys like those of the Allen, Camel, Inny, Fowey and Lynher … are remotest and loveliest Cornwall'.[22]

An 'outsider' who fretted that he did not really 'belong', Betjeman had done his best to side with the locals. Daphne du Maurier, another of Betjeman's contemporaries and another 'outsider' who had taken Cornwall to heart, had attempted something similar. Going further than John Betjeman, she had joined the Cornish nationalist party Mebyon Kernow as an associate member, and in 1969 had written an article for the movement's journal *Cornish Nation*, insisting that a form of self-government for Cornwall was achievable within the next decade.[23] Yet her fiction, at least until the appearance of her last work *Rule Britannia*, was entirely devoid of nationalist constructions of Cornwall, political or cultural, while her comments in her non-fictional *Vanishing Cornwall*, published in 1967, seemed critical rather than supportive of Cornish nationalism.[24] Betjeman meanwhile, who steadfastly eschewed party-political affiliation and had never sought to flirt with Mebyon Kernow, was in his own work more subtly Cornish nationalist. For, in addition to his siding with the locals – and his critical estimation of the worst excesses, as he saw them, of the tourist industry – was his all-important literacy embrace of the Cornish Celtic Revival. It was this 'Revival' that had underpinned the emergence of modern Cornish nationalism – in both its cultural and political guises – and which has helped perpetuate the belief into this millennium that Cornwall is not England.

'Celtic missionaries from Wales and Ireland'

The post-industrial re-invention of 'Celtic Cornwall' had begun in earnest by the time of Betjeman's birth in 1906. Henry Jenner's *Handbook of the Cornish Language*, a milestone in the iconography of Cornish Celtic revivalism, had appeared two years earlier, in 1904, as had the Great Western Railway's guidebook *The Cornish Riviera*, a volume which brought Cornish revivalist assumptions to a wider, English public beyond the Tamar. From the first, as this juxtaposition of titles suggested, there was a paradoxical alliance of sorts between the enthusiasts of the Cornish Celtic Revival and the purveyors of the rapidly developing Cornish tourist industry, each feeding off the other's desire to create a highly differentiated post-industrial Cornwall in the aftermath of mining's collapse. John Betjeman, as we have seen already, was later caught in this paradox, and understood that his energetic embrace of 'Celtic Cornwall' (not least in publications and broadcasts designed for an essentially English audience) had the undesired effect of promoting the mass tourism he so abhorred. However, he also knew that he was writing for a more discerning and imaginative public, one which shared his horror of the destructive edge of unrestrained tourism but appreciated the worth of Betjeman's project. 'Outsiders' of the thinking kind felt reassured that they were being presented with an authentic insight into the 'real' Cornwall that eluded the mass tourist, while 'insider' adherents of the Cornish Celtic Revival could be persuaded that here was a construction of Cornwall which was sympathetic to their cause and with which broadly they could agree.

Betjeman's work on Cornwall – poetry as well as prose – is shot through with Celtic revivalist imagery and allusions. Cornwall's Celticity was ancient and enduring, and Cornwall was part of a wider Celtic world whose strands of common culture went back to medieval times and beyond.:

> Before Southern England was Christian, Cornwall had been visited by Celtic missionaries from Wales and Ireland. Their names survive as those of saints ... The Celtic saints were hermits who lived in beehive cells and are said to have recited the Psalms waist-deep in cold streams. The crosses of their age survive, and so does the siting of their churches, for the parochial system came late to Cornwall, and the church on the site of a Celtic hermit's cell is often remote from the chief village in the parish.[25]

In fashioning this view, Betjeman acknowledged the influence of the Cornish Celtic Revivalists – the early romantic Sabine Baring-Gould (1834–1924), whose flights of fancy were a perpetual annoyance to serious scholars, and the far more scholarly Gilbert Hunter Doble. Made a bard of Gorseth Kernow (the Cornish Gorsedd), that most prestigious of revivalist organizations, at its inception in 1928 (taking as his bardic name *Gwas Gwendron*, Servant of Wendron), Doble produced an impressive series of studies on the Cornish saints, focussing especially on their links with the other Celtic lands. As Betjeman informed his listeners in a broadcast in July 1949:

> The late Revd S. Baring-Gould, the most readable and enjoyable writer on the Celtic Church is, alas!, regarded as unreliable. To him I owe all my early enthusiasm. The late Canon Doble, a scholar who did more than any man to find out about Cornish saints, wrote mainly for scholars ... If a wireless talk can be dedicated to anyone's memory, this should be to that of Canon Doble, vicar of Wendron.[26]

This was in a talk on the 'strange and sweet-sounding saints of Cornwall – Morwenna, Menofreda, Endelienta, Ladoc, Cadoc, Kew, Cuby and Tudy and ... the greatest of your number, Holy Petroc Abbot and Confessor'.[27] As Betjeman was of course aware, Petroc – as well being, along with St Piran, chief among Cornish saints – was especially connected with North Cornwall: Betjeman's own corner of the Duchy. Padstow was anciently Petrockstowe. Bodmin, with the largest parish church in Cornwall, was dedicated to St Petroc, as was Little Petherick near Wadebridge – 'one of the most attractive churches in the Duchy', according to Betjeman, 'a shrine of Anglo-Catholicism'.[28] Like Hawker of Morwenstow, St Petroc was for Betjeman somehow overwhelmingly emblematic of that part of Cornwall for which he felt the most intense affection, and where he felt most at home. 'The Celtic Church tinkled in Cornwall with the bells of its saints expecting Christ at any moment', said Betjeman: 'Here on Bodmin Moor it would be no shock to see the bearded form of Petroc, with stags, poultry, and wolves following him; not bothering to eat one another, for devotion to the saint'.[29]

'Into Betjemanland'

The North Cornwall of Parson Hawker and St Petroc stretched from Padstow and the Camel estuary to the Devon border, then tumbling into that debatable land east of the Tamar but west of Dartmoor which so often seemed more Cornish than Devonshire. Lew Trenchard, for example, firmly in Devon, was anciently dedicated to St Petroc, its church overwhelming Cornish in appearance, with Celtic saints commemorated inside, its squarson – squire and parson – for many years none other than Sabine Baring-Gould. Coincidently, the North Cornwall railway – the sprawling branch system of the Southern (formerly London and South Western) Railway – covered much the same territory. Known by detractors (and affectionately by friends) as the 'Withered Arm', the North Cornwall left the main Waterloo-Exeter-Plymouth main line at Meldon Junction, west of Okehampton, and traversed the wild debatable land to Halwill Junction. Here the line divided, one branch continuing on to Bude, the other turning south-westerly, crossing into Cornwall at Launceston and skirting round the northern edge of Bodmin Moor to Wadebridge and, eventually, Padstow. From Wadebridge, a short branch also ran south to Bodmin, with spurs to Wenford Bridge and Ruthern Bridge.

In its territorial extent, the railway mirrored – almost defined – Betjeman's North Cornwall. This was 'Betjemanland', as T. W. E. Roche dubbed it in his little book *The Withered Arm*, published in 1967, a nostalgic railway enthusiasts' volume which celebrated the former Southern Railway lines of North Cornwall and West Devon. A chapter, 'Into Betjemanland', was devoted to the stretch from Launceston to Padstow, making the most of the Tamar as the border between Cornwall and England, as Betjeman had done, and quoting (not altogether correctly) from Betjeman's verse autobiography *Summoned By Bells* to evoke the journey made via remote wayside stations such as Egloskerry and Tresmeer.[30]

What Betjeman made of Roche's booklet, we cannot know. But we do know that he was a committed railway enthusiast, numbering among his many literary friends the railway historian and artist C. Hamilton Ellis (who sent him a signed copy of his history of the Midland Railway), and in his personal working library was a copy of *The Withered Arm*.[31] Betjeman was certainly a devotee of the North Cornwall. He once described the rail journey from Wadebridge to Padstow, along the ever broadening Camel estuary, as the most beautiful he knew. He also delighted in the separate identity that the railway lent North Cornwall, distinguishing it from the rest of Cornwall where the rival Great Western held undisputed sway. 'I like to think', he said, 'how annoying it must be to tidy-minded civil servants to have to put up with green Southern Railway carriages coming right into this brown-and-cream Great Western district of Cornwall'.[32] He had travelled to North Cornwall by train for family holidays, the long journey part of the ritual of 'going to Cornwall', the slow progress and the continued dividing of trains at junction stations west of Exeter seeming to add to the sense of penetrating a far-off land. 'Can it really be', Betjeman asked, 'That this same carriage came from Waterloo?'.[33] When he wrote his book on London railway termini, Betjeman discussed Waterloo. He enthused about the suburban electric network and the fast main lines to Portsmouth and Southampton. But somehow Padstow, Wadebridge and the North Cornwall had slipped from view, as though these were quite separate places divorced from the everyday life of metropolitan Waterloo, a gulf that mirrored his own sense of there being a vast chasm between his two orbits: Cornwall and London.[34]

'Clinging farms/hold Bible Christians … hamlets given over to magic, cruelty'

The tract of North Cornwall defined by the Southern Railway's branch system was, notwithstanding the massive, ancient quarry at Delabole (which the railway skirted closely) and the remains of old metal mines at St Teath and elsewhere, the least industrialized part of Cornwall. Much of it was moor or high wind-swept plateau, with few towns of any size. The landscape was a pattern of scattered farms and lonely churchtowns, where distances seemed considerable and where the population was sparse, the latter partly a result of rural depopulation in the mid-nineteenth century when the agricultural districts of North Cornwall experienced what was called at the time a 'Rage for Emigration' to the United States and Canada.[35] It was a landscape punctuated by the tall towers of the churches beloved by Betjeman, with their Celtic dedications, and in the churchyards or in remoter spots down dark lanes or on moorland tracks were the ancient crosses and holy wells that were for Betjeman the stuff of Celtic Cornwall. Perhaps here, more than anywhere else in Cornwall, it was possible to construct an imagined landscape of remote Celtic rurality.

For John Betjeman, the rural landscape of North Cornwall – including the dramatic coastline and seascape – *was* quintessentially Celtic. It was also a hidden, mysterious landscape – one which one had to work hard to understand and to get to know. It was a landscape of varying mood, and in Betjeman's imagination it was by turns benign and light, dark and sinister. It was, perhaps, a dichotomy that reflected his own complex personality – light-hearted and optimistic one minute, gloomy and pessimistic the next – one that mirrored in the landscape his innermost struggles, not least those of religious faith. In its smiling, welcoming guise, North Cornwall was a fastness of Christian goodness. Alongside the timeless Celtic saints, who had filled the land with Christian blessings when southern England was still pagan, were the more recent adherents of John Wesley's faith who inhabited the scattered farms and hamlets. '[C]linging farms/ Hold Bible Christians',[36] wrote Betjeman, referring to the Methodist sect that had had its origins in the North Cornwall-North Devon border country in the early nineteenth century, the simple piety of these country folk seeming to saturate the landscape with benevolence. Alongside their plain nonconformist chapels were the medieval churches, their ancient towers visible beacons of hope in the landscape. 'Lin-Lan-Lone' rang their cheery bells, said Betjeman, echoing Tennyson. He knew them all – St Mabyn, St Issey, St Kew, and the rest – but his favourite was St Endellion. 'St Endellion! St Endellion! The name is like a ring of bells',[37] he wrote.

Late one summer evening, Betjeman explained, he had arrived in Cornwall by motor car, the road becoming increasingly familiar, with gaps in 'the high fern-stuffed hedges' now and again showing 'sudden glimpses of the sea ... Port Isaac Bay with its sweep of shadowy cliffs stretched all along to Tintagel'.[38] He passed the old 'granite manor house of Tresungers with its tower and battlements', and as he neared St Endellion church he heard the bells, with 'their sweet tone', being rung for practice. 'It was a welcome to Cornwall', he felt, and he remembered the benevolent words of the Ringer's rhyme painted on a board in the belltower:

> Let's all in love and Friendship hither come
> Whilst the shrill treble calls to thundering Tom
> And since bells are for modest recreation
> Let's rise and ring and fall to admiration.[39]

This was warm, safe, benign North Cornwall. But there was another, darker, pagan North Cornwall that lurked just beneath the surface, ready to reveal itself at any moment. When he was a child, Betjeman had been taken by his parents to the May Day festivities at Padstow. He had been impressed – perhaps even terrified – by the 'Obby 'Oss, with its lurid mask and swaying dance, and was mesmerised by the rhythmic beating of the drums and the haunting, endlessly repetitive May Day tune. Here was something 'strange and secret',[40] as Betjeman called it, intimations of another North Cornwall. Evening jaunts 'Past haunted woods and oil-lit farms' and 'Imagined ghosts on unfrequented roads'[41] had also hinted at this other place, with 'remoter hamlets given over to magic, cruelty',[42] something observed in his poem 'Trebetherick':

> From where the coastguard houses stood
> One used to see, below the hill,
> The lichened branches of a wood
> In summer silver-cool and still;
> And there the Shade of Evil could
> Stretch out at us from Shilla Mill.
> Thick with sloe and blackberry, uneven in the light,
> Lonely ran the hedge, the heavy meadow was remote,
> The oldest part of Cornwall was the wood as black as night,
> And the pheasant and the rabbit lay torn open at the throat.[43]

Some parts of Cornwall could 'feel intensely evil',[44] Betjeman thought, especially the border country out towards Baring-Gould's Lew Trenchard where even in recent times 'places really were remote: white witches, the evil eye, ghosts and strange customs'.[45] Figures from Cornish folklore peopled this threatening landscape. There was Coppinger, the notorious north-coast wrecker-smuggler – 'Cruel Coppinger haunts me today', Betjeman confessed – 'and the ghost of Jan Tregeagle and his hounds of hell'.[46] This North Cornwall was hardly safe, and certainly not benign. Yet there was a 'happy terror' that Betjeman could enjoy when, safe indoors at night and protected from all that stalked outside, he could 'escape to a fire of driftwood' as 'the wind howls up the chimney'.[47] Ultimately, the sinister face of North Cornwall fascinated rather than repelled, complementing rather than negating the alternative landscape of warm embrace.

The 'Quest of the Sangraal'

The 'Withered Arm' railway system defined North Cornwall territorially. Within this imagined space, Betjeman placed those figures who, for him, gave North Cornwall its literary identity, and who mediated those sometimes conflicting, sometimes complementary landscapes that existed in his mind's eye.

In the first half of the twentieth century there had been two really great novelists in the British Isles, Betjeman considered: James Joyce and Thomas Hardy.[48] Betjeman claimed particular affinity with Hardy because he was also a poet. Moreover, Hardy had been an architect – a profession about which Betjeman knew a great deal. In his personal life, too, as well as in his literary work, Hardy had had his own intimate connections with North Cornwall: he met his first wife there (glimpsed in his novel *A Pair of Blue Eyes*) and, years later, after her death, it was on that coast that he wrote some of his finest verse. What Betjeman would have made of Hardy's construction of North Cornwall as 'Off Wessex' we can only guess, but we do know that he looked forgivingly upon his restoration, when a young man, of the church of St Juliot, deep in the North Cornish countryside. Although, in later life, an embarrassed Hardy liked to distance himself from such early 'restoration' work, Betjeman felt that his efforts were far more sympathetic than those of the notorious Victorian restorer, J. P. St Aubyn, who had dealt with neighbouring Lesnewth church 'far more violently'.[49] At St Juliot, Hardy had taken care to preserve seventeenth-century bench-ends and the medieval screen, Betjeman noted approvingly, and in general his approach had much in common (Betjeman argued) 'with the advanced architects of his time, that is to say, Norman Shaw and Philip Webb ... and the Arts and Crafts as practised by William Morris'.[50]

The Arts and Crafts movement sat well in North Cornwall, Betjeman thought, and indeed many of those metropolitans of 'a more sophisticated taste, inspired by the Morris movement and a love of the simple life', had by the late nineteenth century 'found solace' among 'the rugged fishermen of Cornwall'.[51] The movement's penchant for pre-Raphaelite Arthurian themes fitted neatly with Tintagel and its supposed Arthurian affiliations, which was itself a kind of romantic Celtic Revivalism. Here again was the all-pervading influence of Sabine Baring-Gould, Betjeman detected. Much more so than Hardy, of course, it was Baring-Gould who had fashioned the literary construction of Celtic-Arthurian North Cornwall that so appealed. His books were eminently readable, Betjeman said, and 'must have been the inspiration of many young children and nourished the first love and pride in Devon and Cornwall that those children remember. I was one such child'. It was fashionable now for scholars to look down upon Baring Gould, he added, but 'I suspect that many of those archaeologists and historians who despise him today took up their careers on account of Baring-Gould's enthusiasm'. At any rate, Betjeman was happy to acknowledge that it was his 'books of antiquarian lore ... [that] first stirred me to marvel at rough pieces of granite, hewn centuries ago, seen lying in tamarisk-sheltered churchyards or in similar manner on Bodmin Moor'. It was 'Baring-Gould who brought to life for me the strange-named saints of little holy wells. He peopled high Cornish lanes with ghosts and hinted at curses and tragedy round some sheltered, feather-grey slate manor house of Elizabeth I's time, now a decrepit-looking farm'.[52]

As Betjeman also observed, for all those ghosts and curses and tragedies, 'Baring-Gould was a thorough Tractarian, an old-fashioned High Churchman'.[53] He was an Anglo-Catholic at a time when Anglo-Catholicism in Cornwall was linked explicitly to Celtic revivalism, most noticeably in the efforts of the Rev Wlasdislaw Somerville Lach-Szyrma (1841–1915), vicar of Newlyn, who, amongst other things, was a Cornish-language enthusiast and encouraged the flying of St Piran's banner as the national flag of Cornwall. This was an Anglo-Catholicism that spoke directly to John Betjeman, appealing to his religious sense of reverence, ritual, mystery and beauty, as well as to his growing Celtic enthusiasms, and which had the profound effect of locating his religious faith, to a very considerable degree, in his own North Cornwall. It was an intimacy reflected in his poetry:

> A flame of rushlight in the cell
> On holy walls and holy well
> And to the west the thundering bay
> With soaking seaweed, sand, and spray,
> Oh good St. Cadoc pray for me
> Here in your cell beside the sea.[54]

Significantly, this was a literary entwinement of faith and place which echoed that of Robert Stephen Hawker. Like Baring-Gould, Hawker was also 'an old-fashioned High Churchman', said Betjeman, although, paradoxically, he was 'well in advance of his times' – a Celtic revivalist who foresaw prophetically the imminent flowering of interest in the ancient 'Celtic Christianity' of Cornwall, and whose own prescient work was a prelude to the revivalist movement.[55] Baring-Gould had written an entertaining, if unreliable, biography of Hawker, much enjoyed by Betjeman. Betjeman thought that the two men, Baring-Gould and Hawker, had much in common, with their complementary literary enthusiasms, their Anglo-Catholicism, and their twin connections with North Cornwall. Like Baring-Gould, Hawker's life and work reflected – almost personified – the conflicting landscapes that Betjeman had imagined so vividly. On the one hand, 'His Church was his home ... he thought himself back in the Eternal Past and lived in the old Celtic church of Cornwall ... To Hawker, Morwenstowe (sic) was the shrine of St Morwenna, the Celtic saint who founded her church there'.[56] But on the other, Hawker also had his fair share of ghosts and curses and tragedies in that wild country – not least the battered bodies of dead sailors from shipwrecks cast up in great storms on that fearsome shore. And, Betjeman said, there were also abroad in Morwenstow 'evil superstitions with which

Parson Hawker had to contend. Life was war for him: war against the Devil, who was almost a tangible person in evil cottages where witches lived, witches who were consulted by his parishoners'.[57]

In this war between good and evil, Hawker turned inevitably to the high allegory of Arthurianism, with its heady mix of medievalism and epic drama, played out against a 'Celtic' background in which Cornwall – 'From grey Morwenna's stone to Michael's tor',[58] as Hawker put it – featured so prominently. Arthurian allusions peppered Hawker's work, with its visions of 'Dundagel throned', and, as Betjeman pointed out, 'Hawker's angels, his faith, and the ancient Celtic church of which he was a member are expressed in that magnificent poem of his about the Holy Grail, the Cup which Our Lord used at the last supper and which was said to have been brought to England by St Joseph of Arimathea'. This great composition, perhaps Hawker's finest, was his celebrated 'Quest of the Sangraal'. As Betjeman explained, it was a poem 'about King Arthur and Tintagel', a work that brought together in brilliant synthesis all that Betjeman admired in Hawker and his literary-religious construction of North Cornwall.[59]

The Secret Glory

As Betjeman no doubt mused, the Quest of the Sangraal – the Holy Grail – mirrored his own personal quest for Cornwall. It was also, as Betjeman might have agreed, a wider reflection of other strivings in his life, not least his struggle for religious faith, and a metaphor for the many anxieties, angsts and guilts with which he wrestled daily. As he explained in *Summoned By Bells*, this identification with the Holy Grail was given an unexpected dimension when, as an adolescent exploring inland North Cornwall in the early 1920s, he encountered the Rector of St Ervan:

> Dear lanes of Cornwall! With a one-inch map,
> A bicycle and well-worn *Little Guide*,
> Those were the years I used to ride for miles
> To far-off churches. One of them that year
> So worked on me that, if my life was changed,
> I owe it to St Ervan and his priest
> In their small hollow deep in sycamores.[60]

Betjeman found the 'bearded Rector' of St Ervan ringing the bell for Evensong, and after the service the priest invited him for a cup of tea into the 'large, uncarpeted' Rectory with its 'waste of barely furnished rooms', where 'Clearly the Rector lived … all alone'. The Rector 'talked of poetry and

Cornish saints', and when Betjeman admitted that he thought of religion as 'mostly singing hymns/And feeling warm and comfortable inside', the kindly priest decided that he should 'Borrow this book and come to tea again'.[61]

This book that was to have such a profound effect upon John Betjeman was *The Secret Glory*, first published in 1922, a semi-autobiographical novel by Arthur Machen (1863–1947). The Rector of St Ervan, unnamed in *Summoned By Bells*, who decided that young Betjeman must read the book, was Wilfred Johnson, priest of that parish from 1915 until 1955. A useful pen-picture of him appears in Moira Tangey's recent portrait of St Ervan.[62] A Prebendary of St Endellion, Wilfred Johnson was a leading member of the Anglo-Catholic movement in Cornwall in the first half of the twentieth century. Like other Anglo-Catholics, he was also a Cornish-Celtic revivalist. Alongside his interest in Cornish saints, he was a friend of Charles Henderson, the distinguished Cornish antiquarian, and contributed a chapter to a commemorative volume on the life and work of Bishop Walter Howard Frere (1863–1938), the Anglo-Catholic Bishop of Truro from 1923 until 1935.[63] Johnson later crossed swords with Bishop Hunkin, Frere's Low Church successor at Truro, fixing his colours all the more firmly to the Anglo-Catholic mast.[64] In recommending *The Secret Glory*, Johnson detected the appeal that the book would have for Betjeman – the withering satire aimed at the English public school system (in which Betjeman had suffered more than most, as perhaps he had told Johnson) but also its full-blown advocacy of 'Celtic Christianity', and with it a plot enmeshed in a quest for the Holy Grail.

Arthur Machen (the pen-name of Arthur Llewellyn Jones) was born in 1863 at Caerleon-on-Usk in Gwent (as he termed it) in South Wales. Long before *The Secret Glory* had appeared, Machen – whose adopted surname was supposed to rhyme with 'blacken' – had made a name for himself as a writer of supernatural horror. In novels such as *The Great God Pan* (1894), he had acquired a reputation as perhaps the most outstanding British writer of *fin de siecle* supernatural fiction, and had an enthusiastic following of readers and admirers to match. An occultist, Machen was a member of the Hermetic Order of the Golden Dawn, a secret magical order which practised theurgy and which, in the late nineteenth and early twentieth centuries, had a deep impact upon western occultism. Significantly, a number of Celtic revivalists was drawn to its ranks, notably William Butler Yeats, the Irish nationalist poet and purveyor of 'Celtic Twilight' literature, and Aleister Crowley.[65] The latter, famously dubbed 'the most wicked man in England', was for a time active in Cornwall, as was his associate Philip Hesseltine, who – in an echo of Llewellyn/Machen – changed his name to 'Peter Warlock' and (among other things) apparently learned Cornish and set some of Henry Jenner's Cornish-language poems to music. (Interestingly, Heseltine had his own North Cornwall connections, he and his girlfriend 'Puma' staying with D. H. Lawrence – who also found Cornwall 'pagan' and 'pre-Christian' – at Porthcothan before the Great War).[66]

Here was a fraternity of 'pagan' Celtic Revivalism to which Machen was happy to belong, and he revelled in his Welsh origins in the pagan-Celtic land of Gwent. However, by the spring of 1922, when *The Secret Glory* appeared, Machen had begun to alter his position. His *The Great Return* of 1915, about a return to the Wales of the Holy Grail, had presaged this change, and by the time his autobiographical *Far off Things* appeared in 1922, he had effectively recanted. Although he was to continue to write stories of horror and the supernatural, he recognized that hitherto he had mistaken 'awe' for 'evil'. As he put it:

> I have told, I think, how I was confronted suddenly and for the first time with the awe and solemnity and mystery of the valley of the Usk, and of the house called Bartholly hanging solitary between the deep forest and the winding esses of the river. This spectacle remained in my heart for years, and at last I transliterated it, clumsily enough, in the story of *The Great God Pan*, which, as a friendly critic once said, 'does at least make one believe in the devil, if it does nothing else'. Here, of course, was my real failure; I translated awe, at worst awfulness, into evil'.[67]

As *The Secret Glory* made plain, this 'awe' was essentially Celtic-Christian. In the book, the 'hero' – Machen's *alter ego*, Ambrose Meyrick, a schoolboy approaching manhood – struggles against the public school system which threatens to suppress his enthusiasms and creativity (which includes, like Betjeman, a passion for architecture), all the while nurturing a childhood vision of the Holy Grail hidden deep in his native Gwent. As Bevis Hiller, Betjeman's biographer, has commented, it is no surprise that the book made such an impression on the young Betjeman: 'It was suffused with a poetic romanticism, a passionate nostalgia for old saints, grail-quests, holy wells and holy bells of Celtic Wales, which chimed in perfectly with his interest in primitive Cornish saints'.[68] As Hillier added, the book also chimed with Betjeman's 'own supposedly Welsh ancestry'.[69] John Betjeman's great-grandfather had married one Mary Annie Merrick in 1830, and family tradition insisted that they were descended from the Merricks – anciently Meyricks – of Bodorgan in Anglesey, North Wales. For Betjeman, if he was not really English and could not become Cornish, then here at least was a genuine Welshness – a Celticity which allowed him to make some common claim to Cornwall. That the hero of Machen's book was also a Meyrick was an uncanny co-incidence, and – as Betjeman knew – many of the saints of

North Cornwall were also those of Machen's Gwent, the off-spring of King Brychan who was said to have arrived in Cornwall from South Wales with three wives and twenty-four saintly children. Their dedications – among them Endellion, Issey, Kew, Mabyn, Teath – peppered North Cornwall. In the footprints of Brychan and his off-spring, Betjeman felt able – as perhaps he imagined it – to plant his own 'Welshness' in North Cornwall, a device somehow sanctioned by the enthusiasms of Arthur Machen and Wilfred Johnson. At the very least, he felt an affinity with fictional Ambrose Meyrick, and for Meyrick's (and Machen's) Gwent read his own North Cornwall:

> There were laughs
> At public schools, at chapel services,
> At masters who were still 'big boys at heart'–
> While all the time the author's hero knew
> A Secret Glory in the hills of Wales:
> Caverns of light revealed the Holy Grail
> Exhaling gold upon the mountain-tops;
> At 'Holy! Holy! Holy!' In the Mass
> King Brychan's sainted children crowded round,
> And past and present were enwrapped in one.[70]

We should not underestimate the extent to which Betjeman took seriously the 'Celtic' identity lent by his Merrick/Meyrick descent. When, as an undergraduate at Oxford, he insisted on taking a Welsh-language option he was not merely, as others have suggested, being difficult and perverse in the face of authority, but was expressing his sense of ancient kinship.[71] Likewise, during the Second World War, when he was in Dublin working for the British government, he took the trouble to try to learn Irish, and regretted that 'The history of the English in Ireland does not make elevating reading ... There is reason for this hate. Irish history is full of "If only England had ... "'.[72] He was also a devotee of the Isle of Man, noting only slightly tongue-in-cheek that, in the unlikely event of him being offered the Lieutenant-Governorship of the island, he 'would change my name to Ewan Quetjeman and work for Manx independence'. Gravely, he observed that 'Whenever an English monarch visits the Isle of Man, a mist hangs over the island'.[73] Similarly, Betjeman insisted in a *Spectator* article – again only half in jest, and with echoes of Machen – that 'I have not been able to sleep lately for thinking of Monmouth. Is it Welsh or English?'. After much inquiry, he said, he had been told by the *South Wales Echo* 'that culturally it is Welsh, but that the Men of Gwent [Monmouthshire] regarded themselves as neither Welsh nor English'. Absurdly, Betjeman concluded that 'As a keen Manx Nationalist I am in favour of total independence for Monmouth, Berwick-upon-Tweed and the Soke of

Peterborough'.[74] But this was less a reduction to make Celtic nationalists look silly; more a typical example of Betjeman making fun of himself, laughing at his own pre-occupations and enthusiasms. Betjeman really did delight in the diversity of these islands, and had a horror of 'Whitehall' imposing the dead hand of sameness and central control. He could also be very serious on the subject when necessary. He wrote approvingly of Rev R. S. Thomas,[75] the Welsh nationalist poet, and of de Valera he declared that he 'is no Nazi, no sympathizer with Germany, no bomb-thrower and I suspect that he regrets the old hatred of England'.[76] When in less serious mood, Betjeman would purchase supplies of Manx postage stamps, to use instead of English ones on his routine correspondence and letters to friends.

'Red Matyrdom'

In *Summoned By Bells*, first published in 1960, Betjeman observed curiously that 'I would not care to read that book [*The Secret Glory*] again'. His explanation was that he might be disappointed. After the passage of all those years, he said, it might not ring so true: 'It so exactly mingled with the mood/ Of those impressionable years, that now/ I might be disillusioned'.[77] However, there were perhaps other reasons for Betjeman's discomfort, and for his growing ambiguity towards the book over time.

In the second of his autobiographical volumes, *Things Near and Far*, published in 1923, Machen had quoted at length from a review of *The Secret Glory* that had appeared in *The Nation and the Athenaeum*, penned by J. Middleton Murry. It is a review that Betjeman must have seen. He had continued to read Machen's work, and after Machen retired to Buckinghamshire, Betjeman (then living nearby in Berks) was an occasional visitor. Inevitably, the two men compared notes, and Betjeman must have been reminded of Middleton Murry's scathing words. Murry thought Machen's 'onslaught' on the public school system unconvincing. But even worse was the character of Ambrose Meyrick:

> Ambrose Meyrick, if he could be jerked for a moment by his creator into a semblance of real existence, would justify the worst outrages wrought upon him by his equally incredible *alma mater*. He is a sentimental philanderer with aesthetic Catholicism, a mystical Celtic dreamer, a Soho Bohemian (before Soho was ruined, of course); but these crimes are nothing compared to his incorrigible penchant for 'poetic prose'. Mr Machen has encouraged him in it. He will have a great deal more to answer for in the day of judgement than the schoolmaster who tried to beat him out of it.[78]

Betjeman always fretted that he would himself have a great deal to answer for on judgement day, and, having identified so closely with Ambrose Meyrick, here in Murry's review was a critique that (he might have thought) could apply equally to him. To suggest that Betjeman was a 'sentimental philanderer' in any sense is going too far, although it is true that he had a (usually platonic) weakness for beautiful and intelligent women, forever experiencing 'crushes' on those interesting young ladies that he met in the course of his work. More seriously, there was the never-to-be-resolved tension in his life between his love for his (increasingly estranged) wife Penelope and his constant lover-companion, Lady Elizabeth Cavendish. Nor was Betjeman a 'sentimental philanderer' in Murry's sense that he dallied uncritically with 'aesthetic Catholicism", although his wife Penelope, much to his regret, did go over to Rome. Yet he *was* drawn to the aesthetic 'Celtic church' (those Cornish saints waist-deep in cold streams), and to the Anglo-Catholic church in Cornwall which he held to be its direct inheritor: to that extent the accusation levelled against Ambrose Meyrick also applied to him. Moreover, as we have seen, he was certainly 'a mystical Celtic dreamer', and possibly also a 'Soho Bohemian' in the sense that Murry meant it. But most of all, Betjeman had an overwhelming penchant for 'poetic prose' – which was, ironically, perhaps the best description of his blank verse *Summoned By Bells*.

To the discomforting observations posed by Middleton Murry was added the fate of Ambrose Meyrick himself. Put simply, in the pages of *The Secret Glory* Meyrick found salvation – and martyrdom – through his embrace of Celtic Christianity and pursuit of the Holy Grail. He was driven by the twin imperatives of kicking at his public school in dullest England and hankering after the secrets of the Grail locked in deepest Wales. At his 'hideous school', set amid 'the weary waves of dun Midland scenery bounded by the dim, hopeless horizon', his 'soul revisited the faery hills and valleys of the West'. He longed for 'the whole company of the Blessed Saints of the Isle of Britain', for the 'deep apple-garths in Avalon', and 'all the dear land of Gwent'.[79] He watched trains 'vanishing into the west ... away towards the haven of his desire', and celebrated in his heart 'the Ancient Mass of the Britons ... the religion that led me and drew me and compelled me was that wonderful and doubtful mythos of the Celtic Church'.[80]

Thus far, Betjeman's identification with Ambrose Meyrick was complete. He too, when weighed down by the daily routine of London suburbia, knew that 'west of westward, somewhere, Cornwall lay', and that 'Somewhere among the cairns or in the caves/ The Celtic saints would come to me'.[81] But, thereafter, there was much to discomfort him. First of all, as Ambrose Meyrick was initiated into the secrets of the Holy Grail, so it became clear that this rare privilege also carried a terrible responsibility and an inevitable, terrifying destiny. To pursue the Holy Grail was to condemn oneself to a life of perpetual search, perpetual yearning. But to come close to the Grail was to earn a dreadful fate, that of martyrdom. And then, in his journeying, Ambrose Meyrick strayed and stumbled, as did so many of those who allowed themselves to be distracted in their lifetime's quest. Still rebelling against his school, he took up with one of its domestic servants, Nelly Foran, absconding with her. He could not quite believe it: 'I cannot feel she is really Nelly Foran who opens the door and waits at table, for she is a miracle ... [a] wonderful, beautiful body shining through the darkness':

> I saw golden Myfanwy, as she bathed in the brook Tarogi.
> Her hair flowed about her. Arthur's crown had dissolved into a
>   Shining mist.
> I gazed into her blue eyes as it were into twin heavens. All the parts
>   Of her body were adornments and miracles.
> O gift of the everlasting!
> O wonderful hidden mystery!
> When I embraced Myfanwy a moment became immortality.[82]

Yet this Myfanwy *was* Nelly Foran. Posing as Mr & Mrs Lupton (named ironically after Ambrose's school), they find lodgings in London. Soon Ambrose has taught Nelly how to smoke, and together they sit up in bed puffing at their cigarettes. At breakfast, 'They laughed so loud and so merrily over their morning tea ... that the landlady doubted gravely as to their marriage lines'. However, 'She cared nothing; they had paid what she had asked, money down in advance, and, she said: "Young gentlemen *will* have their fun with the young ladies – so what's the good of talking?"'.[83] Suddenly it all began to seem a bit sordid, and Ambrose knew it had to end. As he broke the news to Nelly, she looked at him 'with the most piteous longing ... I shall never forget the sad enchantment of her face ... the tears were wet on her cheek'.[84] But it had to be done. Thereafter, Ambrose led a life of relative obscurity until, on the death of its Keeper, the Holy Grail was placed in his charge: 'he received it with the condition that it was to be taken to a certain concealed shrine in Asia and there deposited in hands that would know how to hide its glories forever from the evil world'. He did as he was bid but as he neared his destination he was captured by 'the Turks or the Kurds – it does not matter which'. They insisted that he spit upon the image of Christ Crucified but he refused: 'So they bore him to a tree outside the village and crucified him there'. And thus 'It was in this manner that Ambrose Meyrick gained Red Martyrdom and achieved the most glorious Quest and Adventure of the Sangraal'.[85]

We know that Betjeman was fascinated by Ambrose Meyrick's progress

– evidenced, for example, in his poems 'Myfanwy' ('Golden the lights on the locks of Myfanwy') and 'Myfanwy at Oxford' ('Gold Myfanwy blesses us all') – but his experience was one from which he inevitably shrank. The metaphor of martyrdom was all too powerful, and Betjeman knew that in his own life, with its numerous distractions and his great love of fun and frivolity, he too would stray one way or another from the straight and narrow. Guilt, angst and a wavering, doubtful faith would be his 'martyrdom'. But he kept up his personal quest for the Holy Grail, both in the sense of rooting himself ever more deeply in Cornwall – especially North Cornwall – and in pursuing a religious vision which owed much to Hawker, Baring-Gould and Wilfred Johnson.

Conclusion

Like Arthur Machen, John Betjeman had seen both 'good' and 'evil' in the 'Celtic' landscape, and like Machen he had attempted to mediate these two constructions of place, opting for a North Cornwall which still retained its *frisson* of 'happy terror' but was fundamentally a place of Christian goodness and redemption. *The Secret Glory* had been a revelation and an inspiration, even if its portents were profoundly unsettling, and the book confirmed his own awareness of personal 'Celticity' as well strengthening his commitment to a mystical Anglo-Catholicism. It was in North Cornwall, indeed, that Betjeman was to find his first and last freedoms – freedom from his father (when bicycling inland to places such as St Ervan), freedom from his marriage (when he holidayed at Trebetherick with Elizabeth Cavendish) – and it was there that he died. Fittingly, he lies buried in St Enodoc churchyard.

From the beginning, Betjeman, so conscious of himself as 'foreigner', had attempted to ally himself with the Cornish, criticising the negative impact of tourism and 'Whitehall', and insisting that Cornwall was not part of England. He deployed his 'Welshness' to build a wider sympathy for the Celtic world – Ireland, the Isle of Man, even Berwick-upon-Tweed – and revelled unapologetically in stories of the Celtic saints and King Arthur. As A. L. Rowse had told him, Betjeman could never expect to be Cornish. But how successful was he in aligning himself with Cornwall? Intriguingly, unlike Daphne du Maurier, who (despite her membership of Mebyon Kernow) was often the butt of Cornish nationalist critics, Betjeman appears to have attracted little hostile attention from such quarters. A clumsy spoof Betjemenesque poem in the journal *Cornish Nation* in the mid-1970s was one of few critical pieces.[86] By contrast, Donald R. Rawe – author, poet, playwright, publisher, Mebyon Kernow activist and Stannary Parliament member – was moved after Betjeman's death to contribute a lengthy poem to the magazine *Cornish Scene*, couched in Betjemanesque language and implicitly affirming Betjeman's vision of Cornwall.[87] In this context, imitation was the sincerest form of flattery: doubly so, since Rawe was a native of Padstow and had written the definitive history of the 'Obby 'Oss.[88] Later, at the centenary of Betjeman's birth in 2006, the nationalist magazine *An Baner Kernewek/ The Cornish Banner* ran an affectionate memorial article, outlining in approving manner Betjeman's life-long links with Cornwall.[89]

A bit like his days in Ireland, perhaps, when the IRA decided that he was a decent fellow and removed him from its assassination hit-list, Betjeman was seen in Cornwall as a largely sympathetic figure. In a BBC television programme in 2006, celebrating the centenary of Betjeman's birth, the successful restauranteur and TV personality, Rick Stein, compared himself with Betjeman: they were both 'outsiders' who had taken North Cornwall to heart but who, in their celebration of it, were perhaps in danger of spoiling the very place they loved. We might add, however, that, despite Betjeman's own fears on this score, few people had actually accused him of this – in contrast to Rick Stein, whose business ventures in Padstow had led to the coining of the pejorative 'Padstein' and the belief in some circles that his commercial activities were driving local house prices beyond the reach of Cornish pockets.[90] John Betjeman, perhaps, had succeeded in his quest for the Holy Grail in a manner that had eluded others, before and since. Whatever Rowse might have thought, Cornwall – North Cornwall – could rightfully be considered his adoptive home, alongside Hawker, Baring-Gould and Wilfred Johnson.

Acknowledgements

I am grateful to Candida Lycett Green for her encouragement, and for her support of my 'John Betjeman and Cornwall' project, of which this article is a preliminary part, as well as her permission (through the John Betjeman Estate) to quote from Betjeman's work. I should also like to thank participants in the Humanities & Social Science seminars at the University of Exeter's Cornwall Campus for their suggestions, criticisms and advice.

Notes and references

1. See A. N. Wilson, *Betjeman* (London, 2006).
2. John Betjeman, *Summoned By Bells* (London, 1960), p. 4.
3. See Philip Payton, *A. L. Rowse and Cornwall: A Paradoxical Patriot* (Exeter, 2005), p. 239.
4. Betjeman, *Summoned By Bells*, p. 79.

5. Marion Bowman, 'Cardiac Celts: Images of the Celts in Contemporary British Paganism', in G. Harvey and C. Hardman (eds), *Paganism Today* (London, 1996).
6. Bevis Hillier, *Young Betjeman* (London, 1988), pp. 7.
7. John Betjeman (edited by Candida Lycett Green), *John Betjeman: Coming Home – An Anthology of his Prose 1920–1977* (London, 1997), p. 186.
8. John Betjeman, *Betjeman's Cornwall* (London, 1984), p. 20.
9. John Betjeman (edited by Stephen Games), *Trains and Buttered Toast: Selected Radion Talks* (London, 2006), p. 301.
10. Betjeman (Games), *Trains and Buttered Toast*, p. 107.
11. Ibid., p. 105.
12. Ibid., p. 95.
13. Ibid., p. 38.
14. Ibid., p. 38.
15. John Betjeman (edited by Nigel Kerr), *Guide to English Parish Churches* (London, 1958; new edn, 1993), p. 125.
16. Ibid., p. 125.
17. Ibid., 1993, p. 125.
18. Betjeman (Green), *Coming Home – An Anthology*, p. 440.
19. Ibid., p. 441.
20. Ibid., p. 442.
21. Betjeman (Kerr), *Guide to English Parish Churches*, p. 125.
22. Ibid., p. 125.
23. *Cornish Nation*, January–February 1969.
24. Daphne du Maurier, *Vanishing Cornwall* (London, 1967), p. 200.
25. Betjeman (Kerr), *Guide to English Parish Churches*, pp. 125–6.
26. Betjeman (Games), *Trains and Buttered Toast*, p. 204.
27. Ibid., p. 204.
28. Betjeman (Kerr), *Guide to English Parish Churches*, p. 131.
29. Betjeman (Games), *Trains and Buttered Toast*, p. 208.
30. T. W. E. Roche, *The Withered Arm* (Bracknell, 1967).
31. University of Exeter Library Special Collections, Betjeman Library.
32. Betjeman (Games), *Trains and Buttered Toast*, p. 293.
33. Betjeman, *Summoned By Bells*, p. 33.
34. John Betjeman, *London's Historic Railway Stations* (London, 1972), pp. 74–9.
35. See Philip Payton, *The Cornish Overseas: A History of Cornwall's Emigration* (Fowey, 2005), chapter two.
36. Betjeman, *Summoned By Bells*, p. 33.
37. Betjeman (Green), *Coming Home – An Anthology*, p. 242.
38. Ibid., p. 242.
39. Ibid., p. 242.
40. See Hillier, *Young Betjeman*, p. 89.
41. Betjeman, *Summoned By Bells*, pp. 33, 40.
42. Betjeman (Games), *Trains and Buttered Toast*, p. 35.
43. John Betjeman, *Collected Poems* (1958; new edn, Boston, MA, 1971), p. 66.
44. Betjeman (Games), *Trains and Buttered Toast*, p. 163.
45. Ibid., p. 189.
46. Ibid., pp. 107, 191.
47. Ibid., p. 107.

48. Ibid., pp. 140–1.
49. Betjeman (Green), *Coming Home – An Anthology*, p. 472.
50. Ibid., p. 273.
51. Betjeman (Games), *Trains and Buttered Toast*, p. 37.
52. Ibid., pp. 190–1.
53. Ibid., p. 194.
54. Betjeman, *Collected Poems*, p. 98.
55. Betjeman (Games), *Trains and Buttered Toast*, p. 162.
56. Betjeman (Green), *Coming Home – An Anthology*, p. 188.
57. Betjeman (Games), *Trains and Buttered Toast*, pp. 161–2.
58. Cited in Betjeman (Green), *Coming Home – An Anthology*, p. 189.
59. Betjeman (Green), *Coming Home – An Anthology*, pp. 188–9.
60. Betjeman, *Summoned By Bells*, p. 85.
61. Ibid., pp. 86–7.
62. Moira Tangye, *The Book of St Ervan* (Tiverton, 2006), pp. 111–16.
63. Guy W. Hockley and W.R. Johnson, 'Truro', in C.S. Phillips (ed.), *Walter Howard Frere: Bishop of Truro* (London, 1947), pp. 76–103.
64. Edwin Stark, *Saint Endellion* (Redruth, 1983), p. 69.
65. Sharon Lowena, '"Noscitur A Sociis": Jenner, Duncombe-Jewell and their Milieu', in Philip Payton (ed.), *Cornish Studies: Twelve* (Exeter, 2004), pp. 61–87.
66. Paul Newman, *The Tregerthen Horror: Aleister Crowley, D.H. Lawrence and Peter Warlock in Cornwall* (St Austell, 2005).
67. Arthur Machen, *The Autobiography of Arthur Machen* (1951), pp. 120–1.
68. Hillier, *Young Betjeman*, p. 122.
69. Ibid..
70. Betjeman, *Summoned By Bells*, p. 87.
71. Hillier, *Young Betjeman*, p. 192.
72. Betjeman (Green), *Coming Home – An Anthology*, p. 150.
73. Ibid., p. 327.
74. Ibid., p. 326.
75. Bryon Rogers, *The Man Who Went into the West: The Life of R.S. Thomas* (London, 2006), pp. 6, 185, 186–7, 210.
76. Betjeman (Green), *Coming Home – An Anthology*, p. 150.
77. Betjeman, *Summoned By Bells*, p. 87.
78. Machen, *Autobiography of Arthur Machen*, p. 260.
79. Arthur Machen, *The Secret Glory* (1922; new edn n.d.), pp. 43, 49.
80. Ibid., pp. 70, 100–1.
81. Betjeman, *Summoned By Bells*, pp. 19, 88.
82. Machen, *The Secret Glory*, pp. 88–9.
83. Ibid., p. 118.
84. Ibid., p. 140.
85. Ibid., pp. 142–3.
86. *Cornish Nation*, March 1973.
87. *Cornish Scene*, Summer 1988, pp. 72–6.
88. Donald R. Rawe, *Padstow's 'Obby 'Oss and May Day Festivities: A Study in Folklore and Tradition* (Padstow, 1971).
89. *An Baner Kernewek*, November 2006.
90. *Daily Mail*, 14 June 2007; *The Times*, 14 June 2007.

8

Alex Parks, Punks and Pipers

Towards a History of Popular Music in Cornwall, 1967–2007

Alan M. Kent

Introduction: Kool Kernow Agas Dynnargh

In the age of television talent shows like *Pop Idol*, there can be few observers of Cornish culture who have not recognized the impact of the singer Alex Parks (*b*.1984) in putting a Cornish-based artist into the mainstream popular music culture of these islands. Parks, who won BBC 1's *Fame Academy* in 2003, had her first single ('Maybe That's What it Takes') rise to number three in the United Kingdom Top 40 chart. The live final of the show saw members of the audience waving St Piran's flags, as Parks sang her songs. She released her debut album *Introduction* (reaching number five in the album chart) to both popular and critical acclaim This was followed in 2006 by her second album *Honest*.[1] Parks, as both artist and personality, has spoken freely about her sexuality and her identity, and the desire of the Mount Hawke-based singer to return sometimes to Cornwall, away from the media circus and hype of the popular music industry.[2]

Parks is the most famous contemporary Cornish pop star, the like of whom has not been seen before in Cornwall. Her success has not only raised the possibility of a higher profile for a 'kool Kernow', but has also reinvigorated the popular music industry in Cornwall. It is smaller in scale than, say, the artists associated with the rise of New Labour (Oasis, Pulp, and Blur)[3] or the development of Welsh popular music culture in recent years (The Stereophonics, The Manic Street Preachers, Catatonia, Super Furry Animals, Charlotte Church).[4] Nonetheless, there is a perceived shift, and a more aggressive promotion of Cornish artists is now occurring. Retail shifts in Cornwall have also resulted in a new awareness of home-grown talent, with Britain-wide music store HMV opening in Truro (Cornwall's premier shopping location), and offering promotion of Cornish music along 'Made in Cornwall' lines.

Meanwhile, Cornish Studies, in a profusion of work on traditional Cornish subject matter (language, emigration, mining, Methodism) is only just getting to grips with contemporary popular culture. Jonathan Howlett's recent work on 'kitsch' is a step in the right direction, as is Merv Davey's important discussion of 'Darkie Days' at Padstow.[5] As Philip Payton has noted, this late start is not surprising, given the long-term cultural background and development of Cornish Studies as an area of academic enquiry.[6] However, the space and place of popular music in Cornwall is just beginning to be investigated by scholars. In earlier work, I have endeavoured to locate Cornish popular music within the context of wider British youth culture,[7] while observers such as Woodhouse and Davey have attempted to understand popular musicology in previous ages.[8] Likewise, Thornton, although studying Ireland rather than Cornwall, has attempted to understand the commercial construction of contemporary Celtic music, providing insights which have profoundly important implications for Cornish music.[9] There have also been serious studies devoted to defining and understanding Cornish music within the wider field of Celtic music.[10] However, the previous emphasis in musical scholarship has tended to focus on folkloric collecting – so-called 'traditional' songs and ballads – and also how these might best be revived,[11] often at the expense of ethno-musicological study. Certainly in Cornwall, there have been few studies of the relationship between music and ethnicity. It is a new and potentially rich field of research.

There is a conceptual difficulty here, for 'traditional' music was of course once also 'popular'. Additionally, we need to consider the merging that sometimes occurs of the 'traditional' with the 'contemporary',[12] an area which has received little scholarly attention but also merits sustained academic treatment. While it might be tempting to look only at those artists who attempt to generate a purely Cornish identity in their music, such restriction would inevitably limit consideration of the much bigger picture of popular music activity in Cornwall over the last quarter of a century. We must also acknowledge that popular music is not an isolated phenomenon. Indeed, with the development of *iPod* technology, *iTunes*, pod-casts, downloads and the perceived end of 'traditional' record shops as we know them,[13] it is evermore multi-national and eclectic, and this complex mix is now central in our understanding of how popular music operates and develops.

Taking all this into account, we ought to be to offer a coherent discussion of indigenous Cornish popular music. Certain critical questions need to be asked. For example, how far is this music influenced by Cornwall's perceived

'Celticity'? Beyond that, what can we learn from Cornwall about the present state of popular music generally? As I have argued elswehere,[14] there are benefits in analysing traditional and wider popular culture in tandem. This applies especially to music, since the two are closely linked and have co-existed over time in the same cultural space. In the useful words of M. Wynn Thomas, they are 'corresponding cultures'.[15]

Cornish sound-scapes: Melody, methodology and MP3

To many observers of Cornish Studies, popular music may seem of only passing interest alongside 'nation-defining' topics such as language or hard-rock mining. Yet it is this author's contention that the cultural, political and economic impact of popular music (both 'incoming' into Cornwall and 'outgoing') on Cornish culture is significant and undeniable. Since the early 1950s, popular music has grown from comparatively humble origins to a multi-billion pound international industry uniquely linked to youth culture. In the past, studies of popular music have tended to be focused on discrete aspects, such as sociology, musical history or biography, yet popular music can only really be understood through an interdisciplinary method (a methodology fitting well within New Cornish Studies), which should range from, say, the political economy of a particular kind of popular music (such as the late 1990s grunge genre in Newquay) and history and ethnography (the corpus of Cornish 'traditional' music), to issues of semiotics (lettering and fonts), aesthetics (cover designs), iconography (fashion, 'look' and image) and ideology (apolitical or politically committed). The ground-breaking scholarship of sociological observers such as Middleton and Frith[16] has led to other equally important studies in defining the field, such as Savage's work on Punk rock,[17] not to mention a collective cultural awareness of the validity and importance of writings about popular music, as established in the work of Heylin.[18] Likewise, the respected Marxist literary critic, Terry Eagleton, has had to re-investigate the place of popular music in his work.[19]

The intention of this article, therefore, is to draw upon some of the established critical methodologies concerned with popular music. It is not fully comprehensive, or biographical, but explores the popular music field as a whole in Cornwall, drawing on several dialectical conceptions of musical development which range across genres and periods. To this end, I hope to offer something of an initial historical map of this field, which others can build upon and expand. In the process, it will be necessary to draw on existing musical histories, and engage with issues of identity and devolution within a wider historical context, which (paradoxically) often refutes globalization and twentieth- and twenty-first-century 'mass-culture'.

Music-making and hearing is a complex field, and is notoriously difficult to pin down. The components of the music industry are ever-changing and developing. This article is already out of date. The received wisdom is that in a capitalist western society, media conglomerates control particular markets and have succeeded in turning 'popular music' into more and more products and consumables for an eagerly recipient public. Yet this view needs to be contested and modified, particularly when investigating a relatively tiny territory like Cornwall. 'Popular music' is itself an elusive concept. As the on-going debate in Cultural Studies continues to ask, what exactly does *popular* mean? What is 'popular' to one person, may not be for another. 'Popular music' is, however, a convenient label for us to apply to music which is listened to (and engaging for) a sizable proportion of the population. The concept of a musical cultural geography is also important in allowing us to understand the spatial dimension to popular music in Cornwall, and is an essential tool in helping us understand more clearly concert space, gigs, clubs, festivals and other locations for music performance and consumption.

The popular music industry operates globally, and is dominated by five major companies which all belong to conglomerates: Sony Music Entertainment, EMI Music, Bertelsmann Music Group, MCA and Warner Music International. The aim of these conglomerates is to build and develop global empires, and to develop artists who have global appeal. Part of this strategy is sometimes to identify regions of the world which will be more receptive than others to their output. Cornwall is a relatively small region in this equation, but it has implications for the marketing of artists such as Alex Parks or, as well shall see later, for alternative rock bands like Thirteen Senses.

Despite the global dominance of these companies, much music is still circulated by independent record labels and distributors, who seek not always 'global' acts but who have identified niche groups and niche markets. Often this is conducted along subcultural lines: one example might be thrash metal, another punk, or so on. Yet some 'independents' will also market work along ethnic lines. Cornish examples the Withiel-based Kesson and www.CornishMusic.com.[20] There are comparable examples in both Ireland and Wales.[21] Needless to say, given the technological developments of the past twenty years, a more self-supporting, *ad hoc* production network has developed around smaller-selling artists, with home studios using cheap technology and a distribution system based around touring, the internet, word of mouth and mobile phone technology.[22] In many ways, this system of production was based on the ethic of autonomy once propagated by Punk rock. The ascendancy of the CD over all other forms of recordings in the past twenty-five years has greatly contributed to the better distribution and variety of recordings available in the Cornish cultural context. However, perhaps the largest shift in popular music over the past five years has been relationship between the internet and the music industry. Dane and Laing have identified the following shifts:

- the retail of traditional soundcarriers
- the marketing of recordings and other activities
- netcasts or live performances
- the retail of music that is not available other than through the net
- sites set up by stars or artists to provide a range of services[23]

An important issue here is what may be termed 'convergence', since many listeners now have the ability to use a variety of devices as music players: domestic computers, MP3 players, iPods, and so on. The major and minor record labels have felt threatened by the growing use of the internet because music files can be sent and downloaded without recourse to the record labels, which feel they will lose control of the distribution of music, and thus revenue. This raises many issues considered with the cultural exchange of popular music in the future. Yet this new autonomy may end up propagating musical development in new ways, particularly in Cornwall where locally produced popular music has probably only limited global appeal.

Observers such as Frith[24] and Sinfield (in particular)[25] have always argued for the linkages between popular music and teenage subculture. The idea of a youth subculture implies a distinctive group that is separate from, and sets itself apart from, the dominant culture of other young people. Recognizable subcultures such as teddy boys, mods, rockers, skinheads and punks have all been reliant on the music industry and other aspects of wider culture to delineate their style and identity. In this sense subcultures can be regarded as creative in that they can be contrasted with more conformist youth culture, although they are often manipulated by the music industry to the extent that they become 'mainstream' and lose their subcultural edge. We need, therefore, to be cautious, although there are certainly recognizable local micro-subcultures in both past and present Cornwall, most of which have received little academic attention hitherto.[26] Examples of these might include the followers of the West Cornwall 'ska' group Ska'd for Life, the long-established link between the china clay villages and heavy metal, and the rave and grunge music which strongly shaped 1990s youth culture in Newquay. But we must also ask if there is a specific subculture related to Cornwall.

The answer is perhaps no, yet there are some subcultural elements in young people's listening habits and fashion that are geographically and ethnically determined. Surfing, skate-boarding and a certain level of interest in goth-punk and rock may be aspects of this. Bullet for My Valentine is one of only a few goth-rock bands to have played in venues such as Truro's 'Hall for Cornwall' but its presence did much to stimulate interest in the genre and to establish its validity in Cornwall. By 'playing Cornwall' bands also assert the validity of place and, by virtue of their presence and performance, reinforce Cornwall's vibrancy, visibility and identity within contemporary Britain as a whole.[27] This 'validity' and its sense of place allows young people in Cornwall to assess other subcultures with a degree of confidence and criticism. Thus many appear to consider 'Chav' culture an 'inauthentic' English import, located outside their own complex notions of local identity. In this way, perceived cultural differences can be expressed through fashion and music.

These are some of the core debates which surround both the production and consumption of popular music in Cornwall. As can be readily observed, there is much cultural pluralism and diffusion in the Cornish musical scene, together with the changing role of popular music in shaping different imaginings of Cornish youth identities. In investigating these further, it is useful to commence with consideration of the connection between 'traditional' and 'popular' music in Cornwall.

The living tradition

A serious ethnomusicology of the 'traditional' music of Cornwall has yet to undertaken.[28] This section does not claim to be a comprehensive portrait of this genre. Likewise, there are several artists which time and space do not permit me to discuss in full.[29] Instead, my intention here is to try to assess the impact of 'traditional' music upon listeners in Cornwall. I use the term 'the living tradition' to describe a specific set of popular music artists operating within Cornish culture, whose music is firmly rooted in 'traditional' instrumentation or songs, in Cornish language or Cornu-English performance, and in a conceptualization of their work as being part of a Cornish-Celtic and wider Celtic tradition. This is an eclectic category, and one in which some artists sit more comfortably than others. 'Living tradition' best describes how these artists draw upon and adapt Cornwall's traditional musical and linguistic lineage in producing and thus defining their contemporary sound. There is not the need here to explain in detail the various strands of that musical heritage, since, as in most western societies, it contains a range of indigenous surviving works, borrowings, adaptations and inventions,[30] which together have contributed over time to an over-arching folk canon of Cornish music.

For many observers, however, there has been a certain shift in knowledge concerning Cornish folk music. For several decades – especially during and immediately after the early twentieth-century Revival – Cornwall seemed to gaze heavily towards other Celtic cultures, where an apparently 'genuine' or 'authentic' tradition was thought to exist.[31] The reasons for this would appear twofold. Firstly, for many of the Cornish musicians and activists, this gaze was positive and inspirational, and acted as a point of departure for their future work. There was a clear sense that Cornwall had a lot to offer within the Pan-Celtic world, and the Cornish musicians argued that their music had a definite place within this wider Celtic genre. Secondly (and paradoxically) there was a lack of self-confidence in Cornwall, and the gaze served to exaggerate Cornwall's sense of inadequacy. In particular, Brittany and Ireland appeared to be Celtic cultures in which 'organic' social and popular music had survived without recourse to reinvention.[32] It was important, then, it was thought, to look to these 'superior' cultures and to try to emulate them. However, as several scholars have shown subsequently, reinvention had also occurred in those cultures (perhaps they were just better at masking it[33]), while in Cornwall there was – even if hidden sometimes beneath the surface – a unique musical tradition, some of it only recently 'discovered', such as the Boscastle recordings and the Mevagissey corpus of clog-dancing.[34] It was no longer necessary to look to other Celtic cultures to see what was 'authentic', although global perceptions of what constitutes 'Celtic music' are still heavily influenced by Irish performance.[35]

During the late 1960s and 1970s Cornish musicians increasingly lost their 'poor cousin' status, despite some resistance from other Celtic countries (one Cornish musician told me that she remembers being critiqued for playing in 'a non-traditional Celtic key'), and by the 1980s they had begun to articulate a more nuanced criticism of 'Celtic music', in the process asking some difficult questions. For example, if Irish music was so traditional and organic, then why was the main corpus played with mainly English-language lyrics? Did Cornwall really need to fit the type? Perhaps there was other instrumentation that better defined ethnic music in Cornwall. By the 1990s and into the new millennium, the position had certainly changed. Although there remained some pressure to follow the Pan-Celtic model (a phenomenon still visible at the major festival of Celtic music in Cornwall, 'Lowender Perran'[36]), there was now a new group of scholars and musicians which was actively, even aggressively, redefining the 'trad' Cornish sound.

If the change was happening musically, it was also happening in terms of iconography. For much of the post-war period, various artists who had played 'trad' music had combined their performance with dance display teams. These teams exhibited a Pan-Celtic affinity, and so attempted to dress in 'traditional' Cornish costume. At this point, there was no recognized Cornish costume (unlike Wales or Brittany[37]), and so dance display teams wore the 'get up' of bal-maidens (with tartan) and miners (as in the group Cam Kernewek), or simply incorporated gold Celtic knotwork on black skirts (Ros Keltek). The musicians' attire also often matched the way the dance teams dressed, so that overall there was a performance that was explicitly and self-consciously 'Celtic'. Just 'being Cornish' was not good enough if one were playing traditional music; one had to look the 'Celtic' part. Instructional videos such as *Corollyn*, produced at the time, followed the same ideology.[38]

Of late, however, this has altered considerably, and there has been a rejection of this 'false' imagery, together an attempt at adopting a more 'genuinely Cornish' attire. Ros Keltek, for example, has now dispensed with the Celtic knotwork, adopting instead the garb of maritime fish jowsters (using gook headwear), with more than a hint of 'Newlyn School' imagery. A self-conscious rejection of the 'Celtic' dance scene had also been witnessed in the progressive, and at times controversial, work of caller and choreographer Karen Brown, and the young dance group Otta Nye. Group members wore individually designed costumes in colours of turquoise, green and purple, and in its promotion and iconography Otta Nye deliberately linked itself to Rave and Trance.[39] These developments were not always easy, with some groups resistant to change and others forcing the pace, a process which echoed wider tensions within the Cornish Revival at the time and mirrored current debates within the Cornish-language movement. Over time, however, the transition produced a new ethos, one seeking to combine 'living tradition' with dance, a fusion that has resulted in the development of so-called 'Noze Looan'. A more organic and populist conceptualization of traditional 'troyls'[40] or 'ceilidhs', 'Noze Looan' requires only normal clothing and a willingness to take part. There is some debate over the term itself. Some observers assume the term is related to the Breton Fest Noz-style contemporary gatherings, although there is considerable evidence that early Cornish revivalists used the term 'Noswyth Lowen' to label their evenings of music, poetry and storytelling.[41]

Because other Celtic territories covered their album and CD covers in quasi-medieval 'Celtic' lettering and knotwork, Cornwall had followed suit. Many of the products from the 1970s and 1980s projected an iconographically uncompromising picture of Celticity, perhaps in a bid to assert Celtic credentials in the face of a wider Celtic movement that was still sceptical of Cornwall's musical status. Of course, the other reason was that people liked it. That side of Celticity is appealing to a post-modernist audience seeking a more fulfilling past. Once again, there is a number of parallels here with the post-war Cornish language revival.[42] Indeed, many of those active within the language revival movement were also active musicians and dancers.[43] A particular squint was given, therefore, to the cultural politics of the era. In many respects, it was a safe Celtic world, which saw 'fusion' and experimentation as almost dangerous, and perhaps even to be resisted, in the face of the globalizing impact of American – and especially 'English' – popular music culture, which many argued had through long-players, cinema and television 'corrupted' and destroyed an apparently once healthy indigenous culture. The myth was a curious one, but it had been remarkably persistent, restricting the production of what cultural materialist critic Raymond Williams has termed 'emergent culture'.[44]

Yet there was an 'emergent culture' in the making. Perhaps the first piece of contemporary popular music culture to arise from the living tradition in Cornwall was Bucca's *An Tol yn Pen an Telynor/The Hole in the Harper's Head* (1976).[45] The work was assembled by the influential Davey family, who were to become the most important group of musicians of the late twentieth-century, with some lyrical contributions made by the Cornish-language poet Tim Saunders.[46] The brothers Merv, Kyt, Neil and Andy Davey are now names synonymous with the traditional music scene within Cornwall. There was some cultural lag apparent in the sleeve of the piece, which seemed more suited to a progressive rock band of the early 1970s, and yet the album was hugely influential, defining the sound and format of music for the next few decades.

The grandiose title sounded progressive. The intention of the Davey brothers was to draw on the popular tradition in Cornwall, and to reinvent it for the 1970s. It was a brave and bold move, drawing on active language revival and the folkloric heritage of Cornwall. The choice of the band's name – Bucca[47] – gave its identity an edge and suggested deviousness. Up until this point, the outside world's perception of Cornish music had been based upon the work of Brenda Wootton, who notably had many songs composed for her by the poet Richard Gendall. Wootton's status was guaranteed in Cornwall, and in particular in Brittany, and she regularly toured throughout Europe.[48] Wootton's popular status was confirmed when she took over the running of the lunchtime request spot on BBC Radio Cornwall on Sundays during the late 1980s, but her work was not always accessible to the youth culture market.

With Bucca up and running, there was a sense that the Cornish tradition was a corpus worth reconsidering. By the late 1970s, other troyl and dance groups had begun to emerge, which helped further to define and shape the Cornish 'trad' sound. One of these was Cam Kernewek, formed in 1979 and led by Alison (as caller) and Merv Davey.[49] In many ways, the music of Cam Kernewek was progressive but the group found itself competing within the wider Celtic festival and dance events, trying where possible to assert a new Cornish presence. Regulars on the Celtic circuit, Cornish language events, dance displays, and becoming almost the 'Lowender Perran' house band, Cam Kernewek was among the first to 'dust down' some of the older Cornish songs and to identify what the tradition actually was. It interpreted the canonical songs in its own way. Merv Davey, in particular, did much ground-breaking work here.

However, the tradition appeared to be played with a particular Pan-Celtic emphasis. The artwork of the group's cassettes and releases matched this, with the usual knotwork and spirals.[50] In 1980 Cam Kernewek offered a more folkloric motif to its music, linking it with their conceptualization of 'Pengwyn' – a white horse's skull on a stick, surrounded by a black cloak, paraded with the music.[51] Although a partial invention, it offered a Celtic mysticism that linked to other horses in surviving traditions, such as the 'Obby 'Oss at Padstow and the so-called 'mast horse' at Penzance. Cam Kernewek imploded in 1997, with most members of the group continuing as Asteveryn[52] and Tan ha Dowr (the latter featuring the next generation of the Davey family).[53] Asteveryn was primarily a dance band, while Tan ha Dowr encouraged new and youthful musicianship. Although, with hindsight, it might seem easy to criticize Cam Kernewek for its Pan-Celticism, the reality was that it was caught culturally between a rock and hard place. Having to defer to the prevailing demands of Pan-Celticism, it nonetheless did much to popularize the living tradition.

New beginnings: Dalla, Bolingey and Gwenno

The 1990s heralded some important changes. One of the most active Cornish-language enthusiasts and writers during the 1980s had been the then Liskeard-based Graham Sandercock. Sandercock's vision in 1992 was to offer on his cassette *Poll Pri* an electrified and amplified Cornish rock music.[54] This drew on the living tradition, and as well as offering songs about traditional Cornish subject-matter (Daniel Gumb, china clay), was also producing songs about other places and cultures ('Dagrow Sygh un Afrika'). The iconography of the cover had altered too: the band was depicted at Roche Rock. This was more in tune with what was happening in other contemporary popular music, and so was an explicit stab at a modern update. Importantly, Sandercock was not concerned with re-invigorating 'standard' songs, but actually writing and recording new music. A second album *In Gwyn ha Du* followed in 1997, under the Gwyn ha Du name.[55] Out of the *Poll Pri* corpus of musicians, another project had emerged; this time explicitly for presenting popular music for children on a cassette, *Planet Kernow* (1994).[56]

More recently, the revolution in the living tradition of Cornish music has come from a n.s. of groups, which has tried to alter the public's conceptualization of what this kind of music is about. One of the starting points for this development was an all-girl trio of musicians, known as Gwaryoryon.[57] Gwaryoryon used traditional instrumentation, and on their

1996 recording *The Three Drunken Maidens* tried more fully to develop a 'truly' Cornish sound and song repertoire, uninfluenced by other Pan-Celtic musical movements.[58] This has been characterized as a certain 'droning' sound.[59] One of Gwaryoryon's key members was Hilary Coleman, and she was also instrumental in forming a musical project called Captain Kernow and the Jack & Jenny Band, producing an album, *Teeriow Droag* in 1997.[60] The cover iconography was experimental and featured a sad-looking dog with a Cornish flag upon it. Although many of the songs on the album were from the corpus ('Bodmin Riding' and the oft-used 'Cadgwith Anthem', for example) the approach was less 'folksy' and more urgent, displaying more pop music sensibilities than before, and combining this with Modern (Late) Cornish rather than the medievalist Unified or Kemmyn of most other 'living tradition' performers. Importantly too, the album saw songs which had been written by Jim Pengelly, a former mainstay of Cam Kernewek, and Neil Davey of Bucca fame.[61]

The name of this group, was however, short-lived and the band mutated into Sowena, producing in 1999 the album *A Month of Sundays*.[62] This CD remains an important benchmark, since it rejected much of the earlier iconography (the cover featured a lizard in the desert), and for the first time it looked as though it might be possible to place Cornish music in the World Music category in HMV or Virgin Records. Retaining the Modern Cornish lyrical motifs, the feel was also very much post-medieval. Sowena seemed to be imagining a Cornish culture that was resolutely Cornish, but also resolutely modern. The trappings of Pan-Celticism and the medievalist predilections of the Revival could therefore be dropped in favour of a more realist response to Cornish experience.

When Sowena 're-emerged' in 2001 as Dalla, with its mining-themed CD *A Richer Vein*,[63] the transformation was more or less complete, with a re-invigorated popular music. Dalla combined concerts with the notion of Noze Looans around Cornwall – in village halls, at festivals and community events, even weddings – often rejecting hints of self-conscious and increasingly unfashionable revivalism of the earlier period. In 2004 Dalla released the second CD, titled *Hollan Mouy!/More Salt!* which saw a further development of their sound and image, though more recently their 2007 album *Rooz [Red]* sees more of a return to the tradition.[64] Post-modern song titles ranged between English and Cornish, and the music was both traditional and newly composed. Again a range of guest musicians contributed to the work, giving the sense of a wider community of popular music, with the core Dalla musicians being Neil Davey,[65] Hilary Coleman, Simon Lockley,[66] Bec Applebee and Pete Kubrick-Townsend. The community feel was retained the design of the gatefold CD booklet of *Hollan Mouy!/More Salt!*, with pictures of pilchards, Crofthandy Village Hall and a 'Noze Looan' in action. The design took its cue not from other traditional folk albums, but from the ideology and iconography of contemporary pop. Album tracks also linked into Cornwall's established brass band culture, signifying another important development.

Old Celtic, new times: bagpipes, pagans and reggae

While Merv and Neil Davey had helped lead this revolution, their brother Kyt had developed his own band called Anao Atao, which at the time of writing has released two albums, *Esoteric Stones; Music from Cornwall and beyond*... (1994) and *Poll Lyfans/Frogpool* (1996).[67] Alongside the Cornish-inspired tracks, such as the title track 'Ros Keltek's Favourite' and 'Tinner's Puzzle', there were also several Breton-themed pieces, which fits well into the established continuum of links between the two territories.[68] In the meantime, the musician Merv Davey had not only completed much scholarship on the musical traditions of Cornwall, but had played with many of the leading musicians of the era, culminating in his role as parade leader in 'nationalist' events such as the annual St Piran's Day parade over the sand-dunes at Perranporth and the 1497–1997 commemorations, as well being the official piper of the Cornish Gorseth. Davey's particular interest, however, was in Cornish Pipes and bagpipes (musical instruments mentioned in many literary texts and depicted on bench-ends in churches[69]), and so he founded the Pyba project to reignite interest in this form. The agenda was set on the 1999 album *Ilow Koth a Gernow/The Ancient Music of Cornwall* and has been followed by several other releases.[70] The iconography of this music, both in sound and album covers, is quasi-medieval.

Slightly different in feel is the group Bagas Degol (composed of David Twomlow, Rick Williams and Dave Trahair) who with their album *Party like it's 1399*, follow a direction of combining traditional instrumentation (bagpipes, tabor drum and clarinet) with (for example) dub reggae. Their song titles reflect this; for example,[71] 'Bodmin Dubbing' and 'A Pyth yw Dub?' Again, growing out of a community (this time being the Tom Bawcock's Eve 'Torchlight Lantern' procession of Mousehole[72]), their name translates to 'Feast Day Band'. On the band's website, one review calls them 'the darkside of folk' and another comments that they are 'the musical embodiment of a Breugal painting'.[73] Unlike some of the other bands, there was a particular West Penwith slant to their music.

The interest in ancient Cornwall is also reflected in the music of Sue Ashton.[74] Ashton is an established violinist who graduated from the Birmingham Conservatoire. Although her Cornish links seem tenuous (her record company – Genius Loci music – is based in Solihull), she has links to a number of activists within Cornish neo-paganism: Cheryl Straffon, Jo May, Paul Broadhurst and Andy Norfolk. Her song titles indicate these neo-pagan interests – 'Rocky Valley (The Wooded Glen)', 'Beltane Fantasy', 'Madron' and 'Earth Sorrow (Sancreed Holy Well)' – and it appears that her music is marketed at this not inconsiderable neo-pagan market in Cornwall, mainly via the internet. Her CD cover is a highly evocative picture of her standing before Roche Rock with moonlight in an oppressive purple-black sky. Clearly, this imagining of sacred Cornwall is one strand of popular music at present, and similar music can be found from Ireland, Wales, Brittany and Galicia – with Melwyn Goodall probably its most famous proponent.[75]

From Troyl to Noze Looan: community, identity, performance

One particular group has emerged in the late twentieth century and early twenty-first century which seems to defy all usual expectations about contemporary popular music – The Bolingey Troyl Band. Here there is an explicit connection between the community and the music (a conscious link perhaps back to the community-based drama of past Cornwall[76]). Bolingey is a small hamlet near the present epicentre of Pan-Celtic music in Cornwall (Perranporth, home of the 'Lowender Peran'), and the musicians involved in the band are all drawn from the local area, having played initially at the village's annual fair. The model, therefore, is explicitly 'Celtic' and organic, a supposedly true union of musical identity and place. In 1998 the nucleus of the band consisted of Will Burbridge, Graham Cullingford, Brian Davidson, Adrian Evans (orginally from Wales), Andy Green, Pete Hodge and Chris White. Their initial CD release, *Gwengogennow Hag Oll* (1998), contained both new material and re-workings of the established musical canon.[77] Visually, the album displayed established notions of Celticity. Only one of the song titles was explicitly in Cornish (Ros Vur). By 2002, the core of the band remained in tact, but the album released that year (*Out on the Ocean*[78]) was a markedly different affair, both musically and visually. Gone was the Celtic lettering and knotwork, and instead there was a more contemporary picture of a green-blue sea breaking over a beach. Six of the tracks now had Cornish titles, with cover versions of some music by Neil Davey and Will Coleman. Celticity had been retained but the aim now appeared to be to embrace a wider popular market beyond the Celtic music enthusiasts.[79]

This leads us to the early twenty-first century end of this musical continuum – Gwenno Saunders. Saunders was born in 1981 in Cardiff to Cornish and Welsh-speaking parents, and so grew up speaking both languages. At the age of sixteen she toured with Michael Flatley in the Irish-dance show *Lord of the Dance*, performing the role of Faoirse (Freedom).

She went on to play Jody, a lap dancer in the S4C soap opera, *Pobol y Cwm*, then progressing to a career in popular music, first as a solo artist, Gwenno and more recently in the mock-60s' girl vocal trio, The Pipettes.[80] In her solo work, Gwenno combines trance and dance rhythms with Cornish and Welsh lyrics, a kind of popular music akin to the work of Madonna on her 1998 album *A Ray of Light*.[81] Gwenno also uses her sexuality as part of the marketing of her music. Promotional material for her first EP, titled *Môr hud*,[82] saw her sprawled seductively on a rock, with a psychedelic background. While Gwenno's Cornish credentials are primarily linguistic, she is an important phenomenon in contemporary Cornish and Celtic popular music, because she has all the right 'media' credentials. She is an established dancer, has appeared in a soap opera, and like Madonna, she understands that the key to long-term success in popular music is continued re-invention.

The fact that Gwenno appears on *Celtic Crossroads* – the follow-up fusion album to Putumayo's *Celtic Tides* (linked by way of artwork and artists to Melhuish's book)[83] – shows her new position in the order of Celtic music. The album is promoted as being where 'ancient traditions meet modern technology'. On this compilation, Gwenno sits alongside more traditional Celtic recording artists, such as Capercaillie and Alan Stivell, but also with newer artists such as Sinéad O'Conner (whose own Celicity is complex) and Keltik Elektrik. Gwenno also sings on Celtic Legend's *Tristan and Isolde* album.[84] Gwenno's post-punk, post-folk, post-Cornish material has certain similarities to the work of the Welsh group *Hen wlad fy mamau/Land of my mothers*, whose material may given an indication of the post-modern direction some of Cornwall's traditional music may need to take.[85] On their album 'Anhrefn' musical styles and genres are fused together, tying punk, metal, dance, choirs and folk into one soundscape. Tracks such as 'Intro USA', 'Myfanwy' (a satire on traditional songs), 'Methodism got to them Big Time' and 'In This Dis-United Kingdom' (an exploration of devolution) offer a new response to Celtic and Welsh experience.

Mouth abroad: Cornish music in Australia and North America

A number of scholars and observers have traced the migratory trails and linkages between Cornwall and other parts of the world.[86] Awareness of identity – including musical identity – has increased markedly during the latter decades of the twentieth century and onto the twenty-first, a phenomenon Melhuish identifies with Irish and Scottish diaspora communities and groups[87] but which is just as applicable to the Cornish overseas.

In Australia, this has come in the form of Carl Myriad, a singer-songwriter who draws on his Cornish roots for both inspiration and song-titles.[88] His album features 'Delkio Syvy' and 'The Cadgwith Anthem'. In the USA, popular Cornish music has been shaped by the Chicago-based Jim Wearne, whose work and career have already been fairly well documented.[89] His initial recorded output saw him interpret the established canon of Cornish songs such as 'Truro Agricultural Show', 'Little Lize', 'Trelawny' and 'Lamorna', with an eye on Cornu-English as a method of establishing his personal and Cornish identity.[90] Successive albums have seen the integration of more political themes such as '1497' and 'The Tin Mines of Cornwall' (a lament for economic decline),[91] alongside work in the Cornish language, such as 'Delyow Syvy' from the album *Howl Lowen*.[92] Thus, as he has shifted from 'Cousin Jack' culture to more mainstream Cornish political and linguistic culture (becoming a bard of the Cornish Gorseth along the way), so Wearne's musical concerns and themes have also shifted. One of his recent albums, *So Low*, featured a cover which drew for its inspiration on Blues as a genre, with his more America-themed 'Zydeco'-style songs blended with more traditional Cornish components, such as 'Hal-an-tow' and 'Flora Day'.[93] Wearne's success as a recording artist has been to re-popularize many of the lost songs of the canon, and also to write contemporary music about Cornish culture, past and present. In the USA his name is synonymous with Cornish music.

Although she is less prolific than Wearne, we may add the Wisconsin-based singer Marion Howard[94] into the group of musicians celebrating Cornishness in North America. Combining voice, the auto-harp and piano, her music mainly interprets traditional songs from the canon, such as 'Sweet Nightingale' and 'Ringer of Egloshayle'.[95] However, Howard also draws on other sources, among them an interpretation of the poet John Harris' 'My Infant Daughter Falling Asleep in My Knee' and Katherine Lee Jenner's 'A Grey Day', which is a progressive use of established Cornish texts. The cultivation of a stage persona for work in schools and at festivals – a storyteller named Mary Ann – assists Howard in propagating the tradition.[96] Both Wearne and Howard are supreme examples of how independent, small-scale production have contributed to the globalization of Cornish popular music.

One artist infusing the Cornish continuum of popular music with ethereal and soaring female vocalization is the Cornish-Canadian singer Heather Dale. Dale's work fits into a genre of music which has been strongly shaped internationally by artists such as Mary Black, Loreena McKennitt, Maire Brennan and Enya.[97] Dale's work is explicitly 'Celtic' and keenly Brythonic and Arthurian in theme. Her 1999 CD *The Trial of Lancelot* is a romantic exploration of the love triangle between Arthur, Guinevere and Lancelot,[98] and contains songs such as 'Mordred's Lullaby', 'Measure of a Man' and 'Lily Maid'. But there is a deeper awareness of Celtic literature here, in songs like 'The Prydwen Sails Again' and 'Culhwch and Olwen'.

Although much of Dale's material may be inspired by the Society for

Creative Anachronism (name-checked on the album's credits), the co-ordinating body of the various Renaissance Fayres held over North America, there is a seriousness in dealing with her subjects. Comparison could here be made with the work of Candice Night in Blackmore's Night, which follows similar anachronistic lines and themes, and although writing at distance from Cornwall, still manages, like Dale, to incorporate Cornish literary themes – for example, 'Village on the Sand' drawing on Daphne du Maurier's novel *Jamaica Inn*.[99] Dale's follow-up album, *May Queen* (2003) again makes use of Cornish historical and literary material (linking as a whole to Padstow May Day), including her song Tristan and Isolt.[100] The iconography of Dale's CDs is particularly important. Both incorporate very contemporary fonts and images, with *May Queen* being especially effective in its composition of a Pre-Raphaelite Arthurian heroine completed in the style of a stained-glass window. This imagining of her as Celtic artist and as 'beautiful young witch' is particularly important in the age of accessible 'MTV'-style neo-paganism.

Other artists have used Cornwall in different ways as a touchstone for their musical development. The Minneapolis-based group *Woad* (comprised of Kevin Myers, Danny Proud, Martin Proud, Frank Siegle and Scott Siegle) select songs from all Celtic territories, and are regulars at Celtic gatherings across North America. Their album *One for the Woad* (2001) is a scatological and satirical affair which plays games with the lyrical content of traditional songs.[101] Here, the Newlyn Fisherman's Reel is rebranded 'Plethyn Newlyn/Braid of Newlyn' and 'Jowan Bon' is a working of the Helston Furry Dance. The album also features the standard 'Fish, Tin and Copper' and 'Tam [Tom] Pearce'. Another North American group drawing on the Cornish musical heritage is *Navan*. Although they mainly play Irish music, on their debut album is a song 'My Pan Esen Ow Kwandra/As I Was Walking' which is a sequence of text from the opening scenes of *Origo Mundi*, the first play of the Cornish trilogy making up *Ordinalia*.[102] This may hardly be viewed as populist in the sense used generally in this article. However, the very fact that Cornish material is beginning to be played by such North American artists suggests a new awareness of Cornwall's position within wider Celtic music. Nowhere is this seen better than in the Californian-based folk group *Gaelic Storm* (best known as the ceieldh band in the James Cameron film *Titanic*) which has in its ranks a guitarist named Steve Twigger, originally from Looe. The group's debut album featured a song titled 'The Road to Liskeard'.[103]

Cornish festivals overseas have provided much of the performance space for these 'diaspora' artists. The biennial Kernewek Lowender in South Australia, the Gathering of Cornish Cousins in North America, as well as the many smaller local Cornish festivals, such as those held at Grass Valley and Mineral Point, provide opportunities for such music to be aired.[104]

Occasionally, the Pan-Celtic festivals also allow Cornish musicians to play, although generally these are dominated by Scottish and Irish music.[105] Back in Cornwall, the Dewhelans 'home-coming' festival, which celebrates the global Cornish, has also provided a space for such performers.[106]

Cornwall goes Pop: some case studies

From the above discussion, it is apparent that narrow divisions of musical genres have not always been helpful within popular music inside Cornwall, or indeed with Cornish-themed music across the globe. However, a 'post-modern' fusion of styles, instrumentation and lyrics is becoming increasingly apparent, which is reminiscent of how popular music itself came to fruition in the post-war period, with its amalgam of genres such as skiffle, blues and gospel. 'Cornishness' may be explicit or implicit in this fusion, but the artists' sense of place and 'musical landscape' is almost always articulated strongly.

This can be observed in a small-scale in the work of two Cornish-based performance artists, both with connections to 'working-class' Camborne. Harry (Safari) Glasson is a veteran of the pub-club circuit of West Cornwall, as well as events such as Morvah Pasty Day. His repertoire includes many Bob Dylan-esque songs lamenting the loss of mining, together with re-writings of 'Trelawny' and other work broadly nationalistic in tone.[107] Glasson is popular at Cornish festivals globally, perhaps because his work is so resolutely and uncompromisingly Cornish. Different to Glasson is the work of Graham Hart, whose rocked-up 12-bar boogie version of 'Camborne Hill' gave him a minor local hit.[108] The cover of the CD single featured Hart superimposed on the recreation of Trevithick's 'first locomotive engine', with Richard Trevithick himself featured on the inner sleeve. Such was the impact of the song, that it may be considered a contemporary Cornish classic.

The sense of place referred to above is seen nowhere better than in the series of useful compilation albums produced by www.Cornishmusic.com (under the supervision of Tim and Sue Chapple) in their 'Songs from the Hill' series. Inspired perhaps by the original 'Camborne Hill', these give the best flavour of the contemporary popular music, ranging across genres and style. The present three volumes are grouped according to genre, the first one devoted to 'punk, metal and ska'.[109] This album begins with the post-punk of Daywaste's 'Millionaire' and Seed's 'Here it Comes', followed by the doom metal of Fathead's songs such as 'Hubcap' and 'Waiting'. Superskank offer a new imagining of Cornish ska in their song 'Cocaine'. Other acts included are Slightly Viking, Confuse and Headrush. Much of the album is influenced by so-called Orange County-style American punk . The album is an important statement about the vibrancy of contemporary rock music from Cornwall.

The second album in the series is perhaps more influenced by international contemporary singer-songwriters (James Blunt and Katie Melua), and is entitled *Acoustic, Eclectic and Electric*.[110] Borrowing traditional Cornish subject-matter (St Ives, stone circles, oceans), the album contains contemporary 'attitude' lyrics and instrumentation. With high production values (if not high quality artwork), this album gives an impressive sense of confident and optimistic song-writing in Cornwall. The third volume takes the them of 'folk, roots and traditional' music,[111] and some familiar names (Ros Keltek, Dalla, Warm Gold) jostle with a number of new artists, including Ian Marshall, Dave Jenkin, Pentorr, Claire Cavender, Mendy, Paul Jones, The Rhythm Balladeer, Thump Country, Scoot, Peter Marshall and Roger Bennett. Put together, these three CDs give a useful primer of the contemporary popular music scene in Cornwall. A fourth volume is planned.

The transition area between 'folk' and 'popular' music is blurred by the work of bands like Skwardya and Krena. The link member between these groups is Matthew Clarke. Now a veteran of the popular end of song-writing in Cornish, Clarke is a News Presenter with Pirate FM, and has a savvy awareness of new Cornish popular music. Skwardya's debut album was released in 2005. Titled *Some Say the Devil is Dead*, here the Cornish language is aired in a much more contemporary song-writing style; with the material being more working-class.[112] On the www.cornishmuic.com website, Clarke comments that the band produces 'Cornish music with a devilish tinge – we are singing in Cornish because we love the language and want to bring it out into the open'.[113]

It was, however, in his other band, Krena, that Clarke won the 2005 Pan-Celtic Song Competition in Ireland, with their composition 'Fordh dhe Dalvann'.[114] On their website Krena describe themselves as 'rock, funk, blues, punk in the Cornish language', their name translating as 'quaking'. The band take Cornish folk songs, such as 'Lamorna' and 'The Wild Rover', and 'punk them up'. Composed of Matthew Clarke, Tom Phipps, Dan Phipps and Tim Chapple,[115] it seems the band might be able to transcend the 'narrow' niche of Cornish-language recording artists and take their music to a wider audience. This is not an easy task, though might well be helped with new UK government support for the Cornish language.[116]

The name most readily associated with contemporary rock music in Cornwall over the past twenty-five years is that of Bodmin-based Al Hodge (1951–2006). Hodge's impact as a musician is not to be underestimated. Hodge was the one-time guitarist and lead vocalist for the band The Mechanics. According to his website,[117] Hodge began his career in 1963, when he played 'Foot Tapper' (an instrumental by The Shadows) during a music concert at Bodmin Comprehensive School, quickly joining the local band of the time, The Jaguars. His stint with The Jaguars was short-lived and he then joined the Cornish band The Onyx, which released seven singles on the Pye label. The 1970s saw Hodge working as session musician at the Sawmills studio in Golant. He then formed the band Rogue (recording three albums for CBS records). In 1978 Hodge formed The Mechanics with Al Eden (drummer and studio manager of the Sawmills) and Dave Quinn (bass player).

It is The Mechanics with whom Hodge will be forever associated, because the group was very successful in Cornwall and south-west Britain. The Mechanics had a very big sound for a three-piece group and also had the knack of writing good material. During its early phase the band appeared on several of the legendary 101 Club albums with leading performers of the time, and signed a deal with Bronze Records (owned by record mogul Jerry Bron) Yet major success seemed to elude the band. The music of this era is perhaps best captured on the retrospective live album *Live Volume 1 – Fearless!* (1996) which includes many of the important songs from this early phase: 'Ain't that Peculiar', 'Talking to the Wall, 'If I Make My own Bed' and 'Measly Wages Blues'.[118] It was in 1980, however, that The Mechanics found 'success' when they became the backing band for Leo Sayer. In the early 1980s, the band toured internationally and recorded with Sayer. When Sayer's career began to down-turn,[119] the band returned to Cornwall, with Hodge co-writing the song 'Rock n' Roll Mercenaries' which was recorded by Meat Loaf and John Parr.

In the 1990s, as well as writing new material, Hodge toured in Cornwall with a revamped The Mechanics (headlining a concert at the Cornwall Coliseum in 1992 to almost 2000 people), resulting in the music captured on another retrospective live album – *Live Volume 2: Proper Bloody Job!* (1996).[120] By now, Hodge was realizing that his 'Cornishness' was actually his core marketability. For example, this album contained a translation guide between Cornu-English and English ('You buggers are fearless tonight!' reads in standard English as 'Thank you. You're a wonderful audience'). At the end of the decade, Hodge was working with artists such as Elkie Brookes, and by 2001 was recording with Suzi Quatro. He had also diversified into composing more soundtrack material, as well as assembling a range of AOR (adult-orientated rock) solo albums: *Wind of Change, The Best if Yet to Come, Wish* and the overtly Cornish *Wozon*.[121]

The major transition in Hodge's career came in 2003 when he composed the music for a new short film titled 'Prime Fillet', which was produced by Marie and John Macneill and shown at the Cornwall Film Festival in November of that year. The link with the Macneills also allowed Hodge to compose the music for the play *Hellfire Corner* (April 2004), which was performed at Truro's 'Hall for Cornwall'.[122] Written by D. M. Thomas (b.1935), the drama celebrated the life of Bert Solomon, Redruth's star rugby player of the early 1900s. Solomon was picked to play for England in 1910, yet he remained uncomfortable with selection (perhaps because English rugby of the time was elitist and resolutely upper class), and so he never became the international player he might have been. It is clear that Hodge empathized with Solomon. He was an international popular music artist, yet his awareness of his own ethnicity and Cornish identity was very important in terms of his creativity and the choice of projects with which he was associated. 'Cornishness' had become an increasingly important resource for Al Hodge but its potential was never fully developed, for he died suddenly in 2006.

Musically, far removed from Krena and Hodge is Thirteen Senses,[123] a Cornish alternative rock group. This group epitomizes the success of the contemporary scene in Cornwall, having had three singles in the Top 40: 'Do Not Wrong', 'Into the Fire' and 'Thru the Glass'. The band had recorded an independent album titled *Falls in the Dark*, but their major label debut, *The Invitation*, was released on Mercury Records in 2004. The press described their music as 'soaring dreamy pop', mixing 'the windscreen ambition of Radiohead with the melodies of Coldplay'.[124] The band was formed when its members were still at school; the present line-up consisting of Will South (vocals, guitar, piano), Tom Welham (lead guitar), Adam Wilson (bass) and Brendon James (drums). Originally playing the smaller venues of Cornwall, such as 'Bunter's Bar' in Truro, the band have quickly progressed to more major venues, such as the 100 Club and the University of London Student Union, and the South by South West Festival in the USA.

Although, retaining Cornish links (the band is regularly featured on BBC Radio Cornwall, and played a recent home-coming gig at the 'Hall for Cornwall'), there is a sense that Thirteen Senses might 'tick all the right boxes' for reception in a global market. Certainly, comparisons to critical and popular favourites Coldplay and Radiohead will help. There is a sense of ambition to the group. 'Into the Fire' was used in the Season 2 preview trailer for the major America comedy-drama televison show *Rescue Me*, as well as in the pilot episode of the medical drama *Grey's Anatomy*. This was a technique that worked well for an American-based band, Filter, in providing the soundtrack for a Cornish-themed film, *Saving Grace*,[125] so perhaps the reversal of this could be successful for Thirteen Senses. Such work proves how the band needs to compete internationally if it is to be retained on a major record label. The band has also performed at some of the UK's major festivals – 'Glastonbury', 'T in the Park' and the 'V Festival' – and has been well-supported by BBC Radio 1 and XfM, with songs such as 'Do No Wrong' featuring on the all-important Radio 1 playlist. The process behind this success is documented in an interview with Will South on BBC Radio Cornwall's website, which explains the positive reception of London-based media to the band's 'Cornishness':

BBC Cornwall: Let's talk about home. Are you missing Cornwall?
WS: Yes – I think in June we've all got some time off so we're all going to come back home at some stage and go to the beach.

BBC Cornwall: Have you had any feedback from anyone in the music industry who have said, 'Oh, you're from Cornwall!'
WS: Yeah, everyone. When we first started getting interest, that was like a talking point that we're from Cornwall – hidden away in this landscape that not many of them venture down to.

BBC Cornwall: Do you think it opened a few doors for you?
WS: When the demos went out and people heard them, they really liked them and then when they heard that we were from Cornwall, they thought, 'This is different – it doesn't usually happen like this'. I think it intrigued a few people as to how we managed it. I think a lot of bands form cos they get into a certain scene – say a band forms in London they get into the new rock revolution that goes on. So a lot of bands sound the same – I think we sounded a bit different to what else was going on at the time in London so I think people got a bit excited.[126]

From this interview, it would appear that it was 'Cornish difference' that lent Thirteen Senses its unique appeal, and helped gain its record deal. HMV and Solo Records in Truro have given the band heavy promotion, and it may be that – like Alex Parks – Thirteen Senses is evidence of a reinvigorated popular music scene in Cornwall. But, despite its prominence in Cornwall, Thirteen Senses is still at the start of its international popular music career, in what is, sadly, a fickle industry.

Space and place: venues and festivals

For new Cornish bands such as Thirteen Senses, one difficulty is finding appropriate venues to play in Cornwall. Mention has already been made of the importance of performance space within the Cornish context, and we have seen the significance of 'Lowender Perran', of Cornish festivals overseas, and the Pan-Celtic Song Competition. Venues past and present in Cornwall have given opportunities for both touring bands and indigenous artists to promote their music, and it is this aspect of popular music culture in Cornwall to which we now turn. Venues of the 1950s and early 1960s need more documentation, but the late 1960s are better remembered.

Two venues define the late 1960s popular music culture for many people in Cornwall. The first was the 'Flamingo Club', actually located in Illogan Highway but promoted across Britain as 'Redruth'. The club, known locally known as 'Flamingo Ballroom', was on the site of the present Morrisons' supermarket and was demolished c.1980. Influential in its development was the local businessman Charles Simpson, originally from London but who then ran a series of local businesses, investing his money in the club. The 'Flamingo' was a sizeable venue, with a travel lodge for the bands to stay in. Joyce Simpson, Charles' daughter, was the manager of the venue. Advertisements of the early 1960s promote the venue as the 'Dancing and Entertainment Centre of the West'. It had Cornwall's 'largest Ballroom with super sprung floor'. It boasted 'visits of name bands' and 'all-in wrestling shows'. Disc Jockeys, such as Jimmy Saville, were also popular visitors. The Hall hosted numerous touring bands during the decade, such as Gerry and the Pacemakers, Gene Vincent and Tom Jones, as well as Cornish artists such as Roger Dee, The Manny Cockle Blues Trio and The Reaction (featuring a young Roger Taylor). Legendary Torquay-based agent Lionel Digby booked many of the artists. The venue also booked the bands which would define some of the music of the 1970s. Deep Purple played the venue on 18th December 1969, then a day later played the popular 'Van Dyke Club' in Plymouth; a venue which many Cornish fans knew well and which, although situated across the Tamar, was the other defining locality of the late 1960s. Deep Purple had also played there in 1968.[127]

December 1967 saw Pink Floyd play at the 'Flamingo Club'[128]but by the early 1970s both the 'Flamingo' and the 'Van Dyke' were struggling. They were soon competing with the new 'Talk of the West Club'. This club is still recalled fondly by many Cornish people. It was located near Perranporth, and promoted Britain-wide personalities and comedians (such as Bob Monkhouse and Tommy Cooper), as well as internal and external popular music. Cornish bands such as Happy Medium and the Vivian Rob Combo often played the 400 capacity venue, while established touring acts such as The Rockin' Berries, The Fortunes, Alvin Stardust, The Tremeloes and The Dave Clarke Five also graced its stage. The club finally closed in 1981.

The most important performance space in Cornwall during the final decades of the twentieth century was the 'Cornwall Coliseum'. With a 3,000 people capacity, the venue was a mainstay of touring artists in the late 1970s and 1980s. The complex, on Carlyon Bay beach, near St Austell, was initially developed as a resort from a run-down 1930s' country club complex. Originally called the 'New Cornish Riviera Lido', it then became known as 'Cornish Leisure World',[129] and eventually the 'Cornwall Coliseum'. In its early days, the complex was managed and developed by Graham McNally, part of the St Austell-based Exchange Travel Company family which owned the complex. The Coliseum was a major vehicle for asserting Cornwall's identity in the field of popular music, since it sat among the major touring venues in Britain and Ireland. Artists might be playing London's 'Hammersmith Odeon', or the recently developed 'National Exhibition Centre' at Birmingham, then the next night be playing at St Austell.[130] This was somewhat incongruous, but it meant that Cornwall was promoted on the back of tour T-shirts and in programmes, sometimes on a European or indeed global trek. The 'Coliseum' was keen to develop its status as Cornwall's venue, although it drew on audiences from the wider south-west, in particular those from the urban centres of Plymouth and Exeter for whom Bristol was generally the only alternative venue option. Often bus-loads of fans were coached in from over the Tamar.

The Cornwall Coliseum became associated with two particular popular music developments. The first was the rise of so-called New Romantic acts, such as Duran Duran, Adam and the Ants, Spandau Ballet and Ultravox. The second was rock and heavy metal. During the New Wave of British Heavy Metal in the early 1980s, the venue saw Thin Lizzy, Saxon, Gillan, Rainbow, Dio and Iron Maiden all play. Other mainstays included Status Quo, The Jam, The Cure, Genesis, Robert Plant, Motorhead and The Who. Cultural commentators such as Straw have argued that Heavy Metal was fore-grounded in industrial localities (such as the Midlands [Black Sabbath and Judas Priest] and the South Wales Valleys [Tigertailz and Budgie]),[131] so St Austell, with its industrial landscape, this fits type. Importantly, the Coliseum also allowed indigenous musicians and groups to support the large bands; for example, the Cornish heavy rock bands Persian Risk (featuring the St Austell-based guitarist Graham Bath) and St Columb-based Panic Attack.

During the 1980s and early 1990s the Womad (World of Music, Arts and Dance) festival was held at the Coliseum site. Some acts performed in the arena itself, while the larger artists (such as Peter Gabriel and Sinéad O' Conner) performed on a purpose-built stage in the large car park area. Later, Womad was to continue its association with mid-Cornwall, when it moved to the Eden Project. By this point, however, touring artists had become ever more reluctant to move their shows to the 'peripheries' of Britain, and instead there was a new emphasis on persuading audiences to travel to 'metropolitan' venues. The costs of bringing bands to the Coliseum increasingly outweighed what the public in Cornwall and south-west Britain were prepared to pay. The Coliseum went into financial decline, a slide not helped by the development of a new venue in Plymouth, the 'Plymouth Pavilions'. The 'Pavilions' offered a more modern venue which was located in a large city but which was still accessible for people in Cornwall. Although the 'Plymouth Pavilions' has been successful, it has not brought the same range and diversity of artists to the south west of Britain.

As the decline of the 'Coliseum' continued, resulting eventually in its demolition and the new development of 'The Beach' complex, Truro's 'City Hall' was becoming active as a performance venue, hosting theatre, arts events, Cornish popular music and touring bands (such as Hawkwind). The internal infrastructure of the 'City Hall' had remained unchanged for much of the twentieth century, and was in need of an architectural overall. Led by Chris Warner, a campaign was launched to re-designate the 'City Hall' as the 'Hall for Cornwall'. This new 'Hall for Cornwall' would be a multi-space performance venue, hosting theatre and popular music. Although generally successful, the 'Hall for Cornwall' has been somewhat disappointing as a venue for popular music, with gigs organized on an irregular basis and not well-promoted. Recent exceptions have been Bullet for My Valentine and A Hundred Reasons. The 'Hall for Cornwall' still seems to be very much off the touring schedule for most prominent bands (Exeter now being the preferred south-west venue), and there appears to be a lack of interest in popular Cornish music outside the familiar repertoire of brass bands, choirs and opera. The musical identity of the 'Hall for Cornwall' has been shaped by its continuing promotion of so-called tribute bands, such as imitations of Pink Floyd, Queen and Fleetwood Mac, although to be fair this is also a Britain-wide trend.[132] By contrast, however, the 'Princess Pavilions' at Falmouth has recently emerged as perhaps the most important popular music venue in Cornwall ... As well as appealing to the growing student audience of Falmouth and Penryn, the 'Princess Pavillions' has been successful in attracting both up-and-coming and well-established groups to Cornwall.[133] Recent groups and artists have included The Mission, New Model Army, UFO and Asia. Of similar importance is Carnglaze Caverns near Dobwalls, which has developed a particular theme of folk-rocks artists such as Fish and Fairport Convention.[134] Some of the smaller arts venues also host popular music events. 'The Acorn Theatre', in Penzance has seen artists such as All About Eve play there. 'The Barn Nightclub' has also hosted many acts throughout the 1980s and 1990s and into the new millennium, as has the 'Driftwood Spars Hotel' at St Agnes.[135]

Given popular perceptions of Cornwall – 'green', surf-culture, alternative lifestyle, a place of 'down-sizing' – it would seem a logical place in which to locate popular music festivals. Various types emerged during the late twentieth-century. The most well-known was the so-called 'Elephant Fayre' (an image based on the idea that the south-western peninsula resembled a large elephant's trunk), which took place in and around Port Eliot in east Cornwall between 1981 and 1986.[136] The model was the 'Glastonbury Festival': hippy in feel but drawing on Britain's ancient heritage. In 1982, Siouxsie and the Banshees headlined the event in front of some 4,000 people. The following year artists such as The Cure, Roy Harper, Wilko Johnson, and

Robin Williamson played. However, 'Elephant Fayre' began to suffer security difficulties when members of the radical Peace Convoy began to commit crime on the site. This ended the musical aspect of the festival, although the "Elephant Fayre' has now been reinvented as a literary event.

In the wake of this came 'Skinner's Bottom Festival' (1987) near Blackwater and the 'Treworgey Tree Fayre' (1989) at Liskeard,[137] both of which blended hippy culture with the then emergent post-punk traveller culture. These festivals brought in a travelling community which followed a summer schedule of festivals across Britain: Stonehenge, Glastonbury, Cambridge Strawberry Fayre and so on. The point was that Cornwall and places like it offered a 'touchstone' into mythic Britain, which suited the aims of these groups. Celtic and 'stone circle' culture was crucial in their imagining of lifestyle, music and identity. Anathema to both the Conservative Government of the era, and very often to local authorities as well as local communities in Cornwall, such festivals were often 'organic' and unplanned.[138] Similarly, the search for Rave venues in Cornwall involved conflict with the police, land-owners and councils. Typical of this type were the series of festivals which took place on Davidstow airfield, near to Camelford during the late 1980s. A more professionally organised Festival was 'Penwith 83', which saw one of the first major musical concerts organized in post-war Cornwall. The event was headlined by Meat Loaf and 10cc, both at the height of their chart success, and support was offered by reggae artists Aswad, Renaissance, The Opposition and Sid's Taxi. Billed as Cornwall's 'largest ever open-air concert' the event was ambitious but did not generate the crowds needed to sustain the event.

A series of smaller venues has been crucial is maintaining popular music culture for both indigenous and touring artists. In the 1980s the very Cornish-named 'Demelzas' or 'Winter Gardens' in Penzance hosted a series of gigs for rising groups, most notably a very young U2, whereas in Falmouth 'The Pirate' became the place to play in the 1990s. In the early twenty-first century, the youth culture picture of Falmouth and Penryn has been transformed with the opening of the Combined Universities in Cornwall campus in Penryn; the buildings there offer performance space, but not yet of the kind associated with other 'University campus' tours of Britain. Newquay has always offered a range of venues, which have often linked to surfing festivals and the 'Run to the Sun' rally. Core long-term performance space has always been 'The Victoria Bars' (famed for hosting rock and heavy metal) and 'The Bowgie' as both a grunge/alternative and a dance/electronica venue. In the 1980s and early 1990s, 'Tyacks Hotel' in Camborne and 'The London Inn' in Redruth were core venues for both external and internal bands.

Another group of important performance spaces was the working men's clubs and band clubs of mid-Cornwall. The china clay villages in particular formed an important audience for local rock bands during the 1970s, 1980s and early 1990s. Bugle, Foxhole, St Dennis, Roche, Nanpean and St Stephen-in-Brannel had an infrastructure which facilitated the development of indigenous music (well-know local groups like Beaver[139] and Tosh, and new bands such as Freedom Run[140]) but also allowed the occasional touring band to perform. 'The Carlyon Arms', 'The Duke of Cornwall' and 'The General Wolfe' public houses of St Austell also had a very active musical profile during the 1980s and 1990s, an ethos which is perhaps only now embedded in 'St Austell Band Club'. This club was the most active of all these clubs during this period, in terms of bringing in more major touring acts but also in promoting Cornish music. It presently offers a range of gigs, but has maintained the cultural tradition of rock. Of late, like most venues of its size across the UK, it has turned its eye to tribute bands. Truro continues to offer several venues. 'Bunter's Bar' and 'Shout' have provided space for touring tribute bands and local rock acts (for example, Bates Motel and The Vision). Nightclubs in Penzance, Newquay and Truro have also provided venues for the various DJs and mixing artists of Cornwall.

Continuity around St Austell has been provided by the 'Eden Sessions'. These have been a series of summer concerts at the Eden Project, usually tied in with a BBC6 radio live audience.[141] They began in 2001 in Eden's first year of operation. Eden's vision in these sessions has been to offer exposure for new and interesting groups and musicians. 2006 witnessed performances from Goldfrapp and The Magic Numbers, supported by José González. Previous headliners at the Eden Sessions have included Keane, Moby, Basement Jaxx, Doves, Pulp, Air and Embrace. An exception to this ethos of the new was the inclusion in 2004 of Brian Wilson (ex-Beach Boys), perhaps embraced because of his surfing and Californian past. Generally, the emphasis at the Eden Sessions has been on UK-wide trends and hype, and not always on what might be classed as popular in Cornwall itself. Perhaps predictably, the 'Eden Sessions' has displayed a curious lack of interest in local Cornish music, even after the success of Alex Parks and Thirteen Senses.

As a popular music space, Cornwall was also to feature in the twenty-year 'Live 8' anniversary concerts celebrating 1985's 'Live Aid'.[142] The 2005 concerts were part of a wider international project titled 'The Long Walk To Justice', a campaign devoted to ending poverty in Africa. A smaller version of the main 'Live8' concert was held at the Eden Project, and was titled 'Africa Calling'.[143] The compares for the event were Peter Gabriel, and Johnny Kalsi (former band member of Asian Dub Foundation and Afro-Celt Sound System). The acts included Youssou N'Dour, Akim El Sikameya, Angelique Kidjo, Ayub Ogada, Chartwell Dutiro, Coco Mbasi, Daara J, Emmanual Jay, Frititi, Geoffrey Oreyma, Kanda Bongo Man, Mariza and Maryam Mursal. The concert drew on the status and iconography of the Eden Sessions but also echoed the earlier WOMAD ethos dating from Cornwall Coliseum days. The 'Africa Calling' theme and the global project reflected Eden's self-proclaimed environmental awareness but, in its embrace of the exotic and the non-metropolitan, it was also mirrored wider constructions of Cornish 'difference'.

Rock pilgrimage: Guitars and Ranamins

As yet, there is no Cornish book on popular music to equate to Barry Sowden's impressive documentation of rock and roll in Devon.[144] But there is any amount of 'urban legend' material, and Cornwall – long since a 'pilgrimage' destination[145] – has found itself on the contemporary rock pilgrimage trail. A typical piece of popular music 'pilgrimage' folklore concerning Cornwall relates to Queen's drummer, Roger Taylor. He was actually born at King's Lynn, in 1949, but is often quoted as hailing from Truro. In fact, he moved to Truro when aged three, attending Truro Cathedral and Truro schools. During 1963 he and some friends formed a band. According to www. queenworld.com, 'they called themselves the Cousin Jacks',[146] drawing on Cornish emigrant culture. Taylor was initially their rhythm guitarist, but he did not enjoy this position and subsequently took over on drums where he felt more comfortable.[147] The band split after a year. In 1965 Taylor joined a local band called Johnny Quayle and the Reaction. On 15 March 1965 they considered themselves competent enough to enter 'The Rock and Rhythm Championship', an annual event run by the local Round Table in Truro City Hall at which bands from all over Cornwall would compete. Johnny Quayle and the Reaction came fourth and that served to start them off in the Cornish music circuit. Shortly after, Taylor moved to London. There he met the other three members of Queen, progressing thereafter to commercial and critical success.

Another example of this kind of interaction between Cornwall and the world of popular music is that of Mick Fleetwood,[148] the drummer with Fleetwood Mac. He was born in Redruth on June 24th 1942, so this makes his birth-place a site of 'rock pilgrimage'. Likewise, the *West Briton* newspaper of May 4th 2006 tells its readers – with a whiff of folklore and myth – that Status Quo 'have an affinity with the county, having played the Cornwall Coliseum on several occasions and [they] wrote their hit Caroline on a table napkin in the dining room of a hotel in Perranporth in 1970'.[149] The Headland Hotel and its environs at Newquay also features in numerous rock n' rolls guides to Britain, for this is where The Beatles filmed part of their September 1967 *Magical Mystery Tour* film.[150] Indeed on www.lennon.net, one Beatles fan reports how he 'managed to interest the Tourism Association with the ideas of an official commemorative plaque which was unveiled by the Mayor of the Restormel district'.[151]

Numerous biographies of major recording artists chart how they often decamped to Cornwall to write or record, seemingly picking up inspiration and a certain vibe along the way. Several groups illustrate this phenomenon well. The early 1980s folk and progressive rock group Solstice recorded their *Silent Dance* at the Isle of Light Studios in Boyton, North Cornwall. Lyrically, the record is influenced enormously by the 'stone circle' and 'neo-pagan' culture of Cornwall, with song titles such as 'Earthsong' and 'Sunrise'. The music's packaging sports images of men-an-tol, druidic groves and Celtic knotwork.[152] Although from a completely different musical tradition, a similar effect can be seen in the 1989 album *Thunder and Consolation* by New Model Army, which was recorded at the Saw Mills studio at Golant on the River Fowey. The album again features a Celtic knotwork cover by the punk artist Joolz and contains a song called 'Ballad of Bodmin Pill'. There is even a 'Celtic' instrumentation on some of the tracks on the album, in particular the song 'Vagabonds'.[153] Influenced in the same way as New Model Army, by traveller and anarchic culture in Britain, are The Levellers. Their 1995 self-titled album features a song titled 'Men an tol'.[154] Long-standing folk-rock group Steeleye Span wrote a song entitled 'Padstow' for their 1989 album *Tempted and Tried*.[155]

Cornwall has always been a place of refuge or retreat for artists of all genres seeking their temporary or personal 'Ranamins'.[156] It is an image captured in Jethro Tull's 1973 concept album *Thick as a Brick*, which contains the absurd but well-observed lyric: 'They're all resting down in Cornwall – writing up their memoirs for a paper-back edition of the Boy Scout Manual.'[157] Another example of a famous musician 'pitching up' in Cornwall (and aiming to promote indigenous music) is Tony Butler, the one-time bass player of Big Country, who owns studio space in Launceston and runs the record label Great West Records. He was instrumental in helping to organize the Castle Rock festival at Launceston Castle in 2005 to promote jazz, folk, blues, reggae, funk, ska, punk, rock and metal.[158]

Rave by the sea: dance, drum n' bass and DJs in the Duchy

By the very nature of the genres of dance and DJ culture, their 'product' is less visible than other aspects of popular music performance. It is the 'event' itself which defines both identity and subculture. It is also less well-recorded, in that much of its culture is 'subversive' and 'underground'; a culture summarized in the fiction contained in Champion's 1997 volume, *Disco Biscuits*.[159] The promotion of events is usually undertaken by flyers, websites and illegal bill-postering. Nonetheless, out of the hedonistic Rave traditions of the 1990s there is an identifiable musical force in Cornwall in which dance, drum n' bass and DJing are central. This musical area in fact, owes much to the production values of punk, since much of it is not linked to multi-national record companies. Instead, there is perhaps the status and quality of the DJ, who mixes and defines the music. Thus DJ culture is highly transportable and mobile, and does not require the larger 'load in' of rock artists.

The emphasis on 'do-it-yourself' means that the music can be radical and fusionist in feel, with particular DJs taking musical themes of motifs into their work. There is an obvious attraction of holding dance and DJ events in Cornwall, since the concept of 'surfing' by day and 'clubbing' by night makes for an attractive experience; hence for example, St Ives's and Newquay's status in becoming two of the key places in Britain in which to celebrate New Year's Eve. Newquay, in particular, is a 'ritualistic' rite-of-passage location to which many young people travel after completing GCSE and GCE Advanced Level examinations.

A common promotional device is the concept of the 'Rave by the Sea Weekender'. In 2006 one of the largest 'weekenders' was held between 26 and 28 May at Newquay's 'Tall Trees'. It featured acts such as Breeze and Styles vs Dougal and Gammer, Nu Energy Live, Heaven Y, Jon Doe Live, Robbie Long, Kate Lawler, A. J. Gibson, Miss Behavin, Phil Reynolds, Billy Bunter, DJ Hype, Sub Focus and Ban Ban. There was a combination of Cornish and visiting DJs. *Pitpilot* magazine also promoted an Easter Sunday event on 16 April 2006, which featured Kosheen at the 'Barracuda Club' in Newquay. 'Koola Club' featured a touring act – Ugly Duckling – a 'ground-breaking hip-hop duo from Long Beach California', so sustaining and nurturing Newquay's surf vintage. Truro is also an important location, especially venues such as L2 and Eclipe; the latter featuring on 15 April 2006 (for example) a 'Rehab Audio Therapy' event, with J. Majik, Section 8, Devinyl, Leroy and Sasquatch.[160]

Conclusion: *Cumpas* and Heavy Metal Morris Men

As the above shows, despite its relatively small geographical size, Cornwall has witnessed a considerable diversity of popular musical activity over the past forty years. The genres of the living tradition, internal pop, rock and dance music have grown and diversified exponentially in a short space of time. Increasingly, there are signs of further fusion between pop and folk, in ways which the original Revivalists in Cornwall could not have dreamed of, as well as a rekindled of interest (particularly in youth culture) in Cornwall's 'living tradition'. Two young groups seem to embody this energy and confidence, once so lacking in Cornish groups performing on the Pan-Celtic musical playing field. The first is the St Day-based band The Red Army, a group formed by the brothers Philip and Steven Burley, whose music combines dreamy female vocals with folk-rock. The group features the emerging fiddle player Richard Trethewey. Secondly, there is Pentorr, a much more traditional band formed by Will Manley. Both groups' origins lie in the Youth Service in Cornwall and the 'Bagas Crowd' fiddle group. To this contemporary list, we might also add Naked Feet, featuring the singing talents of Julie Elwin. Elwin won the International Pan-Celtic Song Competition with Mor Menta Sewia (Follow Me) in 2002, with her sometime group Naked Feet playing an 'additive blend of traditional folk, latin, rock and dance'.[161]

In terms of venues, more and more spaces seem to be opening up for both internal and external acts. At Lanhydrock, near Bodmin, in the face of mounting criticism that the National Trust only put on 'classical' music events, there has in recent years been a regular summer rock concert held in the grounds of the estate. Likewise, the perceived arch-enemies of Cornish nationalists, English Heritage, announced that Status Quo and Westlife would be performing at Pendennis Castle in Summer 2006.[162] At Colliford Lake Park on Bodmin Moor there is the recent establishment of a Solstice Fayre, harking back perhaps to the travellers' festivals of 1980s, featuring among others Dalla, Pendans (a new Penzance-based group) and Seth Lakeman.[163] Meanwhile, Dalla and Otta Nye continue to establish further venues for Cornish dance and music, recently playing the Breton-linked Aberfest (at Falmouth and St Michael's Mount): the *Cornishman* newspaper described the event as 'Timeless music on the Mount during Aberfest'.[164] One of the organizers of this event, Frances Bennett, has long-worked to see Cornish music better established, working initially with Hilary Coleman on outreach work in schools and other areas via projects such as Hubbadillia!, and more recently through the Cornish Music Promotions organization called *Cumpas*.[165] *Cumpas* is a charitable company set up to promote Cornish music through education, performance and research. Bennett is also engaged in an ethno-musicological study of Cornwall (at the Institute of Cornish Studies), her academic work bringing together her twins skills and perspectives as performer and researcher.[166]

Bennett's enquiry will investigate further many of the core issues identified in this article. One of the core debates in the future will be that over the 'division of labour' within music. Relatively few Cornish musicians can operate professionally at present. Several are semi-professional; most are still amateur. Is there a need for an Agency to more actively promote Cornish music both at home and abroad? Can Cornish music be more of a world-player, particularly in the important American market-place? Yet despite these difficulties, the greater confidence that now exists in Cornish music-making means that musical fusion is now much more of a possibility than before, with a great many doors knocked down by artists such as Will Coleman and Bagas Degol and dance groups like Otta Nye.

Popular music in Cornwall is still relatively undocumented. In particular, further research is needed on the way in which 'Cornishness' has been expressed in popular music, as well as the way in which it has developed historically in Cornwall. This chapter has only scratched the surface of this topic. Regardless of the long-term future of Alex Parks, her success in *Fame Academy* has been a pop-culture high-water mark for Cornwall and has done much to stimulate interest in popular music here. The potential for the future, perhaps, is seen in bands such as Thirteen Senses. In the near-distance are the 'new punks', making their own music regardless of globalization and the cultural-imperialist strategies of international record companies. Pipers, with eyes on fusionist strategies of other musicians, see the potential for new collaboration. Nowhere was the potential for fusion in popular music in Cornwall – traditional and rock – demonstrated better than on May Day 2006 when crowds at St Mawes were entertained by 'Heavy Metal Morris Men'.[165] If such innovation is possible, then pop music in Cornwall has an exciting future, with the prospect of past and present musical traditions meeting together in new and dramatic ways. Have your *iPod* ready.

Acknowledgements

Sincere thanks to Frances Bennett, for her helpful observations on this chapter. My thanks also to Jim Pengelly, Hilary Coleman, Matthew Clarke, Christopheur Payne, Danny Merrifield, Freddie Zapp, Roger Dee, Jock Lindsay and Richard Rastall for their comments on its development, and to Kim Cooper and Vanessa Bourguignon of the Cornwall Centre, Redruth. To Neil Kennedy, special thanks, for debating some of the above issues with me for a number of years.

Notes and references

1. Alex Parks, *Introduction* (London, 2003), *Honest* (London, 2005). See also Various Artists, *Fame Academy: The Finalists* (London, 2003), and http://www.alexpark-sofficial.com. One site is devoted to 'the sisterhood of Alex Parks … Alex bys vykken'. See http://www.xsorbit25.com – the site of the Alex Parks fan club.

2. Parks is often featured on the David White Show on BBC Radio Cornwall.

3. See Jo Croft 'Youth, culture and age' in Mike Storry and Peter Childs (eds), *British Cultural Identities* (London, 1997), pp. 163–200; John Harris, *The Last Party: Britpop, Blair and the Demise of English Rock* (London, 2004).

4. Pwyll ap Siôn, 'Welsh music: [4] contemporary', in John T. Koch (ed.), *Celtic Culture: A Historical Encylopedia* (Oxford, 2006), pp. 1768–9.

5. Jonathan Howlett, 'Putting the Kitsch into Kernow', in Philip Payton (ed.), *Cornish Studies: Twelve* (Exeter, 2004), pp. 30–60.

6. For an overview of the process, see Philip Payton, 'Introduction', in Philip Payton (ed.), *Cornish Studies: Ten* (Exeter, 2002), pp. 1–23.

7. Alan M. Kent, 'Celtic Nirvanas: Constructions of Celtic in Contemporary British youth culture', in David C. Harvey, Rhys Jones, Neil McInroy and Christine Milligan (eds), *Celtic Geographies: Old Culture, New Times* (London and New York, 2002), pp. 206–26.

8. Harry Woodhouse, *Cornish Bagpipes. Fact or Fiction?* (Redruth, 1994); *idem, Face the Music: Church and Chapel Bands in Cornwall* (St Austell, 1997); Merv Davey, *Hengan: Traditional Folk Songs, Dances and Broadside Ballads collected in Cornwall* (Redruth, 1983).

9. Sharon Thornton, 'Reading the Record Bins: The Commercial Construction of Celtic Music', in Amy Hale and Philip Payton (eds), *New Directions in Celtic Studies* (Exeter, 2000), pp. 19–29.

10. See the various entries in Koch, *Celtic Culture*; Richard Rastall, *Minstrels Playing: Music in Early English Religious Drama Volume II* (Cambridge, 2001), pp. 307–36.

11. See Davey, *Hengan*; Ralph Dunstan, *Cornish Dialect and Folk Songs* (Truro and London, 1932); Richard McGrady, *Music and Musicians in Early Nineteenth-century Cornwall* (Exeter, 1991), *Traces of Ancient Mystery: The Ballad Carols of Davies Gilbert and William Sandys* (Redruth, 1993); Geoffrey Self, *Music in West Cornwall: A Twentieth-century Mirror* (Camborne, 1997).

12. Exceptions are Martin Melhuish, *Celtic Tides: Traditional Music in a New Age* (Kingston, Ontario, 1998). Interestingly, although Melhuish was born in Penzance and makes much of his Cornish heritage, he does not write about Cornish music. For another perspective, see Martin Stokes and Philip V. Bohlman (eds), *Celtic Modern: Music at the Global Fringe (Europea, Ethnomusicologies and Mondernities)* (Lanham, MD, 2003).

13. See Michael Leonard, 'Superhighway to Hell', in *Classic Rock*, no. 20 (2000), pp. 50–9.

14. Alan M. Kent, *The Literature of Cornwall: Continuity, Identity, Difference, 1000–2000* (Bristol, 2000).

15. M. Wynn Thomas, *Corresponding Cultures: The Two Literatures of Wales* (Cardiff, 1999).

16. Simon Frith, *Sound Effects: Youth, Leisure and the Politics of Rock 'n' Roll* (London, 1983); Richard Middleton, *Studying Popular Music*, Milton Keynes, 1990.

17. Jon Savage, *England's Dreaming: Sex Pistols and Punk Rock* (London, 1991).

18. Clinton Heylin (ed.), *The Penguin Book of Rock & Roll Writing* (London, 1992).

19. Terry Eagleton, *After Theory* (London, 2003).

20. See http://www.kesson.com and http://www/cornishmusic.com. A useful sampler of music is given on Various Artists, *Mammyk Ker: All the Best from Cornwall* (Cornwall, 2002).

21. See the companies *Crai* in Wales, and *Jape*, *Dolphin* and *Dara* in Ireland.

22. An idea embodied in the work of the Dartmoor-based recording artist Seth Lakeman. See Seth Lakeman, *Freedom Fields* (London, 2006).

23. Cliff Dane and Dave Laing, *The UK Music Industry: Some Recent Developments in*

Cultural Trends, no. 31 (1998), p. 4.

24. Frith, *Sound Effects*.

25. Alan Sinfield, *Literature, Politics and Culture in Postwar Britain* (Oxford, 1989), pp. 152–81.

26. See Paul Barker, *The Other Britain* (London, 1982); Simon Elmes, *Talking for Britain: A Journey through the Nation's Dialects* (London, 2005).

27. The rock group Feeder are a good example of this. In the early 1990s, the bands regularly toured Cornwall, and in 2006 are the headline act at a Newquay Surf Festival. *Cumpas*, the Cornish Music Promotions group completed a Global Links project on Identity and Culture project at Brannel School, St Stepehen-in-Brannel. Anti-Racism Cornwall also promoted the event. When asked to give words associated with Cornwall one student replied with 'Open air, seagulls, ocean, pasty'. When asked about St Stephen-in-Brannel, the same student responded with 'Oldies, boring, walk your dogs here, full of Chavs'.

28. Cf. John McLaughlin, *One Green Hill: Journeys Through Irish Songs* (Dublin, 2003); Karen Farrington, *The Music, Songs and Instrumentation of Ireland* (Berkeley, CA, 1998). However, Mike O'Connor, Merv Davey and Frances Bennett are all completing research in this field.

29. The contribution of Benjamin Luxon is important.

30. The Cornish corpus is full of this. See for example, Robert Morton Nance's notes on 'Tom Bawcock's Eve' in Dunstan, *Cornish Dialect and Folk Songs*, p. 7. However, so are the Irish, Scottish, Welsh, Manx and Breton traditions. For a perspective on this cultural process, see contributors in Eric Hobsbawm and Terence Ranger (eds), *The Invention of Tradition* (Cambridge, 1992).

31. See Amy Hale, 'Genesis of the Celto-Cornish Revival? L. C. Duncombe-Jewell and the Cowethas Kelto-Kernuak', in Philip Payton (ed.), *Cornish Studies: Five* (Exeter, 1997), pp. 100–11.

32. See the observations on this in Marcus Tanner, *The Last of the Celts* (New Haven, CT and London, 2003), pp. 69–128, pp. 250–84, and in the sleevenotes to Various Artists, *Celtic Tides* (New York, 1998). See also Alfred Perceval Graves (ed.), *The Celtic Song Book: Being Representative Folk Songs of the Six Celtic Nations* (London, 1928).

33. See the various entries on music in Koch, *Celtic Culture*.

34. A full picture can be gained from the following sources: W. Herbert Thomas, *Cornish Songs and Ditties ... and Other Rhymes* (Penzance and Camborne, publisher unknown, 1904); Ralph Dunstan (ed.), *The Cornish Song Book/Lyver Canow Kernewek* (London, 1929); Inglis Gundry (ed.), *Canow Kernow: Songs and Dances from Cornwall* (Cornwall, 1966); Kenneth Pelmear (ed.), *Carols of Cornwall* (Redruth, 1982); *idem* (ed.), *Songs of Cornwall: Chiefly Drinking Songs* (Redruth, 1985); Racca, *Cornish Tunes for Cornish Sessions* (Calstock, n.d.); Merv Davey (ed.), *Ertach: Traditional Cornish Music Source* (Withiel, 1999).

35. See the observations made by Lisa Gerard-Sharp and Tim Perry (eds), *Ireland* (London and New York, 2004), pp. 22–3.

36. For a explanation of the origins and current budget of this festival, see Kenneth McKinnon, 'Cornish/Kernowek', in Diarmuid Ó Néil (ed.), *Rebuilding the Celtic Languages: Reversing Language Shift in the Celtic Countries* (Talybont, 2005), p. 265. See also *West Briton*, 21 October, 2004, pp. 40–1.

37. An issue explored in Marion Löffler, *A Book of Mad Celts: John Wickens and the*

Celtic Congress of Caenarfon 1904 (Llandysul, 2000).

38. See Cam Kernewek and Ros Keltek, *Corollyn* (Cornwall, 1990). For a useful Britain-wide context, see Georgina Boyes, *Step Change: New Views on Traditional Dance* (London, 2001).

39. See http://www.secondwavedance.co.uk. A 2nd Wave leaflet, 2007 offers the following: 'traditions, noze looan, processions, serpent dancing, ritual and ceremony'.

40. Troyl or troil is a Cornish word which actually means 'whirl, revolve or spin' but which has come to represent the Cornish equivalent of a ceilidh.

41. Some observers feel that 'Noswyth Lowen' was actually another borrowing, from Welsh.

42. See McKinnon, 'Cornish/Kernowek', pp. 211–75.

43. A leading dancer in the *Ros Keltek* group, Jenefer Lowe, was appointed Cornish Language Project Manager for Cornwall County Council in 2006.

44. See Raymond Williams, *Problems in Materialism and Culture* (London and New York, 1980), p. 42. For 'Celtic' fused with 'Acid Jazz' see the work of Galliano, *The Plot Thickens* (London, 1994).

45. Bucca, *An Tol yn Pen an Telynor/The Hole in the Harper's Head* (Cornwall, 1976).

46. See Tim Saunders, *The High Tide: Collected Poems in Cornish 1974–1999* (London, 1999).

47. A bucca is a mischievous sprite or goblin.

48. A useful compilation album is Brenda Wootton, *The Voice of Cornwall* (London, 2000); see also Sue Luscombe (ed.), *Brenda Wootton: Pantomime Stew* (Hayle, 1994).

49. See the useful article on Cornish music by Alison and Merv Davey, Cornish Traditional Dance and Music', in Myrna Combellack Harris (ed.), *Cornish Studies for Schools* (Cornwall, 1989), pp. 11–12.

50. See Cam Kernewek, *Cam Kernewek* (Cornwall, 1991), *Cornish Troyl Band* (Cornwall, 1991). Cf. Oysterband, *Trawler* (London, 1994).

51. For a detailed exploration of this, see Jason Semmens, 'Guising, Ritual and Revival: The Hobby Horse in Cornwall', in *Old Cornwall*, Volume XIII, No. 52 (2005), pp. 39–46.

52. See *Asteveryn* on www.kesson.com. Asteveryn translates to 'Let us replenish!'. Core members of the group include Jim Pengelly, Alan Pengelly, Peggy Morris, Andrew Morris, Julian Whiting and Tamsyn Whiting.

53. Tan ha Dowr, *Loer* (Cornwall, 2000).

54. Graham Sandercock, *Poll Pri* (Liskeard, 1992).

55. Gwyn ha Du, *In Gwyn ha Du* (Cornwall, 1997).

56. See Various Artists, *Planet Kernow* (Liskeard, 1994).

57. The members were Hilary Coleman, Jo Tagney and Liz Davies. Tagney went on to form Caracana. See Caracana, *For the Love of It* (Cornwall, 2005). The original line-up of Gwaryoryon also featured Will Coleman and Matthew Spring.

58. Gwaryoryon, *The Three Drunken Maidens* (Cornwall, 1996).

59. The derivation of this seems based on the clarinet, which works in the same way as the bombard in Breton music.

60. Captain Kernow and the Jack and Jenny Band, *Teeriow Droag* (Cornwall, 1997). The title of this translates to 'Badlands'.

61. Members of this group were also operating as part of Neil Kennedy's Cornish-

language classes, and providing the music for what would become the dance group Otta Nye. Another influential musician at this time was Frances Bennett, who guested with many of the above bands when they played live.

62. Sowena, *A Month of Sundays* (St Agnes, 1999). The line-up was Hilary Coleman, Alan Pengelly, Frances Bennett and Simon Lockley. Sowena split up in 2001, but there is some other recorded material around.

63. Dalla, *A Richer Vein* (St Agnes, 2002). This album was re-released in 2006. In reality, Dalla was considered in some quarters to be a separate project. The band had partial origins in another band called Ryb an Gwella, which featured Simon Lockley, Robin Holmes, Alan Pengelly and Padstow-based accordion player Ray Delf.

64. Dalla, *Hollan Mouy!/More Salt!* (Redruth, 2004), *Rooz* (Redruth, 2007). Music from *Hollan Mouy!/More Salt!* was used in play titled *Oogly es Sin* which toured Cornwall in Spring 2007. See Alan M. Kent, *Oogly es Sin: The Lamentable Ballad of Anthony Payne – Cornish Giant* (London: Francis Boutle, 2007).

65. Davey had considerable experience of the world-wide Celtic tradition, playing at many festivals and touring with the band Anam.

66. Lockley has now left Dalla to pursue other musical interests.

67. Anao Atao, *Esoteric Stones; Music from Cornwall and beyond ...* (Withiel, 1994), *Poll Lyfans/Frogpool* (Withiel, 1998).

68. In the late 1990s Anao Atao ran a regular series of 'troyl' events at Lanjeth Village Hall.

69. See Woodhouse, 1994.

70. Pyba, *Ilow Koth a Gernow/The Ancient Music of Cornwall* (St Erth, 1999). See also, Pyba, *Pibrek* (Withiel, 2005). Cf. Gaiteros De Beluso, *Gaiteros Galegos* (Madrid, 1994). Another piper operating in Cornwall is Will Coleman, who combines his musicianship with storytelling. Coleman himself has been a key figure in marrying popular and traditional music. He is the brother of Hilary Coleman.

71. Bagas Degol, *Party like it's 1399* (Cornwall, 2004). This is a satire of the Prince song, '1999'.

72. See Dunstan, *Cornish Dialect and Folk Songs*.

73. See http://www.bagasdegol.com

74. Sue Ashton, *Sacred Landscapes: Music Inspired by the Sacred Celtic Landscape of Cornwall* (Solihull, 1999). The CD also pictures St Nectan's Kieve in North Cornwall. Gordan Giltrap is a guest guitarist on the album.

75. See Marion Pearce (ed.) *Pentacle*, no. 16 (Southend-on-Sea, 2004), p. 71.

76. See Brian Murdoch in Alan M. Kent, *Ordinalia: The Cornish Mystery Play Cycle, a verse translation* (London, 2005), pp. 3–16.

77. The Bolingey Troyl Band, *Gwenognnow Hag Oll* (St Agnes, 1998).

78. The Bolingey Troyl Band, *Out on the Ocean* (St Erth, 2002).

79. The Bolingey Troyl Band also plays rock and blues.

80. See www.thepipettes.co.uk

81. Madonna, *Ray of Light* (New York, 1988).

82. Gwenno, *Môr hud* (Llandwrog, 2002).

83. Various Artists, *Celtic Crossroads* (New York, 2005).

84. Celtic Legend, *Tristan and Isolde* (Brittany, 2003). Celtic Legend plan another album in 2006, based around the concept of Lyonesse. Gwenno will also appear on this album.

85. Hen wlad fy mamau/Land of my mothers, *Anhrefn* Wales, 2000. Cf. the music of the Galician musician Carlos Nuñes.
86. There are numerous texts here, but see A. L. Rowse, *The Cornish in America* (Redruth, 1991 [1969]); Philip Payton, *The Cornish Miner in Australia: Cousin Jack Down Under* (Redruth, 1984). See also Philip Payton (ed.), *Cornish Carols from Australia* (Redruth, 1984).
87. See Melluish, *Celtic Tides.*
88. Carl Myriad, *Carl Myriad* (New South Wales, 2000). Myriad has toured with Frank Zappa and Roy Orbison. Myriad's Cornish family name was Tregonning. See Alan M. Kent, *Cousin Jack's Mouth-Organ: Travels in Cornish America* (St Austell, 2004), p. 17.
89. Kent, *Cousin Jack's Mouth-Organ*, pp. 14–35; See also Mick Catmull, *Dewhelans: The Homecoming* (A38 films and Westcountry, 2002).
90. Jim Wearne, *Songs of Cornwall Captured Alive! Festival Recordings, Live from Washington DC* (Elmhurst, IL, 1997).
91. Jim Wearne, *Me and Cousin Jack* (Elmhurst, IL, 1998).
92. Jim Wearne, *Howl Lowen* (Elmhurst, IL, 2001).
93. Jim Wearne, *So Low* (Elmhurst, IL, 2003).
94. See Kent, *Cousin Jack's Mouth-Organ*, pp. 53–5.
95. Marion Howard, *The Nightingale Sings: Eos an Howsedhas/Nightingale of the West* (Mineral Point, WI, 2002).
96. Marion Howard, *Tales and Tines of Cornwall by Mary Ann and Try Henath* (Mineral Point, WI, 2003).
97. See Melluish, *Celtic Tides.*
98. Heather Dale, *The Trial of Lancelot* (Toronto, 1999).
99. Blackmore's Night, *Fires at Midnight* (Hanover, 2001).
100. Heather Dale, *May Queen* (Toronto, 2003). Cf. Celtic Legend, *Tristan and Isolde*, and Waltraud Meier and Sigfried Jerusalem, *Wagner: Tristan und Isolde* (Germany, 1995).
101. Woad, *One for the Woad: Traditional Celtic Music* (Minneapolis, MN, 2001).
102. Navan, *An Cuimhin Leat* (USA, 2000).
103. Gaelic Storm, *Gaelic Storm* (France, 1998).
104. See *Kernewek Lowender, World's Largest Cornish Festival, 9–16 May 2005*, Programme; www.the13thgathering.com; *10th Annual Cornish Festival 27–29 September, 2002, Mineral Point, Wisconsin*, Programme; *Grass Valley: Where to Go and What to Do, 2002*, Programme. For more traditional Cornish music, see The Grass Valley Carol Choir with the Grass Valley Male Voice Choir, *When Miners Sang* (Grass Valley, CA, 2001).
105. See for example, *5th Celtic Highland Hames of the Quad Cities*, Saturday 22 August 2003. Festivals such as Festival Interceltique de Lorient in Brittany and Yn Chrunnaight on the Isle of Man (and the others above and below here), do facilitate an important exchange of Cornish music.
106. *Dewhelans 2004, Festival of Cornwall*, Souvenir Guide.
107. Harry (Safari) Glasson, *Because I Was Born Here* (Camborne, 2001).
108. Graham Hart, *Camborne Hill* (Cornwall, 2004). Activists in Cumpas comment that this song is very popular when used in schools.
109. Various Artists, *Songs from the Hill, Volume One: Punk, Metal and Ska. The Sound of Cornwall* (Cornwall, n.d.).

110. Various Artists, *Songs from the Hill, Volume Two: Acoustic, Eclectic and Electric. The Sound of Cornwall* (Cornwall, n.d.).

111. Various Artists, *Songs from the Hill, Volume Three: Folk, Roots and Traditional Music from Cornwall* (Cornwall, 2004).

112. Skwardya, *Some Say the Devil is Dead* (Cornwall, 2005). See also Shwardya, *Arta* (Cornwall 2005). Cf. Beth Patterson, *Hybrid Vigor* (Louisiana, LA, 1999).

113. http://www.cornishmuic.com

114. http://www.cornish-language.org/krena. Other previous Cornish winners were the song-writer and guitarist Pete Berryman, with *An Arvor/The Shore* in 1996 (the lyrics to the song were written by Pawl Dunbar, and the song was released as a cassette single). Julie Elwin represented Cornwall in 2002 and again won the competition. See below.

115. The founder of the 'Songs from the Hill' series.

116. See McKinnon, 'Cornish/Kernowek'.

117. See http://www.alhodge.com

118. The Mechanics, *Live Volume 1 – Fearless!* (Farnborough, 1996). The band was championed at this point by David Rees, the editor of *A New Day*, a Jethro Tull fanzine. Both albums were released under the A New Day record label.

119. Despite a mid-career malaise, in 2006, Sayer had a Number 1 hit with a remixed version of 'Thunder in My Heart'.

120. The Mechanics, *Live Volume 2 – Proper Bloody Job!* (Farnborough, 1996).

121. See http://www.alhodge.com

122. See *Hell Fire Corner*, Programme, 2004. See also D. M. Thomas, *Dear Shadows* (Truro, 2004), p. 17.

123. See http://www.thirteensenses.co.uk

124. Thirteen Senses, *The Invitation* (London, 2004). These comments come from *Time Out* and *The Guardian* respectively.

125. See my observations on this in Alan M. Kent, 'Screening Kernow: Authenticity, Heritage and the Representation of Cornwall in Film and Television 1913–2003', in Philip Paton (ed.), *Cornish Studies: Eleven* (Exeter, 2003), p. 124.

126. http://www.bbc.co.uk/cornwall/music/features. See also 'Everybody knows where we come from' in *Western Morning News*, 15 March, 2005.

127. See Michael Heatley, *The Complete Deep Purple* (London, 2005). Some material is found on the Flamingo Halls in *Camborne/Redruth: The Official Guide* (1961), p. 57.

128. Glenn Povey and Ian Russell, *Pink Floyd: In Flesh, The Complete Performance History* (London, 1997).

129. *Cornish Leisure World*, Promotional leaflet, c.1979.

130. See Iron Maiden, *Live after Death* (London, 1985). Concerts following the Coliseum date included London, Hammersmith Odeon and Cardiff, St David's Hall.

131. Will Staw, 'Characterizing rock music: the case of heavy metal', in Simon During (ed.), *The Cultural Studies Reader* (London and New York, 1993), pp. 368–81. An interesting comparison of this kind of cultural determinism is found in Seattle's grunge scene. See Gus Van Sant in *Daily Telegraph*, 27 August 2005, p. 9. Here Van Sants argues that, 'Aberdeen is about logging and fishing, and I always felt Kurt Cobain's guitar resembled a chain-saw and Nirvana's bass and drum sounded like trees crashing – those unmistakable sounds, the sounds they lived with. His music

was a complete product of the Northwest and he couldn't handle it.'

132. See Michael Heatley, 'Tonight, Matthew we're going to be ...', *Classic Rock*, no. 49 (2003), pp. 48–55.
133. See *West Briton*, 23 April 2006.
134. See *Fairport Convention Newsletter*, Spring 2004, p. 1.
135. *West Briton*, 23 April 2006.
136. See 'New chapter for a country estate' in http://www news.bbc.uk
137. Fiona Earle, Alan Dearling, Helen Whittle, Roddy Glasse and Gubby, *A Time to Travel? An Introduction to Britain's Newer Travellers* (Lyme Regis, 1994), p. 31.
138. See Peter Gardner, *Mediaeval Brigands: Pictures in the Life of Hippie Colony* (Bristol, 1987).
139. Beaver, *Live at St Austell Band Club 8/9/91* (Cornwall, 1991). Beaver's members: Will Coon, Buckley Wallbridge, Reg Hancock, Tony Cousins and Arthur Curwen were all mainstays of the mid-Cornwall music circuit.
140. See Freedom Run, *The First of Freedom Run* (Cornwall, 1985).
141. See http://www.edenproject.com
142. Peter Hilmore, *The Greatest Show on Earth: Live Aid* (London, 1985).
143. See http://www.live8.edenbookings.com
144. Barry Sowden, *Oh No! It Local Rock and Roll ... but I like it! A Fond Look Back at the Roots of Rock and Roll in Mid-Devon, 1954–1979* (Tiverton, 2002), *Oh No! It Local Rock and Roll ... but I like it! A Fond Look Back at the Roots of Rock and Roll in Exeter and East Devon* (Tiverton, 2003).
145. John Lowerson, 'Celtic Tourism – Some Recent Magnets', in Philip Payton (ed.), *Cornish Studies: Two* (Exeter, 1994), pp. 128–37.
146. http://www.queenworld.com
147. http://www.rogertaylor.co.uk
148. See Dan Formento, *Rock Chronicle* (London, 1982), p. 179.
149. *West Briton*, 4 May 2006, p. 1.
150. See 'Beatles Mystery Film discovered. Some rare footage of the Beatles' visit to the South West has been unearthed in the BBC library in Plymouth' on http://www. bbc.co.uk/1/hi/england/devon
151. See http://www.lennon.net
152. Solstice, *Silent Dance* (London, 1984).
153. New Model Army, *Thunder and Consolation* (London, 1989).
154. The Levellers, *The Levellers* (London, 1995). For more on this, see Kent, 'Celtic Nirvanas'.
155. Steeleye Span, *Tempted and Tried* (London, 1989).
156. See Kent, 'Celtic Nirvanas', p. 174. See also Paul Newman, *The Tregerthen Horror: Aleister Crowley, D. H. Lawrence and Peter Warlock in Cornwall* (St Austell, 2005).
157. Karl Schramm and Gerard J. Burns (eds), *Jethro Tull: Complete Lyrics* (Heidelberg, 1993), p. 66.
158. See http://launcestonlive.co.uk. Bands featured include Fleeing New York, TAT, Offshore, The Needles, We Were For, Driverdown, B* Movie Heroes, Sanguine, Died Smiling, Adverse Polarity, Warwick Avenue, Burning Coalition, The Hitchcock Rules, Redwing and Ska'd for Life. For Tony Butler, see http://btconnect. com/greatwestrecords/bio
159. Sarah Champion (ed.) *Disco Biscuits: New fiction from the Chemical Generation* (London, 1997). See also Storry and Childs, *British Cultural Identities*.

160. Selection of posters observed opposite Redruth train station, 2006.

161. See www.naked-feet.com. The group released one EP in 2001 called *Fire*. It was recorded at the Sawmills Studio near Fowey. Another influential folk-rock group of the late 1990s was *Sacred Turf*.

162. See *West Briton*, 23 April 2006.

163. Solstice Fayre flyer, 2006.

164. *Cornishman*, 20 April, 2006, p. 8.

165. See http://www.cumpas.co.uk. Cymaz (Cornwall Youth Music Action Zone) has also been very influential in involving young people in music and recording. For a fictional look at the rock music scene in Cornwall, see Alan M. Kent, *Proper Job, Charlie Curnow!* Tiverton, 2005.

166. *West Briton*, 23 April 2006.

9

Economic Theory and Cornwall

John Dirring

Introduction: economics and the new Cornish studies

The avowedly interdisciplinary nature of the New Cornish Studies has led to an emerging general approach which intertwines strands from the individual social sciences, with very few instances of a 'pure' application of any one of them. Indeed, the essence of interdisciplinary studies is that all dimensions of an issue, rather than particular but limited aspects, come under investigation. Peter Wills, in his 1998 evaluation of Cornish regional development, places it in a wider context; 'moving away from the limits imposed by "pure" economic factors, to examine the total environment within which regional economies operate'.[1]

Bernard Deacon, writing in 2002,[2] considers the extent to which the New Cornish Studies can be thought of as a 'rhetorically defined space'; elaborating on this, it can be seen that further 'rhetorical spaces' are also being defined for some of its actual or potential 'sub-disciplines'. However, while there is distinctly a 'New Cornish Historiography', everything else tends to become subsumed in a 'New Cornish Social Science', the integrity and coherence of which has been assessed by Malcolm Williams.[3] The claim to what will here be referred to as the 'New Cornish Economics' was first staked out by Ronald Perry in 1993,[4] reviewing earlier work in the field, and setting the tone in the early stages for an empirical discourse based on the interpretation of economic statistics. This lack of theoretical sophistication is admitted by Williams,[5] who regards it nevertheless as being appropriate to present purposes.

Economics as a discipline has come to set itself apart from the other social sciences through its highly abstracted theoretical constructs and its ongoing dependence on mathematics. There was a time, however, in the mid-twentieth century, when the social sciences generally seemed to be acquiring a mathematical orientation; this is seen in textbooks of the period such as that by Bishir and Drewes,[6] current in the early 1970s, and containing many examples from the literature across the range of disciplines. This can be thought of as a culmination of modernism, in which the ever-changing and essentially non-formal nature of social behaviour was being generalized as rational, convergent and homogenizing, conformable to norms derived from the determinisms of civil society. It was a further step to apply symbolic logic to the analytic processes involved, and but a short step beyond that to reason in mathematical terms towards formulaic reductions. The increasing proliferation of statistics of all kinds, accumulating since the nineteenth century, fostered this essentially quantitative approach. As the social norms that had been held as axiomatic up until the 1960s began to fade, there was a growing awareness that social behaviour was becoming increasingly diverse and less resolvable into general 'principles'; formulaic reductionism, though continuing to be practised, seemed increasingly inappropriate.

Postmodernism has turned away from mathematics towards linguistics: symbols, rather than representing absolute values connectable by irrefutable logic, can also have relative meanings derived from context and usage; systems of equations can be supplemented by the analysis of representations within semiotic frameworks. The realization in the social sciences generally is that the 'mechanisms' that can be 'identified' or *a priori* hypothesized are not clockwork or deterministic in character; but represent complex processes which, though describable by complex mathematics, seem more amenable to treatment as discourses. However, Williams points out that 'there are non-linguistic limits upon discourse and indeed discourse itself can have non linguistic consequences. Often the linguistic and non-linguistic are enmeshed in complex ways'. He makes a strong case for a 'methodological pluralism' in which the most appropriate approach for the task in hand can become privileged above others which may also be applicable but less effective.[7] To go further: if the subject matter is complex, as it often can be in Cornish Studies, then a variety of approaches and relevant discourses may need to be successively privileged as the analysis proceeds.

Discourses, and the meta-narratives arising from them, have always dominated the ways in which economics and society are considered. Marxists, for example, would argue that all social, political and cultural relationships are functions of fundamental economic relations of production; the full epistemo-logical implications of this are evident in a 1987 review article by Perry Anderson.[8] Christian discourses will assert that spiritual and moral values are paramount; whether in the revolutionary gospel of 1970s liberation theology,[9] or in the familiar Protestant work ethic as elaborated by Max Weber.[10] Nineteenth-century Cornish Methodism put faith and spirituality foremost in facing up to the physical dangers and economic risks of the mining industry; it offered a means of resolving practical experience into what can be called a 'community of being', enclosing and subsuming (or embedding) the realm of action (or 'doing'). The poetry of John Harris provides a literary insight into this process.[11] Every ideological standpoint will have its own equivalent resolution of economic activity, its own discourse and rhetoric.

Economic action can be seen as being embedded in the formal and informal relations of civil society;[12] and it can be considered as being potentially exploitative or alienating when it becomes detached from socially determined moral values. This has been an effect of the growth of once-local financial institutions into large-scale global organizations, reactions to which have led in recent times to the worldwide development of various community-based schemes of alternative finance. Credit unions are the prime example; and the emergence of Local Exchange Trading Schemes (LETS) in Cornwall as elsewhere is indicative of a conscious move towards the re-embedding of economic transactions within the social fabric.[13]

It is social theory that has tended to become privileged in the eclecticism of the New Cornish Studies during the first decade of progress;[14] and the concept of social embeddedness provides a means whereby the particular 'rhetorical space' for the 'New Cornish Economics' can be negotiated within this socially oriented approach; a space in which the economic aspects of Wills' 'total environment within which regional economies operate'[15] can begin to be analysed. So far, it has been seen that this space has been occupied by an empirical discourse of numbers; thoughts now turn to the consideration of what manner of theory might begin to be developed into a suitably Cornish analytical framework.

Some general characteristics of economic theory

The realm of economic action, however embedded, is created by quantitative decision-making processes. Its analysis has to assess tangible, measurable quantities (or tangible qualities with a potentially quantifiable nature); thus discourses derived from mathematical abstraction seem appropriate. However, some of the tangible elements quantitatively conceptualized within 'pure' economic theory, and marginal analysis in particular, are unquantifiable in practice: 'utility', for instance, is a tangible quality of goods and services that contributes to their value, and is a concept that can be theoretically manipulated; yet it is an abstract notion that eludes quantification. Mathematical treatment of the subject is thus more of a conceptualizing device, rather than a derivation of formulae applicable to collected data; proving the presence of mathematically defined relationships can be attempted instead through the use of statistical techniques: as one example among many, Shanmugam *et al* use such an econometric approach in a recent assessment of the Malaysian money supply.[16]

Mathematical methods have provided the means whereby economics has moved, over a very long period, from the comparative-static analysis of equilibrium conditions through partial-equilibrium and dynamic models towards the consideration of stocks and flows. The impossibly esoteric elegance of much of the resultant theory, and its divergence from observed realities, led to the emergence alongside this erstwhile 'modern economics' of an alternative behavioural, evolutionary discourse, in which decisions are pragmatic rather than optimal, theory qualitative rather than quantitative.[17] As the theory of the firm was developed into the mid-twentieth century, a period in which economic activity became increasingly dominated by large-scale organizations, it became apparent that corporate business objectives and behaviour in particular are a complex mix of survival, necessity, satisfaction, and maximization; and that analysis might be better served by investigating decision-making processes:[18] choices in particular are not made in short-term isolation, but set off chains of consequential further choices along evolving pathways of change for better or worse.

A striking feature of the development of the wider discipline over the past generation is its increasing diversity, with the emergence of many specialized interests as the distinction between macro- and microeconomics is becoming blurred, as are hitherto sharply differentiated and conflicting schools of thought; though the debates continue, the overarching meta-narratives of former times are fading away. Keynesianism replaced classicism as the conventional wisdom, until its predictive powers failed in the mid-twentieth century era of high inflation, high public spending and high unemployment. Monetarism replaced it, but is now discredited in turn by subsequent experience; there is seemingly no new dogmatism emerging to replace it. Diversity replaces generalization; application is emphasized over 'pure' theory. These shifting economic paradigms are usefully summarized by Kevin Morgan,[19] who is concerned to identify an emerging 'network' or 'associational' paradigm; while Herman van der Wee, writing in the early 1980s, places the rise and fall of Keynesianism in the historical context of world economic development amid the successes and failures of economic policy.[20]

Economic studies of Cornwall

The 'New Cornish Economics' sits firmly within this latter trend of diversity in application as, following Perry, it continues to be offered to the world as an 'opposition' economics (as Williams does in his 2003 discussion of

Cornish poverty and in-migration[21]), with the intent of offering a critique of policy decisions affecting Cornwall made both within and beyond its borders. These decisions, and the reports which provide their base and articulate an apologetic, are pragmatic in approach, being framed in accordance with political considerations: the response has accordingly been empirical in nature, appropriately (according to Williams[22]) answering particular points in the same language in which they have been made. In particular, the assembly and analysis of datasets of economic statistics has been a key part of this dual discourse of apologetic and critique. The underlying theoretical assumptions and techniques used on both sides are on the whole implicit, rather than being explicitly stated. Somewhat overshadowed by economic despair, the 'New Cornish Economics' takes upon itself the imperative of providing normative answers to contemporary problems. With little scope allowed for self-reflection, it looks for accessible empirical solutions, rather than trying to apply techniques derived from economic theory.

The 'New Cornish Economics', in its adopted 'oppositional' role, might therefore be thought of as a putative economics of welfare, and more particularly the welfare economics of a region; Deacon[23] makes a historical case for Cornwall as an economic regional entity. The historical dimension is well to the fore in Cornish economic thought, as considerations of regionality are grounded in a developed theory of stages of peripherality.[24] This perspective has led to economic issues being addressed firmly but empirically in their embedded context; several of the principal areas of concern in Cornwall – tourism, housing, low incomes, the extractive industries, transport, migration, centralized control – have been investigated in this way under the umbrella of Cornish Studies, usually with alternative policy prescriptions in mind.[25] Beyond this, in the wider British context, Peter Wills identifies two basic approaches that have been used in regional economic studies; the first 'without reference to abstract theory', the second intent on the 'construction of models to explain existing systems'.[26] The actual regional scope of such studies has been in general politically determined; with Cornwall more often than not taken as part of a larger South West area. The resulting conclusions, however, have been for the most part commentaries on the results of statistical analysis, digests of the data; their recommendations might be valid for the agglomerated area as a whole, but disadvantageous for its constituent parts: focusing on Plymouth as an urban growth centre is not offset by considering Truro-Falmouth-Camborne/Redruth as an equivalent 'growth triangle'.[27] While external studies may be empirical or have some theoretical standpoint, but fail to take sufficient account of Cornish embeddedness, Cornish studies have generally lacked a Cornish viewpoint explicitly grounded in economic theory; a grounding which would surely enable more powerful explanations to be generated.

Developing the 'New Cornish Economic'

Appropriate areas of economic theory can be suggested by the structuring of the data. Most statistical data in Cornish economic studies relate to distinct units of economic activity, whether individuals, firms, households, or other groupings. The common approach in economic statistics is to begin analysis with classification into categories according to identified criteria. In an early consideration of the tourism industry, Paul Thornton[28] uses data on service providers to indicate the level of business concentration, later assessing it in terms of the effectiveness of industry training, and of adaptability to changes initiated by policy decisions. The welfare implications, though described, are not fully worked out in theoretical terms. Utton[29] discusses how industrial concentration came to be regarded as a statistical measure of some importance as a welfare indicator. Theories of imperfect or monopolistic competition, developed as rational extensions to classical equilibrium theory, predict that larger and fewer units in an industry would not be achieving an optimum equilibrium owing to inherent structural inefficiencies. Moreover, attempts to reorganize declining industries in this way (as happened in the 1920s with the Lancashire cotton industry) merely offered protection to inefficient units of production. The conclusion in such cases from the developed theory is that performance is sub-optimal, and that welfare within the industry is not maximized. In the modernist centralizing economy, formed of industries organized into ever-larger units to benefit from economies of scale, industrial concentration is considered from the perspective of bigness. The demonstration by Thornton that the typical operator in the Cornish tourist industry is a sole proprietor implies that a welfare theory of industrial concentration constructed rather from the perspective of smallness is requisite. Wills[30] also implies this in his critique of agglomeration economics; the lure of economies of scale to be gained through the centralization of economic, and social, activity leads to spatial concentrations inappropriate for Cornwall. However, this approach remains empirical, and fails to engage directly with the main body of economic theory, and welfare theory in particular.

There has always been a willingness in New Cornish Studies generally to import ideas and techniques, and to try to apply them directly to the job in hand; but on the whole there is an 'eclectic pick-and-mix approach to theory'.[31] Worldwide, there have been many theoretically based studies of particular economic issues; and some of these, though undertaken in a remote context, will have some bearing on Cornish concerns. Some have resulted in the construction of regional models which seem ready for direct installation in a Cornish context; others are less appropriate.[32] With education and training linked to innovation and enterprise identified as a key Cornish issue, Wills[33] points to the need for an explicit engagement with applied evolutionary theory concerning 'learning economies'; as expounded by, amongst others, Gregersen and Johnson, and Morgan.[34] Other approaches elsewhere have resulted in the elaboration of region- or sector-specific techniques which might be appropriate. In particular, the all-pervasive and well-tried methods of cost-benefit analysis have come to be used in a wide range of fields, from medical practice to road construction, to evaluate many different kinds of projects. This proliferation has led to attempts to evaluate non-economic factors in the reckoning, as the problems of the social embeddedness of economic decision-making gradually come to be addressed. The quantification of an expanding range of non-economic values has enabled their incorporation in economic analysis. Sources of such quantification can include valuations in litigation settlements, charitable contributions for conservation or 'heritage' projects (which can be used to measure the 'existence value' of an unused or preserved resource), and measurements of a 'willingness to pay' for the avoidance of environmental consequences through investment in preventative measures.[35]

It is worth taking a look at how cost-benefit analysis has been used in a very relevant context elsewhere – road construction in Norway. A study by Fridstrøm and Elvik[36] attempts to penetrate the decision-making process of national road planners, and investigates how they make their choices: whether strictly governed by the recommendations of economic and social analysis, or swayed by other considerations. Non-economic variables are incorporated by assigning probabilities to each criterion that might be chosen, and using the results to build up a model of revealed preference amongst decision makers. Features of this study applicable in the Cornish context are: first, that if strategic decisions concerning trunk roads are made centrally (as they would be with the A30 in Cornwall), then the questions need to be asked at the centre, and not about Cornwall in isolation; and secondly, that non-economic factors need to be given an economic value and brought into the analysis. That the decision-making process is politically driven is readily recognized in narratives like that of Perry's;[37] this Norwegian study goes further in showing how other elements of choice are subsumed to it: technical choices about road and bridge design might be decided according to the needs expressed by a road haulage lobby; or preferences for pedestrian accessibility or cycle tracks would come to the fore in a climate of 'green' politics. In all cases, 'sound economic reasons' are found for decisions actually made according to other, non-economic criteria.

It is a characteristic of economic theory, and neoclassical theory in particular, that the ongoing developmental process is one of careful addition to a long-standing cumulative body of abstract thought. Thus Charles Blackorby[38] builds his partial-equilibrium welfare model on foundations of Paretian optimality and the theory of second best (Paretian optimality is achieved when all of a set of necessary conditions have been fulfilled and welfare is maximized; in the theory of second best, one condition is not met and the others may consequentially be no longer desirable, but choices still have to be made for the better): this is a deep theoretical base extending back through Lipsey and Lancaster[39] to Alfred Marshall.[40] Nor does welfare theory stand alone; it is erected on the developed concepts of production and utility functions and indifference curves, which in turn are projected from classical equilibrium analysis. 'Pure' neoclassical theory, slowly adding new concepts and deploying advanced mathematical techniques, has something of a timeless quality in its ongoing coherence; but also a level of abstraction that can make it seem irrelevant and inaccessible. Constructed from first principles abstracted from an 'observed' reality, it represents a self-sustaining body of abstract thought; to be of use, it has to be proven on the ground in particular contexts as well as in the air. The complexities of mathematical economics demand the application of sophisticated and abstract techniques. This raises an important issue in interdisciplinary studies generally: in addressing a particular field of enquiry, highly technical arguments emanating from a particular specialization may be fully relevant, but difficult to follow for practitioners outside that specialization. It becomes necessary to translate technical discourses into a wider interdisciplinary language, not least in the context of Cornish Studies, if useable frameworks for the organization and analysis of actual data are to be constructed using abstracted theory.

The process by which the body of neoclassical economic theory has been painstakingly built up over such a long period has been entirely construc-tionist, though not without its misgivings.[41] The rarefied technical discourse of this constructionist approach, being self-sustaining and apriorist in nature, has also been the means of its isolation and inaccessibility. To gain access for non-specialists, the discourse must be deconstructed in some way, linguistically or otherwise. Economists, of course, have been keenly aware of the inaccessibility issue; yet there has always been a resistance within the established theoretical viewpoint to innovations in technique or presentation. This has been met in the past by interpreting new ideas in traditional ways (such as Robert Dorfman's exposition of mathematical programming techniques in terms of marginal analysis, 'purged of the algebraic apparatus which has impeded their general acceptance and appreciation'[42]), or by presenting mathematical or textual argument in graphical form (as in Warren Smith's diagramming of the Keynesian system[43]).

The mathematical content itself may be approached through an analogy with developments in the technology and practice of electronics over the last fifty years. When applications were constructed entirely of discrete components (such as individual transistors) both design and diagnostics depended on a direct knowledge of the workings of every item. When integrated circuits or 'microchips' (groups of components packaged and operational as a single working element) first appeared, this remained the case; but it was also possible to view complete applications as consisting of assemblies of these integrated elements: knowledge of the inner workings of each was not necessary; only its external function mattered. As large-scale integration (with many thousands of components on a single chip) became the norm, only external functions could be considered, as the internal workings were no longer accessible to the user.

The analysis of theoretical economic discourse can begin by regarding its mathematical sections as linked sets of closed integrated elements, in which the nature and validity of the mathematical techniques used are not investigated. Such an approach is valid because the notation employed is already forming abbreviated notional symbol systems. This is illustrated by random examples: Lipsey and Lancaster[44] use general functions of the form $A = f(x,y,z)$, explicitly working separately through the partial derivatives; whereas Palley[45] bundles similar functional arguments together with their derivatives into single analytical units. It becomes possible to represent such a mathematical sequence as a closed system by describing its process and outcome in other terms: the function defines the relationship between the variables, and their relative rates of change are represented by the function's derivatives.

Such an approach is also applicable to other forms of technical discourse; by containing the technical progression within closed integrated elements, it becomes possible to isolate the 'moments' which are linked by them, and around which the new discourses of reinterpretation can gather (this is derived from the work of Leclau and Mouffe, as cited and qualified by Bernard Deacon[46]). Through comparisons between these 'moments' and their equivalences in the empirical discourses being assessed, linkages between the theoretical and empirical can be established. For instance, Blackorby[47] stresses the importance for welfare theory of choosing an appropriate, commonly used and socially acceptable *numéraire* commodity (the value of which is used to measure the worth of all other commodities, and which can become the medium of exchange); while Perry[48] describes the use, by Terry Thorneycroft and the Cornwall Industrial Development Association, of the conceptual 'mile of Camborne bypass' as a measure for assessing economic and social choices in Cornwall. At first a means of political comment, its actual appropriateness as an economic measure might now be determined in a theoretical context. Taken as a signifier, its range of possible meanings becomes enlarged by the clustering of discourses around it as a 'moment'. If it were a kilometre of Norwegian road, then the work of Fridstrøm and Elvik already cited has shown something of the range of preferred meanings that can be attributed to it, and which can be rationalized by cost-benefit analysis to show trade-offs and reveal a deeper *numéraire* representation. This approach can also show more particularly how the dominant road-building discourse has led to suboptimal policy making, as measured by quantified lost opportunities.

The theory of second best suggests that, if Paretian optimality (in which the economic welfare of every element in the economy is maximized) cannot be obtained, then continued pursuit of the ideal by partial methods will detract from the achievement of attainable objectives. This is already a strong theme in Cornish 'oppositional' economics, and can now be given a more general theoretical underpinning. A concept articulated on both sides of the dual empirical discourse, by planners and their critics alike, is that of 'population-led growth'; it is a 'moment' around which rival discourses have clustered, producing different interpretations stemming from different emphases of the same data.[49] The result on both sides, however, remains empiricist in tone; there is no explicit engagement with any specifically economic theory which might also become clustered in this area. There is consequentially no apparent 'informed' discourse of 'growth', no rigorous economic statement of its suitability, or otherwise, for Cornwall.

As inward migration has steadily increased beyond expectations in the post-war period, the course of economic development has been pushed beyond any plan by the aggregated results of choices made by many individuals, acting independently according to their own judgments and desires. It has been turned aside from intended outcomes into other paths, successively leading into new situations with new welfare choices, and new criteria for decision-making. Neoclassical welfare theory assesses the resulting new states as partial equilibria, second-best solutions, but maybe located along optimal pathways to some 'final state'.[50] The alternative approach of evolutionary economics is to consider outcomes as behaviourally 'path-dependent'. Its own deep theoretical base can be taken to begin with Joseph Schumpeter in the early twentieth century: who was concerned, amid the uncertainties of the period, that the equilibria predicted by the classical theory of a more stable age were no more than transient stages in ongoing processes of continual change; processes which were instigated, not by overall market mechanisms or central planning, but by the multiplier effects of individual innovations as they become adopted across the economy and across the culture.[51] In regional economics, this has taken up a central position in the notion of 'learning economies'; and the linking together of education, training and innovation as a matter of deliberate policy has received attention within the emerging 'New Cornish Economics'. The underlying theory, briefly considered by Wills,[52] is given a somewhat fuller consideration by Perry,[53] linked to a critique of the Payton/Deacon model of stages of peripheral development; he offers an alternative view derived from a path-dependent analysis of the historical data. There is, however, no strong invocation, or detailed assessment, of evolutionary economics as a suitable theoretical framework for analysis of the Cornish experience.

The concept of 'learning economies' is also implicit in recent work in Cornish migration studies. Sharron Schwartz[54] suggests that the localized particularity of migration streams is due to the presence or absence of transnational networks; and that these contribute to the social capital that supports a 'process of learning through interaction'. These networks are regarded as essential to the understanding of the dynamics of migration flows, rather than the comparative-static models of Harris and Todaro[55] cited but not enlarged upon. These, from a mid-twentieth-century standpoint, attempt to offer economic explanations for migration within 'developing' economies from viable or even prosperous agricultural sectors to areas of mass urban unemployment. The role of remittances, in both directions, is discussed in these models; but, within the analytical framework, only with reference to the attainment of equilibria. If such a framework could be adapted as the basis of a new evolutionary model of migration into poorer Cornwall, it would contribute towards the understanding of one of the original concerns of the 'New Cornish Economics'.

Towards a theory of 'embedded choice'

Economic theory has always been about choice; but it has generally tried to predict behaviour exclusively in rational economic terms. In practice, the pathways of economic development might be deliberately chosen; or they might be stumbled into by default, and otherwise followed by the choices made by individual decision makers who do not by and large make rational economic choices, but do what seems best to them according to a whole range of constraints, perceptions and desires, some better-informed than others. To understand and evaluate the courses taken through the pathways that can be mapped out by evolutionary economics, a more general theory of choice, and in particular choice in Cornwall, is required. The 'New Cornish Economics', set in a space where there are interfaces with a whole range of concepts and methods in a multidisciplinary environment, is thereby able to dispense with the elaborate reasoning needed by economic orthodoxy for relaxing its crucial assumption that choice is rational. The discourse generated by this reasoning extends back to the thought of David Hume, for whom Political Economy was a particular application of a more general post-Enlightenment philosophy.[56] The 'New Cornish Economics' would gain considerable integrity from being underpinned by such deep justification; but, rather than disputing the rationality of economic choices, it is possible instead to view them as being embedded in social, political and cultural value systems.

A theory of 'embedded choice' might begin by identifying tensions between opposites, of whatever kind, some of which have already been touched upon here – centre and periphery, inward and outward migration, progress and paralysis, large-scale organization and individual enterprise, central and local decision-making, 'being' and 'doing'. The opposed pairs of discourses thus identified can be clustered around 'moments' which can be resolved into an 'economic' trajectory and a 'social/cultural' trajectory. These trajectories in turn can be represented graphically (after the manner of the familiar economic diagram) as the vertical and horizontal axes defining a generalized data field, which can be characterized as a multi-layered surface. The 'economic' axis can be taken as representative of quantifiable values, whereas the 'social/cultural' axis will conceptually depict qualitative valuations. From this general model, particular axes and data fields can then be abstracted for particular purposes. On the field defined by these abstracted axes, individual choices (such as, for an example, those determining inward migration into Cornwall) can be located according to the quantifiable economic element and the qualitative social and cultural factors which determined the choice. The clustered discourses underlying the abstracted axes ensure the due recognition of the embeddedness of the individual actions being investigated; the axes are not merely labelled, but can be consciously related to their wider contexts, thus helping to prevent the analysis from becoming superficial or artificial. Actual collected data will commonly relate to specific periods in time; the individual points in each periodized data set can be conceptually connected

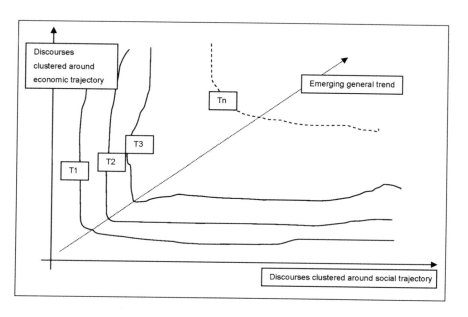

by statistical 'lines of best fit' (T1, T2, T3 ... Tn in the diagram). The shapes of these as drawn here are of course entirely arbitrary; but are suggestive of an *a priori* notion that social and economic choices are in some degree mutually exclusive. Aggregation through successive time periods will indicate emerging historical trends, which can in turn suggest evolutionary pathways of future development.

In practice, workable abstractions appropriate to the job in hand will need to be made from this general model of choice. For instance, if alternative financial institutions are being investigated, such as LETS or credit unions, then it is their particular social and economic functions which are measured on the axes, and the degree to which individual participation is determined by economic need or social awareness becomes the subject of evaluation. On the 'economic' axis, the size of the deposit or loan is measured; while the 'social' axis depicts a coded qualitative assessment of social and cultural motivation. Examples of surveys yielding this type of data include those undertaken as part of the investigations into low-income debt by the Institute of Fiscal Studies.[57]

Conclusion

The starting point for what is here called the 'New Cornish Economics' is seen to have been a pragmatic and empirical, and mostly narrative, commentary on pre-existent datasets concerning Cornish economic issues. It has yet to make the transition to a fuller theoretical approach which establishes a framework within which the type and amount of quantification required can be determined, and within which qualitative factors can be incorporated. This is, however, foreshadowed in some of the newer writing on economic themes, and the enabling methodological apparatus is beginning to be put in place; although it will remain rhetorical in character until given practical application. This article has, in making comparisons with economic theory old and new, attempted to show how the discourses within that body of theory may be deconstructed; so as to release it from the technical complexities of its original construction, and enable it to be usefully deployed in an interdisciplinary setting. Whereas hitherto theories and techniques have tended to be uncritically installed in a Cornish context, it is hoped that theoretical concepts will become central features of the future discourse of a more sophisticated 'New Cornish Economics', combining a deep theoretical base with a long historical perspective at a local level within Cornwall.[58]

Notes and references

1. P. Wills, 'Cornish regional development: evaluation, Europe and evolution', in P. Payton (ed.), *Cornish Studies: Six* (Exeter, 1998), p. 144.

2. B. Deacon, 'The New Cornish Studies: new discipline or rhetorically defined space?', in P. Payton (ed.), *Cornish Studies: Ten* (Exeter, 2002), pp. 24–43.

3. M. Williams, 'The new Cornish social science', in P. Payton (ed.), *Cornish Studies: Ten* (Exeter, 2002), pp. 44–66.

4. R. Perry, 'Economic change and "opposition" economics', in P. Payton (ed.), *Cornwall Since the War* (Redruth, 1993), pp. 48–83.

5. Williams, 'The new Cornish social science', pp. 50–1.

6. J. W. Bishir and D. W. Drewes, *Mathematics in the Behavioral and Social Sciences* (New York, 1970).

7. M. Williams, 'Discourse and social science in Cornish studies – a reply to Bernard Deacon', in P. Payton (ed.), *Cornish Studies: Thirteen* (Exeter, 2005), pp. 14–22.

8. P. Anderson, 'The figures of descent', *New Left Review*, 161, January–February 1987, pp. 20–77.

9. A contemporary assessment from the inside is offered by J. M. Bonino, *Revolutionary Theology Comes of Age* (London, 1975); this is reviewed from a conservative evangelical standpoint by J. P. Baker in *Themelios*, 2/3 (May 1977), p. 96. A retrospective view from a similar angle is given by S. Escobar, 'Beyond liberation theology: a review article', in *Themelios*, 19/3 (May 1994), pp. 15–17. This modern evangelical position is not far removed from the outlook of nineteenth-century Cornish Methodism.

10. M. Weber, *The Protestant Ethic and the Spirit of Capitalism* (1904; translated by T. Parsons, London, 1930). Salient points are represented in the extracts from pp. 155–83, reprinted as 'Asceticism and the spirit of capitalism', in T. Burns (ed.), *Industrial Man* (Harmondsworth, 1969), pp. 15–23.

11. An ethos summarized by Alan Kent in *The Literature of Cornwall: Continuity, Identity, Difference, 1000–2000* (Bristol, 2000), pp. 111–17.

12. M. Granovetter, 'Economic action and social structure: the problem of embeddedness', *American Journal of Sociology*, 91/3 (November 1985), pp. 481–510.

13. L. Thorne, 'Local Exchange Trading Systems in the United Kingdom: a case of re-embedding?', *Environment and Planning A*, 28 (1996), pp. 1361–76.

14. Williams, 'The new Cornish social science', pp. 45–50.

15. Wills, 'Cornish regional development', p. 144.

16. B. Shanmugam, M. Nair, and O. W. Li, 'The endogenous money hypothesis: empirical evidence from Malaysia', *Journal of Post Keynesian Economics*, 25/4 (2003), pp. 599–611.

17. J. Fagerberg, 'Schumpeter and the revival of evolutionary economics: an appraisal of the literature', *Journal of Evolutionary Economics*, 13 (2003), pp. 135–6, 144–5.

18. G. L. Nordquist, 'The breakup of the maximization principle', *Quarterly Review of Economics and Business*, 5 (1965), pp. 33–46.

19. K. Morgan, 'The learning region: institutions, innovation and regional renewal', *Regional Studies*, 31/5 (1997), pp. 491–2.

20. H. van der Wee, *Prosperity and Upheaval: the World Economy, 1945–1980*, translated by R. Hogg and M. R. Hall (Harmondsworth, 1986), pp. 32–81, 225–7, 314–44.

21. M. Williams, 'Why is Cornwall poor? Poverty and in-migration since the 1960s',

Contemporary British History, 17/3 (2003), pp. 55–70.

22. Williams, 'The new Cornish social science', pp. 50–1.

23. B. Deacon, 'Proto-regionalization: the case of Cornwall', *Journal of Regional and Local Studies*, 18/1 (1998), pp. 27–41.

24. P. Payton, *The Making of Modern Cornwall: Historical Experience and the Persistence of Difference* (Redruth, 1992).

25. Examples with an economic content and not otherwise cited here include C. M. Bristow, 'Wealth from the ground: geology and extractive industries', P. Mitchell, 'The demographic revolution', and M. Williams, 'Housing the Cornish', all in P. Payton (ed.), *Cornwall Since the War* (Redruth, 1993); and the following articles in the series *Cornish Studies* (ed. P. Payton, Exeter): M. Buck, M. Williams and L. Bryant, 'Housing the Cornish: containing the crisis' (*One*, 1993, pp. 97–119); M. Williams and E. Harrison, 'Movers and stayers: a comparison of migratory and non-migratory groups in Cornwall, 1981–91' (*Three*, 1995, pp. 176–93); M. Williams and T. Champion, 'Cornwall, poverty and in-migration' (*Six*, 1998, pp. 118–26); R. Elzey, 'In-migration to Newquay: migrants' lifestyles and perspectives on environments' (*Six*, pp. 127–42); T. Chapman, 'The National Dock Labour Scheme in Cornwall' (*Twelve*, 2004, pp. 215–48); T. Chapman, 'Nationalized Cornwall' (*Fourteen*, 2006, pp. 204–28).

26. Wills, 'Cornish regional development', p. 146.

27. Ibid., pp. 146–7.

28. P. Thornton, 'Tourism in Cornwall: recent research and current trends', in P. Payton (ed.), *Cornish Studies: Two* (Exeter, 1994), pp. 108–27.

29. M. A. Utton, *Industrial Concentration* (Harmondsworth, 1970).

30. Wills, 'Cornish regional development', p. 147.

31. B. Deacon, 'From "Cornish Studies" to "Critical Cornish Studies": reflections on methodology', in P. Payton (ed.), *Cornish Studies: Twelve* (Exeter, 2004), pp. 13–29.

32. Wills, 'Cornish regional development', pp. 148–52.

33. Ibid., pp. 156–9.

34. Morgan, 'The learning region'; B. Gregersen and B. Johnson, 'Learning economies, innovation systems and European integration', *Regional Studies*, 31/5 (1997), pp. 479–90.

35. R. O. Zerbe, 'Should moral sentiments be incorporated into benefit-cost analysis? An example of long-term discounting', *Policy Sciences*, 37 (2004), pp. 305–18.

36. L. Fridstrøm and R. Elvik, 'The barely revealed preference behind road investment priorities', *Public Choice*, 92 (1997), pp. 145–68.

37. Perry, 'Economic change and "opposition" economics'.

38. C. Blackorby, 'Partial-equilibrium welfare analysis', *Journal of Public Economic Theory*, 1/3 (1999), pp. 359–74.

39. R. G. Lipsey and K. Lancaster, 'The general theory of second best', *Review of Economic Studies*, 24 (1956), pp. 11–32.

40. A. Marshall, *Principles of Economics* (1890; 8th edn London, 1920).

41. Blackorby, 'Partial-equilibrium welfare analysis', pp. 372–3.

42. R. Dorfman, 'Mathematical, or "linear" programming: a nonmathematical exposition', *American Economic Review*, 43 (December 1953), pp. 797–825.

43. W. L. Smith, 'A graphical exposition of the complete Keynesian system', *Southern Economic Journal*, 23 (1956), pp. 115–25.

44. Generally throughout the exposition of their 'theory of second best'.
45. T. I. Palley, 'Endogenous money: what it is and why it matters', *Metroeconomica*, 53/2 (2002), pp. 152–80.
46. Deacon, 'From "Cornish Studies" to "Critical Cornish Studies"', pp. 14–19.
47. Blackorby, 'Partial-equilibrium welfare analysis', p. 368; C. Blackorby and D. Donaldson, 'Market demand curves and Depuit-Marshall consumers' surpluses: a general equilibrium analysis', *Mathematical Social Sciences*, 37 (1999), pp. 139–63.
48. Perry, 'Economic change and "opposition" economics', pp. 66–7.
49. See Williams, 'Discourse and social science in Cornish studies', pp. 17–20.
50. R. Radner, 'Paths of economic growth that are optimal with regard only to final states: a turnpike theorem', *Review of Economic Studies*, 28 (1960), pp. 98–104.
51. Fagerberg, 'Schumpeter and the revival of evolutionary economics', pp. 128–36, 149–50.
52. Wills, 'Cornish regional development', pp. 156–8.
53. R. Perry, 'The making of modern Cornwall, 1800–2000: a geo-economic perspective', in P. Payton (ed.), *Cornish Studies: Ten* (Exeter, 2002), pp. 166–89.
54. S. P. Schwartz, 'Migration networks and the transnationalization of social capital: Cornish migration to Latin America, a case study', in P. Payton (ed.), *Cornish Studies: Thirteen* (Exeter, 2005), pp. 257–9.
55. M. P. Todaro, 'A model of labor migration and urban employment in less-developed countries', *American Economic Review*, 59/1 (1969), pp. 138–48; J. R. Harris and M. P. Todaro, 'Migration, unemployment and development: a two-sector analysis', *American Economic Review* 60/1 (1970), pp. 126–42.
56. See S. A. T. Rizvi, 'Preference formation and the axioms of choice', *Review of Political Economy*, 13 (2001), p. 141; and A. Viskovatoff, 'Rationality as optimal choice v. rationality as valid inference', *Journal of Economic Methodology*, 8 (2001), p. 313.
57. See S. Bridges and R. Disney, 'Use of credit and arrears on debt among low-income families in the United Kingdom', *Fiscal Studies*, 25/1 (2004), pp. 1–25.
58. Deacon, 'The New Cornish Studies', p. 37.